HITLER'S SUPPRESSED
AND STILL-SECRET WEAPONS,
SCIENCE AND TECHNOLOGY

Henry Stevens

Dedicated to the Memory of
Heiner Gehring who left us
much too soon.

**Hitler's Suppressed and Still-Secret
Weapons, Science and Technology**

Published by
Adventures Unlimited Press
Kempton, Illinois 60946 USA

www.adventuresunlimitedpress.com

ISBN-10: 1-931882-73-8

ISBN-13: 978-1-931882-73-6

Printed on acid free paper in the United States of America

Cover artwork by J. R. Schumacher

10 9 8 7 6 5 4 3 2

Introduction

Much of the material presented in this book came to me by accident, as the result of fifteen years of research into German flying discs. In my first book, Hitler's Flying Saucers A Guide to German Flying Discs of the Second World War, some of that research was presented. What was not presented in that book are the many references to truly amazing technology which seems to have vanished right off the face of the earth. References to this technology are not mentioned by the victorious former Allied Powers for reasons known only to them.

Slowly, at some point in my investigation of German saucers, the fact that other types of technology had been suppressed became apparent to me. From that point on I began to collect references to unknown technology stemming from the Third Reich, which came to me in addition to references made by other researchers.

Some references are better than others. This fact was hammered home in my first book. The topic in question then, German flying discs, was a loaded one socially and politically. No monkey business could be tolerated. That book had to be iron clad and so it had to be written with an iron fist, so to speak. To date, no challenge has been made to my first book on the basis of content or facts. This turn of events is surprising to me as it was aimed at the UFO world and the overwhelming specter of the mass media, neither of which cares much for the concept of German flying saucers. This later force is almost omnipotent and grips much of our entire planet in a Matrix-like-world of ignorance on so many vital issues.

This "grip" is one of the reasons for this book. We realize that the movie, The Matrix, was fiction on the physical level. We are not housed in glass tubes being fed nutrients and given a digital identity and reality as in a computer generated game. But on the intellectual level this is not too far from the situation when it comes to secret technology.

Remember Galileo? He knew the world was not flat but could not advocate this truth because of the church dogma of the times. But there certainly was an underground of thinkers who took his proposition as truth. This underground was obliged to mouth dogma in public, only discussing the truth in secret, among trusted comrades. The proof of this is the New World, for Christopher Columbus knew the world was round before he ever set sail. No man, intelligent or otherwise, would knowingly sail off the side of an abyss. Columbus knew the truth but could not speak it. Yet he must have used this knowledge as a selling point to the very religious queen of Spain, Isabella, as he made his plea for funding. Queen Isabella mouthed the dogma but knew the truth or she would have never funded Columbus. Queen Isabella represented the elite of her time but she was willing to forgo dogma, she was willing to use her suppressed information at this particular moment to make a huge gain for herself and her country.

Today, dogma exists in every body of knowledge. Anybody with half a brain who has been through our educational system knows that something is terribly wrong. We know deep down inside that there are truths not being told. When we do independent research, we find inconsistencies in the data and the theories and explanations we are given. There seems to be something, perhaps many things, which are missing. It almost seems that we are educated, not to further explore the mysteries of life for which we have been "trained", but to explain the existing dogma to those outside of our individual specialty.

But why should there be missing technology? Science and technology deal in facts without political implications in spite of the efforts of those who have found a comfortable niche in life masquerading in "scientific ethics".

Missing technology is a clue that something is wrong. Missing technology is missing because it has been suppressed. If technology is suppressed, then there is a suppressor. This "suppressor" will eventually use this technology for individual gain. At the right time this technology will surface much as a stock trader illegally uses insider information. If technology is suppressed then, in short, there is a conspiracy to do so. It is my opinion that this conspiracy is large is scope, just as it was in the day of Christopher Columbus and Queen Isabella. The conspirators can be found at the nexus of military, industrial, political, financial and media circles. The exact nature of this conspiracy is really beyond the scope of this book.

In presenting the material in this book I am not as concerned in building the air-tight case as I did for German flying discs. This time around, I am interested in presenting as many examples of lost technology as possible. The only caveat being that the particular technology must be of some interest to me. For this reason some real breakthroughs made by the Germans will be omitted. For instance, breakthroughs in synthetic fabrics and fabric dyes will not be discussed other than to say now that it seems that the Germans can make anything from coal tar from aspirin to plastic. References are given immediately after each chapter so that interested individuals can verify what is said and begin their own research from there.

The stories and tales gathered herein do not constitute the entire collection of lost German technology. Far from it. Remember, the German Patent Office lost thirty boxcars of material to the Allies when the war ended. But even that is not the end of the matter, however. The SS never even bothered to notify the German Patent Office of that institution's advances, thinking itself well above mere patents. In addition to this there were individual inventors in individual laboratories throughout Germany, Austria and the occupied countries whose wartime breakthroughs were taken by known or unknown entities when the conflict ended.

This is not a book about the organization of German wartime research. German wartime research was administered in a complicated way and was always changing in its organization. As far as I am concerned, the only important thing to remember is that as the war progressed the SS secured an ever-increasing control over German research. Some facilities remained independent to the end but probably continued to do so only at the pleasure of the SS command. By the end of the war a whole new research and production command and control structure had been set up which reduced or replaced the

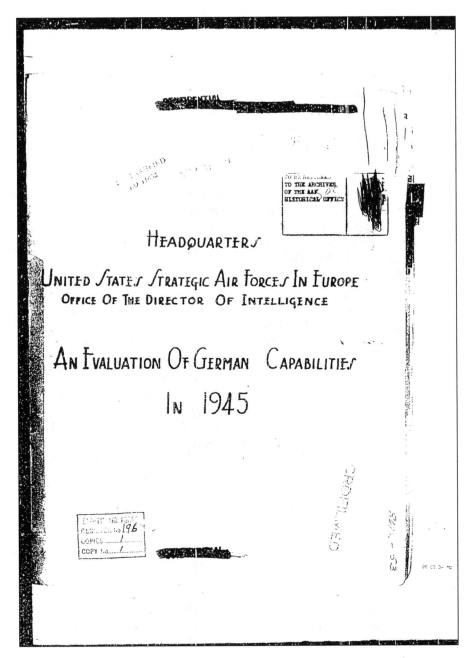

Headquarters

United States Strategic Air Forces In Europe
Office Of The Director Of Intelligence

An Evaluation Of German Capabilities

In 1945

An Evaluation Of German Capabilities In 1945 – The "Rosetta Stone" This intelligence document was instrumental in finally cracking the U.S. government's wall of silence regarding World War Two German high technology. This document supplied the government's names for German projects. Using German names or using our own vernacular, our government always claimed a "no record" response to requests for this information. Using their own names for things, the government had no option but to produce the documentation under provisions of the Freedom Of Information Act. For instance, our words are foo fighters but their words are phoo bombs. Another example is Motorstoppmittel vs. Magnetic Wave. We now have evidence for all the weaponry discussed in this report. This document continues for the next two pages.

PART SIX - OTHER WEAPONS

1. In the following paragrpahs are listed the actual or potential weapons which the Germans may use against USSTAF operations in 1945. For the most part they include the so-called V weapons. No consideration is given to those for which there is lacking evidence of possible use for some time to come. Both V-1 and V-2 are considered in the analysis because, even though they are, in effect, long-range artillery, they do possess the ability to affect our operations by hitting airfields, and supplies enroute and in concentrations.

2. V-2:

    a. Present status. The V-2, or rocket projectile, with a warhead of a, proximately one ton, and a current range of 225 miles; is being fired at London at the rate of 180/250 per month, and against Continental ports at the rate of approximately 300 per month.

    Against London its accuracy is currently rated at 3.2/1,000 per square mile at the main point of impact. Against Continental ports it is estimated at the least 6.1/1,000 per square mile at the main point of impact. The best record was 75 in a twenty-four hour period within a four square mile area of the Antwerp Docks.

    b. 1945 Potential: The German plan calls for an increase in monthly production from 600 to 1200. It is known, however, that any increase would be at the expense of the aircraft industry in radio equipment and certain essential components. An increase in accuracy would depend upon increased firings and increased use of already proved radio equipment, without which the majority of firings are conducted today. It is thought unlikely that range will be materially increased. Accuracy begins to fall off somewhere between 165 and 190 miles, and becomes increasingly inaccurate to the maximum of 225 miles. Whether or not V-2 becomes an increased menace in 1945 must depend upon the position of the aircraft industry and its requirements. Its potential lies in stabilization of the expanding aircraft program.

    Larger rockets (68 feet in length as against 45 feet) are known to exist, and may appear in small quantities during the year. They would have a considerably larger warhead.

3. V-1:

    a. Present Status: The so-called Flying Bomb is being fired from launching ramps against Continental targets, ports and supply concentrations, at the rate of 600 per month, and against England by airborne launchings, at the rate of 250 per month. Accuracy against Continental targets is now between 11.0/1,000 per square mile at main point of impact, and against England at 3.3/1,000 per square mile at main point of impact.

    b. 1945 Potential: Here again, the German plan calls for an expansion in production, but, as in the case of V-2, this expansion must be at the expense of other vital industries. Authoritative estimates state that airborne launchings against England may reach 450 per month, and that a very substantial increase of launchings on the Continent will take place. On the other hand, the number of He-111s available for airborne launchings is distinctly limited, and the demands of other industries are such that the expanded production may not be carried out as planned.

4. "PHOO" BOMBS: Occasionally reports by pilots and the testimony of prisoners of war and escapees describe this weapon as a radio-controlled, jet-propelled, still-nosed, short-range, high performance ramming weapon, for use against bombing formations. Its speed is estimated at 525 mph

and it is estimated to have an endurance of 25 minutes. These bombs are launched from local airfields, and are radio-controlled, either from the ground, or possibly by aircraft. The few incidents reported by pilots indicate no success. They have passed over formations, and performed various antics in the vicinity of formations. It is believed that in order to be effective some 100/200 would have to be launched against a formation, and it is also believed that they will not be produced in sufficient quantities to prove a real menace in 1945.

5. MAGNETIC WAVE: The best information available is from very secret and reliable sources, and forces the conclusion that this weapon exists as a possibility. It is designed to cause failure of various electrical apparatus in aircraft. Technically it does not appear to be a possible serious threat in 1945. At most it would be effective at a few locations for preventing ground strafing. Evidence to date indicates that it could have little effect against high level attack, since the apparatus would be too cumbersome to permit its use in aircraft.

6. GASES APPLICABLE TO AIRCRAFT: Two types of gases applicable to aircraft are known. One is designed to cause pre-ignition, blowing the heads off cylinders; and the other is designed to break down the viscosity of lubricating oils. Under laboratory conditions, free from operational considerations, these gases are a distinct possibility. It is doubtful, however, that with proper fighter escorts a sufficient concentration of either of these gases could be thrown against our formations to have any serious effect. Similarly, it is doubted whether sufficient anti-aircraft guns are available to produce an effective concentration, and it is probably that any possible concentration would be no more effective than a similar amount of well-directed flak.

7. ATOMIC BOMB: Close check of every report, and close surveillance of the area in which tests are alleged to have taken place lead to the conclusion that such bombs are not a likelihood in 1945.

figures we normally think of as running the Third Reich such as, for instance, Herrmann Goring and Albert Speer. When the Allies finally forced the collapse of Germany and began interrogating the officials with whom they were familiar, they had to learn a whole new set of names and locations in deciphering the new weapons research and development chain of command. First and foremost of these was General Dr. Ing. Hans Kammler and the super-secret organization which he set up to research and catalog scientific findings within the Reich, the Kammler Group.

We will start off with some simple, seemingly isolated reports.

We may see some of them again in a completely different setting or in an advanced form, so please bear with me and read from start to finish without jumping around.

What happened to all this stuff? I have reports and lots of questions myself but not many answers as to where it all went or why. You will have some ideas about what happened before you finish this book. I will save my speculation for the Conclusion.

Contents

1 | The Kammler Group

The Kammler Group or Kammler Staff owes its name to Hans Kammler. Kammler was born on August 26, 1901 at Stettin in northern Germany. He was a Doctor of Engineering. Kammler specialized in the very rapid construction of bombproof underground facilities. His ability to work ahead of schedule impressed all those around him and caused his rapid rise within the military-engineering world and from the Luftwaffe to the SS.

Parallelling Kammler's meteoric rise was the rise of the SS itself. The SS increasingly usurped power from the military but it also usurped industrial and scientific research and development, as well as economic functions which had previously been in civilian hands. This transfer of power exploded following the August, 1944 attempted assassination of Hitler. From that moment on, Hitler seems to have relied on the SS primarily.

Meanwhile, Kammler's SS Works Division C was busy burrowing into German soil and burying and hiding its industry there. He built countless underground installations, some of which remain unknown and unexplored today. To do this, Kammler had at his disposal, a slave-labor force which could have been as high as 14 million.

Eventually, Kammler became the number three man in the SS, behind Heinreich Himmler and SS General Oswald Pohl. And besides overseeing construction projects Kammler was also given responsibility for missile production in Germany as well as jet aircraft production. At this point Kammler began sucking in

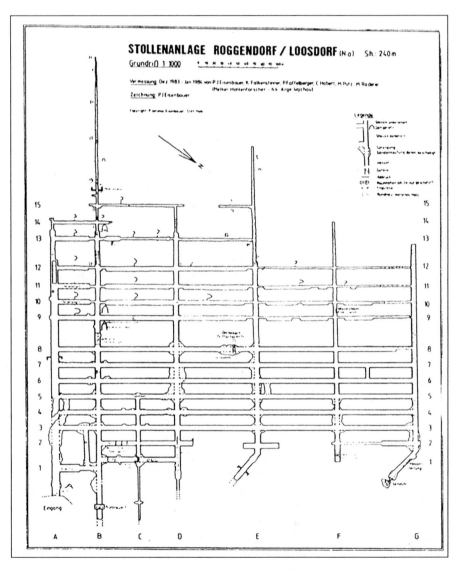

This is diagram of Kammler's facility in Austria code-named "Quarz". This was nearing completion as the war ended. It would have been Kammler's private nest and headquarters.

6. OSENBERG declared that his records contain a number of recent addresses of Development Commissions and other establishments connected with the concentration scheme.

7. He stated that until a few weeks ago the heads of the Technisches Amt, including Karl Otto SAUR and Friedrich GEIST, had been operating from evacuation offices in an underground installation at ILFELD, north of NORDHAUSEN (S. of the HARZ mountains). The installation was known under the code name MITTELWERK. The place was an emergency evacuation headquarters (Notverlagerung). OSENBERG thought that the greater part of the Speer Ministry, including Speer himself, were until quite recently still in Berlin. KAMMLER, a high SS leader known to be in charge of underground plant construction, and according to OSENBERG also in charge of the V-1 and V-2 programs, was also said to have had his HQ at ILFELD.

These are two statements made by Professor Osenberg in a Combined Intelligence Objectives sub-Committee report, number 51, dated June 2, 1945. Osenberg was head of the Reichs Research Council. Professor Osenberg was a very influential scientist and one who steered the course of scientific research and development within Nazi Germany. In this report, Osenberg actually says the name "Kammler", which is one of the very few times Kammler's name was allowed to be reproduced in this official documentation.

projects and responsibility far beyond the alleged scope of his duties. Eventually, virtually every priority or secret technology and weapons system fell under his control.

This was a big responsibility, even for a guy like Kammler, but Kammler solved or perhaps controlled this problem as he had solved all his other challenges, by organization. Kammler put together a think-tank. This involved finding and organizing a technical staff who could take potential war-winning ideas and research these ideas, develop them to the point of practicality, coordinate their production with an appropriate industrial firm, and deliver them to the field, usually to the Reich's soldiers of choice, the Waffen SS. This means that by war's end, the Kammler Group ending up sitting on a huge library: a nest-egg of German research secrets.

The Kammler Group needed a secure home in which to operate. They needed the use of technical laboratories and machine tools. Kammler found the environment he was looking for in the Skoda Works at Pilsen in what is now the Czech Republic. During World War Two, this region had been annexed by Germany and was part of the Greater German Reich. For a period of time Reinhard Heydrich administered the region with an iron fist resulting in a relatively stable occupied population. The population contained Czechs and also Germans. The Skoda Works relied on German supervisors or German-trained Czech supervisors and a skilled work force of Czechs.

Skoda did many things and must be thought of like one of the major technical industrial manufacturing firms in the USA today. Examples of these are Boeing, General Dynamics, General Electric, Lochkeed or perhaps even General Motors. Skoda was not, however, considered as a core "German" company by the German military since it was outside Germany proper and had a history going back to Austro-Hungarian times. This was perfect for Kammler. Kammler spoke Czech. Skoda had countless sub-facilities in the area. Skoda, technically, had everything Kammler needed.

Security was the last piece in the puzzle. It is a puzzle today because Kammler's security was never breached. It was not breached by the U.S., British Intelligence or even Soviet Intelligence which thought they knew everything. Kammler was able to pull Albrich's Cloak of Obscurity over himself and his staff using a tripple-wall of counterintelligence. There were three counterintelligence divisions at work in the Kammler Group. These were the military counterintelligence unit, the political counterintelligence unit and the industrial counterintelligence unit.

This security arrangement was so successful that when the Allies began advancing into Germany in the early spring of 1945, nobody asked the local population anything about Kammler or the Kammler Group. Neither side knew anything about it. By the time the "boots on the ground" realized who Dr. Kammler and his organization really were, his very name became a forbidden subject. This was probably so lest the other Allied Powers, especially the Soviets, learn of any potential treasure-trove of scientific secrets.

Remember, Kammler administrated up to 14 million slave-laborers. I think we can all agree that this was probably illegal and this led to the deaths of some, if not many, conscripts. Yet Kammler was not charged with war crimes at the Nuremberg hearings. Kammler's name only came up twice and nobody, none of the Allied Powers conducting these hearings, bothered with follow-up questions about Kammler. Also remember that Field Marshal Hermann Goering was tried, convicted and sentenced to hang for using slave labor. What is going on here?

Dr. Ing. Hans Kammler's life and "death" are full of mysteries. Unfortunately, we only have so much time and space, so this discussion of Kammler and his Kammler Group must be limited to secret weapons and high technology activities. Kammler would have had knowledge of everything described in the pages of this book. As a matter of fact, this book as well as everything ever written about Kammler, German secrets, and German secret weapons is probably only a tiny drop in the whole bucket of his nest-egg.

SOURCES

1. Agoston, Tom, 1985, *Blunder How the U.S. Gave Away Nazi Supersecrets to Russia*, Dodd, Mead and Company, New York

2 | The Stonewall and Undervaluation

Before describing some of this lost technology itself a couple of things should be mentioned. Getting real information out of the government of the United States is not as easy as it should be if you read the Freedom Of Information Act. For some reason, the government is very reluctant to disclose anything once classified. Sometimes it even goes beyond this, however. Sometimes information is declassified but then filed away where the light will never shine, without index or filing records. In fact, the information was classified, declassified and then, in the de facto sense, re-classified. Here is how it works.

The Army, or Air Force or Navy has wartime records. After awhile, they decide these records are old news and reassign and ship them to the U.S. National Archives and Records Office for storage, safe keeping and perhaps declassification and dissemination. The National Archives are stingy with their index system. They have a computer-based system, known by their acronym, N.A.I.L. but using this system a person cannot even find records previously produced by the National Archives. This secret-keeping regarding their holdings allows them to generate a "no record" at will. Any argument or appeal is met with the refrain "we don't do research". The U.S. National Archives honestly believes pulling a file is research. The only working methodology is to request a list of their holding for a particular topic as a separate Freedom Of Information request and then use it against them. Even with box numbers, file numbers, group numbers, etc., the National Archives frequently claim the item is out of file or lost. So, even with all the appropriate identification, so their clerks can walk right to the filing cabinet, open the drawer and go right to the information requested, they then seem to want to know which of their two hands is holding the file in question. This is their stonewall strategy and it is their first line of defense.

The German U-boat, U-234, and its cargo are an infamous example of this secrecy. Briefly, U-234 was a mine-layer, converted into a cargo submarine which left Germany for the Norwegian fjord of Kristiansand in the middle of March, 1945, the dying days of the 3rd Reich. Aboard were two Japanese officers, reels of microfilm on super-secret German weaponry, an entire disassembled Me 262 (the jet fighter) German scientists, specialists and technicians, and ten barrels of uranium oxide each weighing 56 kg each. This was not normal uranium oxide. It had been irradiated in an atomic reactor (or perhaps enriched by some other process) and converted into uranium 235, the uranium required for an atomic bomb.

This U-boat allegedly bound for Japan, ended up surrendering to U.S. authorities on May 19th, 1945, off the east coast of the United States. The story of the enriched uranium falling into the hands of the Americans in this way is legendary and has been cited many times. Remember, the Germans surrendered on May 8, 1945 and the United States was still at war with Japan at this time. The first atomic bomb detonated by the U.S. authorities was not until July, 1945. There has always been the hint or suspicion that the uranium carried by the U-234 found its way into the American uranium bomb dropped on Nagasaki.

I set out to verify this naval legend. I wanted to actually document the uranium on the German U-234. I wrote to the source always given, the U.S. National Archives. They generated a bill for copying and a statement denying fissionable material being aboard U-234 (see the copy of the National Archive's letter). I requested the bill of lading anyway and there was no uranium on their list, as they stated. Naturally, I appealed and got nowhere.

Originally, U-234 had surrendered to the U.S.S. Sutton. A request was made to the agency which would have originally held this information before transfer to the National Archives, the Naval Historical Center, Washington Navy Yard. To my surprise, it was no secret or mystery at all and they were perfectly willing to send me a micro-fish copy of the cargo list for $5.00. Sure enough, the cargo list was exactly as sent by the National Archives except for the fact that the uranium oxide canisters were present and listed as the reader can see. This is in contrast to the list provided by the National Archives. Had the U.S. National Archives actually lied? Not only did they lie, but had they altered records and then covered up the whole thing? I wondered how they would react over a request for truly sensitive information?

The second big problem encountered is the undervaluation of German technology by the Allies. They seem to do this as a matter of course. This may have originated during the war itself. After all, did we really want to tell our 18 year-old soldiers that the German soldier was better trained than he was? Or did we want to tell him that the Germans had better small arms, machine guns, or tanks? Of course the answer is no. This undervaluation extended to matters of higher technology as well, especially aircraft and missiles. After the war re-use of this dis-information technique proved to be a successful way of minimizing German achievements in comparison to ours as part of some sort of nationalist, cold-war reasoning. Let me cite one example.

During the war, the Germans experimented with tailless, flying wing aircraft. The ones described here were made by the firm Horton, owned by the Horton brothers. There were several flying wing designs under development during those years for various purposes but the one in question is the Horton 9.

The Horton 9 was a tailless, jet-powered, flying wing fighter. Only three were ever built. The first Horton 9 (V-1) was never given engines and used as a glider for test purposes. The second Horton 9 (V-2) was given jets and tested. The third aircraft was actually produced by another company, the Gotha firm who was to mass-produce this aircraft. This one aircraft was given the designation Gotha 229 and was never fully assembled and never flew. It fell into the hands of the Americans while still in pieces.

So, it was only the second Horton 9, the V-2 version that flew at all. In fact, it flew very well. Remember, this was a tailless flying wing that flew before computer avionics made such aircraft possible in the USA. Evidently, the Horton 9 was so well thought out that a mere human pilot could fly it. But the Horton 9 was somewhat more than just an ordinary fighter aircraft. During flight testing it was noticed that the radar return for this aircraft was almost absent. The Germans got busy with this idea and planned to paint the Horton 9 with radar

National *Archives* at College Park

8601 Adelphi Road   College Park MD   20740-6001

December 9, 1997

Henry Stevens
German research Project

Dear Mr. Stevens:

This is in response to your November 17, 1997, letter concerning cargo lists for the captured German submarine U-234.

We examined the files relating to U-234 in the ONI, OP-23-F-2, records. We located one folder identified as "Cargo Lists", comprising 46 pages. Our current fee for electrostatic (paper) copies of these pages is $20.00. Please be aware that their are any number of additional manifests and cargo lists scattered within this file. We are unable to identify and provide reproduction information for all of them. These records have been heavily used by those seeking to identify plutonium or other nuclear substances which were reported to be on board this U-Boat. None of those researchers has located any nuclear material on these lists.

If you wish to order by check or money order (payable to "NABT-NWDT2"), send it with the enclosed order form to the National Archives Trust Fund Board, P.O. Box 100793, Atlanta, GA 30384. If instead you wish to pay by using a MasterCard or VISA credit card, you should return the enclosed form (annotated with type of credit card, account number, expiration date, and your signature) to the Cashier (NABT), National Archives at College Park, 8601 Adelphi Road, College Park, MD 20740-6001. Your account will be verified before the copies are shipped.

Sincerely,

Barry L. Zerby

BARRY L. ZERBY
Archives II Reference Branch
Textual Reference Division

Enclosure

National Archives and Records Administration

U-234 Deceptive Response – U.S. National Archives. Please note the last two sentences in the second paragraph. Was this information altered?

OP-20-3-G1-A

SECRET

234/6

BILLS OF LADING

and

PACKING SLIPS

U - 234

BuShips

Translated from German
28 May 1945

This is the cover of the U.S. National Archives and Records Administration Document regarding U-234. This document omits all reference to uranium on board U-234.

POS. NR.	DESTINATION NR.	LABEL & NR.	REPACKED IN LABEL & NR.	NUMBER OF BALES	HOW PACKED	WEIGHT IN KG.	TOTAL WEIGHT	CONTENTS	RECIPIENT
1	2	3	4	5	6	7	8	9	10
31	2542B	3Ø213/1-2	3Ø213/1/2A-B 3Ø213/2/2A-B	4	PACKAGES		11.Ø	RECEIVERS	JAP NAVY
1	12306	ST 1704 1569/13-21	A-C /13-17,19-2ØA-M	3	PACKAGES		6.5	DOCUMENTS	JAP ARMY
		ST 1773	/18A-E,/21A-G A-E.	103	PACKAGES		317.Ø	STEEL BALLS	JAP NAVY
		ST 6058/385		5	PACKAGES		8.5	DOCUMENTS	JAP ARMY
		/255							
		/385		3	CASES		219.Ø	ARMAMENT PARTS	"
		ST 244		1	PACKAGE		6.Ø	PLANOSPHERICAL LENS	"
		ST 1255/7	/7A-B						
		/9		4	PACKAGES		25.4	DYES	"
		/10							
2	2863	2863/1-2Ø	/6-8,10-11,13-17, /2ØA-G,/12A-O, /18-19A-D	39	PACKAGES		214.5	FUG X	JAP NAVY
		1172Ø6	K 168	1	PACKAGE		2.5	CABLE	"
3Ø		ST 127Ø/1-1Ø		1Ø	CASES		56Ø.Ø	URANIUM OXIDE	JAP ARMY
51		ST 6157/1-17		17	PACKAGES		62Ø.5	STOCK PARTS FOR PERCUSSION CAPS	"
3Ø		ST 1257		1	CASE		25.Ø	HEMOGLOBIN	"
1		ST 1255/1-2		2	PACKAGES		59.Ø	DYES	"
61	2851	3Ø215/1-8	/1-2,/4-7A-B " /3A-8,/8A-B	57	PACKAGES		107.Ø	COILS	JAP NAVY
		31Ø7/1-8	/1,3,6-7A-H /2,5A-G/4A-F /6A-I	61	PACKAGES		271.9	RAW GLASS SHAP- ING RINGS	"
		3Ø114/1-25	/1A-E,/2A-F,/3,4,11 12,14A-G,5,29A-J 9 1ØA-I 6 23-25A-H,8A-" 13,17A-K,15,18,21A-L 16,2Ø 22E-N,/7A-Z UE,AE,OE,CK,CH,AI,EI						
71	31	ST 1239/1-21	JE A-Y	262	PACKAGES		1275.Ø	RAW GLASS	"
				525	PACKAGES		1312.5	PLASTOCHIN	JAP ARMY

Copy of the U.S. Navy's cargo contents for U-234. Note that uranium oxide is clearly part of the cargo. The U.S. Navy sends records to the U.S. National Archives for safe keeping. It is lucky that the Navy kept a copy for themselves.

absorbing paint that they had developed for another purpose. The fact is that the Horton 9 was the world's first stealth aircraft. Unfortunately, during a landing one of its two engines failed and the one flying Horton 9 crashed.

So what do we know about the Horton 9 in flight? All we now know about the performance of this legendary aircraft is what Allied technical teams said about it and this is the way it has been reported to us down through history via semi-technical aircraft history journals and books.

For instance David Masters, in his book German Jet Genesis, lists the speed of the Horton 9 at 540 mph with a ceiling altitude of 52,490 feet. The same authority reports the Gotha 229 (which never flew) as having a maximum speed of 590 mph at sea level and 640 mph at 21,320 ft. with a ceiling of 51,000 ft. This compares with the Me 262, the operational German jet fighter with which we are familiar, whose top speed Masters lists at 538 mph at 29,560 ft. with no ceiling given.

Surprisingly, both jets were powered by the same two Junkers Jumo 004B-1 engines. Yet the Horton 9 had the cross-section of a knife while the Messerschmitt cross-section was much more typical for an aircraft of the time. How could their performance be nearly identical? How would the Allies know what the performance of the Horton 9 actually was since they never got their hands on a working example?

Perhaps it was extrapolation. Perhaps they simply wanted to under value this sleek German jet simply because it looked so advanced for its time and there was nothing comparable in the Allied arsenal. Without contradictory evidence, the word of the American experts was repeated and became part of history as we know it. The funny thing is that now contradictory evidence has surfaced and has somehow slipped by the American censors.

The document in question is a Memorandum Report, dated March 17, 1945 while the war was still in progress. The "Subject" of this report was data obtained on the German tailless jet propelled fighter and Vereinigte Leichtmetalwerke (United Light-Metal Works). The "Purpose" of the report:

> "To present data of immediate value obtained on C.I.O.S. trip to Bonn on 11 March to 16 March 1945. Travel performed under AG 200m 4-1, SHAEF, dated 9 March 1945."

MEMORANDUM REPORT

SUBJECT: Data obtained at Bonn re: tailless jet propelled fighter and Vereinigte Leichtmetallwerke.

A. PURPOSE: To present data of immediate value obtained on C.I.O.S. trip to Bonn on 11 March to 16 March 1945. Travel performed under AG 200.4-1-AGP, SHAEF, dated 9 March 1945.

B. FACTUAL DATA:

1. Mr. F. V. Berger was found at the former home of the Horten brothers. Berger has been a draftsman for Horten brothers while they were developing their tailless aircraft and gave a detailed description of the Horten series of aircraft. The models described are discussed below.

2. H1, H2, H3, H4, H5, H6 - Parabola. Prewar gliders and small airplanes.

3. H7 - Twin engine trainer now being built at Minden by Peschka. Now being tested at Oranienburg. RLM No. 226. An explosive hub for jettisoning propellors has been designed. Two Argus 240 hp engines.

4. H8 - Post-war commercial transport being built at Reichsautobahnen, Meisterei. Span is 48 meters, powered by six 600 hp, BMW-6 pusher engines. Range about 6,000 km, at 300-350 km/hr, cruising at 1,000-2,000 meters. Should fly in about 8 months.

5. H9 - Single seat jet-propelled fighter-bomber now in experimental stage. Span 16 meters. Two BMW jet engines, static thrust of 500 kg each. Wing loading 180-190 kg/m², Gross weight 8,000 kg, including 2,000 kg. of bombs (2 bombs), four 37 mm. cannon, full fuel. Maximum speed 1,160 km/hr @ 6,000 m.

(Informant quoted Me262 at 900 km/hr. Arado 234 at 800 km/hr; stated H9 with bombs would get away from Me262 without bombs.)

Estimated take off run 1,000 meters with full load, without assisted take off. Landing speed 130-140 km/hr. Endurance with full load 4½ hrs. Equipped with tricycle landing gear. Armor and leak-proof tanks are not provided on the experimental models. Spring operated catapult seat is provided. No de-icing provisions on experimental models. Informant did not know load factors.

The first experimental design was H9 V1. Enlarged engine diameter forced re-design as H9-V2. H9-V1 was tested as glider; H9-V2 is being tested at Oranienburg now.

A re-design for production is being made by Gotha and is called H9-.3.

The H9-V4 is a two-seater version of H9-V2 for night fighting. It has a larger pointed nose.

A 3-view drawing of H9 was obtained, also snapshots of the engine installation. The appearance of H9 is very similar to H5.

6. H10 - This is an H3 with either movable wing tips or sharply swept back wings. Probably being built at Hersfeld.

7. H11 - Acrobatic single seat glider about 8 in. span, being built at Hersfeld.

8. H12 - A two-seat side-by-side with 50 hp. DKW engine. Designed at Gottingen, built at Kiertorf. Similar to Horten III. Should have flown by now.

9. The Informant did not know of any radio-controlled tailless aircraft.

10. The Vereinigte Leichtmetallwerke were visited. No precision parts were found. The plant seemed in fairly good condition, might be easily used.

C. 1. The H9 should be watched for.
2. The H8 is interesting and should not be destroyed by bombing or artillery.
3. The Vereinigte Leichtmetallwerke might be useful.

Being built at Reichsautobahnen Meisterei, this is on road leading from Autobahn to Göttingen, about 100 meters from Autobahn.

/s/ RAY GOODALL,
Capt., A.C.

Microfilm copy listing Horton aircraft.

- Single seat jet-propelled fighter-bomber now in experimental stage.
Span 16 meters. Two BMW jet engines, static thrust of 500 kg each.
Wing loading 180-190 kg/m^2. Gross weight 8,000 kg, including 2,000
kg. of bombs (2 bombs), four 37 mm. cannon, full fuel. Maximum
speed 1,160 km/hr @ 6,000 m.

(Informant quoted Me262 at 900 km/hr. Arado 234 at 800 km/hr; stated
H9 with bombs would get away from Me262 without bombs.)

Estimated take off run 1,000 meters with full load, without assisted
take off. Landing speed 130-140 km/hr. Endurance with full load
4½ hrs. Equipped with tricycle landing gear. Armor and leak-proof
tanks are not provided on the experimental models. Spring operated
catapult seat is provided. No de-icing provisions on experimental
models. Informant did not know load factors.

The first experimental design was H9 VI. Enlarged engine diameter
forced re-design as H9-V2. H9-V1 was tested as glider; H9-V2 is
being tested at Oranienberg now.

A re-design for production is being made by Gotha and is called H9-..3.

The H9-V4 is a two-seater version of H9-V2 for night fighting. It
has a larger pointed nose.

A 3-view drawing of H9 was obtained, also snapshots of the engine
installation. The appearance of H9 is very similar to H5.

Enlargement of the Horton IX discussion in which a maximum speed of 1,160 km/hr or about 719 miles per hour. The informant spoke during |the war, while the last example of the Horton IX was still flying. Data about all other German aircraft is correct. Was there an intentional cover up concerning the performance of the Horton IX by the Allies?

So what we have here is raw intelligence to be compiled into a Combined Intelligence Objectives Sub-Committee report by SHAEF personnel.

Under "Factual Data" we learn that their German informant, Mr. F.V. Berger, is a draftsman for the Horton organization during the time that the Hortons were designing the tailless aircraft. To add to Berger's trusted position, he was actually found in the former home of Horton brothers by the intelligence agents.

Mr. Berger describes the Horton aircraft, models H1 to H12 but most of the discussion centers on the H9, the jet-powered, tailless, flying wing fighter-bomber. Berger goes on to list the weight, bomb load and cannons used but then states that the maximum speed for the H9, which was still being tested as this report was being written, was 1,160 km/her at an altitude of 6,000 meters.

This last statement must have shocked the SHAEF team to the core. The speed given, 1,160 kilometers per hour works out to slightly over 719 miles per hour! The Allies weren't even thinking about flying that fast in those days.

In the next paragraph it is evident that the intelligence team has been transfixed by Berger's statement and is double-checking his veracity. They asked him about the speed of the Me 262 and the Arado 234. Allied intelligence knew both these operational German aircraft and their capabilities by this time even if they had not gained an example of each aircraft. Berger gave the speed of the Me 262 at 900 km/hr and the Arado 234 (jet-powered bomber-reconnaissance aircraft) at 800 km/hr. This works out to 558 mph for the Messerschmitt and 496 mph for the Arado. These figures are right on the money and lend credibility to Berger's evaluation of the Horton 9.

Then Berger made another astonishing statement. Berger stated that the Horton 9, loaded with bombs (weighing 2,000 kg.) "would get away from Me262 without bombs".

Berger went on to describe the Horton 9 V-1 correctly as being tested as a glider and the Horton 9 V-2 as a fully powered aircraft. He goes on to say that the Horton 9 V-2 "is being tested at Oranienberg now." So at the time of this interview, the Horton 9 V-2 was still flying and had not crashed yet.

Perhaps we could back up a little bit and go over what we already know. The Horton 9/Gotha 229 had a low radar return. The Germans knew this and planned a radar repelling type of paint for it that was already used on submarines. These features would make the Horton 9 the first stealth aircraft, a fact much mentioned concerning the history of the American B-2 bomber. In fact, American engineers visited the remaining partially assembled Gotha 229 in Maryland to get ideas for the B-2.

But the speed given by Berger, 719 miles per hour, puts the Horton 9 in a class by itself. By this it is meant that this speed and ceiling altitude exceed both the Soviet Mig 15 and the American F86 Sabre of Korean War vintage, five or six years later.

If we listen, we can hear echoes of the undervaluation of German aircraft at the highest levels, even within the American aerospace industry. Aircraft legend Howard Hughes owned a captured Me 262. Hughes was a big fan and participant in something called aircraft racing during those post-war years. Towering pylons would mark out a course of several miles in the California desert and aircraft would race around this course. When Hughes' rival company, North American Aviation came out with its F-86 Sabre, Howard Hughes challenged the US Air Force to a one-on-one match race of their new Sabre jet against his old German Me 262. The Air Force declined. Obviously, there is some unspoken fact behind the Air Force decision.

The Sabre was said to be "trans-sonic" or having a top speed of about 650 mph. with a ceiling of 45,000 ft. If the US Air Force wanted no part of a contest with the real Me 262, not the paper projection, what would they have thought of a head to head match with the Horton 9?

Yet, the Horton 9 was a stealth aircraft. The Americans didn't even recognize what a stealth aircraft was until over 30 years later and even then they always wanted to couch the comparison of the Horton 9 to the B-2 stealth bomber. That comparison is fallacious and perhaps designed to hide something else.

Let's compare the Horton 9 to the F-117 stealth fighter instead. The F-117 has vertical control surfaces and may be, in fact, less stealthy than the Horton 9. Both had special radar absorbing paint. But the F-117 is not supersonic. The F-117 is generally conceded to fly about 650 mph, about the same as the F-86 Sabre, while the Horton 9 could be faster at 719 mph. Another difference is that the Horton 9 carried two 37 mm cannons while the F-117 has no guns or rockets and so is really not a fighter at all but only a first-strike bomber.

There are other examples but we should both watch for these tactics and recognize that the government is reluctant to fully credit the Germans for their advances during the war and we should recognize that they will go to some lengths to maintain the secrecy status quo. These tactics also include false comparisons and outright deception.

3 | German Digital Computers

Quite frankly, nothing is quite as boring as a computer discussion. However, computers have the ability to make rapid mathematical calculations and to take mountains of raw data and organize it for us in ways which give us new insight into problems. This organizational ability was picked up on immediately by Dr. Kammler.

Dr. Kammler had the benefit of knowledge, hardware and software that was developed by the computer pioneer, Dr. Konrad Zuse. In spite of everything churned out by the computer industry and "history" as we know it, Dr. Zuse built the first digital computer in 1938[1] and the first programmable software language, "Plankaikuel"[2]. He was also instrumental in developing magnetic tape as a computer storage medium[3]. By 1944 the Germans were using computers, the Zuse-built Z-3, to plot the course of ballistic attack by the V-2 at Peenemuende and Nordhausen[4].

After the assassination attempt on Hitler in July, 1944, power, on many levels of German cultural, technological and military life was transferred to the SS. Old-time Nazi bosses such as the Minister of Armaments, Albert Speer, sat back and watched helplessly as most of his empire was usurped by Dr. Hans Kammler. This included Dr. Kammler taking over the most promising and most highly technical wartime projects. Dr. Kammler was able to assume this role in addition to his other responsibilities and to handle them all with the excellence for which he was known. There is no doubt that Kammler had a genius

Fig.43b (Left). The Methfesselstraße in Berlin (1999). The Z3 and Z4 were constructed in a house on this plot of land (just to the right of the red car). Fig.44 (Right). Konrad Zuse (1989) at the entrance of the Methfesselstraße 7

The Z4 Computer

The goal of the Z4, which was developed between 1942 and 1945, was to build the prototype for a machine that was intended to be produced in the thousands. Unfortunately, the war destroyed my father's hope, which was that his machines should support the work of engineers of the time.

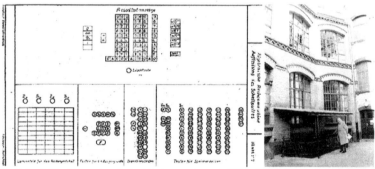

Fig.45 (Left). The Z4's input and output devices, as drawn in 1942 by Konrad Zuse. Fig.46 (Right). Konrad Zuse at the building of the Oranienstraße 6 in Berlin-Kreuzberg (1989), where the Z4 was almost finished in 1944/45.

It took more than four years to build the Z4, which ended up being much smaller than was originally planned. In the case of the Z4, Konrad Zuse wanted to implement a sub-program principle. For this reason he planned six punch tape readers and two punch tape writers. However, lack of materials, the almost daily air raids (Fig.47 and Fig.48), and the increasing difficulty of living in Berlin (which worsened daily) made it impossible to finish the Z4 completely.

Die rekonstruierte Z3 im Deutschen Museum in München

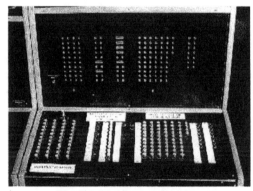

The Z4 *Planfertigungsgerät.*

Above: is the reconstructed Z-3 computer. This machine was most likely used in the headquarters of the Kammler Group as well as to calculate trajectories of the V-2 rocket.

Below: is the "Planfertigunsgeraet" (plan completion apparatus) which produced punched tapes as a program. Programming
of the Z-4 could be learned in three hours.

The Z4.

Memory unit of the Z4.
This picture was kindly made available by Dr. Kistermann.
It was taken at an exhibition at ETH Zurich in 1981.

Top: picture is the reconstructed Z-4 computer.

Bottom: memory of the Z-4

for organization, but he had some digital help.

Perhaps we can imagine the Kammler Group Headquarters, somewhere in Czechoslovakia, probably underground and perhaps near Prague or Pilsen. There, behind a triple wall of security which the Allies never managed to break, Kammler's think-tank and laboratories selected and directed the production of weapons and secret technology for the Reich. One of Kammler's secrets was that his organization was completely computerized[4]. Hollerith, Z-3, and Z-4 computers, software computer languages and magnetic tape storage devices made Kammler's headquarters look more late 1960s like than mid-1940s. In fact, German computers were so advanced that the Allied scientists and technicians failed even to understand the future when it stared them in the face.

The citation comes from a British Intelligence Objectives Sub-Committee report:

> "D. Calculating Machine of Dipl. Ing. K. Zuse Associated with Ernst (Josef Ernst who is mentioned elsewhere in this book—author) were a group of people headed by Dipl. Ing. K. Zuse, of the Zuse Apparatebau, Berlin, who had been evacuated to Hinterstein in the last days of the war. They claimed to have invented and developed a new and exceptionally versatile calculating machine, which had an application in the solving of, for example, aerodynamic, ballistic, and statistical calculations. The apparatus itself is at Hinterstein, but is not assembled. Another team of specialists led by Dr. Simms, of the Ministry of Supply, who were passing through the area at the time were consulted, and one of their members, who had considerable experience of calculating machines gave it as his opinion that the apparatus did not embody any special features which were in advance of Allied knowledge."[5].

The fact that Zuse and his computers were so advanced that the Allies didn't know what they were seeing, comes from the fact that they waited five years to approach Zuse, under Operation Paperclip, and offer him work in the United States. When they did realize their error, at least two government missions were sent to Germany, with the backing of the US computer firm Remington-Rand. Dr. Zues

22

resisted these advances since he had found work in Germany. In fact, he was directing his own computer company by this time and had found the funding to do so which was hard for that time and place. Eventually, a trip to the USA was planned but canceled. It is unknown if he ever gave the US computer maker the benefit of his knowledge[6].

Today Dr. Zues is held in high esteem in Germany and any Internet search using the words "Konrad Zuse" produce a plethora of old pictures and documentation.

SOURCES

1. Georg, Friedrich, 2003, page 23, *Hitlers Siegeswaffen Band 2: Star Wars 1947* Teil A: Von der V-1 bes zur A-9: unkonventionelle Kurz-und Mittelstreckenwaffen, Amun-Verlag, Schleusingen.

2. ibid

3. Georg, Friedrich, 2003, page 24

4. Georg, Friedrich, 2003, page 31

5. British Intelligence Objectives Sub-Committee report number 142, "Information Obtained From Targets Of Opportunity In The Southofsi Area, page 9, London

6. File of Konrad Zuse, Foreign Scientist Case Files, Record Group 330, box 186, (Paperclip Scientists), US National Records and Archives, College Park, MD.

German Flying Discs Update
Witness to a German Flying Disc

Shortly after the release of Hitler's Flying Saucers: A Guide To German Flying Discs Of The Second World War, I was contacted by a radio talk-show host, Jeff Rense, to do a live interview on his show. This radio show centers around the "unknowns" or "barely knowns" in life. Although Jeff's show originates from the Pacific Northwest, he has contacts throughout the country, if not the world. During our chit-chat off the air he mentioned another researcher, Lea McDonald, who had made contact with an individual who had actually seen a German flying disc take off during the war. Jeff was most gracious in providing an e-mail address for Lea. This seemed like a hot lead so I could not wait to make contact with Lea. Lea McDonald was as gracious as Jeff had been and gave me the telephone number of "Leo".

I don't want to give out Leo's last name at this time but he is known both to Jeff Rense and Lea McDonald. Leo is a friendly, elderly gentleman who took time to rely his sighting to me. I, in turn, do not want to appear ungrateful, so I don't want to be responsible for his telephone ringing off the hook at all hours of the night by people interested in verifying this story.

Leo's story is that he saw a flying disc ascend from the Prague airport. He does not remember the exact year, nor does he have details which can be gotten through question and answer sessions. The reason for this is that Leo was a child when he made this sighting. He saw the disc rise and ascend out of his line of sight from a school room at the Prague airport.

At first, this testimony, that of a child, might be

deemed less reliable than a competent adult's testimony. To be sure, it is not as good as J. Andreas Epp's sighting, which may have occurred on the exact same day, in terms of detail, let alone the photographs Epp took. Nevertheless, I know from personal experience how accurately a child can see things.

As a child, I grew up near Los Angeles International Airport. The period of which I an speaking was the 1950s. During that time both commercial and military aircraft landed at "LAX". Almost always all the aircraft took off to the west, into the wind. The difference between flight patterns of commercial and military aircraft centered on their landing. Military aircraft landed near the south side of the airport and so circled in by making a turn over the south side of the airport. This turn took the military aircraft directly over my home, sometimes so close I could see the pilot.

I learned each aircraft operated by the U.S. military during those times and which company made it. Further, if there was some sort of inconsistency regarding this landing routine, such as military aircraft landing from the east or a new type of aircraft landing, I recognized it instantly. I could even tell aircraft by their signature engine sound. My eyes were not the eyes of a trained observer but my eyes did count for something.

Likewise, Leo probably saw and was disrupted by, many aircraft coming and going while in his classroom at the airport. The fact that this particular aircraft was something special is the reason that memory of it has been retained all these years. Leo simply saw an unusual disc-shaped, jet powered flying craft noisily ascend from the vantage point of a classroom window. He watched its ascent until his line of sight was obstructed by the building. His sighting could not have lasted more than a few seconds.

The fact that the disc was spinning on its axis indicates that it was either the Schriever or the Habermohl saucer. Both projects were stationed at the Prague airport. The Miethe discus may have been brought to the Prague airport from its place of development in Breslau at some time but its exterior skin did not spin as did the others. Since, by his own admission, Schriever says his saucer never flew, and since we have photographic evidence as well as testimony of a functioning disc at Prague, we must assume that it was the Habermohl version[2].

SOURCES

1. Interview with witness. Leo

2. Stevens, Henry, 2003, *Hitlers Flying Saucers A Guide To German Flying Discs of The Second World War,* pages 41-52, Adventures Unlimited Press, Kempton, Illinois

5 | The Electromagnetic Vampire

What I am calling the "electromagnetic vampire" is so unique that I feel it must be discussed. Its implications in the modern world, in our current "Security State", are obvious.

The uncovering of this device is not my work. This report comes to us from Dr. Axel Stoll in his book *Hochtechnologie im Dritten Reich*[1]. The topic of interest arises as Dr. Stoll is discussing a German base in Tibet during the Second World War. He mentions that Tibet fought with the Germans in this conflict and that SS men were actually trained in Tibet. This association argues for a German underground base in Tibet and Dr. Stoll goes on to describe possible provisions for security in German underground bases and describes an example of a German electromagnetic security system.

The example he uses is the early Reich Chancellery. The lower floors of the Reich Chancellery were flooded during the latter stages of the war. This tactic was used numerous times on high-value underground facilities to prevent the advancing Allied Powers from learning Nazi secrets. Therefore, there may be other examples still out there.

The device under discussion is some sort of electromagnetic cage. Dr. Stoll calls it an "energetischen Kaefig" or "elektromagnetische Birne". Within the area of this cage a special electromagnetic field was present. This cage would be used to surround a specific room or area within the larger facility. Presumably, within this room, objects of tremendous value would be stored and therefore needed ultimate security, even more security than simply housing them within this high-security underground facility.

Dr. Stoll is unable to name his sources for security reasons, but goes on to tell a fascinating story. In the former East German Democratic Republic (DDR), strong, able-bodied divers, who were former members of the State Security Service (MfS) of that communist government were detailed to dive into the Reich Chancellery and surrounding vicinity with the goal of recovering documents, material stores and technology.

These operatives were not boy scouts, nor was East Germany a worker's paradise in the 1970s and 1980s, which is the period in which our story takes place. The DDR is the country which spawned the dreaded secret police, the "Stasi". Stasi was one of the most efficient, innovative and ruthless intelligence organizations ever conceived. Stazi could be thought of as the KGB coupled with German innovative efficiency. It is from this hard background that the divers were lowered by ropes into the black pool which were the lower floors of the Reich Chancellery.

What the divers encountered in the blackness was terror itself. Some of the divers, described by Dr. Stoll, surfaced with prolific symptoms. Their faces were contorted into a horrible grimaces. The problem was that this terribly distorted expression would not relax. Their contorted faces were frozen into a masks of permanent deformity. Not only were they disfigured but somehow they had been aged during the dive. Now they appeared to be visibly older, perhaps aging up to fifteen years in a few minutes. But that was not all.

Functioning like an almost perfect security system, the divers could not remember what had happened during their dive. Their memories had been blanked out. This was not temporary amnesia. This amnesia proved to be life-long.

Dr. Stoll, a Geophysicist, explains the workings of the device this way. Within the cage, "Kaefig", which is the space to be secured, a human body encounters an almost null-point of energy near the physical center of the device. At this point, energy is actually drawn out of the human body! This withdrawal of energy alters the human body and the human being, as a rule, for the worst. This sucking away of human energy can lead to death.

This electromagnetic or psychic vampire constitutes the ultimate in security systems. Imagine marketing a home security system boasting to suck the life out of intruders. Imagine this system in place in all truly sensitive government facilities today.

SOURCES

1. Stoll, Axel, Ph.D., 2001, *Hochtechnologie Im Dritten Reich Reichsdeutsche Entwicklungen und die vermutlich wahre Herkunft der "UFOs"*, Amun-Verlag, Schleusesiedlung 2, D-98553 Schleusingen, Germany

6 | Liquid Air

It seems that the Germans were on to a new way to make and store energy. It was the process of liquefying air. Air is a combination of many gases but its main components are nitrogen and oxygen in a ratio of roughly seventy percent and twenty percent, respectively.

There is a history of research and breakthroughs regarding means to liquify air prior to World War Two. A commercial means to liquify air was developed by the Frenchman, Georges Claude, who worked with the Germans[1]. Given a method to liquify air, liquified air seems to have been produced and stored by the Germans for later use.

There may also have been a breakthrough in storage. To make it a liquid, the gas must be artificially cooled until it reaches a temperature were it turns from a gas to a liquid. Some gases are harder to liquify than others. Usually, the difficulty comes from reaching a temperature low enough to liquify the gas. Once a gas has been liquified, it can usually be stored under pressure. This means storing the liquified gas in steel containers.

One source says that liquid hydrogen as well as liquid air can not be stored under pressure because of their low boiling points. Instead, it must be stored at normal atmospheric pressure in thermos bottles or Dewar flasks[2]. This is a system in which a metal bottle is encased within another metal bottle with a space in between where the air has been removed. With a vacuum between the two bottles, the inner bottle is filled with the liquid to be kept cold. The vacuum is an excellent insulator and so the contents of the bottle are kept cold or hot, depending on application, for an extended period of time. Additionally, a small hole or valve can be placed in the bottle, allowing a measured quantity of liquid gas to escape and expand to a gas. Heat is absorbed in this expansion process, cooling the remaining liquid gas in the bottle to offset any heat entering the bottle.

This thermos-at-atmospheric-pressure explanation is fine but somehow does not conform to what was observed during the war. Apparently, the Germans were making liquified air, storing it under pressure, and extracting its stored energy at a later date.

As early as 1930, the Reichsarbeitsgemeinschaft, the Reichs Works Association, concerned itself with liquified air and its energy potential almost as much as it concerned itself with sources of new energy[3]. This organization was set up with the express purpose of energy independence for Germany. The exact application to which the liquified air was to be put was not explained but it was given a considerable volume of print in their publications.

During the war, all sorts of plans were made to utilize the liquid air that must have been on hand. Plans were made to ignite it in new engines[4]. Liquified air facilities fell under the control of the SS, which is a sure sign that this was a valued commodity with a real role to play in the war[5]. These roles included powering submarine as well as aircraft engines[6]. But the information that tells us the Germans were able to store liquid air, presumably under pressure in a closed container, comes from their work to used liquid air as an explosive in artillery shells.

This information comes from a G-2 source working in conjunction with the U.S. Seventh Army, on or about October 21, 1944[7]. In that source a prisoner of war was interviewed. The prisoner claimed that 105 mm howitzer cannons had been modified to fire a liquid air-filled shells. The German word "Pressluft" is inserted into the English text and presumably was the word employed by the prisoner. The barrel of this gun was about half meter longer than the normal German 105 mm howitzer, and, on both sides of the breech there was a vent 2-3 cm wide. The projectile itself is somewhat longer that the standard for that gun. The new shell, without the powder charge is about the same as the length of the normal 105 mm projectile and the cartridge case combined.

The firing of this gun was somewhat out of the ordinary. The firing crew stood off 10 meters away from the gun at time of firing. The explosion made a muffled sound and smoke came through the vents in the breech. The smoke itself was described as having the effect of vomiting gas and caused the lungs to ache which way why the crew withdrew to the 10 meter distance. This description seems to indicate that the projectiles themselves were fired using liquid air as a propulsion source.

In test firings, 30 cows and horses were spread out over a 2.5 km diameter area. Four projectiles were fired. All the animals were killed. It was discovered that the animals died because their lungs had been crushed. At time of the tests a Col. Kruse, the commanding officer of the artillery school made an odd comment:

> "Let us hope that in the field the same result will be attained. Then V-2 will be achieved".

The first sentence is not surprising. Every military man hopes his weapons will work in practice as they do in testing. It is the second statement which is noteworthy and which raises the question as to if liquid air was intended as an explosive warhead for the V-2 rocket. According to one source, this is exactly what was in the works and an American OSS report from October 8, 1944 is cited—a date very close to the one discussed here[8].

The use of liquid air as an explosive is probably only one small part of its significance. During the period of the Third Reich, the Germans envisioned liquid air as a source of energy. They did not need to go abroad to get it, the raw material, air, was everywhere. No prospecting equipment, pipelines or refinery was necessary. Liquid air could be manufactured at leisure, then bottled and stored for later use. Its energy could be extracted halfway around the world.

The ultimate German flying machine may have been a saucer that manufactured and burnt its own liquid air as it flew. This is an idea hinted at by flying saucer pioneer Renato Vesco[9] and which has recently been taken up again by researcher Klaus-Peter Rothkugel who has written me about this on many occasions.

In the liquid air howitzer shell and the V-2 warhead, we think of the utilization of liquid air as a burning or explosive force. To do this, of course, liquid air must burn. Oxygen itself doesn't really burn; it supplies the oxygen necessary for combustion. We seem to be left with nitrogen as the combustible material under consideration. Nitrogen is

Ref No 578

LIQUID AIR SHELLS

SOURCE

~~████████~~, Pvt, Signal Pl, 1316 Arty Regt, 16 Inf Div. An 18-year old, intelligent electro-mechanic from BRESLAU. He was security-minded at first but later became cooperative.
Rating: C-3 Date of Information: Up to 21 Oct 44 Interrogator: A.Z.

From 5 Feb 44 to 28 June 44 PW attended an arty radio course at the KRIEGSCHULE, at BROMBERG. Here he was taught that the German 105 mm gun-howitzer, with a few minor alterations, could be adapted to fire liquid air-filled shells (PRESSLUFT-ORANATEN). The barrels of these guns, when used for this purpose, are about .5 m longer than the normal guns, and on both sides of the breech there is a vent 2-3 cm wide. The projectile is somewhat longer than the usual 105 mm projectile. Its length without the powder charge is about the same as the length of the normal 105 mm projectile and the cartridge case combined. The weight of the projectile is 2.3 kg. The new powder charge is about 25 cm long.

In BROMBERG PW witnessed target practice with the new guns. The gun crews remained about 10 m away on both sides of the guns when the firing took place. The gun was fired with a lanyard. The explosion made a muffled sound and smoke came through the vents in the breech. The smoke has the effect of vomiting gas and causes the lungs to ache; this is the reason why the gun crew remained about 10 m away when it was fired. Almost no whistling of the projectile is heard.

During the practice fire demonstration which took place in BROMBERG and which PW witnessed, about 30 old cows and horses were dispersed in an area about 2.5 km in diameter. All the animals were killed as a result of the firing of four projectiles. The lungs of all the animals had been crushed. At the conclusion of the demonstration Col KRUSE, the C O of the Arty School at BROMBERG, delivered a short speech to the students, ending with the following: "Let us hope that in the field the same result will be attained. Then V-2 will be achieved".

1316 Arty Regt is composed of three bns. In Sept 44, 2 Bn withdrew through France to SCHERWEILER, Alsace, and 1 Bn to TIEFENTHAL Alsace. PW does not know the location of 3 Bn.

On 1 Oct 44 PW was sent to a point about 2.5 km NORTH of BROUVELIEURES with about 80 men, to build a defense line. Lt KOLTERMANN, C O of the work detail, told PW on 21 Oct that 2 Bn was moving from SCHERWEILER to the front lines after having been equipped with the new guns. The lieutenant emphasized the word "new". (This is the only evidence PW was able to furnish that the 105 mm gun-howitzer firing liquid air projectiles will be in operation in this theater.)

25 October 1944

MU 500, CSDIC (WEST) SEVENTH ARMY

PAUL KUBALA, Maj, Inf,
Commanding.

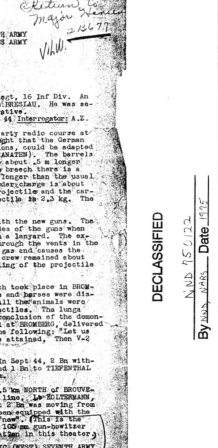

(g) Liquid air bomb

As the research on the atomic bomb under Graf von Ardenne and others was not proceeding as rapidly as had been hoped in 1944, it was decided to proceed with the development of a liquid air bomb. Experiments using ordinary powdered coal were not at all successful, but extremely good results were obtained from a mixture consisting of 60% finely powdered dry brown coal and 40%

liquid air. The technical man responsible for this work was Dr. Zippelmeier. The first trial was made on the Döberitz grounds near Berlin using a charge of about 8 kg of powder in a thin tin plate container. The liquid air was poured on to the powder, and the two were mixed together with a long wooden stirrer. Kreutzfeld did this himself, and was present at the ensuing test. In an area of radius 500 to 600 metres trees etc. were all completely destroyed. Thereafter the explosion started to rise and only the tops of the trees were affected, although the intensive explosion covered an area 2 km. in radius. Zippelmeier then had the idea that a better effect might be obtained if the powder was spread out in the form of a cloud before the explosion. Trials were made with a paper container impregnated with some waxy substance. A metal cylinder was attached to the lower end of this container and hit the ground first, dispersing the powder. After a short time interval of the order of 1/4 second a small charge in the metal cylinder exploded and ignited the dark funnel shaped dust – liquid air cloud. The bombs had to be filled immediately prior to the departure of the aircraft. Bombs with charges of 25 and 50 kg. of powder were dropped on the Starbergersee, and photographs of the explosion were taken. Standartenführer Klumm kept a photograph of the result and showed it to Brandt (Himmler's personal adviser). The intensive explosion covered an area 4 to 4.5 km. radius, and the explosion was still felt on a radius 12.5 km. When the bomb was dropped on an airfield, much destruction was caused 12 km. away, and all the trees on a hillside 5 to 6 km. away were flat. On a radius of 12.5 km. only the tops of the trees were destroyed.

A Dr. Hahnenkamp was also concerned in this work with Dr. Zippelmeier, and both scientists were working for the R.L.M. in the laboratories of a research institute near Vienna. About the end of September 1944 Zippelmeier was moved to the Horn Gyroscopic compass factory in Plauen, Vogtland (Saxony), but was probably evacuated before the Russians occupied the area. The materials of the explosive were made by the specialists of the Nobel company.

BIOS Report Number 142: Liquid Air Bomb. A liquid air bomb design using coal dust may have been a forerunner to Dr. Zippermayr's fuel-air bomb.

usually thought of as an inert gas. This is true as a practical matter in our daily lives, but nitrogen will burn if it gets hot enough. Thunder is evidence of this.

During a discharge of lightning, atmospheric nitrogen is burnt by the heat generated by the lightning. Nitrogen rapidly combines with atmospheric oxygen, causing a low-pressure area in its wake. Thunder is the sound generated by the gasses of the atmosphere slamming that pocket of low pressure, burnt nitrogen, shut once more. The fallout is "fixed nitrogen", molecules of nitrogen combined with oxygen, falling to earth which are used by plant life as fertilizer. The point is that nitrogen will burn given enough heat.

A second method to extract energy from liquid air involves its rapid transformation from a frozen liquid (liquid nitrogen at-147 degrees C.) to a gas as the result of heating. Here we encounter the patent of Karl Nowak. Nowak was an Austrian who found that when matter in its cold, liquid state is heated rapidly, for instance injected into a combustion chamber on an engine, it expands with a tremendous rate of force. Nowak made all sorts of claims as to the power of that force but for us it is probably only necessary to recognize the principle. If liquid air were injected into a combustion chamber, such as that of an automobile engine, and it was sufficiently heated, such as with a high voltage discharge, not only would a force of expansion arise from the burning of the gasses, but prior to the burning and just before ignition, a force would have generated based upon the rapid heating of the liquid air by the spark discharge. A second expansion would take place upon the burning of the fuel itself, a reaction with which we are all familiar.

The basics of this liquid air discussion are that the Germans succeeded in finding a simple new source of energy, one that was not based on foreign sources and which could be produced and transported relatively easily and one that has apparently been forgotten today. We will add to this discussion of liquid air when we review the work of Dr. Mario Zippermayr.

SOURCES

1. Vesco, Renato, *Intercept UFO, 1976*, page 164, Pinacle Books, Inc., New York

2. Van Nostrand's Scientific Encyclopedia, 1958, page 979, D. Van Nostrand Company, Inc., New York

3. Weltdynamismus Streifzueg durch technisches Neuland an Hand von biologischen Symbolen, 1930, commissioned by the Reichsarbeitsgemeinschaft "Das kommendende Deutschland", Otto Wilhelm Barth Verlag, Berlin

4. Vesco, Renato, Intercept UFO, 1976, pages 93, 134-136, 163, 164.

5. Vesco, Renato, 1976, page 93

6. Vesco, Renato, 1976, pages 135, 164

7. Office of the Director of Intelligence (G-2), file: MU 500, CSDIC (West), Ref. No. 578, Interrogation Reports and Correspondence on Prisoners of War ("Mis-Y"), 1943-1945, The National Archives, Record Group 165: Records of the War Department Genera and Special Staffs

8. Georg, Friedrich, 2003, *Hitlers Siegeswaffen Band 2: Star Wars 1947 Teil A: Von der V-1 bis zur A-9: unkonventionelle Kurz – und Mittelstreckenwaffen*, page 116, Amun-Verlag, Zella Mehlis

9. Vesco, Renato, 1976, pages 135-136, 163, 168

7 | Synthetic Penicillin Substitute "3065"

During the 1950s, penicillin, an antibiotic, was touted as a "wonder drug". It was so effective against a myriad of bacterial infections that it single-handedly replaced "sulfa-drugs" which were previously in use against infection. Penicillin saved countless lives. It ushered in a whole medical age of similar antibiotics.

Now we know that antibiotics were over prescribed and over used by doctors. Bacteria, being adaptable and quickly reproducing organisms, evolved into strains resistant to penicillin. Newer antibiotics constantly had to be developed to stay one step ahead of the latest super-bacteria. Today, we live in fear of these evolved bacteriological super-bugs. Of course, the elite can have any prescription that money and power can buy but penicillin is now prescribed only as a last resort for the general populace.

But perhaps this sad situation was not the inevitable consequence of medical and pharmaceutical history. What if there were a non-antibiotic based treatment which was just as effective or even more effective against infection as penicillin? What if it were cheap and easy to manufacture compared with penicillin? What if this medicine really did exist yet all knowledge of it were suppressed? Do you think this sounds like "fringe" or "kook" medicine, something which can easily answered by the current resident doctor on CNN? Well, let's see if the debunkers can deal with this.

Penicillin substitute 3065 was the brainchild of Professor and Doctor Richard Kuhn. We learn from the Combined Intelligence Objectives Subcommittee had warlike application. (Address of RWA - 120 Sanrianustrasse, Berlin).

Kuhn had no direct knowledge of CW activities, any information he had coming from casual sources, such as servicemen (e.g., he had heard of Stickstofflost from a soldier, but had no knowledge of any other CW agent). He supposed that, as in the last war, research was going on at the KWI, Berlin. Professor Flury who worked at the KWI Berlin during the last war was now at Wurtzburg. Kuhn had no knowledge of Spandau.

7. ACCOUNT OF WORK ON "3065"

Kuhn et al have synthesised simple derivatives of benzil which they have found to have the same order of effect as penicillin, and in some cases to be much more effective.

The most effective derivative, termed 3065 is the 2:2' dihydroxy-5:5'-dibromo benzil

This may be readily synthesised by condensing 2 mols salicylaldehyde (hydroxy groups protected by methylation); bromination may be carried out in the initial or in the final stage. 3065 is stable towards heat (m.p. 215) (cf. penicillin), is little soluble in water, but is soluble in weak alkalis and forms a water soluble (5-10%) complex with boric acid.

Other benzil derivatives (e.g. tetrachloro-) are effective but not as good as 3065. The synthesis of some analogues is given in Ber. 1943, 76.900. (Kuhn, Birkhofer and Möller).

Interest in the benzil derivatives was stimulated by the discovery that 4:4'-diamino benzil was a powerful antagonist to p-amino benzoic acid--this was the first example of an antagonist which was not a sulphonamide drug.

The clinical application of 3065 will be covered by a report from a medical assessor. Briefly, it rivals penicillin in its effects, especially in the case of staphylococcus (claimed to be 300 times more effective); the MLD is of the same order as the sulphonamide drugs except that the patient is more

Synthetic Penicillin—"3065" A copy from the actual text showing the chemical structure of "3065".

evaluation reports number 75, report 1, dated April 20, 1945 and marked "Secret"[1] that Dr. Kuhn was not a quack. On the contrary, he was President of the German Chemical Society since 1938. In wartime Germany, Dr. Kuhn was the Director of the organic chemistry division of the Reichforschungshaft, second only to Professor Thiessen. Dr. Kuhn did pure research while at the Reichforschungshaft, that is, it was not militarily oriented. Dr. Kuhn was responsible for work on nutrition, vitamins and war infection and disease. Since Dr. Kuhn worked in a purely research setting, any discoveries were given to a development (Entwicklung) facility or appropriated by the Reichamt fuer Wehrschaft Ausbau (Reich Bureau for Military Consolidation) for purposes of practical application. Dr. Kuhn was very cooperative with Allied interrogators who believed in his sincerity and efforts to set down the facts correctly. Additionally, Dr. Kuhn spoke excellent English. This meant that there were no misunderstandings about the properties of "3065".

The account of the work on 3065 is well described and seems to lack mystery. From the report cited we learn that Dr. Kuhn and his team "synthesized simple derivatives of benzil (benzol or benzoyl?—author) with they have found to have the same order of effect as penicillin, and in some cases to be much more effective". For those interested in chemistry, 3065 is described further as a 2:2' dihydroxy-5:5'-dibromo benzil. A chemical diagram is pictured in the report. 3065 may be synthesized by condensing 2 mols salicylaldehyde (hydroxy groups protected by methylation); bromination may be carried out in the initial or in the final stage. 3065 is stable towards heat (m.p. 215), is little soluble in water, but is soluble in weak alkalis and forms a water-soluble (5-10%) complex with boric acid.

This CIOS report goes on to say that a detailed report of the clinical value of 3065 will be covered by a report from "a medical assessor". It does state, however, that 3065:

> "rivals penicillin in its effects, especially in the case of
> staphylococcus (claimed to be 300 times more effective;
> the MLD is of the same order as the sulphonamide drugs
> except that the patient is more sensitive when narcosized
> e.g., by morphine; it has been very effective against
> sulphonamide resistant gonococcus."

Clinical application in Germany was in the early stages and was interrupted by Allied occupation. Manufacture of 3065 was being carried out by I.G. Wuppertal-Elberfeld.

Reference is made to the investigation of the physiological workings of 3065 which was being done by introducing radioactive bromine, prepared by Professor Bothe at Heidelberg. This statement is confirmed by another Combined Intelligence Objectives Subcommittee report, number 75/155 "Cyclotron Investigation at Heidelberg Interview with Prof. Walter Bothe[2] in which Dr. Bothe confirmed collaboration with Dr. Kuhn in producing tracer materials.

In addition to his work of 3065, Dr. Kuhn also worked on the medical application of a synthetic rubber derivative said to be a deep blue liquid that was effective in treating mustard gas burns. The liquid was applied prior or two hours after exposure. It was also an anti-inflammatory and provided protection from B. coli infection.

What can be said of Dr. Kuhn and 3065 in summary? Dr. Kuhn did not disappear after his CIOS report. He went on to be a Paperclip scientist, coming to the USA to work after the war. The final outcome of 3065 is somewhat unclear: in fact it is unknown. It just seems to have fallen off the face of the earth. Why was this? Was this pressure from the pharmaceutical companies, which were busy developing antibiotics? We simply do not know. But at one time there was the possibility of a world in which both antibiotics and medicines such as 3065 coexisted. Perhaps bacteria would have rapidly evolved defenses against 3065 just as they have to penicillin and other antibiotics. On the other hand, 3065's method of killing bacteria would have been totally different from that of an antibiotic. Therefore, its effectiveness and usefulness would have complemented antibiotics. If this is true, no near universal reliance on antibiotics would have been necessary. In this senecio, bacteria would not have had the universal exposure to nor built up the tolerance to penicillin and other antibiotics as they have done today. If penicillin was a "wonder drug" and we lost the opportunity for a complimentary drug equal to it, then we seem to have lost more than another wonder drug and we seem to have somehow gained, unnecessarily, super bacteria resistant to all antibiotics we can throw at them. Is it too late for 3065 to be of value to us?

SOURCES

1. Combined Intelligence Objective Subcommittee evaluation reports 75, April 30, 1945, evaluation Report 1, April 20, 1945, CIOS Target 8/59 (Professor R. Kuhn at the KWI, Heidelberg.

2. Combined Intelligence Objective Subcommittee Evaluation Report 159, June 30, 1945, Target C-9/327, Cyclotron Investigation at Heidelberg Interview with Prof. Walter Bothe

8 | Synthetic Blood

Imagine, in our world where the fear of AIDS transmission though blood transfusion is a constant worry, what if that worry did not exist. What if our blood supply was safe? What if it had always been safe? What if countless lives had been saved through the transfusion of uncontaminated blood and what if those individuals had not passed the disease on to others? Is this possible? Yes it is and yes, it always was.

It is possible because during World War Two, the Germans invented not only synthetic blood plasma, but actual synthetic blood itself.

Rudolf Lusar wrote a book from memory. He was a German engineer who worked it the German Patent Office. He was privileged to only those patents filed officially at that time and not the secret SS patents, but even these official patents are truly impressive. The Allies took these patents and left no record or receipt. All that remains of boxcar loads of seized patents is Lusar's memory of them.

Lusar mentions that the method to produce synthetic blood plasma was invented by the Germans during this time period.[1]

An even more revealing glimpse into this suppressed science comes to us from a 1946 American magazine article titled "Secrets By The Thousands" which ran in Harper's Magazine.[2] Before describing the article, a little explanation is necessary.

In 1946 the war was over. The troops were coming home. The world looked so good that it spawned a "baby boom" in the United States. The Cold War had not started yet. In this brief moment of good feeling the censors were lifted and the press was allowed to print whatever they wanted to print. It was in this brief glow of good cheer that the Harper's article appeared. The article is a real window into exactly what was taken from Germany.

That article was only a few pages in length and only attempted to list the booty taken. The article says in part:

> "German medical researchers had discovered a way to produce synthetic blood plasma. Called capain, it was made on a commercial scale and equaled natural plasma in results. Another discovery was periston, a substitute for the blood liquid."

Another secret, lost.

SOURCES

1. Lusar, Rudolf, 1964, *Die deutschen Waffen und Geheimwaffen des 2. Welkrieges und ihre Weiterentwicklung*, page 365

2. Walker, C. Lester, October 1946, *"Secrets By The Thousands"*, Harper's Magazine, page 333.

9 | Human Nutrition and Performance Enhances

Worldwide, humans eat a surprisingly varied diet. Some people eat almost no meat at all, yet other people eat almost nothing but meat. The diets of peoples originating in Europe and East Africa contain large amounts of dairy products while peoples originating outside those areas find dairy products undigestible. We, as individuals and as members of distinct human populations, have varying nutritional needs. The United Nations has tried repeatedly to establish minimum daily requirements regarding calories and vitamins but has failed miserably.

In the western world, especially in the United States, we are swamped with nutritional studies in our mass media. Many times, these studies contradict earlier ones. Even our official governmental organizations, such as the USDA, only seem to be telling us to eat whatever foods that we have in abundance.

Compounding this confusion is the fact that some of the testing done in the United States is sponsored by the companies which stand to gain from favorable findings regarding the foods or vitamins they produce. These companies know of human diversity and variability and they, therefore, know how to manipulate the results of a "clinical study" by using a carefully selected, small, statistically insignificant test group.

In the meantime, we are marketed food, vitamins, performance enhances and "engineered foods" Madison Avenue style, each coming with their own "proof". What are we to believe?

Wartime Germans were under particular stress. Young males almost universally wore a uniform.

Everyone else was mobilized in some form and worked for the war effort. There was a labor shortage. Slave laborers were drafted from prisoners as well as foreign civilian and prisoner of war populations. German efficiency demanded that the maximum return be gotten out of each calorie of food and out of every vitamin and mineral. German nutritional studies of those times were conducted with the necessary scientific rigor and were devoid of commercial considerations. It is for these reasons that the results of this work is still valid today and should be heeded.

Information used in this presentation was based upon a September 1, 1945 report by the Headquarters, United States Air Force In Europe, Office of the Surgeon, Aero-Medical Research Section which was titled "Interrogation of Major Gunther Lehmann Medical Officer, German Luftwaffe". *The information in question was done by the Kaiser Wilhelm Institute for Medical Research at Dortmund and Baden.* Major Gunther Lehmann was the director of this project. Before joining the Luftwaffe, Major Lehmann was a medical doctor and professor and had already been with the Kaiser Wilhelm Institute for Medical Research since shortly after his graduation from medical school in 1923. His miliary commission was largely ceremonial as was his Nazi party affiliation. Major Lehmann was told to remain at the institute and to continue his civilian research. Two additional topics of research were given him. One was to test the effectiveness of drugs in combating fatigue. The other was the effect of oxygen on fatigue.

The Germans were very interested in drug stimulants. They wanted to know if an individual's productivity could be increased. If workers and soldiers could be stimulated into increased productivity, obviously the entire German war effort would benefit. Dr. Lehmann actually began this work in 1933. These experiments led to later research with Professor Kraut which was performed on volunteers at the Kaiser Wilhelm Institute.

Subjects continued to work all night and were given a stimulant before breakfast. They were then tested for endurance on a bicycle ergometer. Pulse rates and pulse pressure were graphically recorded. The ergometer test continued until the product of the pulse rate times pulse pressure reached 10,000 which was considered the exhaustion threshold.

Initially, Dr. Lehmann administered caffeine as the experimental stimulant. In 1942 Dr. Lehmann switched to pervitan, which he believed to be the superior drug in all respects. Pervitan was found to alter the "vegetative energy reserve" or "work capacity", terms coined during this research, little, if at all. Pervitan was, however, found to double or even triple the ability to carry on over and above the ordinary exhaustion threshold or "energy ability". This energy ability is entirely a function of the brain cortex according to Dr. Lehmann in somewhat of a complex relationship.

In addition to drug stimulants, Dr. Lehmann did some rather interesting experimentation with adrenalin, which is nature's own stimulant. He concluded that there were actually two types of adrenalin secreted by the body, each with a different purpose. One, called the "activated form" causes the familiar flight or fight response. The other, called the "inactivated form" is secreted constantly by the body.

Dr. Lehmann found that subjects who tested the highest on the bicycle endurance test also had the highest levels of adrenalin in their blood streams. Dr. Lehmann determined that trained athletes invariably had higher blood levels of adrenalin than non-athletes. Finally, Dr. Lehmann determined that the ability to secret adrenalin could be trained or increased simply by the conditioning derived from the daily bicycle ergometer testing.

It can be seen that adrenalin levels figure into the vegetative energy reserve, the Adrenalin Level and Vegetative Compensations on Lehmann's chart that he used to measure drug stimulant response.

Dr. Lehmann also studied oxygen's relationship to fatigue, both mental and physical. As before, rigorous testing was conducted to measure both the physical and mental fatigue of subjects while controlling for oxygen in an altitude chamber. Dr. Lehmann found that both muscular and mental performance was positively increased in fatigued subjects by breathing 100% oxygen as measured at ground level. A tested efficiency increase of up to 50% was observed.

Dr. Lehmann and Professor Groff had already begun performance nutritional studies before the war. These studies continued with the directive that the effects of thiamin (vitamin B-1) on exercise be investigated. In addition to thiamin, glucose, simple sugar, was also a subject for testing. For this testing subjects were chosen from a nearby glass factory and their work was graded and classified by an industrial expert assigned to Dr. Lehmann's staff. Dosages were fifty grams of glucose and five mgms. of thiamin given after breakfast.

About 40% of the factory workers were already thought to have a thiamin deficiency.

The results of this testing were that neither glucose nor thiamin had any affect on work tolerance or efficiency if given separately. If combined, however, there was a noticeable improvement in both work tolerance and efficiency. In view of these findings thiamin enriched bread was ordered to be given to the Luftwaffe in 1943 and 1944 and employees in mines and glass factories were given sweetened tea and thiamine tables each day.

In 1941 Drs. Lehmann and Kraut began investigations on human protein requirements. Their methods were revolutionary for the times and were later incorporated by East European coaches for monitoring their strength athletes. Drs. Lehmann and Kraut measured the nitrogen content in their test subject urea. All protein is composed of nitrogen. Neither fats nor water contain nitrogen. The test subjects, like all humans, break down bodily proteins in relation to their activity. The more activity and the harder it is, the more protein is broken down and excreted through the urine as nitrogen. The subjects for this test were female statistical clerks in a nearby factory and a bridge building crew composed of Russian prisoners. This is quite a range of physical activity.

In order to measure protein intake, Dr. Kraut employed the "best chefs available" to "ingeniously mask changes in protein content". The doctors running the study could then measure protein or nitrogen input vs output while using essentially two sample populations, one sedentary and the other composed of hard laborers. The exact amount of protein required for a given activity could roughly be determined using this protein balance method.

The results were interesting. The absolute minimum protein intake necessary daily to maintain a positive urinary protein balance is 40 grams for sedentary office workers. The figure increased to 55 grams for laborers. The most interesting finding was that for work efficiency to reach its highest level, that is for the workers to work at peak performance, whether sedentary or laborer, the stated minimum protein intake figures had to be doubled.

These findings were immediately marked "Secret". The diets of Luftwaffe personnel, upon which depended the protection of the Reich, were supplemented with 15 grams of additional protein. That

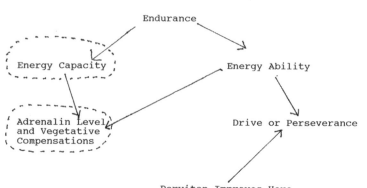

Endurance

Energy Capacity

Energy Ability

Adrenalin Level and Vegetative Compensations

Drive or Perseverance

Pervitan Improves Here

Ergometer measures those factors encompassed in dotted lines.

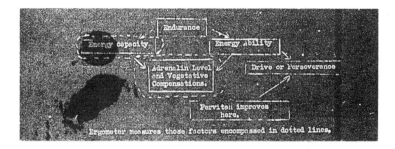

A chart from the text showing the relationships involved. Ergometer measures those factors encompassed in dotted lines. Above: redrawn chart, Below: original chart.

brought the dietary figure up to an average content of 85 grams in 1943 and 1944.

Caloric intake also effects work performance. Dr. Lehmann found that work efficiency increased in direct proportion to caloric intake up to 3,000 calories per day for office workers and 4,500 calories per day for laborers. Interestingly enough, it was found that there was a time lag of approximately three weeks between improvement in the diet and increased work efficiency.

American intelligence summaries of this type hardly ever make conclusions or even assess the implications about the research reviewed. Why this was so remains somewhat of a mystery. Some implications can be drawn, however.

The conclusions involve those individuals engaged in physical exertion, whether it be hard labor or athletics. Drug stimulants can greatly increase the capacity of an individual to do work after that individual has reached his or her exhaustion threshold. Exceeding the previous work capacity causes an increase in the level of blood adrenalin. Increased levels of blood adrenalin allow that individual to exceed his or her previous best. What is being described is a kind of performance enhancing feedback loop or step-by-step increase begun using drug stimulants.

It was found that pure oxygen increases physical and mental ability.

It was found that work efficiency could be doubled using a combination of vitamin B-1 and glucose.

It was found that a 40 grams per day protein consumption can be considered a minimum, even for sedentary individuals, while individuals doing heavy manual labor, and presumably athletes, can benefit from a diet containing up to 110 grams per day of protein.

It was found that there is a daily caloric requirement needed for peak output which varies positively with the degree of activity involved.

All this may mean that those small, canned energy drinks whose main ingredients are caffeine, B vitamins and simple sugars may actually work. They may be used when the individual is exhausted and actually build further endurance. This research also means that more oxygen, even the deep breathing as done by boxers between rounds, is probably beneficial toward recovery.

It also means that individuals restricting caloric intake to lose weight will not be at peak performance. Boxers and other athletes who must "make weight" usually do this during training for their next contest. The training period employed for most boxers, for example, is about six weeks. It takes about six weeks to bring a boxer to his peak. If less time is allocated, then the boxer will not be in proper condition. If more time is taken, the boxer runs the risk of overtraining and going stale. But it can be concluded from the research presented above that if the boxer is restricting himself calorically, he will never achieve optimum performance. This research indicates that the wiser course of action might be to diet to make the weight before the six-week training period commences as opposed dieting during the training.

There is an addendum to this story. The reader may be wondering exactly what pervitin is. And the reader may be wondering if it was ever actually used by the German military. In other words, were the Germans on their way to inventing "Universal Soldiers", drugged to enhance performance?

Freedom of Information Act requests were made for "pervitin". One did come back which was obviously only a piece of a much larger story. This involved the 1946 post-war world of Occupied Germany and the culture that sprung up there overnight. This file was marked "secret" at the time and was titled "Report on Deadlock". This file took on both the aspect of a criminal as well as a military investigation because it dealt with a black-market conspiracy to sell pervitin and another stimulant called "hykola" by a former military man of questionable motives.

The concern on the part of the military seems to be the history of the principal character in the investigation who was a former SS man. It seems that their concern was that the funds derived from this black market sale not go to any surviving SS organization. As far as we are concerned, the file is mostly trivial nonsense except for the fact that the drug pervitin was produced in wartime Germany by a company called Tem_ler Werke (one letter cannot be read) and that a sizeable store of these pills was in the possession of the Wehrmacht at the end of the war[2]. No records could be found concerning its field use by the German military but we now know that Pervitin was what we now call methamphetamine.

Sources

1. Head Quarters, United States Air Force In Europe, Office of the Surgeon, Aero-Medical Research Section, September 1, 1945, "Interrogation Of Major Gunther Lehmann, Medical Officer, German Luftwaffe.

2. CSDIC(WEA), "Report on Deadlock", page 5, May 25, 1946, (ref IB/A1/PF 13520 dated 22 May 46 and IB/A1/PF 6467 dated 25 May 46.

10 | Magnetofunk and Himmelskompass and Point 103

The Magnetofunk and Himmelscompass were passive defenses used by the Germans in conjunction with their secret arctic base, which Wilhelm Landig calls "Point 103". To gain some understanding of these devices it is necessary to discuss this base but to do that we must digress even further to include the Nazi post-war writer Wilhelm Landig and one of his detractors.

In 1993 Joscellyn Godwin published Arktos The Polar Myth in Science, Symbolism, And Nazi Survival. Godwin summarizes Landig's contribution as best as possible in six pages. Godwin's point in this summarization was to paint Landig's attempt to air the Nazi point of view as Godwin puts it:

> "Goetzen gegen Thule is in one sense a massive work of revisionism, or, to put it plainly, of whitewashing the Nazis."[1].

Godwin is part of a time-tested tradition. He cites and uses the work of known Nazis, but, to do so and to get his work published, he must mumble an anti-Nazi formula as penitence. The effect is to discredit Landig. Unfortunately, because of the language barrier, this has become the "accepted party line" view of Landig in the English-speaking world.

Wilhelm Landig died in 1997. Since then we have learned that he was in the SS and was in charge of security at the Prague Airport, the site were the Habermohl saucer lifted off[2]. In all probability, he oversaw, on at least one occasion, not only the Habermohl model, but the Schriever and Miethe designs as well. Landig was a responsible person within the security structure of the 3rd Reich and probably came across many other items of interest during his duty, which he passes along to us in his writing.

After the war, Landig wrote three novels describing things and events that went on in the war and immediately afterward. He prefaces these works by telling the reader these are novels full of realities. This was code because in the post-war world of Germany and Austria one was not allowed to state in fact what Landig stated in "fiction".

One of these "facts" was Point 103. Point 103 was a secret German base somewhere in the Arctic. Landig tells us it was in Canada but, in fact, it could have been most anywhere. Point 103 was a military base in every sense of the word in "Goetzen". It had hangers, runways, housing, storage facilities, shops, laboratories, and maintenance facilities, all contained in huge caverns blasted from the arctic rock.

One main function of Point 103 was to serve as a weather station since northern storms move from the West before arriving in Europe and accurate weather forecasting on the part of the Germans for their military operations could help mitigate Allied air superiority. The Battle of the Bulge is a great example of how the Germans used bad weather to their advantage.

This base was always sought out by Allied aircraft. Landig tells us that this base survived this aerial onslaught and survived the war. In fact, Landig's story picks up at Point 103 after the war has ended. It is the technology that allowed this base to survive which is our topic in this chapter. These devices, according to Landig, were the Magnetofunk and the Himmelskompass.

The magnetic north pole, the "North" of compasses, is not as close to the geographical North Pole as one would imagine. It is located near 70 degrees of North Latitude, near 90 degrees West Longitude, on the Boothis Peninsula in the Northwest Territories of Canada.

"Funk" in German has to do with our word "radio". Therefore, Magnetofunk is magnetic and delivered by radio waves. The job of the Magnetofunk was to deflect the magnetic lines of force in the instruments of Allied aircraft ever so slightly. Over the vast tracks of the Arctic, this slight deflection was designed to steer the search aircraft safely around Point 103 [3].

But if the magnetic compasses of the Allied aircraft were altered, how would it be prevented from confusing the compasses of the

Germans? How would the base ever be resupplied, for instance?

The answer is the other device under consideration, the Himmelskompas or heavenly compass. This compass did not use the magnetic north pole to orient itself but oriented itself using the position of the sun instead. This compass was so sensitive to sunlight that it could even function in twilight or if the sun was below the horizon. The explanation given is that a portion of the sunlight striking the earth is polarized. This effect is said to be strengthened by the focused magnetic field in the region of the poles. This polarized light was measured and a position relative to the pole fixed[4].

Its ability to function below the horizon is based on its ability to register polarized light which would only appear above the horizon. Not only could this light be used for directional purposes but it could also be used to indicate the aircraft's attitude from the horizontal. This horizonal ability may be the cause of some confusion in its name.

So, Landig claims that through use of these two devices the German polar base's secret location was kept from the Allies while its exact position was known to the Germans. Is this a fairy tale as Godwin implies? Is there any proof?

Nobody has ever found Point 103, or, if they have, this information has been kept from us. Nobody has ever come up with a Magnetofunk as far as I know. But there is independent evidence that the Himmelskompass did exist. And the evidence comes from United States intelligence documents.

These two references are brief and rather cryptic as are many such documents. They are more interested in identifying the devices to be studied without divulging classified details to the casual reader. Remember, the United States military already had plenty of horizon devices which were mounted in the cockpits of aircraft and indicated to the pilot the degree of level flight of the aircraft. Therefore, we are not discussing the usual cockpit horizon device in these reports.

The first report comes from a prisoner of war, Kurt Kreutzfeld, involved in German high technology. In the report in question he also discussed German glide bombs, rocketry, devices for projectile direction, as well as microfilmed SS technology. He describes an "Artificial horizon" as:

"A self regulating artificial horizon for use in aircraft was invented by Dr. Knappstein, who had a factory in Berlin –

NO.	TO	FROM	DATE	

PAGE NO. 2

1174 – RESTRICTED – 9 June 1945
Subject: "Mother Horizon"

Request received from Technical Data for one (1) "Mother Horizon", as the Germans called it. It's a remote indicating gyro horizon device. Equipment Lab seems to be the interested agency.

D. L. PUTT,
Colonel, A.C.
Director of Technical Services.

(e) Artificial horizon

A self regulating artificial horizon for use in aircraft was invented by Dr. Knappstein, who had a factory in Berlin-Schoneberg. He worked in collaboration with Henschel, Berlin-Königswusterhausen. The horizon was not affected by any aerobatic manoeuvres.

Above: copy of HQ, U.S. Strategic Air Forces in Europe document discussion "Mother Horizon".

Below: part of a British Intelligence Objectives Sub-Committee report number 142, page 4, discussing an artificial horizon.

Schoneberg. He worked in collaboration with Henschel, Berlin-Koenswusterhausen. The horizon was not affected by any acrobatic maneuvers".[5]

The second document is strange indeed. It is a two-page extract of a certain Lt. Newton's diary, copied and sent to a Col. Deyarmond on 6/21/45 by Col. D.L. Putt, Director of Technical Services. This was a month and a half after the war in Europe ended. The first entry concerned communications problems in forwarding an "engine" to Wright-Patterson AFB and how to avoid such problems in the future. The second entry describes the lack of qualified technical people involved in the "V-1" project (the American investigation) and how it would be great to find qualified Germans to explain it all. The third entry is the shortest and most cryptic:

"1174-Restricted–9 June 1945
Subject: "Mother Horizon"

Request received from Technical Data for one[1] "Mother Horizon", as the German's call it. It's a remotely indicating gyro horizon device. Equipment Laboratory seems to be the interested agency."[6]

These documents are reproduced here.

Incidently, the US military spent huge amounts of time, money and manpower in the years following the war in secret missions, flying over the Arctic. This is no secret now since we have the testimony of Col. Wendele Stevens who took part in these operations while serving in the USAF. In these operations, B-29 bombers were outfitted with the latest electromagnetic sensing gear and flown all over the American and Canadian Arctic allegedly looking for "flying saucers". According to Wendele, when they were sighted, they were filmed and the film and recorded measurements were spirited way to Washington D.C. Nothing was ever heard of them afterward.

It may be no coincidence that something like this was the method used to track down German weather stations during the war. It is also even possible that the origin of these post-war, artic flying saucers was this base or others like it.

SOURCES

1. Godwin, Joscelyn, 1993, page 68, *Arktos The Polar Myth In Science, Symbolism, And Nazi Survival*, Phanes Press, Grand Rapids, MI.

2. Chatwin, Margret, 1999, page 1, Ahnenerbe, UFOs, Neonazis: Wilhelm Landig, Informationsdienst gegen Rechtsextremismus, http://www.idgr.de/texte-1/esoterik/landig/landig.html

3. Landig, Wilhelm, 1971, pages 121, 132, *Goetzen gegen Thule Ein Roman voller Wirklichkeiten*, Hans Pfieffer VerlagGmbH, Hannover

4. Landig, Wilhelm, 1971, page 27

5. British Intelligence Objectives Sub-Committee report 142, page 4, Information Obtained From Targets Of Opportunity In The Sonthofen Area, London,

6. Unmarked document, undated, titled "Carrier Sheet", page two, microfilm numbers: A-1007, 1652

11 | **German Free Energy Research**

The Germans like people everywhere in the 20th century, were experimenting with free energy or new energy inventions. Among those well-known inventions are the Hans Coler devices and the Karl Schnappeller device. The Karl Schnappeller device was described in an earlier book, Hitler's Flying Saucers: A Guide To German Flying Discs Of The Second World War. The Hans Coler device is one of the best-known devices thanks to the British having declassified their analysis of his work and their publication and translation of earlier evaluations[1]. Beyond these two, there is the work of Georg Otto Erb, which was also briefly touched upon in Hitler's Flying Saucers.

Besides working on field propulsion systems, Dr. Erb also worked on "Electric sources of energy of various kinds" as well as "Apparatus for turning the energy of the sun's rays into electrical energy"[2]. A page of the microfilm report is reproduced here. Beyond this report there is no information on Dr. Erb or his research during or after the war.

The devices of Hans Coler are quite another matter. Information about them can is only a mouse-click away using the search words "Hans Coler". Indeed, the entire British Intelligence Sub-Committee report is reproduced on-line, in full. So perhaps instead of a full review of his work, our time would be best spent in discussion of Coler and his ideas as they are contained in that report.

Hans Coler incorporated permanent magnets into both of his devices. There were two of these, the

Statement of the work of Dr. Otto ERB

1. Before the war, Dr. Erb developed measuring instruments of all sorts. The following are examples of his work:

(i) Measuring apparatus for interference free determination of the hardness and temper of steel.
(ii) Electrical measuring apparatus for automatic control of storage temperature.
(iii) Apparatus for conversion of residual heat into electrical energy.
(iv) Electrical medical apparatus of various sorts.
(v) High tension apparatus.
(vi) Warning mechanisms for excessive temperatures.
(vii) Electric fire fighting apparatus.
(viii) Electric sources of energy of various kinds.
(ix) Apparatus for turning the energy of the sun's rays into electrical energy.
(x) Rearward impulse propulsion for vehs and aircraft.
(xi) Wood gas generator for high performance.

After outbreak of war he had to devote his research to armament work.

CIC 75/139   - 1 -   Enclosure

Government file on Dr. Georg Otto Erb. Note his interest in new sources of energy.

SOLID STATE - AMPLIFYING TRANSFORMERS
HANS COLER - CURRENT FLOW DEVICE & MAGNET CURRENT FLOW APPARATUS

Hans Coler, a German energy researcher from the period from 1936 to 1945 evolved several promising solid state electrical energy sources using permanent magnets, various shaped coils, copper plates and condensers (capacitors).

Two significant devices were produced from this war-time research, the first being the *"Stromerzeuer,"* or *Current Flow Device*, which consisted of a central transformer comprised of two flat coils, with the ends of the secondary flat coil connected in series with the South poles of two permanent magnets. The North poles of the two permanent magnets are linearly connected to two flat copper plates.

The output leads were connected to the ends of the copper plates, all in accordance with the accompanying diagram.

The input to the primary flat coil was at the wattage level provided by a standard dry cell battery, presumed to be the 1½ volt size. It was claimed that when the battery energized the primary circuit, a separation of charge takes place, influenced by the two magnet polarities, within the linear circuitry. When the battery source was switched off, a reversing current is supposed to flow, in the secondary circuit, but the magnets are not supposed to influence a polarization effect on this reversing.

Several size versions of the "Stromerzeuger" were built, one small ten watt unit, a larger seventy (70) watt unit and finally a large unit built in 1937 reportedly produced 6 KW output.

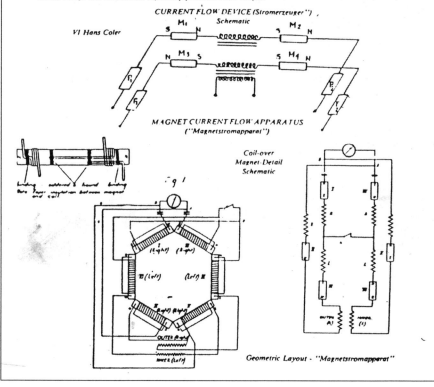

German Free Energy Devices: *Above* is the Stromerzeuger which greatly interested the German Navy.
Below is the agnetstromapparat, a demonstration device.

"Magnetstromapparat" and the "Stromerzeuger". The Magnetstromapparat was fully developed and completed by 1933 with the help of von Unruh and Franz Haid of Siemens-Schukert. This means that the Siemens firm, inspire of later denials (or memory losses), has known of free energy and specifically the Hans Coler device since the early 1930s. In 1933, as part of a test, the Magnetstromapparat was locked in a room in the Norwegian Legation in Berlin. During the time it was locked away, the Coler device continued to produce electric tension of thirteen volts

No further work was done by Coler on the Magnetstromapparat after this time. His entire energies were focussed on the Stromerzeuger. In 1943 Coler and his work ended up at the O.K.M., or the German Navy. At this time Coler had achieve an output of 6 kilovolts for the Stromerzeuger. This was just the basic unit, meaning that additional sections could be grafted onto this unit for a much increased output.

The official "party line" is that no further developments came after this time, meaning that the German Navy never used this device. The story gets even more definitive in that it is claimed that the Coler devices were destroyed in an air raid. For what purpose do you suppose the German Navy might have used this device? I have only one clue to offer. By this time in the war the German Navy was really nothing more than the German U-boat service. Imagine a U-boat running on electricity generated underwater without an air-consuming diesel engine? Do you think they just might be interested?

It was only after the war, in 1946, when Color found himself in the British occupation zone, that the Magnetstromapparat was rebuilt at the request of the British. The British supplied material but the device was re-created in Germany. The British also asked for a materials list for the much more powerful Stromerzeuger, but information on its re-construction is lacking.

The Stromerzeuger was not one device or model but several. In reading the descriptions given by scientists who studied the device for fraud, it is evident that these devices varied in size and output as well as design details.

The Stromerzeuger consisted of two separate devices, a primary connected via induction to a secondary. The primary was activated by battery. The primary was opened and closed inducing a reaction in the secondary. The output from the secondary was said to have been many times that of the primary's input. Additional "secondaries" could be added, further increasing output.

Coler said that ferro-magnetism has an oscillation of a frequency of 180 kilohertz. The interaction of this frequency and that of opening and closing the circuit is thought by Coler to have built up an electrical tension.

Coler thought this tension was further enhanced by what he called "Raumenergie" or "space energy". Coler believed that this additional outside energy, "space electrons" flowed from "repelling spaces" to "attracting spaces" in his device. These were located in the flat copper plates he used as part of the circuit. This attracting-repelling space sounds very much like the semiconductor theories presented in modern textbooks. The space energy is still unrecognized by accepted science, yet the British confirmed that the Magnetstromapparat worked and could not be explained by conventional electrical theory.

The British report on Coler was not de-classified until 1978 or 1979, well after the first energy crisis. If this were just mad ravings, then it would have never been classified and would have been used for propaganda purposes to discredit German science, thus removing it from the notice or interest of "enquiring minds".

It sounds like when the flat copper plates were activated, they acted like an open drain-plug, allowing this "space energy" to enter the circuit.

Hold on, we are not quite done with German free or new energy devices and research and I promise you a big surprise when we return to it.

SOURCES

1. British Intelligence Objectives Sub-Committee report no. 1043, item no. 31,
   The Invention Of Hans Coler, Relating To An Alleged New Source Of Power,
   1946, London, W.1.

2. Combined Intelligence Objectives Sub-Committee report number 146,
   Dr. Georg Otto Erb

12 | Technical Infrastructure

Just as established history tells us that there are no new energy sources or new energy devices, established history also tells us that it was not the Germans, but the Americans who detonated the first atomic device. German atomic research is often described in establishment history as consisting of a crude atomic pile in someone's basement or backyard which would have either exploded or the faulty device would have killed everyone involved with radiation. This is the classic undervaluation, minimization story.

But if the Germans were able to do far more than they have been credited, wouldn't there be some sort of corroborating technical evidence? In other words, wouldn't there have been a supporting technical infrastructure?

Thanks to the intensive efforts of Allied intelligence to investigate every aspect of the technical underpinnings of the German war effort, we have the evidence in the form of the Combined Intelligence Objectives Sub-Committee reports, the British Intelligence Objectives Sub-Committee reports, the F.I.A.T. reports and other similar research gathering reports and organizations. All these agencies published findings and summary reports, even if they have not all been de-classified today. It would take volumes of books to bind and organize this material but I would like to discuss one or two that have a bearing on past and future topics.

Through much of the war, research was directed by the Reich's Research Council. From here it was organized in three phases. Basic research was done at a

List of Equipment, etc., Evacuated by Mr. Horsley of
T.I.C. from 21 A.G.Area.l, July, 1945.

No Originals except Dr. Muller's Betatron Notebooks
and Misc. Magnetron Data from C.H.F. Muller.

BOX 1. A. Muller Drawings re. Tubes 300 Kv. Rectifier, etc.

B. Siefert Data.

C. Miscellaneous (Electron Microscope Phillips Valve
Works data, Seifert Industrial X-Ray book, Infrared data etc.)

D. Muller Underwater Sound Unit assembly drawings.

E. Muller Patent Applications.

F. Muller Magnetron Parts.

G. Muller gas filled Communication Tubes and Special
resistance Wire.

H. Siemens & Halske ThreePart Anode.

BOX 2. 2 M.V. Betatron Tubes.

BOX 3. A. Muller Drawings of New Tubes and Dental Head

B. Muller Neutron generator Drawings.

C. Muller Technique and Sales Bulletins, Phillips
Organisation Chart, write-up of Hydrogen Casting
and Throiated Filament Processes.

D. Muller Patent Applications.

E. Phillips Technical Roundups.

BOX 4. A. Muller Drawings of New Tubes and Dental Tube Head

B. Muller, Neutron Generator Drawings.

C. Muller Technique and Sales Bulletins, Phillips
Organization Chart, write-up of Hydrogen Casting
and Throiated Filament Processes.

D. Muller Patent Applications.

E. Phillips Technical Round-up.

F. 15 M.V. Betatron Drawings

G. 200 M.V. Betatron Layouts.

H. Kulenkampff Paper.

I. Wrist Generator Data.

J. Wrist Patent Applications.

K. Contact Therapy Book.

From the Combined Intelligence Objectives Sub-Committee report number 174, C.H.F. Muller, A.G. This is a list of recovered items in boxes. Note: box 3, letter B and box 4, letter B, "Neutron Generator Drawings". Also note in box 4, I and J which concerng a wrist generator data and patent application. Magnetrons and betatrons are also discussed.

"Forschungs" (research) facility. After the basic concept had been tested and verified, the idea, machine, weapon, etc., went on to an "Entwicklung" (development) facility where the idea was worked out in practical terms. From here the idea was carried to a production facility that was a manufacturer, usually a commercial manufacturer. The larger manufacturers have names which are familiar to us, Heinkel, Siemens, I.G. Farben, etc. But it could also go to a smaller, less known manufacturer.

Having described a chain of events, it should be added that there were many exceptions to this sequence. Some of the manufacturing companies did their own research. Universities and technical colleges did research besides and in addition to that sponsored by the government. Every branch of the German military did independent research. There were many private inventors and scientists working on their own projects that were of special interest to them. Finally, the SS had a vast system of research by the end of the war and actually appropriated facilities and people from other organizations.

Government intelligence reports are not explicit but what I would like to do is use them to describe a couple of these research facilities and a small manufacturing firm who made devices necessary for the development of some of the more exotic devices we will encounter later. Also, a description of one or two of the completely researched concepts from those days might prove interesting.

Let us first look at the C.H.F. Muller, A.G. Company. This was a small manufacturing company, employing about 500 people with about 80,000 square feet of floor space.

C.H.F. Muller made x-ray machines and similar electronic devices that were employed in the nuclear effort. They made x-ray machines for use in the medical realm. They also made a "cascade" high voltage generator, 900 to 2,400 Kv. for use as a deutron generator. A deutron or deuteron is the nucleus of the deuterium atom. Deuterium is an isotope of hydrogen meaning that it has the same chemical properties as hydrogen but a slightly different atomic structure. Both hydrogen and deuterium form oxides, hydrogen oxide and deuterium oxide. We call hydrogen oxide "water" and deuterium oxide "heavy water".

C.H.F. Muller made magnetrons of apparently their own design. A magnetron is used to generate very high frequency wavelengths. They also made betatrons of three kinds. The betatron had only been recently invented and it was used to generate very high-energy electron beams as well as extremely powerful beams of x-rays. The x-rays generated using a betatron have very great penetrating power. C.H.F. Muller made electron microscopes, a "wrist generator" (a patent application for this device was also found at C.H.F. Muller) and there were plans found for a Muller neutron generator. Let's look at the last two in more detail.

A few years back, a retired USAF Colonel, Philip Corso, made some claims about finding a dead alien in a plastic body bag at some US Air Force base in his book titled, The Day After Roswell. Well, he couldn't produce the dead alien for his book or even a picture of it or another witness to corroborate his testimony, so, to bolster his argument he linked this alleged dead alien with examples of to-that-time unknown technology which he claimed were of alien origin. The two big unknown technologies he cited as coming from with the alien universe were the transistor and night vision equipment.

Night vision equipment is well documented as having been invented by the Germans during World War Two. In fact, the device described below must have been some sort of light amplification device. This particular device was said to have been powered by a truly miniature generator.

> "He showed me then what had been two of the most
> closely-guarded technical secrets of the war: the infrared
> device which the Germans invented for seeing at night
> and the remarkable diminutive generator with operated
> it. German cars could drive at any speed in total blackout,
> seeing objects clear as day two hundred meters ahead.
> Tanks with this device could spot targets two miles away.
> As a sniper scope it enabled German riflemen to pick off
> a man in total darkness.
>
> There was a sighting tube, and a selenium screen out
> front. The screen caught the incoming infrared light,
> which drove electrons from the selenium along the tube
> to another screen that was electrically charged and
> fluorescent. A visible image appeared on this screen. Its
> clearness and its accuracy for aiming purposes were
> phenomenal. Inside the tube, distortion of the stream of
> electrons by the earth's magnetism was even allowed for!

25. Cable Technology
    (Kabeltechnik)   Dr KADEN

B. SIEMENS-HALSKE Production Plants

   These plants are under the supervision of Direktor Dr LUESCHEN:

26. F-Werk   Dir SEIFER
                                      Dir WECHER   Bldg 10

27. M-Werk: Measuring Instruments
    (Messinstruments)   Dir Dr SCHLEICHER
                                      Dir PFEIER   Bldg 11

28. T-Werk: Telegraphic Devices
    (Telegrafengeraet)   Dir STOVIK   SPANDAU

29. Fg-Werk: Telephone Devices
    (Fernsprechgeraet)   unknown   SPANDAU

30. Y-Werk: amplifying Devices
    (Verstaerkergeraet)   Dir Dr RABANNUS   Bldg 10

31. EL-Werk: Electrochemical plant
    (Elektrochemie)   Dir Dr ILLIG

C. Research Laboratory

32. Research Laboratory   Prof Dr HERTZ*
33.   (Forschungslabor)   Prof TREUDELNBURG**
                                                          corner of
                                                          Rohrdamm &
          * a nephew of Heinrich HERTZ   Motardstr.,
         ** accoustic specialist   in cellar
                                                          of new bldg.

34. The main research work is at present concerned with the destruction of atoms (Zyklotron). Experiments are conducted in accordance with
principles formulated by U.S. scientists. Prof Dr HERTZ witnessed some of
these experiments in the States in 1939.

This is part of a page from a Secret report, dated October 1944 but issued in March, 1945, titled: Coil Research Laboratory Siemens Halske Berlin (6824 DIC/MIS/NOT-533) Please note item 34. At this radio research and development laboratory the Germans experimented with a "Zyklotron" with is their spelling of cyclotron. A cyclotron is a particle accelerator, still used in atomic research and development to this day.

> The diminutive generator-five inches across-stepped up
> current from an ordinary flashlight battery to 15,000
> volts. It had a walnut-sized motor that spun a rotor at
> 10,000 rpm—so fast that originally it had destroyed all
> lubricants with the great amount of ozone it produced.
> The Germans had developed a new grease: chlorinated
> paraffin oil. The generator then ran 3,000 hours!"[1].

The C.H.F. Muller wrist generator fits this description. Please remember this context as we will return to the super lubricant in a later chapter.

The other development mentioned in the intelligence report is the neutron generator. In order to cause a chain reaction, on demand, resulting in an atomic bomb, a method to generate a stream of neutrons is usually thought necessary. The fact that the C.H.F. Muller A.G. had designed some sort of neutron generator indicates that one piece in the puzzle concerning the detonation of an atomic device had been solved.

Along these same lines there was another company in production of electronic devices necessary for an atomic infrastructure. This was the Siemens Halske firm in Berlin who made, among other things, a cyclotron[2]. A cyclotron is a machine that uses a magnetic field to propel heavier nuclear particles. It is a particle accelerator. There have been rumors that the Germans even used a particle accelerator as one method to enrich uranium.

Next we turn to a pure research organization, the Flugfunk Forschungsinstitut Oberpfaffenhofen, abbreviated F.F.O. The F.F.O. was an organization specializing in aeronautical radio research for the Luftwaffe. This organization seems to have specialized in work of jamming radar. This was a large organization and had many physical sites of operation. When the war drew to a conclusion, all the secret research done at the F.F.O. was burnt. What we know and what remains consist largely of what was remembered by the individual scientists involved and their private libraries. It is not unreasonable to assume that some secrets went forever unspoken after those ashes cooled, however.

The F.F.O. developed three types of magnetrons and several types of klystrons. A klystron tube is used to produce ultra-high frequencies but they seem to have been smaller than magnetrons. Klystrons seem

to have been the hot ticket at this time and were employed to generated frequencies in order to jam radar. Klystrons were employed in
the famous "Feuer" devices of which there was more than one[3]. This
name "Feuer" is "fire" in English and has given rise to speculation
that klystrons were employed in the alleged jamming devices on the
German Feuerball (foo or phoo fighter). The klystron tube could very
well have been the transmission apparatus for the Magnetic Wave or
Motorstoppmitel device we will discuss later.

The F.F.O. also did some interesting work in "crystal detectors", as
named by the Americans. But before discussing that topic, perhaps
two examples of completed projects should be pointed out as well as
one involving some very futuristic research:

ELECTROSTATIC ANTI-AIRCRAFT SHELL FUSES

"The principle involved in these fuses is similar to that
used in measurements of electric fields. The shell or
projectile has a small aerial sticking out on one side. The
whole shell rotates about its axis in the normal manner
and this causes the aerial to develop an alternating
voltage if any electrostatic fields are present. This voltage
is fed to the grid of a cold-cathode thyratron tube causing
it to conduct when the voltage is large enough. The
anode of the tube is fed by a condenser that was charged
while the shell was in the gun. The discharge of this
condenser through the thyrotron blows a small electric
fuse and explodes the shell.

The shell is fired from the ground where the electrostatic
field is usually about 1 Kv per metre (it varies between
0.1 and 10 Kv/m). Consequently, the shell has an appreciable charge induced on it by this field before it loses
contact with the earth. During flight this charge gives a
field that is symmetric and produces no alternating
voltage in the aerial. When the shell approaches an
aircraft or large conducting body the induced fields are
asymmetric and can induce alternating voltages of the
order of tens or hundreds of volts in the aerial."[4]

Today, we call this a proximity fuse but it is evident in this careful description by the CIOS that this concept was revolutionary at that time.

GUIDED MISSILES

"A remote control steering mechanism for a falling bomb has been developed by the group of Ing. Kreil at F.F.O. Grafolfing. It consists of an airborne transmitter at 25 mc/s and a receiving system inside the bomb. The aerials are stretched diagonally between the tail fins of the bomb to make them less susceptible to jamming coming from the front of the bomb. The apparatus was unsuccessful owing to electrical discharges (corona, etc.), from the bomb during fall affecting the receiver and causing the bomb to zig-zag. The work was stopped in 1944.

Ing. Kreil said that the Luftwaffe had subsequently found a cure for this by trailing wires with resistors or threads of semi-conducting materials behind the bomb to cause the electrical discharges to take place slowly and without oscillation in the frequency range used for controlling the bomb.[5]

In other words, the F.F.O. invented the first "smart bomb".

STEALTH RESEARCH

"Measurement on the conductivity and dielectric properties of flame gases are being conducted by Dr. Lutze at Seeshaupt. They are intended to provide knowledge of the effects to be expected with radio control of rockets and to say how much the flame and trail of a V-2 contributes to radar reflections."[6]

So the F.F.O. was measuring the conductivity and radar reflectional properties of exhaust gases? Placing a cathode in the exhaust of a jet or rocket was the Flame Jet Generator of Dr. T.T. Brown[7]. This procedure induced a negative charge to the exhaust. A corresponding positive charge is automatically induced on the wing's leading edge. This combination bends

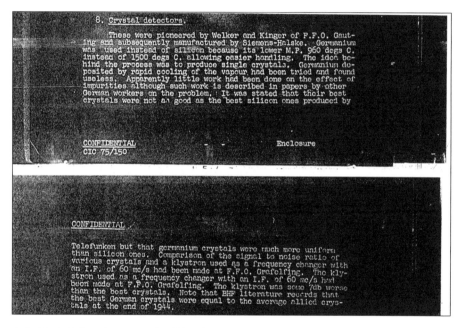

8. Crystal detectors.

These were pioneered by Welker and Kinger of F.F.O. Gauting and subsequently manufactured by Siemens-Halske. Germanium was used instead of silicon because its lower M.P. 960 degs C. instead of 1500 degs C. allowing easier handling. The idea behind the process was to produce single crystals. Germanium deposited by rapid cooling of the vapour had been tried and found useless. Apparently little work had been done on the effect of impurities although such work is described in papers by other German workers on the problem. It was stated that their best crystals were not as good as the best silicon ones produced by

Enclosure

Telefunken but that germanium crystals were much more uniform than silicon ones. Comparison of the signal to noise ratio of various crystals and a klystron used as a frequency changer with an I.F. of 60 mc/s had been made at F.F.O. Grafelfing. The klystron used as a frequency changer with an I.F. of 60 mc/s had been made at F.F.O. Grafelfing. The klystron was some 7db worse than the best crystals. Note that BHF literature records that the best German crystals were equal to the average allied crystals at the end of 1944.

Work of the Flugfunk Forschungsinstitut Oberpfaffenhofen (F.F.O.) on "crystal detectors" involving silicon, germanium and a discussion of impurities within these materials. Engineered impurities in silicon/germanium form the basis for modern semiconductors.

radar signals around the aircraft and is one method used by the B-2 bomber.

Let's back up a second. The Horton 9, described earlier, had recessed intake and exhaust ports. It had no vertical control surfaces. Therefore, its radar reflection was already super-low. We certainly have no trouble imagining this aircraft painted with radar absorbing paint as was planned. How about inducing a radar-bending envelope of charged particles around this aircraft? And how about fitting this aircraft with a klystron tube in its nose pumping out the same frequency used by Allied radar, jamming it or making the aircraft invisible to radar? If we can imagine this, so could the scientists with the F.F.O. If the war had lasted another year, the Allies might have faced not only a 700 mile per hour Horton 9, but a Horton 9 which was also a true stealth aircraft in the modern sense.

Finally, "crystal detectors" should be mentioned. According to the CIOS report, both the F.F.O., the firm Telefunken, and Siemens-Halske worked with this and related ideas, the pioneering work having been done by Welker and Kinger of the F.F.O., Gautling facility. Single crystals were involved which originally were made of silicon. This is the same silicon used today in our modern semi-conductor industry. This technology broke upon the scene with the introduction of the transistor.

The transistor, invented in 1947 by Dr. William Shockley, replaced the glass vacuum tube as a valve or switching device in electronics. The transistor works because it allows electrons to flow only in one direction, on demand. Transistors could make a gate or valve in a three-way connection. It does this using special impurities in the crystal structure which facilitate electron flow.

Philip Corso, in his book The Day After Roswell, claims that aliens invented transistors and they just suddenly appeared on the scene. These transistors just fell into the hands of Dr. Shockley at Bell Laboratories, according to Corso. Of course nobody in the scientific community agrees with Corso. But what would be evidence for the terrestrial development of transistors? It would be a history of development of transistors and related devices right here on earth leading up to the transistor.

Not only was the F.F.O. and other institutions working with silicon in electronics during the Second World War, they were also working with the other crystal substance always mentioned in discussion of semi-conductors, Germanium. In fact, the CIOS report describes manufacturing methods involving both of these crystals and compares the results of silicon vs. Germanium.

Of course, there are those who will say that working on crystals is not necessarily the same as working on semi-conductors. But the discussion of impurities within a discussion of silicon or Germanium would indicate a discussion of semi-conductors. From the CIOS report:

> "Apparently little work had been done on the effect of impurities although such work is described in papers by other German workers on the problem."[8]

At first, this may sound like negative evidence but it is not. It says that the Germans were not working on semi-conductors at the F.F.O. but they had recognized the concept and were not only working on the problem somewhere else, they had written about it. This report is dated July 1, 1945, just after the war in Europe ended. This pre-dates the alleged Roswell crash. It documents that research in semi-conductors or leading to semi-conductors took place on planet earth shortly before their disclosure in the form of the transistor. I really do not know if the Germans invented the transistor and if it was later funneled into the hands of an American company or not. But this CIOS report does document that the Germans were at the very least involved in this research which not only argues for their high-tech status, it strips the late Col. Corso of any corroborating physical evidence for aliens besides his body-bag testimony.

What these examples show is that the technical infrastructure which was present in Germany during this period of time was more than advanced enough to supply research scientists with machines and devices they needed to do advanced work. This technical infrastructure was at least the equal of anything found in Britain or the United States at the time.

SOURCES

1. Walker, C. Lester, "Secrets By The Thousands", October, 1946, page 331, Harper's Magazine

2. Coil Research Laboratory Siemens Halske Berlin Oct 44, March 14, 1945, reference numbers 0136094, 6824 DIc/Mis/Noi-5633, VicaMed. Afbq No R-1198/455

3. Combined Intelligence Objectives Sub-Committee report number 139, "Drs. Kleen & Larbs,1 July, 1945, page 2

4. Combined Intelligence Objectives Sub-Committee report number 156, "Report On Flugfunk Forschungsinstitut Oberpfaffenhofen F.F.O. Establishments, 1 July, 1945, pages 9 and 10

5. ibid

6. ibid

7. Stevens, Henry, Hitler's Flying Saucers A Guide To German Flying Discs Of The Second World War, 2003, pages 132-136, Adventures Unlimited Publishing, Kempton, Illinois

8. Combined Intelligence Objectives Sub-Committee report number 156, "Report On Flugfunk Forschungsinstitut Oberpfaffenhofen F.F.O. Establishments, 1 July, 1945, pages 7 and 8

13 | German Atomic Test

For some readers of history the very idea that Germany built and tested an atomic device during World War Two is heretical. Conventional history has drilled it into our heads that American scientists of the Manhattan Project built the first atomic weapons. They allegedly succeeded in accomplishing this goal in July of 1945 with the first atomic weapon was tested in New Mexico. Beginning in August of 1945, atomic weapons were dropped on Japan, which brought the Second World War to a close. It is all very neat and tidy. American scientists became heroes, icons in our culture. Buildings and whole institutions are named after Enrico Fermi and Robert Oppenheimer, for instance. At the same time we are told that the weak German effort at building atomic weapons was too little and too late and too disorganized.

Established history does not deny the German atomic program, it only minimizes it. Modern writers cite such evidence as the Farm Hall conversations as proof that the German scientists were years behind the Americans in building atomic weapons. At the same time established history seeks to maximize the British effort to destroy the German heavy water producing facilities in central Norway. This operation is treated as one of the military/technological turning points in the war effort and one that sealed the fate of the German atomic weapons program permanently. So that is it, then, neat and tidy?

Recently, new information has cast doubt on idea that the Germans were incompetent in this area. This new information is based upon evidence in Europe itself rather than simply the controlled information released in post-war America.

Some of this new information is based upon exploration of underground facilities abandoned by the Germans in the closing days of the war[1]. Many of these underground facilities were sealed with explosives as the Germans retreated and never re-opened until after the collapse of the former Soviet Union. Some of this new information is based upon research done in Germany at the Jonas Valley which indicates that a whole atomic infra-structure was set up there during and that this was done after the destruction of the heavy water facilities in Norway[2]. This is not conjecture but based upon eyewitness evidence as well as actual physical evidence which is still on-site. Some of this new information resides in the American government's own declassified words in which they admit the existence of neutron generators, for instance[3], and affix the location and scientists involved.

And finally, some of the new information comes from interconnecting a number of separated and isolated eyewitness and historical sources[4] which would have been impossible only a few years ago. The resulting tableau painted by these facts is shocking, to say the least. What emerges is a detailed step-by-step, date-by-date account of the German atomic program. Actually, it is many programs, not three or even six. Some were secret programs within a secretive Germany, one of these being run by the SS. Thanks to this new research, we have dates, locations, names of scientists who were involved and even the weapons they produced at these individual locations.

The Germans did make atomic bombs. Not only did they make atomic bombs, they made uranium as well as plutonium bombs and other atomic weapons which remain somewhat of a mystery. What the Germans could not do in these dying days of the 3rd Reich, was to match up one of these nuclear warheads with an effective delivery system. The reasons for this differ with each weapon, individually, and run the gambit from mistake to treachery to incompetence[4].

The shocking outcome of these events was that the unexploded German atomic bombs fell into the hands of the Americans at the end of the war in Europe in May of 1945, two months before the "first" explosion of an atomic weapon in the New Mexico desert. What a present for the Americans! All they did was to put new tail fins on the bombs, repaint them, and drop them on Japan. Naturally, the American scientists involved with the Manhattan Project were given credit[4].

As an aside, the fact is that many of those very scientists were spies for the Soviet Union during this time as recently discovered Soviet intelligence proves[5]. I am not talking about simple middlemen like the Rosenbergs. What I am talking about are those very icons in our society who speak for American atomic scientists. I am talking about all those American atomic scientists who found a "conscious" after they realized the atomic bomb would never be used on Germany, as they hoped, but might instead be used on the Soviets after the war was over. I am talking about those "emigre", "peacenik" scientists calling for and "end to war". I am talking about those scientists who posed, smoking a pipe, as someone somehow smarter and morally on a higher plane than you and I.

Here are the facts: "Calibre" was the Soviet code-name for their agent Greenglass. "Editor" was their name for Enrico Fermi and "Star" was the Soviet code-name for their agent Robert Oppenheimer[5]. These men are our cultural heroes. Put your hand behind your ear. Can you hear the KGB laughing all the way from Moscow? Not only were they spies, they conspired to lie about their work and did so. But they are not alone. They got a lot of help from their friends in the intelligence community and the mass media. The amazing truth is that they got away with the whole big lie. The Manhattan Project scientists, failures, unable to build their own atomic bomb, literally fell into the toilet and came out smelling like roses, as far as history is concerned.

I am not going to try to re-tell the whole story of the German atomic projects. Those interested can see the sources below. What I would like to do is tell one story. It is a story of an eyewitness to a German atomic test which took place in October of 1944, nine months before "history" says that was possible.

This report originates in the journal "Defensa", Number 76-77, August-September of 1984. The text was in Italian but a summary and translation appeared in German language and it is from this translation that this report is derived[6]. The report was the life experience of the writer, Luigi Romersa. Mr. Romersa was sent upon a strange mission by Bonito Mussolini, the Fascist leader of Italy and Hitler's ally. The time was April of 1944. The war was not going well for the Axis Powers and Mussolini was summoned to a meeting with Hitler at Castle Klessheim, near Saltzburg, Austria. The meeting lasted three days. With Mussolini came Marshal Rodolfo Graziani and with Hitler were von Ribbentrop, Keitel, Dollmann and Ambassador Rahn. Hitler's allies had been given little information on the development of German wonder weapons until this time. This meeting was the first time Hitler had broached the subject with Mussolini.

Hitler and Mussolini were genuine friends. In the past, Hitler had personally defended Mussolini when he was disparaged by ranking members of the German military. Hitler had personally intervened when the Italian government did a flop-flop and deposed Mussolini, imprisoning him on a mountaintop fortress while entering into negotiations to turn him over to the Allies. This intervention took the form of Colonel Otto Skorzeny, who led a team of commando raiders onto this mountaintop fortress in a daring glider attack. El Duce was freed and flown to Vienna before the turn-coat Italian government knew what had happened. Mussolini was subsequently installed in a Northern Italian government, loyal to Hitler. Mussolini spoke excellent German and had even given a speech or two in that language. So, bearing these facts in mind, it was not lack of trust or lack of communication, which caused the doubt that had arisen in Mussolini's mind after hearing Hitler's discussion of German wonder weapons. But Mussolini did want to know if Hitler's promised weapons could really win the war. In other words, he wanted to do his own appraisal.

The first meeting lasted two hours. By all accounts, Hitler was the master of positive thinking and was also the master of intoning such optimism in the face of adversity. Using this manner, Hitler reviewed the global political and military situation and inundated his guests with impressions and observations. He assured his audience that the war would certainly be won once Germany had deployed its new weapons. Hitler walked through the room as he said:

> "We have aircraft, imperceptible U-boats, giant tanks and cannons, unbelievably powerful rockets and a bomb with a force which will surprise the whole world. The enemy knows this, he attacks us, he destroys us, but through this destruction he will be answered with attack and without launching biological warfare, for which we are also prepared. (…). All my words correspond with the purest truth which will be confirmed."

After the meeting Mussolini quietly returned to Gargnaro, on Lake Garda in Northern Italy, where he had a residence. Mussolini clearly wanted to know more.

In the Fall of 1944, Mr. Romersa was summoned by Mussolini to the villa Orsoline where he was living with his family. Romersa was given the assignment by Mussolini to journey to Germany and find out more about things which had only been presented to him superficially at Castle Klessheim. Mussolini wanted detailed information. Romersa was given credentials and a letter of recommendation for Goebbels and Hitler, respectively.

Romersa traveled to Germany by car. Hitler personally read the letter of recommendation in his headquarters at Rastenburg in East Prussia and allowed Mr. Romersa's presence at some experiments. He began his tour with underground factories that were concentrated in Upper Selesia and Bavaria.

The underground factories were more like small cities buried underground within a mountain. Elevators offered access the inner bowels of these well-camouflaged, well-guarded facilities. The tunnels ran kilometer after kilometer within the earth, all connected by rail, which facilitated transport of personnel as well as material.

The tour of the underground facilities, however interesting, was not the highlight of Mr. Romersa's trip to Germany. Sometime during the night of October 11, 1944 Mr. Romesa was picked up at the hotel Adlon in Berlin. He was told that after this particular trip, he would be received by none other than Minister Goebels himself. Mr. Romersa asked where he was being taken but to his question there was no answer. This was at two o'clock in the morning. A light rain fell that night as he was driven to his goal. At ten o'clock the following morning they arrived and got out of the car. They were on the shores of the Baltic in the vicinity of Stralsund. They took a motorboat from there to the island of Ruegen. Ruegen was within the testing range were many German weapons were completed. This was a secret place, guarded by specialized units. It was an area in which none could even set foot without an approval card from the supreme command of the German military. In fact, Ruegen Island lies just north of Peenemuende.

Once on Ruegen Island, they immediately went into a region that was sheltered by trees. In a flat area within this forest there had been prepared stone houses and a protective bunker made from cement. They went into a half buried underground tower through a metal door that was closed behind them. Besides Mr. Romersa, there were three other men in the party.

One of the military men who had accompanied Romersa began talking. He said that they would now witness a test of an atomic bomb. Nothing could withstand the blast of such a bomb, the man went on, saying that the explosive power of this bomb was the strongest ever discovered. They were only a kilometer from the point of the explosion but, of course, well sheltered from the blast, which was scheduled for noon. Nevertheless, they would have to remain in the bunker until that evening. Romersa was told that the bomb released deadly radiation. The effective circumference of the blast would be a kilometer and a half. The witnesses would, therefore not only be seeing the blast, they would be experiencing it first hand.

The telephone rang. The test had been moved up to 11:45 A.M. Slits in the side of the concrete bunker had been provided which were covered with smoked glass for viewing. Romersa could see trees and a darkened landscape. The telephone ran again with the exact time of detonation. All present synchronized their wristwatches.

Suddenly a blinding light appeared as the concrete tower of the bunker shook. As Mr. Romersa watched, a thick curtain of smoke descended over the landscape and then the cloud covered their position. Nobody spoke. They were entangled in the smoke and the impact of the blast. They felt as if they had fallen over an abyss.

Finally, the driver of their vehicle who was a lieutenant in the army, the branch of the service that had prepared this test, said that the test they had seen and therefore confirmed was extremely important. When ready, he went on, these bombs could be dropped on the Anglo-American invasion troops or on enemy cities. This bomb, he said, should cause the enemy to think twice about the course of this war.

The officer went on: We have done research for years. After long and tiring experimentation, we have finally completed this discovery. We have facilities everywhere. Some were met with and destroyed by the enemy, such as the facilities in Norway, but Peenemuende is intact although the Americans have sought to destroy this facility. In six or seven months the series mass production of these bombs will begin. Everything will change then but some will be perplexed or discon-certed because of or on account of the introduction of this frightful remedy.

Mr. Romersa continues his narrative which is loosely translated here: About four o'clock, the hall dark, there appeared some shadows. They ran to our bunker tower. They were soldiers dressed in what looked like some sort of strange diving suit. These soldiers soon entered the building. They brought with them special garments for those inside to wear as they left the shelter of the bunker. Romersa did not know for sure what the overcoats were made of but they were white, rough fiber-like material that might have been asbestos. The head covering was provided with a slit of mica-like glass at eye level. They were given high but very light boots to wear as well as gloves made from the same material as the overcoats. The soldiers led them out of the bunker tower in single file.

The farther they got from the bunker the more mixed up the landscape looked. The forest looked like it had been swamped by a wave of fire. In this burnt-out setting, Mr. Romera's foot struck something unusual. It turned out to be the carbonized body of a goat. The stone houses and tower that he had seen a few hours earlier were completely swept away. The devastation increased as they moved toward ground zero. Here, the grass had a strange color resembling chamois and the trees that had remained upright were stripped of their leaves. They returned to Berlin that night.

Before the end of October Mr. Romersa met with Minister Goebbels. The meeting took place at Goebbels home. Goebbels was informed of Mr. Romersa's presence at the "Experiment in Ruegen". He told Mr. Romersa that by various means great numbers of these weapons would be manufactured by which the enemy would be "decisively met with". Countermeasures to the weapon, if any, could be thought up later since, by that time, this war would be over.

Goebbels paused and then began discussing delivery systems. He told Mr. Romersa that the bombs would be delivered by special U-boats equipped with snorkels and turbines, from radio controlled V-weapons of unbelievable high speed, from supersonic aircraft, from long-range rockets, A-4 and A-9 with a range of more than one thousand kilometers. For a few months we must bear our teeth and hold out, Goebbles said. "We need time. Twenty-four hours could be decisive".

Goebbels began to discuss the development of the atomic bomb. He mentioned that heavy water facilities were located in Norway as well as on the Northeastern coast of Germany. The Allies knew of these facilities and their meaning. Air attacks and sabotage had been mounted, the latter being successful in Norway but not in Germany. Hitler, according to Goebbels, had not wanted to employ atomic bombs at first because he thought them unnecessary to win the war. In 1942, he changed his mind and inquired as to how long such weapons would take to develop. He was told it would be two years, which he considered too long. He changed his mind again in 1943 at which time intensive work began anew.

Goebbels described other weapons, confirming what Romersa had been told earlier. These included new cannons, and instruments that would allow the Germans to see and precisely shoot in the dark. A dozen new remotely controlled rockets were in the works. A-4 and A-9 rockets were to be equipped with 10 and 15 ton atomic warheads respectively.

Then Goebbels came back to a recurring theme. This theme was the need to hold out until these weapons became operational. He reiterated that six months were necessary. This contest was clearly a war of time since the Allies were dropping tons of bombs, day and night, in the hope that Germany would collapse in the meantime. Goebbel's final words to Romesa were: "Germany's salvation depends upon its genius".

What can be made of Mr. Romersa's narrative? The Germans clearly wanted Mr. Romersa to recount his impressions of the atomic test and the optimistic words he had heard to Benito Mussolini. But by late 1944, Mussolini was not in any real position to assist Germany at this point in the war. German atomic weapons were never deployed. The German atomic programs were discredited by the Allies. Nobody had ever mentioned a German atomic test. One wonders what would have happened to anybody making such a claim in the early days of the cold war. In light of these developments, Mr. Romersa's extraordinary experience on Ruegen Island became a politically incorrect "tale" or at best a baseless "war story". Without confirmation, it is no wonder that he kept the information to himself for so many years.

But Luigi Romersa, himself, did not fall off the pages of history. After the war, somehow, perhaps because of his substantial insider information concerning the Axis Powers, Romersa applied for and was granted a high security clearance with the government of the United States of America[7]. He went on in 1959 to write a ten part series, titled: "Wernher Von Braun Y La America Del Futuro" (Wernher von Braun and the Future of America) for a Spanish

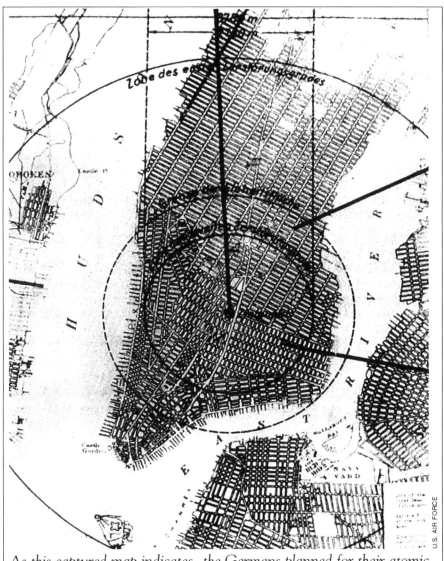

U.S. AIR FORCE

As this captured map indicates, the Germans planned for their atomic bomb—to be delivered by a specially designed V-2 rocket—to explode near Delancy Street and the Bowery in downtown New York City.

This is a German map of New York City showing he projected destruction their atomic bomb would cause. *Source:* World War II, (magazine), Danny Parker.

GESTERN NACHRICHT, HEUTE GESCHICHTE

Die "GEHEIMWAFFEN " von HITLER, etwas mehr als (nur) Phantasie

Von Luigi ROMERSA

Die Geschichte die ich jetzt erzählen werde gründet auf gewissen Erfahrungen/Ereignissen die ich persönlich miterlebte und die damals – als der Krieg noch nicht beendet war – von vielen zu schnell als Phantasien bezeichnet wurden. Die Geheimdienste von Amerikanern, Briten und Franzosen haben am Anfang auch gedacht es wären nur Phantasien, aber diese Meinung musste man ändern um sich mit all den zur Verfügung stehenden Mitteln zu schützen.

Ich spreche über die deutschen Geheimwaffen, welche mit dem Namen oder besser Genie, von Wernher Von Braun verbunden sind. Ich hatte eine brüderliche Freundschaft mit ihm von 1944 bis zu seinem Tod.

Dass Deutschland gegen Kriegsende über ein Waffenarsenal verfügte, dass verglichen mit was von deren Feinden benützt wurde, jede Phantasie herausforderte ist heute eine anerkannte unbestreitbare Tatsache. (...).

In 1945, als er den offizieller Sieg verkündete, sagte Churchill: *Die Entdeckungen die wir vor kurzer Zeit*

[Seite 130]

auf dem deutschen, holländischen und französischem Gebiet gemacht haben zeigen, dass der Zusammenbruch des Feindes Grossbritannien von einer furchtbaren Gefahr rettete, (...). Die alliierten Armeen haben die Schlange in dem letzten Moment in ihrer Brutstätte zerstört, (...). Der Oberst D.L. Putt, vom Kommando der amerikanischen Streitkräfte in den besetzten Gebieten, hat sich nicht wenger deutlich als Churchill ausgedrückt als er die Beendigung der Operationen bewertete. *Nur einige Wochen mehr* – sagte er – *und die Deutschen hätten eine entscheidende Waffe eingesetzt: Atombomben, von denen sie zwei hatten, wären in die V2 eingebaut worden. (...).*

This is the first page of a German translation of an article written by Luigi Romersa in the journal "Defensa", number 76-77, August 1984, titled: "Yesterday's News, Today's History: The "Secret Weapons" of Hitler, Something more than (mere) Fantasy".

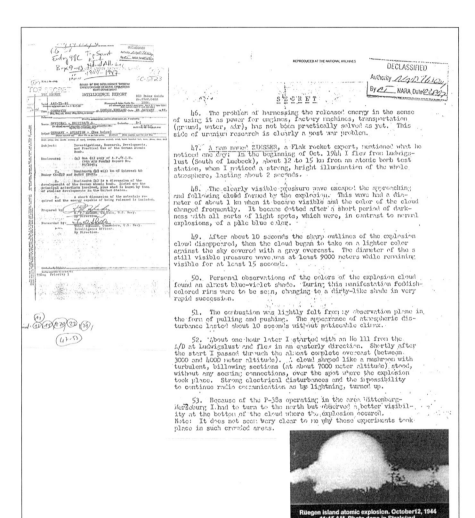

S E C R E T

46. The problem of harnessing the released energy in the sense of using it as power for engines, factory machines, transportation (ground, water, air), has not been practically solved as yet. This side of uranium research is clearly a post war problem.

47. A man named ZUESSER, a Flak rocket expert, mentioned what he noticed one day: In the beginning of Oct. 1944 I flew from Ludwigslust (South of Luebeck), about 12 to 15 km from an atomic bomb test station, when I noticed a strong, bright illumination of the whole atmosphere, lasting about 2 seconds.

48. The clearly visible pressure wave escaped the approaching and following cloud formed by the explosion. This wave had a diameter of about 1 km when it became visible and the color of the cloud changed frequently. It became dotted after a short period of darkness with all sorts of light spots, which were, in contrast to normal explosions, of a pale blue color.

49. After about 10 seconds the sharp outlines of the explosion cloud disappeared, then the cloud began to take on a lighter color against the sky covered with a grey overcast. The diameter of the s still visible pressure wave was at least 9000 meters while remaining visible for at least 15 seconds.

50. Personal observations of the colors of the explosion cloud found an almost blue-violet shade. During this manifestation reddish-colored rings were to be seen, changing to a dirty-like shade in very rapid succession.

51. The combustion was lightly felt from my observation plane in the form of pulling and pushing. The appearance of atmospheric disturbance lasted about 10 seconds without noticeable climax.

52. About one hour later I started with an He 111 from the A/D at Ludwigslust and flew in an easterly direction. Shortly after the start I passed through the almost complete overcast (between 3000 and 4000 meter altitude). A cloud shaped like a mushroom with turbulent, billowing sections (at about 7000 meter altitude) stood, without any securing connections, over the spot where the explosion took place. Strong electrical disturbances and the impossibility to continue radio communication as by lightning, turned up.

53. Because of the P-38s operating in the area Wittenberg-Merseburg I had to turn to the north but observed a better visibility at the bottom of the cloud where the explosion occured. Note: It does not seem very clear to me why these experiments took place in such crowded areas.

Rüegen island atomic explosion. October 12, 1944 11:45 AM. Photo done in Stralsünd. The sky looks dark as contrast to brilliant explosion.

Top Left: Cover sheet of Top Secret US Naval Intelligence report detaining a German atomic test.

Top Right: blow up of the pertinent text.

Bottom: Alleged picture of the German atomic test, October 12, 1944, at Ruegen Island, just north of Peenemuende.

language newspaper in Valencia, "Las Provincias"[8]. One photograph contained within that series of articles shows the two men, Romersa and von Braun, standing together as von Braun points to a rocket model. One can only wonder what these two men discussed in their private moments. Ruegen Island is located at the tip of the peninsula where Peenemuende was located. Both were privy to insider information, which could have changed the popular world-view of the history of science and technology. They must have had a lot to discuss.

It was only years later, in 1984, after von Braun's death, that he went public with the atomic test on Ruegen Island.

SOURCES

1. Jesensky, Milos, Ph.D., and Robert Lesniakiewicz, 1998, *"Wunderland" Mimozemske Technologie Treti Rise*, AOS Publishing, Czech Republic

2. Faeth, Harald, 1998, *1945-Thueringens Manhattan Project Auf der Spurensuche nach der verlorenen V-Waffen-Fabrik in Deutschlands Untergrund*, CTT-Verlag und Druckerei Foester, Schleusingen, Germany

3. Combined Intelligence Objectives Subcommittee Evaluation Report 174, July 9, 1945, *C.H.F. Muller, A.G.* Hamburg, Fuhlsbuttel, Rentgenstrasse 24, Target No. CAFT 1/132a

4. Georg, Freidrich, 2000, *Hitlers Siegeswaffen Band 1: Luftwaffe und Marine Geheim Nuklearwaffen des Dritten Reiches und ihre Traegersysteme*, Anum Verlag, Schleusingen and Heinrich-Jung-Verlagsgesellschaft, Gmbh, Zella-hehlis

5. Jesensky, Milos, Ph.D. and Robert Lesniakiewicz, 1998, page 149

6. Romersa, Luigi, German language translation of article in Defensa, Number 76-77, August-September, 1984, *Gestern Nachricht, Heute Geschichte Die "Geheimwaffen" von Hitler, etwas meher als (nur) Phantasie*, (English translation of the German title is: Yesterday's News Today's History The Secret Weapons of Hitler, something more than only Fantesy)

7. Mayer, Edgar and Thomas Mehner, 2002, pages 150-154, *Die Atombombe und das Dritte Reich Das Geheimnis des Dreiecks Armstadt-Wechmar-Ohrdruf*, Jochen Kopp Verlag, Rottenburg

8. ibid

14 | La Fusee Pilotee "T"

This tale comes to me via a French researcher, Joseph Altairac. It is an article from the magazine "Au dela du ciel". The date is unknown. This article was translated into English for me by the writer, editor, environmentalist, activist and free energy advocate, Remy Chavilier.

This article has much to do with the previous discussion of the German atomic tests and also concerns a subject which we will come to shortly, unknown large German rockets. This article may be a confirmation of the atomic test seen by Mr. Romersa but if that is so it is seen through different eyes, which add some additional detail. Also, the focus is different because this story is primarily about the rocket or flying craft sent to deliver the bomb.

This article claims that device was the Triebflugel. The Triebflugel was an aircraft shaped very much like the V-2 but with three wings at its center and rotating around the craft like a helicopter. At the end of each rotor was a ram jet. The three ram jets powered the craft which could rise vertically and then transition into horizontal flight. There was no rocket exhaust at the tail of the craft as in the V-2. In fact, the resemblance to the V-2 was superficial.

The Triebflugel was an interceptor. It was never intended to be used to deliver a bomb. Further, only models of the Triebflugel were built to the best of our knowledge, no full-scale versions actually flew.

What all this means is that, in my opinion, this device's designation as a Triebflugel is almost certainly

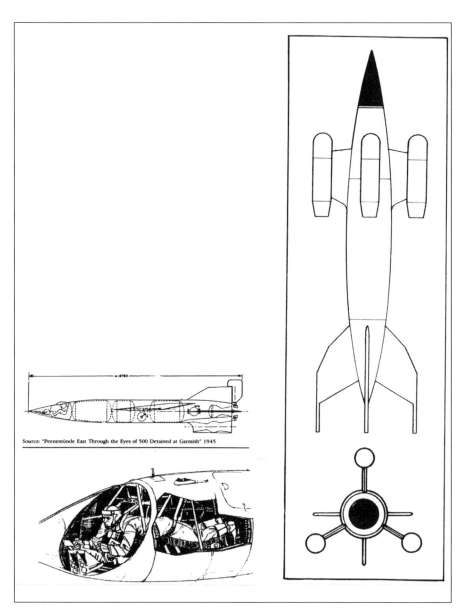

Source: "Peenemünde East Through the Eyes of 500 Detained at Garmish" 1945

Top Right: La Fusse "T". Below-Center: manned version of the A-4 or V-2.

Below-Bottom: detail of the pilot in the cabin of the V-2.

wrong. On the other hand there were manned rockets under consideration by the Germans and this could have been any one of those prototypes. The list includes the A-9, the V-1, and the Saenger stratospheric vehicle. It may have even been some sort of hybrid machine, a manned A-4b for instance, which was a V-2 with large wings, intended to glide to its target rather than free-fall. The article begins stating that this rocket delivery system exists but without giving it a name or other designation.

The test occurred in Northern Germany just as in the Romersa description. In the heather of that region a target town was erected with concrete buildings, low cost houses, two and three-storey buildings, offices and metallic constructions. Different types of cars were parked on the streets. There was a small train station, rail tracks, locomotives, gardens and winding trees added a to complete the picture of a town.

Two miles away from the town a shelter was constructed from which to observe the test. In that shelter there were Luftwaffe technicians and army officers.

The article says that "witnesses" saw "the rocket" rise vertically. The three flaming engines could be plainly seen. The missile leveled off at 8000 meters and flew in a rather zigzagging manner toward the target. Nearing the target the missile seems to have made a wide turn, under power, which could be heard by the witnesses below. The power was then cut and the missile started downward. At 5000 meters the transparent nose broke away and the pilot bailed out. A few seconds later his white cloth parachute could be seen slowly descending in the vicinity of the shelter.

"The rocket landed almost in the center of the buildings with a deafening detonation. There was a huge flame and everything was covered with a dense, gray heavy smoke, while a warm breath cutting puff of air spread rapidly. It took more than one hour for this dense curtain to clear. From the buildings, only debris remained. Metallic constructions stuck out of the ground shapeless and melted. The tall trees were no more than burned trunks."

At the point of impact, the ground was literally furrowed with deep crevasses, actually burning in some points and dug as if subjected to an enormous pressure. The cars parked in the street were reduced to debris, or violently thrust by the explosion against the houses on fire. The concrete train station had partly collapsed. The locomotives had resisted the blow but the smashed and tipped over wagons showed their insides."

The article goes on to say that a great number of French prisoners witnessed these rockets in the hands of the Germans and being destroyed prior to the Allied advance.

"The Germans went to great length to hide these experiments. The Allied information services found out about them only after the peace was declared, and competent technicians thought it was a nuclear explosion."

The article goes on to describe what they believed to be the facts of the rocket used to deliver the weapon, the Triebflugel. One obvious shortcoming of using this device as a bomber is mentioned:

"It is to be noted at this point that the weakest part of what our witness relates lies in the fact that, according to a few American technicians, the explosions were of a nuclear kind, in which case, the pilot being ejected near the launching place would make no sense at all because of the harmful radiations of the bomb which would have had a considerable effect thousands of meters away."

Here it is stated a second time. The bomb was nuclear or considered such by the investigating American technicians.

It is to be noted that the real dangers of atomic radiation were only appreciated much later, not in the 1940s, or 1950s, but only later did the real enduring nature of atomic radiation sink home in the minds of most individuals.

This story would be considered just another post-war tale if it were not for some of the other evidence offered here and by the German investigators working in the area of the German atomic bomb. The validity of the German atomic bomb and exactly how this story meshes with the tale of Mr. Romersa will be left for the reader to decide.

SOURCES

1. La Fusee Pilotee "T", an article from Au dela du ciel (magazine), 1958, author unknown.

15 | Mysterious German Bombs

In this chapter a few fragmentary accounts are explored which deal with truly strange bombs on which the Germans were said to be working.

There are sporadic accounts of a German bomb, which is sometimes said to kill all life within its blast radius. The interesting thing about this bomb it is alleged to do this by absorbing all the oxygen within this area. The first report shown here from late 1943 is typical in that it gives few details. It says only that the projectile in question contains phosphorus and other chemicals that absorb oxygen within a radius of a few hundred meters from the spot of detonation.

The second report referenced "Nordhausen", the site of the huge underground V-1 and V-2 rocket production facility, adds some detail to our picture of the oxygen bomb. This report says that the bomb has been under development for three years and it is huge. The dimensions given are: Length 17 meters (about 55 feet) with a diameter of 7 meters (almost 23 feet). This would make it larger than a V-3 rocket! Its kill-zone is said to be several kilometers.

The third report of this device is marked "Polish Intelligence". It repeats the active ingredient as phosphorus compounds and then goes on to say that the radius of action of this bomb is larger than present incendiaries.

The facts that the bomb itself was very large and that its killing radius was also very large are worthy of note. Details are lacking but this same basic theme has come from different sources. For the moment, perhaps, we should set aside evaluation and perhaps return to it at a later time.

The next very strange bomb is the endothermic bomb or cold bomb. Like the oxygen bomb, little reports of this device crop up throughout the wartime intelligence reports. In the "Polish Intelligence" report we learn that it works though some unknown chemical agent. The chemical agent is disbursed by the bomb, evaporates, and the result is a sudden drop in temperature for the area within the bomb's working range. Freezing kills life forms. Some property damage also results such as the breaking of water pipes and some cables.

Some confirmation of this device comes from another intelligence report on a related weapon, "icing gas". As we all know from recent airliner crashes, an airplane wing does not work well when it is iced over. Airports work long and hard with dedicated crews and special chemicals to keep aircraft wings free of ice before take off.

According to the report, the Germans wanted to use ice to down Allied aircraft. They planned to send a aircraft, or even a robot aircraft, ahead of a flight of a bomber squadron and discharge this specific chemical. The chemical would drift back, ice over the bomber's wings and cause them to fall from the sky.

The substance forming the active ingredient was called "Azote" which was a mixture of liquid nitrogen (minus 250 degrees C.) and liquid air. We know the Germans were making liquid air projectiles shells for cannons. Air is largely nitrogen, so it is not surprising that a chemical cocktail wasn't being considered by the Germans for use as a bomb.

The last item in the "Polish Intelligence" document, item (c), is a very brief description of a third bomb. This is described as the H.B. bomb "of great power". This H.B. was to be used with the other two bombs for maximum efficiency. What was this H.B.?

Could it be a hydrogen bomb? Is that really so far-fetched considering what has already been discussed? Well, if you think this idea was not under consideration by the Germans, please suspend judgment until we review some of Dr. Richter's work.

Perhaps the most mysterious bomb of the Second World War is called the molecular bomb or M-bomb. Indeed, a respected German researcher has told me that the account of Luigi Romersa as discussed above, was not exactly an atomic bomb in our modern conception of that device but a molecular bomb.

This bomb was said to have been under development through the

Erteilt auf Grund des Ersten Überleitungsgesetzes vom 8. Juli 1949
(WiGBl. S. 175)

BUNDESREPUBLIK DEUTSCHLAND

AUSGEGEBEN AM
8. MÄRZ 1954

DEUTSCHES PATENTAMT

PATENTSCHRIFT

Nr. 905 847

KLASSE 12g GRUPPE 1 01

N 1126 IVb / 12g

Karl Nowak, Wien

ist als Erfinder genannt worden

Karl Nowak, Wien

Verfahren und Einrichtung zur Änderung von Stoffeigenschaften oder Herstellung von stark expansionsfähigen Stoffen

Patentiert im Gebiet der Bundesrepublik Deutschland vom 16. März 1943 an
Patentanmeldung bekanntgemacht am 18. Juni 1953
Patenterteilung bekanntgemacht am 21. Januar 1954

Die Erfindung betrifft ein Verfahren und eine Einrichtung zur Änderung von Stoffeigenschaften oder Herstellung von stark expansionsfähigen Stoffen (bzw. Sprengstoffen) und besteht darin, daß der zu verändernde Stoff bei Tiefkühlung, zweckmäßig möglichst nahe dem absoluten Nullpunkt (im Zustand der Supraleitfähigkeit), unter Druck gesetzt wird oder ist.

Es hat sich erwiesen, daß durch die gleichzeitige Unterkühlung und Druckbehandlung eines Stoffes dessen Atomstruktur geändert werden kann.

Die Erfindung basiert auf der Überlegung, daß es möglich sein muß, durch Ausübung eines äußeren Druckes bei tiefen Temperaturen die Eigenschaft eines Stoffes zu ändern, und zwar insbesondere in folgenden Richtungen:

1. Bei der folgenden Erwärmung des bei Tiefkühlung komprimierten Stoffes bilden sich entsprechende Atomabstände aus, die aber nicht der vorherigen Atomanordnung (Gitter) entsprechen müssen. Insbesondere ist es auf diese Weise möglich, verschiedenartige Stoffe miteinander durch Verkettung ihrer Kristallgitter auf besondere Art zu legieren.

2. Bleibt der Stoff auf sein Kompressionsvolumen beschränkt, so wird er bei der folgenden Erwärmung einen besonderen Expansionsdruck ausüben, stärkste Ausstoß- oder Expansionswirkung zeigen.

Der Erfindungsgegenstand wird an Hand der Zeichnung noch weiter erläutert.

Es zeigt die Darstellung ein Gefäß 1, in welches der zu beeinflussende Stoff 2 durch eine obere Öffnung eingebracht wird, die dann mittels eines Verschlusses 3 hochvakuumdicht verschlossen werden kann. Das Gefäß 1 wird von einem zweiten Gefäß 4

(f) Other work at Camp Mecklenburg

Ernst also stated that work was carried out at this camp on a new liquid air bomb, and liquid air gun (?), while trials on some kind of atomic bomb were made at or near the camp.

HEAD... ...
HEADQUARTERS ARMY AIR FORCES
Target Intelligence Section
AIC 650

COUNTRY	GERMANY	Location & Coord: 51.30 10.46
LOCALITY	NORDHAUSEN	
TARGET	"Oxygen Bomb" Factory.	
CATEGORY	Secret Weapons	SUB CATEGORY Oxygen Bomb. V-2

I. SUMMARY OF CURRENT INTELLIGENCE

Production of the "Oxygen bomb", which is capable of killing all organic life in a circle of several kilometres, is limited to one factory in the Nordhausen area. Construction of the plants started 3 years ago/?Sept 1941/ in a hill.

Dimensions of the bomb are given as Length – 17 metres, Diameter– 2 metres

(OSS. SZ-6585. C– O. d/inf.Sept. 44.)

Type Report	Date	Status & Indications
PW.Int.Bulletin 2.1.45 2/25.		P/W heard from guards at the Buchenwald concentration Camp 9,000 closely guarded prisoners were working at a plant at Salza which was 500 metres underground. (Salza is about 3 km. west of Nordhausen)
OSS. B-1724-2 B-2	3.2.45	V-2 plants are at Nordhausen (RD-12 Saxony).

Top: part of a British Intelligence Objectives Sub-Committee report number 142 discussing exotic bomb research.

Bottom: Intelligence discussion of the oxygen bomb.

A - ?

Source: OSS, SL-4, December 29, 1943.

German Secret Weapon

It is reported from France that according to information obtained from industrial circles Germany's new secret weapon is a long-range heavy gun which fires projectiles containing phosphorus and other chemical substances which absorb oxygen from the air within a radius of a few hundred metres from the spot of the explosion and thus render organic life impossible.

Tales of the oxygen bomb from a second source.

ICING GAS

In their efforts to cope with Allied bombing attacks, it is reported the Germans have introduced their newest weapon - "Icing Gas". The new weapon, it is stated, operates on the principles of accelerated icing induced by an extremely low temperature zone, including crystallization and condensation through a temporary cloud causing the immediate icing of objects passing through it. The equipment is said to consist of a cylindrical reservoir tube secured under each wing of a fighter aircraft These tubes are filled with "Azote", a liquified nitrogen with a temperature of minus 250° C., combined with liquid air, and a gas outlet is affixed.

Proposed tactics consist of cutting across the bomber path perpendicularly and releasing the tube facing the bomber, or, flying over the bomber and diving across its path releasing the gas at close range, the higher the altitude the better the results.

According to German sources, extremely satisfying tests have been made on robot target planes at altitudes of 7-8,000 meters. It is alleged that these targets were brought down at once and that on reaching the earth they were found to have a coating of ice about two inches thick. It is further alleged that German fighters have brought down some isolated heavy bombers by employing this method. Hopes are also being built on this weapon as a good defensive measure against a pursuing plane. (Abract of G-2 Periodic Report No. 99.)

SOURCE: Med. Allied Strategic Air Force, Weekly Intelligence Summary No. 2 (K-92317) date 15 January 1945. Abstracted 12 March, 1945. SECRET.

Icing Gas and its proposed tactics.

(g) Liquid air bomb

As the research on the atomic bomb under Graf von
Ardenne and others was not proceeding as rapidly as had
been hoped in 1944, it was decided to proceed with the
development of a liquid air bomb.. Experiments using ordinary powdered coal were not at all successful, but extremely good results were obtained from a mixture consisting of 60% finely powdered dry brown coal and 40%

liquid air. The technical man responsible for this
work was Dr. Zippelmeier. The first trial was made on
the Döberitz grounds near Berlin using a charge of
about 8 kg of powder in a thin tin plate container. The
liquid air was poured on to the powder, and the two
were mixed together with a long wooden stirrer. Kreutzfeld did this himself, and was present at the ensuing
test. In an area of radius 500 to 600 metres trees,etc.
were all completely destroyed. Thereafter the explosion
started to rise and only the tops of the trees were
affected, although the intensive explosion covered an
area 2 km. in radius. Zippelmeier then had the idea that
a better effect might be obtained if the powder was
spread out in the form of a cloud before the explosion.
Trials were made with a paper container impregnated
with some waxy substance. A metal cylinder was attached
to the lower end of this container and hit the ground
first, dispersing the powder. After a short time interval of the order of 1/4 second a small charge in the
metal cylinder exploded and ignited the dank funnel
shaped dust – liquid air cloud. The bombs had to be
filled immediately prior to the departure of the aircraft.
Bombs with charges of 25 and 50 kg. of powder were
dropped on the Starbergersee, and photographs of the explosion were taken. Standartenführer Klumm kept a
photograph of the result and showed it to Brandt (Himmler's personal adviser). The intensive explosion covered an area 4 to 4.5 km. radius, and the explosion was
still felt on a radius 12.5 km. When the bomb was dropped on an airfield, much destruction was caused 12 km.
away, and all the trees on a hillside 5 to 6 km. away
were flat. On a radius of 12.5 km. only the tops of the
trees were destroyed.

A Dr. Hahnenkamp was also concerned in this work with
Dr. Zippelmeier, and both scientists were working for
the R.L.M. in the laboratories of a research institute
near Vienna. About the end of September 1944 Zippelmeier was moved to the Horn Gyroscopic compass factory
in Plauen, Vogtland (Saxony); but was probably evacuated before the Russians occupied the area. The materials of the explosive were made by the specialists of
the Nobel company.

Reconsider this document again as it shows that several of these exotic bombs had elements in common. We will consider
Zippermayr's fuel-air bomb in the next chapter.

C
C
P
Y

E X T R A C T

Letter from John G. Trump, Director, BBRL, Advanced Service Base Laboratory, APO-887 – U. S. ARMY to Dr. L. A. DuBridge, Director, Radiation Laboratory, Massachusetts Institute of Technology, Cambridge, Massachusetts

"New Weapons"

Probably inspired by the German development of V-1, V-2, and other military devices such as the jet aircraft and rockets, there appears to have developed a very strong "new weapons" psychosis which leads to reports of new and amazing phenomena every other week. I have recently been looking into the evidence for a reported enemy radiation capable of interfering with aircraft ignition up to 3,000 meters and operating i certain high-priority target areas. There is also the reported German pro-knock gas capable of minute concentrations of removing aircraft engine heads. Not so long ago several pilots reported flying through thousands of transparent glasslike bubbles which, although they had no adverse effect, were thought to be a new weapon. A considerable number of ground and air observers saw new-weapon possibilities in an unusual pink cloud phenomenon which persisted for about an hour over the front line, but without any noticeably adverse effects. The explanations for the latter two items seem to be bundles of Window dropped by a preceding high-altitude bomber formation and an actual pink-colored cloud respectively. There is the report of a "freezing gas" for icing up aircraft, and a host of others. Most of them have little effect and are quickly discredited. On the whole, they illustrate the interesting attitude of mind which has developed--but, with V-1 and V-2 as daily evidence, one has to be careful.

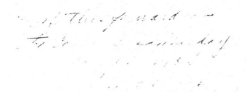

A letter from a U.S. Army lab to the Massachusetts Institute of Technology reporting the magnetic wave (Motorstoppmittel), gas designed to stop engines, mysterious glass-like bubbles and a pink cloud, as well as freezing gas.

POLISH INTELLIGENCE   CONFIDENTIAL

No. 0171/44

GERMANY

Information concerning new German bombs.

The following information has been received:

German chemical experts are now finishing 3 new models of very powerful bombs.

a) The contents of the first bomb: "neige carbonique", which by evaporation of some chemical component, is to cause a sudden drop in temperature which is maintained so long that it can cause the death of every living creature as well as causing material damage such as the breaking of water-pipes, the destruction of cables, etc.

b) The second bomb has a chemical filling made up of phosphorus compounds but of a highly improved type. It is said that the radius of action of this type of bomb is much larger than that of the present incendiaries.

c) The third bomb is a H.B. bomb of great power. It is to be used together with the other two types by waves of aircraft. Thus the highest efficiency of all three types is to be ensured.

Source F
Informant II

The legendary cold bomb described in U.S. government files as well as what may be the oxygen bomb using phosphorus and an " bomb of great power", identified only by an abbreviation which may be H.B. or M.B., the old microfilm copy is unclear.

Source: OSS, EL-6, December 29, 1943.

<u>German Secret Weapon</u>

It is reported from France that according to information obtained from industrial circles Germany's new secret weapon is a long-range heavy gun which fires projectiles containing phosphorus and other chemical substances which absorb oxygen from the air within a radius of a few hundred metres from the spot of the explosion and thus render organic life impossible.

The oxygen bomb described again.

combined efforts of Dr. Kurt Diebner and Manfred von Ardenne in addition to their work on a classic atomic bomb. This is interesting because these are two very different, high-profile individuals.

Diebner was already involved in more than one atomic project and was also involved with a secret SS atomic project. So, in other words, Dr. Diebner was a somewhat clandestine scientist whose primary allegiance belonged to the SS and Dr. Kammler. It may be that he even reported the progress of these other projects in which he was involved directly to the SS.

Manfred von Ardenne ran one of well-known German atomic projects. This was for the Reichspostamt, the German Post Office. Now, in the USA, the Post Office is just about the last place you would want running a high-tech, crucial, war sensitive project but this was not so in wartime Germany. The German Post Office enjoyed a high-tech reputation and organization. It was perhaps on the same order as Bell Laboratories in the US. Manfred von Ardenne was a first-rate scientist and had all he needed to do his work.

My one source says the M-bomb was developed in a middle school in Stadtilm but that no tests were carried out in Thuringia[1]. This bomb was in the widest sense an atomic weapon but very different from both the atomic and hydrogen bombs we are familiar with. This bomb is also known as a super-compression bomb because it was composed of matter that was compressed or "densified" as compared to normal matter. This bomb did generate pressure and heat just as a normal atomic blast does but did not generated radioactive radiation. From this description, it sounds exactly the opposite of a neutron bomb.

From the discussion super-compression, this is reminiscent of the work of Karl Nowak. Nowak was responsible for a process used to compress and so strengthen metals through cooling and pressure. He was also responsible for a new method of power generation within an internal combustion engine in which a super-cooled liquid gas was injected and subsequently expanded, producing power[2]. We might ask if the M-bomb has any relationship to the oxygen bomb or the cold bomb? We should also consider whether or not the work of Nowak was involved in the M-bomb or any of the other bombs described above. Unfortunately, the answers still await exact determination.

Finally, there was yet another type of liquid air bomb. This information comes to us via British Intelligence Objectives Sub-Committee report 142[3], which is a gold mine.

This report involved Dr. Mario Zippermayr whom we will meet in the next chapter and serves as background and introduction to his fantastic work. It seems that in 1944 the progress on the atomic bomb was not as advanced as the Germans expected. It was decided at that it was time to experiment with a kind of "Ersatz" bomb using liquid air and coal dust. Dr. Zippermayr was put in charge of this project and the first tests were done at the Doeberitz grounds near Berlin. A mixture of 60% finely powdered dry brown coal was hand-mixed into a 40% solution of liquid air. Eight kg of powder was mixed together for this test. This was actually done by a man named "Krautsfeld" according to the report, by hand, using a wooden stirrer. According to Krautsfeld, our witness for the report, an area whose radius was 500 to 600 meters containing trees was absolutely destroyed. The explosion started to rise into the air, afterward, so that only the tops of the trees were affected, although the explosion itself consumed 2 km.

At this point Dr. Zippermayr had the idea that a better effect might be realized if the powder was spread out in the form of a cloud before the explosion. This was evidently the idea behind the fuel-air bomb to which we will turn our attention to next.

SOURCES

1. Georg, Friedrich and Thomas Mehner, 2004, page 258. Atomziel New York Geheime Grossraketen-und Raumfahrtprojekte des Dritten Reiches, Jochen Kopp Verlag, Rottenburg

2. Nowak, Karl, Deutsches Patentamt, Patentschrift Number 905847, original patent dates from March 16, 1943

3. British Intelligence Subcommittee report number 142, pages 4 and 5, London

16 | "Projekt Hexenkessel"
The Fuel-Air Bomb

The German word "Hexenkessel" means "witches cauldron" in English. It is only one of the projects run by a true genius of the days of the Second World War, Dr. Mario Zippermayr. Dr. Zippermayr, sometimes spelled incorrectly as "Zippermeyer", was born an Italian of Austrian parents and educated in German speaking institutions. His interests ranged from perfecting color photographic film to the medical benefits of ozone therapy. He is remembered for his wide-ranging weapons research. His involvement with secret weaponry has never been much of a mystery but the true nature of his research has been hidden in layers of secrecy and disinformation until quite recently.

As the war broke out, Dr. Zippermayr was drafted into the Luftwaffe but detailed to begin practical research to facilitate the German effort. Dr. Zippermayr was first posted in Vienna and given his own laboratory where he headed a thirty-five-man research team. Among some of the research objectives he was given at this time were the development of the L-40 torpedo, the development of the Enzian and Schmetterling anti-aircraft rockets as well as the development of a mysterious, high-speed jet airplane.

Suddenly, in March of 1945, Dr. Zippermayr was put in charge of a facility called Talstation, near Lofer. He immediately fired most of its employees. The acronym T.A.L. means Technische Akademie der Luftwaffe. The word "Tal" also means "valley" in English. Talstation, which was actually more than one facility, was located in the mountainous region of the

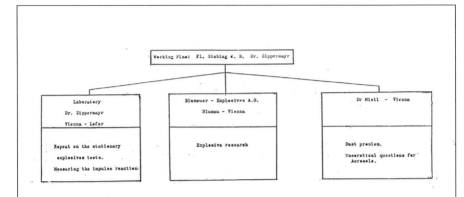

| Working Plan: Fl. Stabing 4. B. Dr. Zippermayr | | |

Laboratory Dr. Zippermayr Vienna - Lofer	Blumauer - Explosives A.G. Blumau - Vienna	Dr Miatl - Vienna
Repeat on the stationary explosives tests. Measuring the impulse reaction.	Explosive research	Dust problem. Theoretical questions for Aerosols.

23. TRIALS WITH COAL DUST EXPLOSIONS

a. Explosive-air mixtures present themselves as media suitable for the production of explosions as described. The substance to be mixed with air may be gas, liquid, or solid. After ignition the character of all these explosive mixtures is that of a gas. With fog or dust mixtures of liquids or solids vaporization precedes the explosion. Of these explosive-air mixtures, those of dusts are of particular interest and especially those formed from brown-coal dust. The coal used should contain a minimum of ash, 5% to not more than 10%, and a minimum of moisture. The explosive range includes mixtures between 80 and 1600 grams of dust per cubic meter (2 1/2 to 40 ounces per cubic yard). The available energy of brown-coal dust is about 5 times that of conventional explosives. Only a small part of the oxygen needed for combustion need be supplied, as that required for the explosion is drawn from the air. The action of dust explosions in confined spaces, as in mines, is well known. Explosions in the atmosphere have not been observed. If a dust cloud is ignited in the air it simply burns.

25. METHODS OF APPLICATION

a. To defend a large space, for example against a close formation of bombers, it is more useful to produce simultaneously a large number of small explosions. This is accomplished by sending up a large number of small rockets and igniting them simultaneously as soon as they have reached the elevation of the attacking aircraft. Thus there is produced in the air a mass explosion similar to a bomb carpet on the surface. It is essential that simultaneous ignition take place, most easily obtained by radio means. Tests on remote ignition were projected and the firm of Prinz Werke, Markt Pongau, was given the assignment of developing a simple igniting mechanism.

of "Enzian" and "Schmetterling" were foreseen. This involves rockets with searching heads and proximity fuses. As far as is known "Enzian" had a capacity of approximately 500 liters of coal dust.

Top: Chart of Dr. Zippermayr's organization.

Bottom: C.I.O.S. report 201 which focus on Project Hexenkessel's use of coal dust explosive as an anti-aircraft weapon.

5. At the meeting on 8 March
ZIPPERMAYER and ████████ were interrogated regarding the results obtained
in coal dust explosion experiments conducted during the war, and ZIPPER-
MAYER's theories on the applicability of the coal dust explosion theory
to other fuels and the potential military value of the project. ZIPPER-
MAYER related how the pressure created by coal dust explosions from a
pipe installed vertically in the ground had been measured at different
distances. He explained how the column of coal dust vapor was ignited
at the bottom, how the vapor was forced by the counter-pressure of the
outside air into a series of vortices, and how the first explosion initiated a chain-reaction of increasingly powerful after-explosions. Unlike conventional explosives, he declared, coal-dust vapor had an explosive
effect on areas rather than points. As a result, he theorized, the pressure could be used preferably for the destruction of large objects, but
would, by changing the atmospheric conditions in a comparatively wide
space, stop - and possibly destroy - aircraft in flight. Coal dust explosions of sufficient magnitude, he maintained, should compare with the
area effect of atomic bomb explosions, and would be infinitely cheaper.
He expressed his belief that rockets loaded with coal dust could, like
atomic bombs, be carried by aircraft to their destination, and could be
launched with destructive effect on cities or other installations. If
necessary, other fuels could be substituted for coal dust; gasoline, for
instance, would constitute a powerful explosive if it were used under
appropriate conditions.   (b)(7)(C)

Conference of CWS officials with Ing Mario ZIPPERMAYER, dtd 18 Mar 49.

ation with Air Force backing, this office arranged for preliminary conferences between CWS officials and ZIPPERMAYER, which conferences were to determine whether the US would offer contracts to ZIPPERMAYER and his associates.

(b)(7)(C)

4. Also present at the conference on 8 March was ███████████ (See Preliminary Interrogation Report, No. 15, this office, dated 20 Sept 1945), another explosives expert and associate of ZIPPERMAYER. A further associate of ZIPPERMAYER's ███████████ a mathematician, (See Preliminary Interrogation Report No. 18, this office, dated 21 Sept 1945), is also considered, with ████ for contract.

(b)(7)(C)

5. At the meeting on 8 March ZIPPERMAYER and ████████ were interrogated regarding the results obtained in coal dust explosion experiments conducted during the war, and ZIPPERMAYER's theories on the applicability of the coal dust explosion theory to other fuels and the potential military value of the project. ZIPPERMAYER related how the pressure created by coal dust explosions from a pipe installed vertically in the ground had been measured at different distances. He explained how the column of coal dust vapor was ignited at the bottom, how the vapor was forced by the counter-pressure of the outside air into a series of vortices, and how the first explosion initiated a chain-reaction of increasingly powerful after-explosions. Unlike conventional explosives, he declared, coal-dust vapor had an explosive effect on areas rather than points. As a result, he theorized, the pressure could be used preferably for the destruction of large objects, but would, by changing the atmospheric conditions in a comparatively wide space, stop - and possibly destroy - aircraft in flight. Coal dust explosions of sufficient magnitude, he maintained, should compare with the area effect of atomic bomb explosions, and would be infinitely cheaper. He expressed his belief that rockets loaded with coal dust could, like atomic bombs, be carried by aircraft to their destination, and could be launched with destructive effect on cities or other installations. If necessary, other fuels could be substituted for coal dust; gasoline, for instance, would constitute a powerful explosive if it were used under appropriate conditions.

(b)(7)(C)

6. All conferees agreed that ZIPPERMAYER's theory was basically sound. ████████ however, pointed out that a major part of the theory remained to be proven in actual experiments. He readily accepted the feasibility of coal dust explosions from a ground-installed pipe. Such explosions, he stated,

2

- 2 -

This is a portion of a U.S. government post-war interview with Dr. Zippermayr, March 8, 1949. In this interview Dr. Zippermayr explained to the U.S. officials the test conclusions he reached during the war blowing coal dust out of hollow pipes. This test method led to a cover story that Dr. Zippermayr had invented a "vortex cannon" by which enemy aircraft would be swept from the sky. This myth still persists to this day and has even been repeated by a prominent and respected historian in a recent British TV documentary. The initial explosion scattering and vaporizing the coal dust must be slow enough to allow a long billowing explosion over a wide area. For this a mathematician was included to verify Dr. Zippermayr's work. Other than this math, the method was so simple and direct that a cover story was needed lest this cheap rival to the atomic bomb fall into the wrong hands. This cover story and strategy worked for decades. Continued on following page

Tyrol, approximately where Germany, Switzerland, Austria and Italy meet. Dr. Zippermayr and his pre-existing staff, now a total of eighty individuals, set up shop in one of the outlying sub-bases just outside of Lofer which was called "Hochtal" (high valley).

Dr. Zippermayr continued his brief tenure at Lofer until May 8, 1945, the day of the German surrender. Days later, American troops reported the presence of 2,000 kilos of explosives at Hochtal and laboratory facilities in an absolutely pristine state. Dr. Zippermayr continued to reside at Hochtal, setting up an open house for any intelligence people or dignitaries who cared to visit. On May 15, 1945 Dr. Zippermayr was arrested and interrogated by military authorities. Shortly thereafter he was discharged from the Luftwaffe with the rank of Major and transported back to Lofer on June 20, 1945 where he apparently continued to host the "open house". The facility was visited by increasingly higher levels of intelligence people, including Colonel Leslie E. Simon, Director of the Ballistic Research Laboratory at the Aberdeen Proving Grounds. Dr. Zippermayr complied completely with all requests for information.

Information used for this report does not come from a review of the existing literature on Dr. Zippermayer or his work. Instead, it comes as a result of a Freedom Of Information request directed to the United States Army regarding Dr. Zippermayr and the facility at Lofer[1]. To this writer's delight, the Army responded with a whole series of reports, each originally more classified than the last, which gave us a whole new perspective on Dr. Zippermayr and his work as well as the nature of the maintenance of secrecy concerning German secret weapons. The Army even persuaded the Air Force to contribute with a report of their own which was known to the Army but now out of their control In all four large reports were received.

Legend and propaganda had it that Dr. Zippermayr was working on a "vortex cannon" at Lofer. It was said that this gun was powered by coal dust and set off in such a way that a huge explosive vortex would be generated. This explosive vortex was said to be powerful enough to blow the wings off enemy aircraft and so was to be employed as an anti-aircraft weapon. Hidden within this story is an element of truth. But the truth is much greater than the alleged story, so much greater that it can only be concluded that the whole vortex cannon concept was created to conceal the nature of this truth. It is unclear if the Germans originally concocted this tale and it was just maintained by the Americans or if it was completely a post-war addition by the Americans.

When Dr. Zippermayr began his experimentation on coal dust the project was code-named "Humus". On March 8, 1945, in the waning days of the war, the project was re-named "Hexenkessel". At this time, coinciding with Dr. Zippermayr move to Lofer, a large-scale, intensive effort was put into this project, involving several agencies besides the Zippermayr laboratory.

Coal contains a surprising number of calories, that is, it has a high energy content even when compared with the explosives of the times. As a matter of fact the amount of energy available in coal is about five times that of high explosive. But to get the highest possible temperatures and pressure from the explosion, it must be an instantaneous detonation. The destructive effects of this explosion are limited by the intensity and duration of the explosive pressure. Explosive pressure at the center produces high heat but at the same time the very nature of the explosion disperses the explosive material eventually to a point were detonation no longer takes place, so limiting the scope of the explosion. But it was found that the effectiveness on an explosion upon a target with flat surface was more dependent upon increased duration of the explosion rather than high intensity. Knowing this, Dr. Zippermayr concentrated upon producing explosions of longer duration.

Coal dust is explosive within a confined space, every coal miner knows this, but to get coal dust to explode in the atmosphere it has to be compressed. The wave of air pressure resulting from an explosion can provide this compression. It was found that this could be done using by packing coal dust around a low velocity explosive charge but not directly next to it. A space between the charge and the coal dust was necessary for dispersion of the coal dust into the atmosphere. Under pressure from this explosive wave, the coal dust of the fuel-air bomb mixes with the atmosphere and uses atmospheric oxygen as its burning agent rather than chemical oxygen in the warhead itself.

To defend a city against a close formation of bombers, used at that time, several smaller explosions would be used at once. The rockets "Schmetterling" and "Enzian" were foreseen for this purpose. Multiple rockets would detonate, spreading their coal dust packages in a large area throughout the atmosphere directly below or above the bomber formation. All the warheads would be detonated at once by radio. A truly monstrous explosion would take place near the squadron, producing a long-duration explosion that would simply break the wings off the heavily laden bombers.

Tests had begun with coal dust being shot out of tubes pointed upward. Something curious was observed. A flaming vortex was observed which spread outward from the center of the column of air as it was shot skyward. From this curiosity was born the cover story of the "vortex cannon". In fact, what was being developed was what we call an air-fuel bomb today. The blast resulting from this kind of weapon is second only to an atomic bomb in destructive power.

According to a later set of declassified documents received under pressure from the Army, Dr. Zippermayr met with U.S. Air Force officials on March 18, 1949. Dr. Zippermayr presented his findings to the Air Force for the use of what would be called the air-fuel bomb for use as an anti-aircraft weapon. The record of this meeting is important because he explained the explosive process in somewhat more detail. According to the report:

> "...He explained how the column of coal dust vapor was ignited at the bottom, how the vapor was forced by the counter-pressure of the outside air into a series of vortices, and how the first explosion initiated a chain-reaction of increasingly powerful after-explosions. Unlike conventional explosives, he declared, coal-dust vapor had an explosive effect on areas rather than points. As a result, he theorized, the pressure could be used preferably for the destruction of large objects, but would, by changing the atmospheric conditions in a comparatively wide space, stop-and possibly destroy-aircraft in flight. Coal dust explosions of sufficient magnitude, he maintained, should compare with the area effect of atomic bomb explosions, and would be infinitely cheaper. He expressed his belief that rockets loaded with coal dust could, like atomic bombs, be carried by aircraft to their destination, and could be launched with destructive effect on cities or other installations. If necessary, other fuels could be substituted for coal dust; gasoline, for instance, would constitute a powerful explosive if it were

used under appropriate conditions."

Three points taken from the general FOIA text on Dr. Zippermayr are worth mentioning at this point. Coal dust or any solid fuel once it is blown into the atmosphere in this way becomes a vapor. This long-duration explosion characteristic of the fuel-air bomb actually seems to be many explosions, each billowing out and creating the next. According to Dr. Zippermayr such an explosion would probably reach a maximum height of one mile.

At the conclusion of the meeting it was recommended that Dr. Zippermayr be hired along with a mathematician for further work.

That was 1949. The fuel-air bomb concept was not spoken of publicly by the government until the United States was ready to invade Iraq during the Gulf War. At that time much was made out of the possibility that Saddam Hussein might possess a fuel-air bomb and use it on U.S. ground troops. Presumably, the technology was known outside the USA. Perhaps this presumed leak came during Dr. Zippermayr's weeks at the "open house" in Lofer when anybody might have simply inquired about this technology. In any event, the Iraqis did not use a fuel-air bomb in the early 1990s. Again, this idea was to sleep for a period of time.

According to recent chatter on the internet, the fuel-air bomb idea has been recently resurrected, now going by the name "a-neutronic bomb" or "electro-hydrodynamic gaseous fuel device". This bomb is said to be the handiwork of the renegade scientist Dr. Michael Ricionoscuito. You may remember Dr. Ricionoscuito for his other work, the famous Promis software, used to spy on individuals by just about every government intelligence agency in the world today.

The a-neutronic bomb consists of blowing a cloud of gaseous, combustible material into the atmosphere whereby a small rocket is launched into its midst trailing a small wire connected to the ground. The wire charges the cloud with electric energy so that the cloud is saturated with electro-static energy. The cloud is detonated with the resulting explosion being on a par with a small atomic detonation. The resulting blast also produces the same long duration as its ancestor. This is evidenced by the fact that it is said that the Nevada test site, which is flat desert, sank about 30 feet after the blast[6].

SOURCES

1. Combined Intelligence Objectives Subcommittee Evaluation Report 201, 7/23/45, Report On Talstation, Lofer, Target Nos. C-4/222 and C-1/667, obtained through Department Of The Army, Fort George G. Meade, MD. 20755-5995

2. Counter Intelligence Corps, Salzburg Detachment, United States Forces Austria, Zell am See Section, 8/4/45, Case Nol S/Z/55, Zippermayr Mario Dr. Ing., obtained through Department Of The Army, Fort George G. Meade, MD. 20755-5995

3. Headquarters Seventh Army, C.I.C. Detachment, 5/16/45, Dr. Zippermayer, (Stabsingenieur) Kreis Zell Am See, Lofer, obtained through Deptartment Of The Army, Fort George G. Meade, MD. 20755-5995

4. Combined Intelligence Objectives Subcommittee Evaluation Report 201, 7/23/45, Report On Talsation, Lofer, Target Nos. C-4/222 and C-1/667, (Expanded Version), obtained through Department Of The ARmy, Fort George G. Meade, MD. 20755-5995

5. Conference of CWS Officials with Ing. Mario Zippermayer, Regraed Unclassified, 7/13/99 by USAINSCOM FOI/PA, obtained through Department Of The Army, Fort George G. Meade, MD. 20755-5995

6. Grabbe, Orlin, "When Osama Bin Ladin Was Tim Osman, www.orlingrabbe.com/binladin_tim osman.html

17 | "Pfiel" (Arrow) Aircraft

In reviewing the new documents sent by the Army concerning Dr. Zippermayr it became evident that he was involved in another project, which had never been reported before. This project was called the "Pfiel Flugzeug" or Arrow aircraft. This "Pfiel" had nothing to do with the Donier projectof the same name.

Anyone familiar with German weaponry of the Second World War knows how much research has been done in tracking down every proposed German aircraft prototype. These prototypes have been fleshed out in illustrations and in projected operational data by interested researchers. These illustrations fill numerous books and magazines as well as several internet web-sites dedicated to the idea of what might have been if the 3rd Reich had lasted another year. Because of the intensity of this work and the number of years that it has been in progress, it is truly gratifying to stumble upon something new and unreported at this late date.

The concept for this aircraft came from his work on another project, the L-40 aerial torpedo. Dr. Zippermayr's solution to the problem of the aerial torpedo led directly to a subsequent project, the Pfiel aircraft.

The standard German aerial torpedo was released at about 50 meters (slightly over 150 feet) from the ocean's surface by an aircraft in horizontal flight at an air speed of about 300 km. per hour or about 180 m.p.h. To release higher or faster would cause the torpedo to impact the water at too great a speed,

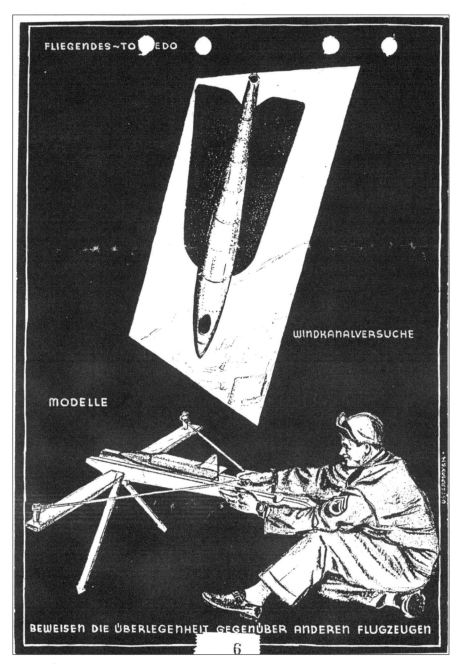

A model of Dr. Zippermayr's new wing design as a glider and for wind canal research.

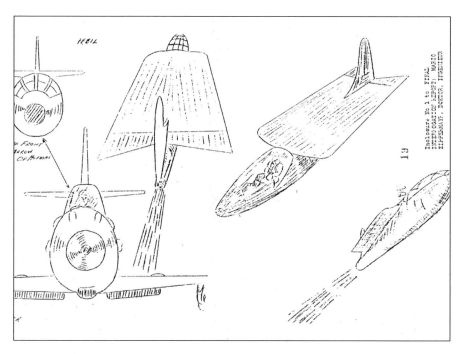

Drawings of the Pfiel in flight and in three views.

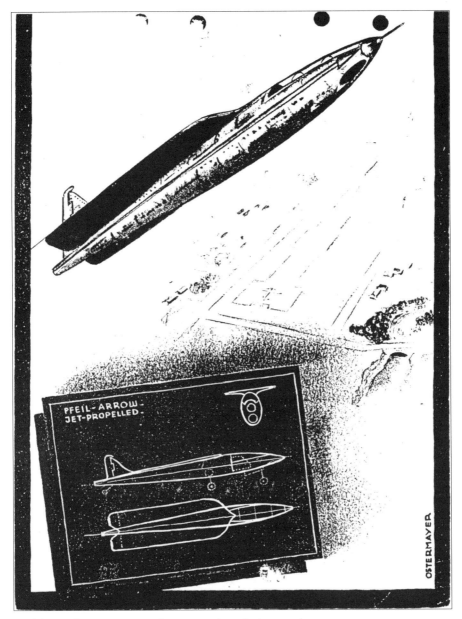

The Pfiel (arrow) design in comparison with a conventional propeller-driven aircraft.

A U.S. built Pfiel design as it would be test-dropped from a B-29.

Blohm & Voß P. 202

Im Verlauf des Krieges wurden bereits eingehende Untersuchungen über die Beeinflussung der Schnellflugeigenschaften durch gepfeilte Tragflügel angestellt, die eindeutig bewiesen, daß bei Pfeilflügeln die Kompressibilitätserscheinungen im schallnahen Bereich hinausgeschoben wurden. Gleichzeitig erbrachten diese Versuche aber die durch den Auftriebsabfall des Pfeilflügels hervorgerufenen schlechten Langsamflugeigenschaften, die Probleme bei Start und Landung auftürmten. Bei der P. 202 wurde versucht, sämtliche Nachteile des Pfeilflügels im Langsamflug durch einen um die Hochachse drehbaren Flügel zu beheben. Beim Start und bei der Landung lag der normale Trapezflügel, mit als Pfanne ausgebildetem Mittelstück, rechtwinklig zur Längsachse des Rumpfes, also in Normalstellung eines eingepfeilten Flügels, bei der sämtliche auftriebserhöhenden Mittel, wie Landeklappen und Vorflügel, wirksam blieben. Beim Schnellflug sollte der Flügel um 35⁰ gedreht werden, so, daß die linke Fläche negative und die rechte Fläche positive Pfeilform aufwies. Der sonstige Aufbau des freitragenden Schulterdeckers war normal. Unter dem Rumpf waren nebeneinander zwei Jumo 004 Luftstrahl-Turbinen geschlungen, das Leitwerk war ungepfeilt. Die einsitzige Maschine sollte als Jagdflugzeug Verwendung finden.

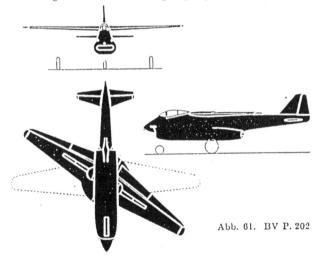

Abb. 61. BV P. 202

Blohm & Voß P. 203

Die geradezu primitiv anmutende Konstruktion der Zelle dieses als Langstreckenflugzeug ausgelegten Aufklärers täuscht darüber hinweg, daß dieses Flugzeug durch seine Triebwerksanlage etwas revolutionierend Neues brachte. Daß der von Vogt beschrittene Weg richtig war, ist be-

A diagram of the Blohm & Voss P.203 scissor-wing aircraft. When folded back for high speed flight, this design resembles the Pfiel. For low speed takeoff, the wings were set in the conventional position.

damaging the torpedo's steering mechanisms. The Germans suffered substantial losses to their attacking aircraft using these weapons and tactics. The low altitude and low speed simply left the attacking aircraft venerable.

What was needed was a new torpedo with a new attack methodology. The Germans needed a torpedo that could be fired from a distance, at a high altitude, and at jet-plane speeds. They wanted the new torpedo to be launched at 1.5 kilometers from the target, at any height, at any angle and at speeds up to 700 km per hour (435 m.p.h.).

Dr. Zippermayr reworked the internal components of the new aerial torpedo with these goals in mind. But what is most interesting were his aerodynamic solutions for the new torpedo. This solution was a new gliding surface that automatically balanced the torpedo in flight. This gliding surface was a new wing with a special shape. It was attached to the top edge of the torpedo and its wings were "V" shaped as seen from the front or rear. This wing design automatically confirmed stability on the flying craft since its center of gravity was directly below what we might call its point of suspension, the mid-point between the V-wing surfaces. Tests were performed in which the torpedo was dropped from an aircraft flying at speeds up to 720kph and from heights of over 1000 meters. The Arado 234 was envisioned as using this weapon. The work was carried out from January, 1944 until the end of the war.

The success of the L-40 torpedo design had obvious implications for high-speed aircraft. Besides Dr. Zippermayr, Messerschmitt, Augsburg, was already present at Lofer for work on the Enzian rocket. Dr. Wurster and none other than Dr. Lippisch worked on this project. Given all this aviation genius, it is no surprise that the Aerodynamische Institute der Technischer Hochschule, Hanover was put to work conducting wind tunnel and other tests of the torpedo design. They passed the opinion that the structure was sound and suitable and could be applied successfully to aircraft. These findings were published in their technical research manuals (Berichten des General-Luftzeugmeinster). Orders were given to Dr. Zippermayr to incorporate the torpedo principles in developing a jet-propelled aircraft capable of extremely high speed.

The first aircraft was to be a high-speed fighter. But, at the same time experiments were to be conducted to determine the value of the new design in the construction of gigantic, high-speed airliners. These plans were said to have been successful as far as they were able to progress before Germany's defeat.

The first step was to build a model glider, complete with instruments to register flying and diving qualities of the aircraft. This model would be released from a tow line at high altitude. The results of these experiments were then used in the construction of the first full-scale glider model. It was during the construction of this full-sized model, about three-fourths complete, that the war ended and construction stopped. At least for a time the model was stored at the Hagen carpenter shop in Lofer.

After flight tests of the full-scale model were completed, work was to begin on a jet-propelled prototype. The Army report states: "Dr. Porche, located at Schuttgut near Zell-am-See had already been assigned the task of supplying the jet-units." Yes, this is the same Dr Porsche whose cars we all know and love.

The Zippermayr wing design had two advantages over contemporary wing design. The first was tremendous speed. Even as the Army wrote up their findings, in July of 1945, two years before the sound barrier would be officially broken, there was already discussion in the report of this wing design going supersonic. The reason these wings were credited with "speed" is that they offered considerably less resistance, drag, to the atmosphere than wings in current usage. In other words, this type of wing was more efficient at high speed.

The second advantage bestowed by this wing design is stability. The stability was especially apparent on the transverse axis, which made the aircraft easy to control. The torpedo prototype flew without any automatic steering device and, even at speeds of 80 to 200 meters per second, was perfectly stable. At an incidence angle of 52 degrees the torpedo showed no tendency to stall nor were their any irregularities in the flight direction. It was also claimed that the wing loading was much less than for conventional wing types.

In engineering, there are always trade-offs. The big disadvantage, although not ever mentioned in the government reports. This would certainly be that takeoffs would be more difficult. Short takeoffs are usually associated with large, straight wings. As we know, the double-decker wings of World War One aircraft are sometimes used, even today, for jobs requiring slow speed and reliability such as crop dusters.

The Germans invented just about every wing type that exists.

Swept wings, both front and back, delta wings and swing wings were all invented by the Germans at this time. The German aircraft makers all shared information during the war. They simply had to do this. Many times aircraft designed by one company were actually built by another firm during the war. This was done to more efficiently utilize resources. Messerschmitt was on-site at Lofer. It is to be expected that knowledge of the Zippermayr wing design was disseminated throughout the German aircraft industry on some level. Therefore, it is not surprising if another attempt was made to utilize the advantages of the Zippermayr design while minimizing the disadvantage.

The design in question is the Blohm & Voss P.203. This wing design is called a scissor wing. At takeoff the wing assumes its customary position, at right angles to the fuselage. After takeoff, when high speed is desired, the wing is rotated from the standard position to a position almost parallelling the fuselage. At high speed, this position would still provide enough lift for flight yet the atmospheric drag would be greatly reduced as in the Zippermayr design. As the drawing shows, the wing is affixed on top of the fuselage as in the Zippermayr design. The scissor wing design would combine the virtues of a standard wing, for takeoff and low speed efficiency, with the reduced wind resistance of the Zippermayr design for high-speed performance. The government documents do not make this connection, nor does any known literature to date, but the similarity of the two designs begs for comparison and possible connection.

The scissor wing has remained on the drawing board in spite of its apparent advantages. Every so often mention of this design or a picture of a futuristic aircraft with scissor wings appears on the cover of a magazine.

SOURCES

1. Combined Intelligence Objectives Subcommittee Evaluation Report 201, 7/23/45, Report On Talstation, Lofer, Target Nos. C-4/222 and C-1/667, obtained through Department Of The Army, Fort George G. Meade, MD. 20755-5995

2. Counter Intelligence Corps, Salzburg Detachment, United States Forces Austria, Zell am See Section, 8/4/45, Case Nol S/Z/55, Zippermayr Mario Dr. Ing., obtained through Department Of The Army, Fort George G. Meade, MD. 20755-5995

3. Headquarters Seventh Army, C.I.C. Detachment, 5/16/45, Dr. Zippermayer, (Stabsingenieur) Kreis Zell Am See, Lofer, obtained through Department Of The Army, Fort George G. Meade, MD. 20755-5995

4. Combined Intelligence Objectives Subcommittee Evaluation Report 201, 7/23/45, Report On Talsation, Lofer, Target Nos. C-4/222 and C-1/667, (Expanded Version), obtained through Department Of The Army, Fort George G. Meade, MD. 20755-5995

5. Conference of CWS Officials with Ing. Mario Zippermayer, Regraded Unclassified, 7/13/99 by USAINSCOM FOI/PA, obtained through Department Of The Army, Fort George G. Meade, MD. 20755-5995

18 | Supermetals

There are reports of super metals being produced by the Germans during the Second World War. There are probably multiple origins of these rumors and perhaps multiple metals or metal alloys involved.

In 1960 Michael X., later writing under the name Michael X. Barton, described a metal called "Impervium" which was allegedly used by the Germans in construction of field propulsion flying discs. Barton's German informant describes an experience from wartime Germany:

> "In Schramberg, South Bavaria, I had a friend who's father was a renowned Metallurgy scientist. He experimented with the chemistry of metals. There is little doubt but that he was one of the world's most brilliant minds, for it was this same scientist who invented a metal harder than diamonds. In 1935-36 the Nazis put this amazing metal—we shall call it IMPERVIUM—to use for the first time in airplanes of the German Air Force.

I recall visiting his fantastic laboratories under a luxurious house at Lake Schramberg. He allowed me to see how the metal glowed with a red-blue florescence when heated to a high degree.

One year later (in the 1940's) I met this scientist and his daughter again, this time at the Polish Embassy. The daughter told me that her father had been called for an audience with Hitler that very night. The scientist's consultation with Hitler concerned secret plans for an OVAL or 'ELLIPSE-SHAPED' aircraft".[1]

The author goes on to state that the source of power for this oval aircraft was "electro-magnetism" or "electrified propulsion system"[2].

The quotation stated "to use for the first time in airplanes of the German Air Force", so might this metal have appeared in other aircraft? According to another source, Wilhelm Landig, it did.[3]

Curiously enough, the word "Impervium" is today the registered trademark of a company called Northwest Research Institute, Inc. and can be found on the internet at:

www.carbideprocessors.com/Knives/Impervium.htm

Their Impervium may not be quite the Impervium described above but there are similarities. This commercial Impervium is twice as hard as stainless steel. It is a stainless steel like alloy of 65% iron as well as Nickel and chromium for carbide formation. It also contains about 10% manganese and about 10% carbon. Then something interesting is described:

"As a final step a gas is introduced as final alloying agent".

This gas is evidently not oxygen since the carbon content has already been fixed by the manufacture and introduction of oxygen is done for this purpose. What was the gas and why was it not named? Maybe we will find out.

At this same website another commercial metal alloy is described in the discussion of Impervium. It is called "Lubricium" and it is described as Impervium that has been "cold reduced". The description of cold reduction is a forging process in which a piece of Impervium is beaten long and hard enough to re-arrange the crystalline structure of the metal, packing the molecules tighter together.

As with Impervium only part of the story is being told and these two metals, while probably very tough, constitute only partial steps of the original German research.

Wilhelm Landig wrote three novels. These novels, he claimed, were based upon reality and we are given to understand in the text of his work that the technology he describes was real or at least under development during World War Two. The fictional aspect of his work seems to be the characters by which this technology is explained. After Landig's death in 1997, it was made public that he was a member of the SS during the war and it was his job to guard German flying discs near Prague.

Landig wrote of other aircraft and weapon's systems besides flying discs. One description involved a peculiar aircraft, a prototype, flown out of Norway called the "Dosthra". This aircraft resembled a giant insect. It was a mid-wing monoplane with a five-cornered fuselage, viewed in cross-section. It was thicker in the front than the rear. The front end of the fuselage was made of glass, giving it the insect-look. The wing-span of the aircraft was about 135 feet, so it was about the size of a B-29. The Dosthra was designed for rough, outlying airfields with tow landing wheels being an incredible four meters in diameter. It's four radial Argus engines each dove a four bladed propeller. A fifth high-altitude engine was positioned in the rear of the aircraft. One the tips of the wings were mounted jet engines as in the B-36, which additionally, could be used for steering. The wings were of a slotted construction, possibly suction wings, whose area was considered small in proportion to the size of the aircraft. The tail section slanted backwards. Top speed for this aircraft was given at 830 kilometers per hour or almost 515 miles per hour. Its range was given at 22,000 kilometers or 13,640 miles. Enough range to be a threat to the American mainland. Its crew consisted of five to seven people. The mission of the Dosthra remains unclear. The most curious thing about this aircraft was that it was armed with a weapon called "Metalstrahl".

Metalstrahl was a type of rail gun that used magnetic forces to attract and repel steel bullets and launch them at tremendous velocity[4]. Whether or not a rail gun was actually mounted in this aircraft or not, it is a fact that such a weapon was under development by the Germans in this time frame[5].

Returning to our discussion of super metals, the other curious thing about this aircraft was that it was said to be made of a special metal. This metal, according to Landig, was made by compression at 400,000 atmospheres of pressure. It is said to have had the highest possible tensile strength and functioned on the Dosthra as a protective armor[6].

This is all good and well if we are talking about "rumors" of super metals, but what actual evidence is there that the Germans managed to realized this technology? There is some evidence coming from government sources, one Allied and one Axis.

As soon as the smoke had cleared off the battle ground, elite teams of Allied scientists began combing Germany and Austria for advanced technology which could be used against the remaining enemy, Japan. These teams of scientists, going by various names, compiled their findings in a series or reports, actually several series of reports. One of these series of reports was the British Intelligence Objectives Sub-Committee reports (BIOS). In report number 142, a German advance in metallurgy is described which seems to have baffled the British scientists of the times.

The reason this is said is that one of the German informants, upon with the British relied for information, is simultaneously given credence and then discredited. The BIOS report says of their informant, Josef Ernst:

> "In the course of interrogation it became clear, that Ernst was not at all reliable, and though there may in some cases be a factual basis for some of his claims, they are as a whole inaccurate and of doubtful value"[7].

This is a pattern seen over and over again in Allied intelligence reports. The question is: Why use information from a source that is unreliable? Why would these scientists report information to their superiors that they themselves believe is wrong or inaccurate? The answer is that they are covering themselves either way. If the information is correct, then they were the first to report it and are to be commended. If it is false, they are on record having warned all those concerned against this information.

The underlying truth about this and other such attempts of Allied scientists to have it both ways in their reports is that these interviewing Allied scientists "didn't have a clue" if the information is accurate or not and are just covering their butts.

Ernst claimed the Germans had developed a method to harden steel and aluminum beyond any means yet developed. He claimed this involved a process of nitrogen bonding to the surface of these metals. The report says:

> "Ernst claimed to have worked for many years on nitriding processes, and to have evolved a method of hardening steels and aluminum alloys. Ernst had been in contact with a Prof. Dr. Thalhofer of the Technische Hochschule, Karlsruhe, who had carried out trials for the army, at Wamberg, Czechoslovakia, and is probably the real inventor of these processes. The method for the harden-

ing of steels, which is claimed to produce a nitride coating up to 0.5 cm. thick with a hardness of up to 1,800 Vickers, is as follows. The steel is heated to 600 degrees C and quenched in 30% aluminum sulphate solution, which etches the surface. When cold the steel is packed in powdered charcoal and heated to 750 degrees C, and on reaching temperature is removed from the charcoal and quenched in a 15% sodium nitrite solution at 35 degrees C. The method is good for drills, and silicon steels."[8]

Ernst goes on to say that all the equipment for operating this process is at the house of Baroness Mangold, at Silcherof, near Weilheim, near Munich. Remember that the site for the Impervium research is also said to be in Bavaria and one wonders if the two reports are possibly describing the same research.

In doing research for this chapter, I spoke on the telephone with a chemical engineer, John Ritzenthaler, who deals with metal surfaces. He told me that this process was carbo-nitriding. Aluminum impurities in the steel react with nitrogen and bond. Carbon is then added as in making steel. The process is called case hardening.

On another occasion, I called a large defense contractor, TRW, and spoke with a metallurgist about German developments in metals during the war. I asked him:

"What about all those super-metals the Germans were supposed to have developed?"

To this sort of open-ended leading question the metallurgist replied that:

"It is true. The Germans developed all sorts of alloys during the war. After the war we took them—some of them were great—we took one and gave it a TRW number, and still market it today—we didn't want to give the Germans credit though".

TRW assigned a "TRW number" to its commercial metals for purposes of designation and marketing.

There is more. Norbert Juergen-Ratthofer describes a method of propulsion based upon a super-cooled, fuel such as liquid helium, injected directly into the combustion chamber of a motor at which time it expands tremendously. The connection to metallurgy is that this same super-cooling, high compression process, needed to utilize this fuel can be employed upon metal to make it super-hard. This is reminiscent of the high-pressure technique described by Landig in describing the compressed metal skin of the Dosthra. This process, according to Juegen-Ratthofer, is based on the German patent of inventor Karl Nowak.[9]

According to Karl Nowak's 1954 German patent, patent number 905847, Class 12g, Group 101, by a process of extreme cooling coupled with pressure, the basic atomic structure of material can be changed. It is reduced, narrowed and confined in terms of atomic, crystalline structure. Nowak's idea was to re-heat this substance in a combustion chamber and reap the rewards of an instantaneous, explosive expansion. The question remains if it is possible to apply this technology toward the hardening of metals. Admittedly, at first the idea of compression cooling as a means to change atomic structure sounds a lot like junk science.

At this point Dr. Gordon Freeman weighs in with some remarkable scientific insight. According to Dr. Freeman, an elements behavior is determined by its arrangement of electrons orbiting the nucleus of that elemental atom. Seven electron shells are present around the core. Under high pressure electrons are shifted to lower orbits and new orbital overlappings are formed. This changes the whole behavior of the element concerning color, boiling temperature, density and so forth.[10]

The trick seems to be to cool and compress the material and then gradually release the pressure. The material will retain its new properties at least for several months.

Dr. Freeman points to a neutron star as an example. A star burns out and turns cold in intergalactic space. "Cold" is very cold, meaning at or near absolute zero. As it burns out it collapses, putting the remaining cold material under unbelievable pressure. Imagine hydrogen, composed of one electron and one proton, as an example. Pressure becomes so great that the electrons are pressed into the core of the atom, that is, pressed into the core of the proton. A new neutron is formed through this process. Repeated billions and trillions of times, a new material and a new type of star is thus formed which is a cold, dark neutron star. This is the most dense and strongest of metals.

A question remains as to if there were whole classes of metals or

(b) Nitriding of steel

Ernst claimed to have worked for many years on nitriding processes, and to have evolved a method of hardening steels and aluminium alloys. Ernst had been in contact with a Prof. Dr. Thalhofer of the Technische Hochschule, Karlsruhe, who had carried out trials for the army, at Wamberg, Czechoslovakia, and is probably the real inventor of these processes. The method for the hardening of steels, which is claimed to produce a nitride coating up to 0.5 cm. thick with a hardness of up to 1,800 Vickers, is as follows. The steel is heated to 600°C and quenched in 30% aluminium sulphate solution, which etches the surface. When cold the steel is packed in powdered charcoal and heated to 750°C, and on reaching temperature is removed from the charcoal and quenched in 15% sodium nitrite solution at 35°C. The method

(d) Nitriding of aluminium alloys

Ernst claimed that experiments on the nitriding of aluminium alloys were carried out at Camp Mecklenburg. Aluminium could be nitrided by active nitrogen produced by alpha particle bombardment. A product of very high strength was obtained, by the use of which the weight of aircraft structures could be decreased by 50%. It was claimed that the surface of aluminium alloys hardened in this way had a hardness of 1,000 Brinell.

Super Metals – British Intelligence Objectives Sub-Committee report number 142.

Top: the hardening of steel through nitriding. This is a chemical process.

Bottom: Aluminium was hardened through bombardment by alpha particles. Alpha particles are similar to nitrogen atoms so the two processes, one chemical the other using irradiation, had similarities. Both are examples of densification technology. Former SS man Wilhelm Landig describes a prototype aircraft built with this super-hardened aluminium in his novel "Goetzen gegen Thule". Was this one of the "realities" he said his novel contained?

other metals whose final step in manufacture is the introduction of nitrogen for purposes of super-hardening? Could other more exotic processes have been involved in nitriding such metals as Michael X. describes? Ernst answers the question in the same Combined Intelligence Objectives Sub-Committee report.

Ernst claims that aluminum was nitrided, strengthened and hardened to the degree that a 50% weight reduction could be achieved in aircraft using this metal. But the most amazing claim Ernst makes is the method for the nitriding process itself. Ernst claims that to achieve this the metal was subject to alpha particle bombardment. Alpha particles are positively charge particles emitted from a nucleus and composed to two protons and two neutrons. This makes an alpha particle identical with the nucleus of a helium atom.

The generation of alpha particles would require special equipment and the presence or absence of this equipment could be considered a test of the veracity of Ernst's testimony. To the best of my knowledge, the minimum piece of equipment required to generate alpha particles is a cyclotron. A search was made and a record for cyclotron research in Nazi Germany was found with no less than the Siemens firm[11].

One can only imagine a cyclotron bombarding the subject metal to be strengthened in some strange underground lab at Camp Mecklenburg, as Ernst describes. It may sound like weird science but it is exactly this sort of Nazi atomic alchemy that we have encountered before and will encounter again. The description of the atomic nitriding of aluminum is beginning to resemble the original words of Michael X. and one cannot help but wonder at the validity of the real Impervium as he describes.

SOURCES

1. X, Michael (Michael X. Barton), 1960, *We Want You Is Hitler Alive?*, page 17, Futura Press, Reprinted 1969 by Saucerian Books

2. ibid

3. Landig, Wilhelm, 1971, *Goetzen Gegen Thule*, page 185, Hans Pfeiffer Verlag GmbH, Hannover

4. ibid

5. Lusar, Rudolf, 1960, *German Secret Weapons of the Second World War,* page 160, Neville Spearman, London

6. Landig, Wilhelm, 1971, *Goetzen Gegen Thule,* page 185.
   Hans Pfeiffer Verlag GmbH, Hannover

7. British Intelligence Objectives Sub-Committee report number 142, page 6,7, 32 Bryanston Square, London

8. ibid

9. Nowak, Karl, 1954, German Patent, Patent number 905847, Klasse 12g, Gruppe 101, page 1,

10. Personal communication to the author, 12/19/02

11. Coil Research Laboratory Siemens Halske Berlin, File Number 6824 DIC/MIS/NOI-533, March 14, 1945, (interrogation of Paul Mehler), Reference Number 0136094

19 | N-Stoff

Shortly after the end of the war in Europe, Allied Intelligence interrogated the former Reich Minister of Armaments, Albert Speer. Speer was an architect who got lucky. Somehow, he became a personal friend to Adolf Hitler and rose in prominence within the Third Reich as the war fortunes of Germany rose. Eventually, he became Reich Minister of Armaments. In this position he coordinated the war industry of Germany. In his interrogation we have the transcript of the answers Speer gave but, unfortunately, not the questions[1]. From his answers, of course, we can deduce the questions in a general sort of way.

From the answers given, we know that the questions centered around the highest technology Germany possessed and its most powerful weaponry. The Allied interrogators prepared for this interview as if they were dealing with a media celebrity. This interrogation is to the point and pointed, as if there time constraints involved, not as if the prisoner is simply languishing in prison. Implicit in the questioning is the understanding that they, the Allied interrogators, are talking to "the man", the one most knowledgeable about these things and the person in overall control of these projects. We now know that this time had long passed for Speer. He had lost position and power to other agencies within Germany during the wane of the Third Reich. Principally, Speer's loss was General Hans Kammler's gain. Speer's answers reflect this "loss" in that there are some projects that were given code-names by the interrogators, for which Speer knows little or nothing at all.

In the third paragraph of the interview, labeled "3.", Speer apparently strays from the point of the question and provides us with a clue to something totally unknown, even today. It reads:

> "3. Questioned on chemical warfare, SPEER said at once that Dr. AMEROS of I.G. Fraben LUDWIGSHAFEN was entirely responsible both for development and production and the sonderausshuss of K-Stoff was virtually the I.G. he mentioned in this connection a new substance known as N-Stoff, which was the only one developed and made not by I.G. Farben but by HWAmt at FALKEN-HAGEN; he was not sure of the exact purpose of this material-it was not real war gas, but he thought it could "burn without oxygen"."

The Germans had code words for some chemical concoctions. There was C-Stoff and T-Stoff, for instance, which were complicated formulas for rocket fuel. Rather than recite or write out a long chemical formula, a codeword such as T-Stoff could be employed and be understood. N-Stoff was, then, a chemical formula rather than a codename for an element. Because of the "N", nitrogen might come to mind but this is not the case since the German word for nitrogen doesn't begin with an "n" and in fact is called "Stickstoff".

What was this N-Stoff that was so secret that even Albert Speer was unclear about it?

There is a clue. It seems the N-Stoff was to be used as the explosive warhead of both the V-1 and V-2[2]. It was a completely new type of explosive. At first, it was being developed by the German Army but the Wehrmacht's progress was deemed too slow by Hitler, so he gave it to a more reliable institution in his mind, the SS[3]. This technological transfer to the SS is the reason Speer seemed so vague about N-Stoff, it had simply escaped his purview and had fallen into the hands of Dr. Hans Kammler.

The development of N-Stoff seems to have gotten quite far along. A test of N-Stoff was actually done[4]. A fifteen-centimeter grenade of N-Stoff burnt a circumference to a distance of 800-1000 meters. Imagine a ton of this explosive in a V-1 or V-2.

This may have actually happened, because during the V-1 and V-2 attacks on London during October to November, 1944, there were extremely strong fires reported as a result of a few of these attacks which was never clarified[4].

According the Freidrich Georg, upon whom we are relying for much of this information, N-Stoff was composed of Chlorine and Fluorine and other substances[5]. This is about all we have on N-Stoff, just enough to perk the curiosity. N-Stoff has always been and remains one of those unsolved mysteries of the Second World War.

SOURCES

1. Combined Intelligence Objectives Sub-Committee report, Evaluation Report 53(b), June 18, 1945, page one

2. Georg, Friedrich, 2003, *Hitlers Siegeswaffen Band 2: Star Wars 1947 Teil A: Von der V-1 bis zur A-9: unkonventionelle Kurz-und Mittelstreckenwaffen,* pages 77 and 113, Amun-Verlag, Schleusingen

3. Georg, Friedrich, 2003, page 77

4. Georg, Friedrich, 2003, ibid

5. Georg, Friedrich, 2003, page 113

20 | Nipolit

Nipolit is another one of the mysterious explosives developed by the Germans during the war. Friedrich Georg describes nipolit as a "Sprengbaustoffen" or an explosive construction material[1]. It can immediately be appreciated that a construction material which itself is an explosive would have tremendous use in a military situation. Imagine, for example, a retreating army making bridges or even roads out of this material, which could be utilized as if it were concrete, yet detonated as the enemy approached or even detonated, as the enemy used it.

Planners at the time had another application. They wanted to form a whole nose cone out of nipolit and mount it atop a V-2 rocket[2]. This V-2 would not just be any rocket, it was to be the first V-2 using a nuclear-powered rocket engine. In this technique, an atomic reactor would be placed where the combustion chamber normally was located and through it or around it would be pumped a liquid gas such as hydrogen, for instance. The liquid hydrogen would cool the reactor but the intense heat would cause the liquid hydrogen not only to vaporize but to ionize. Without an oxidizer, the hydrogen would not burn in the normal sense, but would expand at an even greater rate and be ejected at rear of the rocket, providing thrust.

The nipolit nose cone would have the structural strength to remain intact until impact, presumably without the need of detonating equipment. The effect of this weapon would be further enhanced as radioactive uranium was scattered by the exploding nipolit giving it some of the value of a "dirty bomb".

TABLE NO. 5

Composition and Identification of Nipolit Powders

Identification	Nipolit - Röhren	Nipolit - Stifte
Dimensions	Length 80 mm Diam. 27 mm Hole diam 9.1 - 9.2 mm Hole depth 30 mm Weight 42 grams	Diam. 9.1 - 9.2 mm Length 50 mm
Caloric value	1300	1300
Nitrocellulose % Type	34.1 GU *	29.1 GU *
D.E.G.N. %	30.0	20.0
Stabilit %	0.75	0.75
Mg O %	0.05	0.05
Graphite %	0.10	0.10
P.E.T.N. *2 %	35	50

* Nitrogen content of nitrocellulose used 12.6 - 12.7%

*2 Unwaxed P.E.T.N. used in manufacture of nipolit.

Nipolit as described in a CIOS report by the U.S. government.

Confirmation of the reality of nipolit comes from the Combined Intelligence Objectives Sub-Committee report, on the subject titled: Manufacture Of Solventless Type Smokeless Powder & Nipolit Kraiburg Works, Deutsche Sprengchemie

G.M.B.H. The plant in question was visited by Allied investigators just after the war and nipolit is described in their report[3].

They state it was an explosive and the only explosive make at this particular facility. The other job of Kraiburg plant was to make solventless, smokeless powder for various types of guns. To make these various powders nitrocellulose, nitroglycerin, diglycodinitrate and a mysterious substance, PETN, were used. PETN is an abbreviation. Only nipolit contained PETN in its formula and PETN is nowhere defined.

A table showing the other contents of nipolit as well as the mysterious PETN indicates that it was formed into tubes (Roehren) and spikes (Stifte) which seems to confirm that nipolit was something other than just an explosive powder.

SOURCES

1. Georg, Freidrich, 2003, page 90, *Hitlers Siegeswaffen Band 2: Star Wars 1947 Teil A: Von der V-1 bis zur A-9: unkonventionelle Kurz-und Mittelstreckenwaffen,* Amun-Verlag, Schleusingen

2. Georg, Friedrich, 2003, page 131

3. Combined Intelligence Objectives Sub-Committee report, Item #2, File # XXVll-72, Manufacture Of Solventless Type Smokeless Powder & Nipolit Kraiburg Works, Deutsche Sprengchemie G.M.B.H., G-2 Division, SHAEF (rear) APO 413, October, 1945

Red Mercury

Did the Germans invent red mercury during the war? I have found no records stating that they absolutely did do so but the discussion of red mercury is so closely linked to that of increasing the density of metals, Karl Nowak, and atomic research and methods of making plutonium that mention should be made of the possibility.

What in the world is red mercury? Firstly, it should be said that the U.S. government calls red mercury a hoax and with that denunciation, the discussion of red mercury has been thrown into the realm of the rumor-mill in the United States. The Soviets are said to have invented red mercury, according to the rumor mill, in about 1968. With the fall of the Soviet Union, quantities of red mercury were said to have appeared on the black market. Agents of numerous countries have been trying to buy red mercury from Soviet sources. Other countries may have conjured up their own supply of red mercury, once its existence and samples were made known.

Red mercury is a compound of mercury, antimony and oxygen having the chemical formula of $Hg_2SB_2O_7$[1]. At room temperature and pressure it is a powder. It is red in color. But it seems that there is more to red mercury is not a simple chemical combination.

Legend has it that once chemically concocted; red mercury is put into a nuclear reactor for a period of time in order to charge up. During this charging up process while undergoing neutron bombardment in the reactor, the red mercury powder changes into

Chemistry

Q. What Is Red Mercury?

From Anne Marie Helmenstine, Ph.D.,
Your Guide to Chemistry.
FREE GIFT with Newsletter! Act Now!

A.

The science newsgroups have been a-buzz with tales of a 2-kiloton yield Russian red mercury fusion device, theoretically in the possession of terrorists. This, of course, begs the question: What Is Red Mercury? The answer to this question depends largely on who you ask. Is red mercury real? Absolutely, but definitions vary. If you had asked me before I did a bit of Internet research, I would have given you the standard cinnabar/vermillion answer. However, the Russium tritium fusion bomb is more interesting...

1. **Cinnabar/Vermillion**
   Cinnabar is naturally-occurring mercuric sulfide (HgS), while vermillion is the name given to the red pigment derived from either natural or manufactured cinnabar.

2. **Mercury (II) Iodide**
   The alpha crystalline form of mercury (II) iodide is called 'red mercury', which changes to the yellow beta form at 127°C.

3. **Any Red-Colored Mercury Compound Originating in Russia**
   as in the cold war definition of 'Red'. I doubt anyone is using 'red mercury' in this manner, but it's a possible interpretation.

4. **A Ballotechnic Mercury Compound**
   Presumably red in color. Ballotechnics are substances which react *very* energetically in response to high-pressure shock compression. Google's Sci.Chem group has had a lively ongoing discussion about the possiblity of a an explosive form of mercury antimony oxide. According to some reports, red mercury is a cherry red semi-liquid which is produced by irradiating elemental mercury with mercury antimony oxide in a Russian nuclear reactor. Some people think that red mercury is so explosive that it can be used to trigger a fusion reaction in tritium or deuterium-tritium mixture. Pure fusion devices don't require fissionable material, so it's easier to get the materials needed to make one and easier to transport said materials from one place to another. Other reports refer to a documentary in which is was possible to read a report on $Hg_2Sb_2O_7$, in which the compound had a density of 20.20 Kg/dm^3 (!). Personally, I find it plausible that mercury antimony oxide, as a low density (nonradioactive?) powder, may be of interest as a ballotechnic material. The high-density material seems unlikely. It would also seem unreasonably dangerous (to the maker) to use a ballotechnic material in a fusion device. One intriguing source mentions a liquid explosive, HgSbO, made by Du Pont laboratories and listed in the international chemical register as number 20720-76-7. Anyone care to look it up?

An internet article in which Dr. Anne Marie Helmenstein defines red mercury.

a thick liquid[2]. The charged liquid only has a life of about three months[3], so it must be used within this period of time for it to express its special properties.

Putting material into a reactor to try to change it may seem rather strange. In fact, this is exactly the method used to make plutonium. Uranium 238 is placed into a reactor and irradiated, absorbing neutrons until it finally changes into another element, plutonium. The Germans used this method and made plutonium[4]. Putting things and substances into a reactor in order to change them is a sort of modern alchemy. There have always been rumors of attempts to make gold by the Germans using this method, which is possible but expensive to do using enrichment methods. Following this line of thought, is it is no wonder that these early German nuclear alchemists would think to introduce mercury, a heavy, liquid electric conductor into a reactor for experimentation. If later compounds of mercury were introduced, it should be no surprise.

What is really going on here is that the red mercury put into the reactor is being made denser. The idea is similar to that of Karl Nowak, which is that an attempt is being made to reduce the space between the atoms and so causing the metal, or in this case, a compound, to become more dense. In this irradiation method it is not being done by cooling the existing material but by bombarding it with neutrons, additional material, in a reactor. The red mercury is trapping and retaining neutrons and so becoming denser. Like the Nowak method, the change is only temporary but while it lasts the change causes the compound to have special properties besides being mildly radioactive.

These special properties are numerous and truly unique. Red mercury is said to be able to detonate small nuclear bombs, "mini-nukes". Red mercury is said to burn with very great intensity making it an explosive in its own right[5]. It is also said to be used in the manufacture of semiconductors[6], the production of electricity[7], the production of coatings for military equipment to avoid radar detection[8], and, because of its high-energy explosive content, it is used as a rocket propellant[9].

Of course the main concern here is the use of red mercury for the production of very small nuclear bombs and the use of red mercury for the manufacture of a completely new type of very small nuclear bomb. The historical reason for the concern with mini-nukes is that

Ballotechnics, Pure Fusion and Nuclear Terrorism

According to Sam Cohen, a new type of non-nuclear explosive is potent enough to light off a nuclear fusion reaction between deuterium and tritium. In the usual H-bomb, a fission bomb is needed as a match to light off the fusion. With the new type of explosive, the fission bomb is unnecessary. As nuclear bombs go, the pure fusion bombs have an extremely low blast, equivalent to 1 ton of TNT: a "pop, not a bang."

But they release a flood of neutrons, lethal within 1/3 mile, causing death "from immediately, till shortly after."

They could be made by several countries known to sponsor terrorism, and could be carried in a sandwich bag.

The new type of non-nuclear explosives are called ballotechnic materials. Cohen says that unlike other explosives, they produce no bang, no cloud, keep the same shape while they detonate, "but Boy!, do they get hot!" Ballotechnics may have already led to very small fission bombs as well as pure fusion.

Cohen identifies the mysterious "red mercury" (of TV documentary fame) as a ballotechnic material. He offers this "recipe:" take mercury-antimony oxide, compress it, and bombard with neutrons. He says it is slightly radioactive, with a half-life of a couple of days.

Cohen says the Russians have built and tested mini-nukes, and that Americans and Russians are cooperating on pure fusion. He says that a Russian bomb was brought to Los Alamos ("by Federal Express" from a Russian plane in Washington) and successfully tested.

Dr. Teller agreed with most of this--including the successful test at Los Alamos--but rejected red mercury as "nonsense," possibly "a pure hoax." Cohen was more impressed with the agreement than the disagreement. As he was leaving the building, I heard him say that from now on, he would "quote Teller word for word," and had ordered tapes of the meeting for that purpose.

The terrorist potential of mini neutron bombs is horrifying. One possibility mentioned by Cohen involved a US State Of The Union address. Mere mention of it provoked the founder of DDP, Howard Maccabee to demand that Cohen stop his presentation!

Ballotechnics' potential for good is also great: it could be a route to practical fusion power.

The first page of an internet article Dr. Sam Cohen (father of the neutron bomb) describes making red mercury through compression of mercury-antimony oxide and bombardment of it by neutrons. This densification is reminiscent of Karl Nowak but done more like Joseph Ernst describes in hardening aluminium. Neutron bombardment can happen inside a nuclear reactor or by the neutron generators made by the C.H.F. Muller, A.G. company.

Red Mercury

The WMD no one wants to "officially" talk about... Its deadly potential cannot be ignored!!!

On Friday, September 24, 2004, British police arrested 4 suspects for allegedly trying to purchase a 'highly powerful, radioactive material, originally made in Russia, know as' Red Mercury'.

These four supposedly were willing to pay $ 541,000 a kilogram, on behalf of a Saudi Arabian, (described as sympathetic to the Muslim cause'), whose name was not disclosed.

"The News of the World said that the material was developed by Soviet scientists during the Cold War for making briefcase nuclear bombs that could kill people within a few city blocks."

Sam Cohen, the physicist who invented the neutron bomb, sheds a little more light on the destructive pow of red mercury. As quoted from a June 15, 1997 article by Christopher Ruddy of the Tribune-Review, it stat

> 'Most frightening for Cohen is the relative ease by which neutron bombs can be created with a substance called red mercury. Red mercury is a compound containing mercury that has undergon irradiation. When exploded, it creates tremendous heat and pressure – the same type needed to trigger a fusion device such as a mini-neutron bomb.

> Before, an obstacle to creating a nuclear bomb was the need for plutonium, which when exploded could create a fusion reaction in hydrogen atoms. But red mercury has changed that. The cheap substance has been produced in Russia, Cohen said, and shipped on the black market throughout world.

> Cohen said that when UN inspectors went to Iraq to examine the Iraqi's nuclear weapons capabiliti the U.N. team found documents showing that they had purchased quantities of red mercury. The material means that a neutron bomb can be built "the size of a baseball" but able to kill everyone within several square blocks."

Another article, "The Balance of Terror and the Red Mercury Nightmare" states that 'Iraq possesses "s-megaton" micro-nuclear warheads. These are softball sized two-megaton fusion bombs triggered by an irradiated and compressed compound of mercury antimony oxide. This device doubles the nuclear yield v a hundredfold reduction in weight. Using heavy hydrogen instead of uranium or plutonium to fuel its explosive reaction, this handheld nuclear weapon cannot be detected by U.S. sensors.'

Red Mercury....The CIA says that it does not exist, yet terrorist organizations worldwide are willing to pay outrageous amounts of money to procure it...Scientists have alluded that nuclear weapons containing red mercury, can enter the United States, UNDETECTED, be placed in cities all across the country, and cause cataclysmic destruction...from a nuclear bomb, of incredible power, the size of a softball...I don't know ab you folks, but this REALLY scares me!

Now, what bothers me even more, is that last year, confidential intelligence sources informed me that a Special Ops unit in Iraq had lost track of about a ton of red mercury. I have not heard anything to the contrary, so I am assuming that it is still missing. How could that happen???

According to the research that I have done and talking to the contacts that I have in the Intelligence community, red mercury not only destroys human life, but kills every living thing in its path for eternity!!! other words, where its destructive energy has touched, NOTHING will ever live again, not at least in our lifetime!

Let me go one further, my sources inform me that it would only take a teaspoon of red mercury to kill all living creatures in the Great Lakes.

In another internet article Dr. Samuel Cohen discusses the real danger of red mercury weapons.

the wartime Germans are known to have mentioned nuclear bombs of a very small size. These bombs were sometimes described as the size of small pumpkins or pineapples[10]. This small size greatly confused the Allied Powers when they heard descriptions of it. This is perfectly understandable considering that atomic weapons were usually thought of as being large, heavy and bulky. The description concerning size compares favorably with the description given for a red mercury bomb which is said to be somewhere between the size of a grapefruit[11] and a soccer ball[12]. The question for us is, could red mercury have been one of the missing components in the Allied assessment of the German atomic bomb?

The Americans are said never to have discovered red mercury (or gotten it through any other means)[13]. But how is this possible? We had Robert Oppenheimer. We had Edward Teller. We even had Albert Einstein. We still have Samuel Cohen, "father of the neutron bomb". These people are geniuses. They are icons of our American scientific culture, whose work proves American superiority in the field of nuclear physics. These worked on the Manhattan Project. They know virtually everything about nuclear weaponry. All these individuals, inspire of their denials, spent their life's energy working hard and actively to produce the most efficient killing machines ever invented by man. Like the German rocket scientists who later went on to put man on the moon[14], the American nuclear scientists mentioned above worked, first and foremost, feverishly for the express purpose of killing untold multitudes of people they considered their enemies.

So why, with all this effort and with the financial backing of the government, did the Americans not discover red mercury? Perhaps it is because the role of American discovery in the field of nuclear weaponry has been great exaggerated. This is a theme taken up by many modern European researchers, some cited here and elsewhere in this book. I do not want to open this discussion here, only to mention that this is a possibility.

If the Soviets gained this technology through a German source, then this secret was one of the best-kept secrets of all time, lasting for almost fifty years. The initial secret involved here can be explained by what I call the "Vesco Principle". In Renato Vesco's paradigm, if any one former Allied Power recovered a particular technology and the other three Allied Powers did not recover it, that technology remained secret, perhaps until this very day. He states:

> "In fact, of the numerous revolutionary "new weapons"
> that the Germans developed in that period, we know
> only those— fortunately they comprise the majority—
> that fell into the hands of all, or at least more than one,
> of the four occupying powers."[15]

So if more than one former Allied country recovered a particular weapon of whole technology, then the secret was out and everybody openly discussed it. But if only own former Allied Power managed to get a particular technology, it guarded that secret very, very closely. How it was possible to keep this secret for so long will be discussed at the end of this chapter.

The Germans had nuclear research facilities spread across Germany, Czechoslovakia, Austria, and portions of modern-day Poland. They were looking for breakthroughs and were willing to try most anything. As we will see in a later chapter, in one of these facilities, "Der Riese" in what is now Poland, there were descriptions of a "metallic liquid, mercury-like substance, violet in colour" being used in experiments there[16]. Red mercury can sometimes be violet in color but what is even more important in this description is its state of matter. It is described as a liquid. Dr. Gordon Freeman, in personal communication to me dated December 18, 2002, stated that under normal atmospheric conditions, *all* mercury compounds are *solid.*

By this he means all the known compounds of mercury are solids. The rumor of red mercury is the only compound of mercury ever said to be a liquid. This leaves little doubt in my mind but that the enigmatic violet fluid, in the midst of a wartime German nuclear research facility, was, in fact, red mercury.

One reason why it may have been possible for the Germans to make this breakthrough while the Americans did not is because the Germans and the Americans were working with two different schools of physics in mind. Igor Witkowski, modern-day expert on "Der Riese" and secret German research is quoted by Nick Cook:

> "The Germans ignored Einstein and developed an
> approach to gravity based on quantum theory." Don't
> forget that Einsteinian physics, relativity physics, with its
> big-picture view of the universe, represented Jewish
> science to the Nazis. Germany was where quantum
> mechanics was born. The Germans were looking at

gravity from a different perspective to everyone else. Maybe it gave them answers to things the pro-relativity scientists hadn't even thought of".[17]

Many, many German atomic scientists went East at the close of the Second World War, either voluntarily or involuntarily, just as in the case of the German rocket scientists. The Soviets spared no effort and no expense in setting up the captured German scientists in the Russian motherland.

But the Soviets were interested in big nuclear bombs. Soviet long-range rockets reflected in their design that they were intended to carry a large payload in the form of a warhead. This heavy lifting ability put the Soviets ahead of the Americans in the space race and was a direct result of Soviet desires to carry a large megaton payload to the enemy. As you may recall, it was the Soviets who tested the heaviest thermo-nuclear weapon ever detonated. It was estimated at 50 megatons.

If the German scientists brought knowledge of red mercury with them to Russia, it must have been relegated into the cellar in terms of priorities. It was only with the interest in tactical nuclear weaponry that small atomic bombs resurfaced on the scene.

This brings us to the question of how red mercury technology is said to be able to produce small nuclear weapons. First of all, let us take a look at small nuclear weapons, employing less fissionable material than is normally thought of as being enough to form critical mass. Critical mass is the amount of nuclear fuel necessary to sustain a chain reaction. The actual amount varies with the various nuclear fuel used. The fact is that the large values given for critical mass in the first generation of nuclear weapons has been greatly reduced. Even when discussing "conventional" nuclear devices involving widely known ideas of fission and fusion, a decent discussion of the facts of nuclear weapons miniaturization is hard to come by, at least in the popular press.

One atomic bomb dropped on Japan was made of uranium 235. Approximately 50 kilograms of U-235 (about 10 1/4 pounds) were necessary to constitute critical mass. The chain reaction was started using a neutron gun, which was built into the bomb. Once the gun had split the first atom, the mass of uranium was enough to absorb the "split" neutrons, causing others to split in a chain reaction, resulting in a tremendous release of energy.

In order to reduce the amount of uranium necessary to constitute critical mass, that is, to carry this chain reaction, three things can be done. The bomb can be given "tamper", more neutron reflective ability, and/or be made denser.

The bomb can be made stronger (tamper) which makes it hold together longer, giving the chain reaction more concentration. This is done by using an armored coating around the bomb, which physically makes it stronger for a tiny fraction of a second.

The bomb can be made to reflect more neutrons back toward the focus of the chain reaction instead of going off randomly into space. Special neutron-reflective materials can be used to do this. Beryllium is, for example, one of these materials.

The nuclear fuel itself can be made denser. This is done by surrounding the fissionable material with conventional explosive and detonating it so that the force of the blast focusses the nuclear material inward, on to itself, compressing it. Nuclear scientists sometimes call this "implosion". It is said that Pu-239, used in the Hiroshima bomb must be detonated using the method[18].

Some elements or compounds used for the purposes described above have both the qualities of tamper and neutron reflectability. Some have one or the other. Using these methods the size of atomic weapons have been greatly reduced to the size of large cannon projectiles. The explosive values of these mini-nukes are greatly reduced as compared to the two bombs detonated over Japan.

I promised not to discuss the recent research of the new generation of researchers working on German atomic weaponry but I will say that their interest in mini-nukes is based on German references to their small size and the fact that several detailed, eye-witness accounts of two small nuclear detonations in March of 1945 have been gathered[19].

A fusion bomb is much more powerful than a simple fission bomb. A fusion bomb works by fusing two light nuclei to form a heavier nucleus, which is accompanied by a release of the difference in nuclear binding energy of the products and the sum of the binding energies of the two light nuclei[20]. The materials used for fusion fuel are heavy water (deuterium) and tritium. Tritium is simply lithium which has been placed in a reactor long enough to undergo a trans-mutation (the same method used to enrich uranium and to make red mercury).

A red mercury based nuclear weapon is a pure study in miniatur-

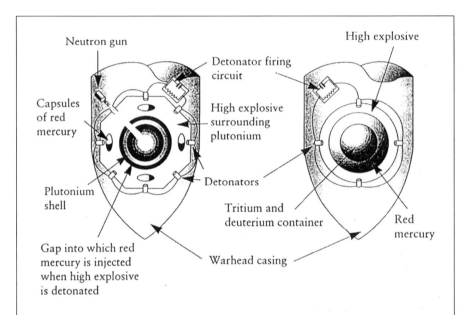

Neutron gun

Detonator firing
circuit

High explosive

Capsules
of red
mercury

High explosive
surrounding
plutonium

Plutonium
shell

Detonators

Tritium and
deuterium container

Red
mercury

Gap into which red
mercury is injected
when high explosive
is detonated

Warhead casing

The diagrams above illustrate the supposed principles of two types of red mercury nuclear weapon. They were published by *International Defense Review* in
1994 in an article by the nuclear analyst Dr Frank Barnaby.

On the left is a fission device: an advanced type of atom bomb. Capsules of
red mercury are embedded in high explosive surrounding a spherical shell of
plutonium. When the explosive is detonated, the red mercury is injected into a
gap around the plutonium. It acts as a neutron reflector, increasing the efficiency of the nuclear fission process, and as a tamper, preventing the plutonium
from disintegrating too quickly. Neutron rich elements known as actinides (e.g.
Californium 252) in the red mercury also give a boost to the fission process,
increasing the yield of the bomb for a given quantity of plutonium.

On the right is a pure fusion neutron bomb. An outer layer of high explosive
is detonated causing the inner layer of red mercury to release an enormous
amount of stored energy. The energy implodes the tritium and deuterium at the
centre of the device, producing enough heat to create a fusion reaction and a
massive release of high-energy neutrons.

Diagrams of two red mercury weapons from Hounam and McQuillan.

Appendix 2: Specification of Liquid Red Mercury

This specification for 'RM 20/20' or 'red mercury' is a translation of a Russian document given to the authors by a government official in the city of Ekaterinburg. It is typical of many that circulate on the black market. Some of the scientific details baffle scientists, notably its density and its being a liquid. In its normal state $Hg_2Sb_2O_7$ is a powder.

Product:	Red Mercury, R 20/20
Density:	20/20
Chemical Formula:	Hg2SB2O7
Molecular Mass:	756.61
Purity:	99.99%
Colour:	Cherry Red
Form:	Liquid, in case of Ro = 1.01325 bar
Melting Temperature:	$-37.87°C$
Flare Temperature:	170. 026°C
Boiling Temperature:	350.72°C
Isotope Temperature:	160.87°C
Natural Radioelements:	SF & SIC Circa in Number 0.784
Gamma FS:	0.440
Reaction K:	0.00015
Reaction R:	9,000–8,000
Reaction Absolute Temperature:	0.062
Reaction VIT Temperature:	1.024
Reaction VDSA:	0.30–0.29
Reaction Ren:	0.794
Warning:	The substance is mildly radioactive, handling is safe.
Package: Possibility No.1:	Retort NY 22
	Gross Weight: 39.5 kg
	Net Weight: 34.5 kg/retort
Possibility No.2:	Wooden box package with 3 standard ceramic carboys, 4 litres capacity, hermetically closed by lead seals with registration number, supplied with ampoules with samples and placed in aluminium vessels.
	Net Weight: 90.89 kg
	Gross Weight: .110 kg
Preparation date:	No more than 15 days
Special analysis:	With samples of 7.5 grammes

Special analysis. Metal content (%):

Co 2 x 10 7	Sn 1 x 10 8	Ag 3 x 10-8
Cr 1 x 10-7	Al 1 x 10-7	Mg 1 x 10-7
Ni 1 x 10-7	Cu 1 x 10-7	Pb 3 x 10-7

Transuranic – Actinide: Lawrencium (Lr – 103)
Isotopic Structures (%):

O 16:	99.76	Hg 196:	0.18
O 17:	0.037	Hg 198:	10.20
O 18:	0.20	Hg 199:	16.80
		Hg 200:	23.10
		Hg 201:	13.22
		Hg 202:	29.80
		Hg 204:	6.80

Specifications for one type of red mercury from Hounam and McQuillan.

ization. The employment of red mercury increases both the tamper and the neutron reflectability of the bomb. Further, red mercury explodes with such amazing energy that it can be used to surround the fissionable or fusionable material, compressing it to a higher density as it explodes. Red mercury delivers all three necessary qualities of atomic miniaturization.

Red mercury can be used in a fission or fusion bomb. The qualities red mercury brings, especially to the small fusion device, vault it into a class of nuclear weapons all on its own. It is no wonder that the bidding on the Soviet material and its underlying technology became so frantic in the early 1990's[21].

The question for us is not if red mercury, as we have come to know it, was Russian. The question is if red mercury had a German father. Was red mercury actually invented by some alchemist during the Third Reich, working underground in a first generation reactor, desperately searching for a war-winning technology and willing to stop at nothing and to rule nothing out in order to succeed? As we have already seen, the Germans knew of methods to make metals denser. The Germans knew how to turn lithium into tritium and how to enrich uranium 238 into plutonium by putting it into a reactor for a time. Were these ideas tried on other substances? They certainly had a supply of heavy water, deuterium, as there still exist today pictures of heavy water storage tanks from the region of Jonastal[22]. There are reports of small pumpkin or pineapple-sized atomic weapons being under development at that time. The Germans had experimented with, according to the report cited above, mercury compounds, which were liquid and violet in color at a site known as a site of nuclear research. The Soviets gained the services of many of the German nuclear scientists from several different German atomic projects after the war. The Soviets did "discover" red mercury but only after their thirst for truly large nuclear weapons had been slaked. Did they return to the German discoveries when the wanted to develop tactical nuclear weaponry? If this is true, then it is only verified by the "Vesco Principle" which states that if only one former Allied Power gained a particular German technology, as opposed to two or more former Allied Powers having it, then it was kept absolutely secret form the other former Allied Powers.

This scenario would explain the origin and hidden history of red mercury but would not explain why the Americans had no knowledge of this secret until the Soviet Union fell apart. How this secret was kept is a topic, which was promised the reader earlier. With all the Cold War spy vs. spy going on one would think that no important breakthrough or technology could totally escape this spy dragnet. The surprising truth, however, is that secret technologies were kept for decades.

Nothing in the Cold War had higher priority than rocket technology. Yet the Soviets made a huge technological breakthrough in rocket technology in the late 1960s and this breakthrough was kept from the prying eyes of the American spy agencies until after the Cold War ended. Here is what happened.

In the late 1960s the race to the moon was in its final stretch. The Americans were actually in the lead. This lead was based upon the Saturn 5 rocket, the vehicle, which would take man to the moon. The Soviets had suffered a setback. Their ace rocket designer died in 1966. The Soviets were behind in designing a rocket capable of delivering man to the moon. The reason for this lag was the difference between the size of the Saturn 5's rocket engines and anything that had been built before. The Saturn's engines themselves were enormous. The Soviets had nothing comparable off-the-shelf. A new engine had to be built.

Realizing they were behind, the Soviets gambled on reworking an old idea, the closed cycle rocket engine, which the Americans had given up as unworkable. At that time what normally occurred was that a rocket engine expended great amounts of energy venting burnt fuel and oxidizer that powered the turbo-pumps, used for pumping fuel to the main engines. These turbo-pumps were actually small rocket engines and it was only with a rocket engine that it was possible to pump the vast quantities of liquid propellants necessary to lift a rocket of this size to the moon. The problem was that the exhaust gases for these rocket-powered turbo-pumps were not being used as thrust, but being vented out of the sides of the rocket. The Soviets began work on another system.

Instead of a separate feed of liquid oxygen to the turbo-pump, the Soviets fed the entire supply of liquid oxygen, for both the turbo-pump and the main engine, directly into the turbo-pump. The excess or unburnt liquid oxygen was then routed out of the turbo-pump as exhaust and directly into the main combustion chamber of the rocket where it combined with more liquid hydrogen, the fuel. After years of failure, this engine was finally perfected and given the designation NK-33 by the Soviets. Amazingly, this engine was 20-25% more efficient that any rocket engine ever built by the American, even to this day.

After the Americans landed on the moon in 1969, the space race was over and the Soviets saw no political gain in building their own moon rocket. Their program was scrapped. The NK-33 engines were slated for destruction and the order was so given. Fortunately, this order was disobeyed. Many engines were secretly stored in a warehouse inside the Soviet Union. These engines remained in storage and in secrecy for the next thirty years.

It was only well after the fall of the Soviet Union that the information was leaked to the Americans. The Americans, at first, did not believe the efficiency figures their Russian counterparts were giving them concerning the secret NK-33 engines. The Americans brought some of these engines to the USA for testing and found they were exactly as stated by the Russians. The Russians, now in partnership with the Americans, modernized the NK-33 engine and it now forms the basis for the new satellite launch vehicle, the Atlas 2.

This story proves that secret technology can be kept secret for a long time. This was true of the NK-33 engine, which was at the heart of a great space rivalry and the subject of intense espionage. Red mercury was a secret for which no spies were searching. A secret not looked for can be kept a secret for a long time. Red mercury was most likely a unique and fortuitous find for the Soviets, based upon German research. Because they alone possessed its secrets, knowledge of its existence remained a top secret. Like the NK-33, red mercury only surfaced after the fall of the Soviet Union at a time when the Russians became interested in marketing a product.

SOURCES

1. Hounam, Peter and Steve McQuillan, 1995, page 190, *The Mini-Nuke Conspiracy Mandela's Nuclear Nightmare*, Penguin Books, New York.

2. Hounam, Peter and Steve McQuillan, 1995, page 58

3. ibid

4. Mayer, Edgar and Thomas Mehner, 2002, page 186, Die Atombombe und das Dritte Reich, Jochen Kopp Verlag, Rottenburg

5. Hounam, Peter and Steve McQuillan, 1995, page 130, 140

6. Hounam, Peter and Steve McQuillan, 1995, page 60

7. Hounam, Peter and Steve McQuillan, 1995, pages 60, 281

8. Hounam, Peter and Steve McQuillan, 1995, page 64

9. Hounam, Peter and Steve McQuillan, 1995, page 90

10. Mayer, Edgar and Thomas Mehner, 2002, page 265, *Die Atombombe und das Dritte Reich Das Geheimnis des Dreiks Arnstadt-Wechmar-Ohrdruf,* Jochen Kopp Verlag, Rottenburg

11. Hounam, Peter and Steve McQuillan, 1995, page 129

12. Hounam, Peter and Steve McQuillan, 1995, page 134

13. Hounam, Peter and Steve McQuillan, 1995, page 195

14. Georg, Friedrich, 2003, pages 41-46, *Hitlers Siegeswaffen Band 2: Star Wars 1947 Teil A: Von der V-1 bis zu A-9: unkonventionelle Kurz-und Mittelstreckenwaffen,* Amun-Verlag, Schleusingen

15. Vesco, Renato, 1976, page 96, Intercept UFO, Pinnacle Books, New York

16. Cook, Nick, 2001, page 191-192, The Hunt For Zero Point, The Random House Group Ltd., London

17. Cook, Nick, 2001, page 194

18. Mayer, Edgar and Thomas Mehner, 2002, pages 251-254, *Die Atombombe und das Dritte Reich Das Geheimnis des Dreiecks Arnstadt-Weckmar-Ohrdruf,* Jochen Kopp Verlag, Rottenburg

19. Mayer, Edgar and Thomas Mehner, 2002

20. Van Nostrand's Scientific Encyclopedia, 1958, page 715

21. Hounam, Peter and Steve McQuillan, 1995

22. Faeth, Harald, 1998, page 151, *1945-Thuerigens Manhattan Project Auf der Spurensuche nach der verlorenen V-Waffen-Fabrik in Deutschlands Untergrund,* CTT Verlag, Schleusingen

22 | Electric Gun or Rail Gun

An electric or rail gun uses forces of magnetic attraction and repulsion to move a projectile. We are all familiar with how opposite poles of a magnet attract and how like poles repel. This idea can be harnessed in what is called a linear motor. This device is set on a rail or rails and alternately attracts and then repels a small car that is set upon the rails. The car is rapidly accelerated down the track. The car's front end is open so that a projectile placed in the car will be shot out when the car reaches the end of its track. The projectile cannot be spun to give it stability in flight as a bullet is spun by the spiral groves in the gun barrel. Instead, fins are attached to the projectile in the manner feathers are attached to an arrow.

The Germans first considered the electric gun for use as a long-range cannon for exactly the same role as the Hockdruckpumpe (HDP), the high-pressure pump or cannon, was ultimately built. This device actually saw service in the Second World War and rained projectiles upon London from facilities located across the English Channel on the west coast of France[1]. The HDP was further developed after the war into long-range weaponry, which finally culminated in the super cannon built by Dr. Gerald Bull.

In 1990, Dr. Bull's nearly completed super cannon was mounted at a 45-degree angle up a hillside in western Iraq and pointed at Tel Aviv. This weapon was capable of launching projectiles the size of Volkswagens into the center of that Israeli city. Fortunately, for the Israelis, the government of the United States, through some slick maneuvering, gave

Saddam Hussein the green light to invade Kuwait and then condemned him for it. These events led to the United States's bombing and destruction of the super cannon in the ensuing Gulf war before it could be used against Israel. Dr. Gerald Bull was assassinated by the Israeli Mossad on March 22nd of 1990. The Americans never wanted to disclose the Machiavellian moves leading up to the first Gulf War and the Israelis were never held accountable for the murder of Dr. Gerald Bull. This is another example of how the winners write the history.

Besides the Hochdruckpumpe, the Germans also had the V-1 and the V-2 for use as long distance artillery. For these reasons it was felt that the rail gun might be better put to other uses[2]. Instead, this technology was to be used for anti-aircraft purposes. A Berlin based company, the Gesellschaft fuer Geraetebau, was put in charge of development of this weapon's system.

At first glance, the rail gun, the idea of inventing a whole new class of machine for use as an anti-aircraft weapon sounds like pure science fiction. Indeed, it still sounds like science fiction. Rail guns have recently been proposed for use as one method to shoot down incoming ballistic missiles as part of a "Star Wars" defense system. But this is not fiction. The basic developmental work necessary to field this weapon was done almost sixty years ago. This fact is made clear by the Combined Intelligence Objectives Sub-Committee report 4/258. The information contained in this report was gathered shortly after hostilities ended and published in mid-June of 1945. This information was based upon a German report issued on 9/10/44.

The CIOS report does two things. It details the finished anti-aircraft device itself and it explains in scientific terms exactly how the device works. It has been said that all machines can be reduced to numbers and this is exactly what the author of the report did. Anyone with a serious interest in this technology should avail himself of this report.

The specifics of the weapon to be produced were that it would have a muzzle velocity of 2000 meters per second and rate of fire of 72 rounds per minute. Each shell would weigh 500 grams. Six 10-meter barrels would be linked to a single power device and fired at once. The whole unit was to be mounted on a 12.8 cm AA gun carriage. This battery would have a burst of fire every five seconds[3].

Based on the report, the chief of the OKL-TLR requested that an experimental plant be set up as quickly as possible, consisting of a complete power unit and a three-barrel gun configuration.

In reading the CIOS report, it should be noted that it was based on some rather stale information, that of 9/10/44. Things were moving very fast at this time in Germany. There was only about seven months left in the war in Europe. Using other sources we can trace the gun's development after it left Berlin.

One of the most reliable sources on German secret technology is Rudolf Lusar. Lusar was an engineer who worked at the German Patent Office during the war. After the war was over, the Allies marched into the patent office and took everything. Lusar says 30 boxcar loads of German patents. After the war Lusar wrote a book on German secret weaponry base on his almost photographic memories.

Lusar reports that work on the electric gun moved from Berlin to the mountainous areas bordering between Bavaria and Austria, to the foothills of the Alps and to the slopes of Mt. Wetterstein to be exact.[45] Two versions of this weapon were tested. These were a 20 mm and a 40 mm version. A top-end muzzle velocity of 2000 meters per second was achieved, although some variants of these weapons had lower velocities. In one version, the 10-meter barrel was actually surrounded by electromagnetic coils, which were activated in succession as the projectile progressed down the barrel. In this mountain experimentation it was found that the large energy requirements of the weapon necessitated a new type of condenser that was developed. High hopes rode with this weapon but the military collapse brought this and all other weaponry research to an end. In the end, this technology fell into the hands of the Americans.

SOURCES

1. Porezag, Karsten, 1996, *Geheime Kommandosache Geschichte der "V-Waffen" und geheimen Militaeraktionen des Zweiten Weltkrieges an Lahn, Dill und im Westerwald,* Verlag Wetzlardruck GmbH, Wetzlar

2. Combined Intelligence Objectives Sub-Committee G-2 Division, SHAEF (Rear), CIOS Target No. 4/258, APO 413, page 5

3. ibid

4. Lusar, Rudolf, 1960, *German Secret Weapons of the Second World War,* page 160, Neville Spearman Ltd., London

5. Lusar, Rudolf, 1964, *Die deutschen Waffen und Geheimwaffen des 2. Weltkrieges und ihre Weiterentwicklung,* page 211, J.F. Lehmanns Verlang, Munich

23 | Electric Gun Part 2

The reason this chapter is called Part 2 is that new information has been received concerning this topic which deserves independent recognition. This information comes by way of Friedrich Georg and consists of two reports from the original company developing the electric gun, Gesellschaft fuer Geraetebau m.b.H. These two reports are dated January 30, 1945 and June, 1945. The Allied CIOS report is dated June 14, 1945 and prepared by H. A. Liebhafsky although a comparison of the two texts from June, 1945 reveals their similarity, even to the signature at the end of the Allied document which reads "J. Hansler". The German language text, titled "Ein Beitrag zum Problem des Elektrischen Geschuetes" was written by Dr. Joachim Haensler and the second text, "Entwurf fuer eine Elektrische 4 cm Flak" is signed by Haensler at its end. Therefore, the Allied CIOS report might be taken for a translation, which it is not. There is certainly a similarity between the two but the German texts are far more detailed and encompassing.

Stated in the reverse, the English text is more general and less specific. Whole discussions have been omitted. This comparison is an example of exactly how Allied post-war security was designed to work. Specific and detailed information was gleaned from German sources about a specific subject. The Americans then would summarize and generalize this specific information that would sometimes even be accompanied by a disclaimer as to the source or accuracy of the information repeated. A name, in this case H.A. Liebhafsky, U.S. Ord. would be attached to

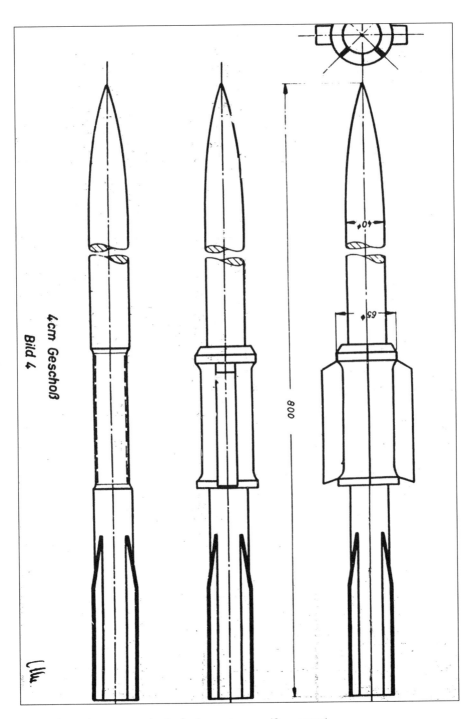

4cm Geschoß

Bild 4

800

⌀40

⌀65

Diagram showing the cross-section of an iron-free linear motor cannon (German report).

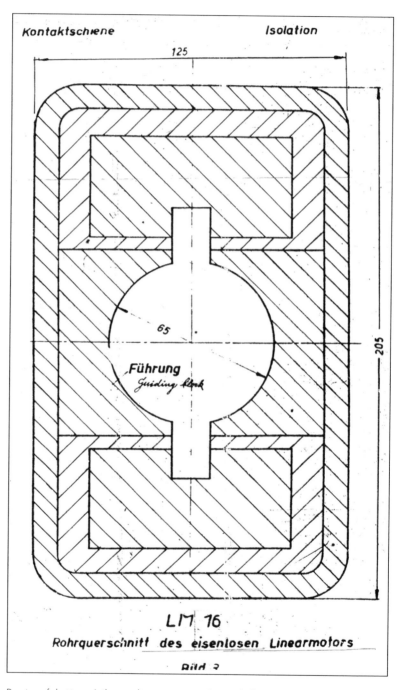

LM 16

Rohrquerschnitt des eisenlosen Linearmotors

Bild 2

Drawings of electric gun (rail gun, or linear motor cannon) projectiles from a German report.

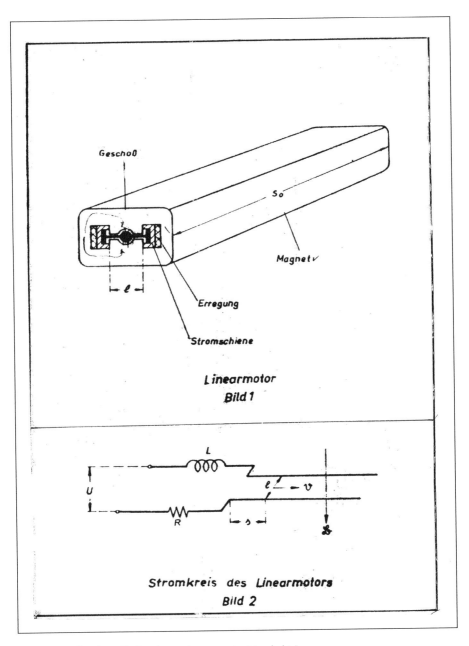

Geschoß

S_0

Magnet v

t

ℓ

Erregung

Stromschiene

Linearmotor
Bild 1

L

U

ℓ — v

R

s

Stromkreis des Linearmotors
Bild 2

Top: The barrel of a rail gun. The finned projectile emerges at point marked "e".

Bottom: Schematic of the linear motor's electric circuit.

the report. The purpose was to supply a lead to the technology but not an exact blueprint to it. For precise information one's security clearance had to be appropriate and then one had to contact the "custodian of records", to use a legal term, in this case H.A. Liebhafsky. He would then fill you in on the details not covered in the CIOS report and presumably provide you with whatever technical information he had. These levels of security indicate that even in an official sounding government rendition of the subject, underlying facts and perhaps secrets remain which are the subject of more secretive reports of in the possession of a designated person.

The two German reports do provide fresh insights and specific facts, which are the subject of this chapter. Both are similar in content, and brief. What has happened is that the earlier one was written during the war and the latter on was written after the war, presumably at the request of G-2 Division, SHAEF (rear). Since they are similar and brief, both reports will be treated together without specific page references.

The Germans had determined that the absolute maximum muzzle velocity for a powder-propelled projectile was about 2810 meters per second. In practice the maximum was only about 2790. For comparison, the German Paris Gun of World War One had a muzzle velocity of about 1600 m/sec. The Germans now needed something better. Analysis had shown that an electric gun's muzzle velocity potential was far higher, as high as 6000 m/sec.

The most pressing need was for a more effective anti-aircraft gun, able to deliver a larger charge at higher altitudes. They wanted to deliver 500 grams of explosive in this new flak weapon. To do this a muzzle velocity of about 2000 m/sec was necessary. The projectile itself would have the length of about 20 cm and a 4 cm diameter. It would have to be fin stabilized since spinning the projectile in the bore of the gun was impractical. Several barrels per anti-aircraft unit were desired. Originally, the Germans wanted ten barrels but, as the project progressed, this requirement was relaxed.

One aspect, only briefly discussed in the CIOS report is the other uses the Germans ultimately planned for the electric gun, beyond simply as an anti-aircraft weapon.

Due to the high muzzle velocities attainable, it was believed that long-range artillery could be fashioned using this technology. Mention of huge batteries of electric guns each vaulting one shot per minute are sometimes encountered in Allied prisoner of war debriefings but this information is not specific and was usually and understandably discounted by Allied intelligence as unreliable. These facilities were to be located in Western France and were always confused with the high pressure gun, known to the Allies as under German development and discussed in the previous chapter on this subject.

But besides flak and long-range artillery, there was another consideration in mind. Using a long track and a very powerful linear motor, the Germans believed it would be possible to boost the performance of their existing and future long-range rockets. There is not a lot of detail given but one can imagine a mile long, sloped launching ramp, as with the V-1 only much larger, in which a huge sled powered by a linear motor carried a large missile up to several hundred miles per hour before flinging it into the air. The fuel normally wasted just inching the rocket off the ground could now be used to extend its range. This would have been suitable to start the ram-jet based Tromsdorff-D-6000 missile or the huge intercontinental Saenger designs.

One major problem that was encountered with the linear motor was the problem of self induction. An iron object moving through a magnetic field itself becomes an electromagnet. When two magnetic fields interact, a kind of magnetic resistance is encountered which, in this case, would slow the projectile down considerably. The Germans identified three areas of self induction. These were the power source, the barrel and the electric leads.

The power source was a huge generator of 7800 kw. It consisted of an 8 cylinder diesel motor rated at 16,000 horse power. Besides the power source, unipolar impulse generators of a new type manufactured by Siemens-Schucker, each weighing 150 tons, as well as a new type of battery were necessary to impart energy to the projectile. An electric generator is a source of magnetic energy. Nothing is stated but one wonders how successful efforts were in reducing the self-induction values for these generators.

The barrel could be modified to reduce self-induction. The answer in this case was to make it iron-free. With an iron free barrel there would be no self-induction as the projectile traveled through it.

Likewise, the electric leads themselves were capable of generating field energy. The solution was to use 8 parallel single leads, each two copper bands with insulation material in between them as well as keeping them as short as possible and contained within the machine itself.

From the description given, these guns were going to be heavy. It is hard to believe that they would be mobil units as the famous German 88 millimeter anti-aircraft cannon had been. It seems more likely that once these units became operational, they would have been stationed near high-value targets for use against bomber formations.

The Germans felt that they had worked all bugs out of this weapon and that it could be realized at that time. Perhaps experimental models were utilized as conditions allowed, but by the end of the war there is no official confirmation of the operational use of these weapons. Nevertheless, the technology is certainly ready to be "ramped up" in a "Star Wars" application or for launching heavy payloads into orbit.

Sources

1. Haensler, Joachim, Ph.D., 1/30/45, "Entwurf fuer eine Elektrische 4 cm Flak", privately published by Gesellschaft fuer Geraetebau m.b.H.

2. Haensler, Joachim, Ph.D., 6/45, "Ein Beitrag zum Problem des Elektrischen Geschuetzes", privately published by Gesellschaft fuer Geraetebau m.b.H.

24 | Means To Stop Engines
Gas

A large part of the Renato Vesco scenario concerning what he termed the "Kugelblitz" flying disc centered around its unusual means for shooting down enemy aircraft. Vesco described German experiments in producing a gas, not harmful to people, but which would case aircraft to fall out of the sky[1]. The method by which this was to be accomplished were special blowers in the Kugelblitz which shot out this special gas ahead of enemy bombers. The enemy aircraft's engine would inhale a small percentage of this gas, along with atmospheric oxygen needed for combustion. The gas would cause the bomber's engines to pre-ignite. This pre-ignition, also called "pinging" or "knocking", compromises the efficiency of the engine's normal ignition advance curve which fires earlier as revolutions per second increase. The efficiency of the advance curve depends on revolutions per minute, engine load, the compression ratio of the engine and the octane rating of the gasoline. In this case the gas in question functioned as if it lowered the gasoline's octane, thus causing it to ignite prematurely and destructively inside the combustion chamber. Depending on the severity of the pre-ignition, the engine would suffer anything from damage to total failure. Vesco even named the research facility responsible for this work and an individual scientist, the "Luftfahrts-forschungsanstalt" (flight research installation) at Volkenrode and Dr. Hans Freidrich Gold, respectively.

This whole idea remained a myth for years. Vesco was always treated with extreme skepticism concerning the Kugelblitz story and the mysterious gas. Now, while evidence for Vesco's manned flying disc designated Kugelbiltz is still largely lacking, the reality and the facts behind the amazing gas able to swat aircraft out of the sky have become known.

Of course, this did not come easily. Numerous requests have been made of the intelligence agencies of the USA for information concerning the Kugelblitz. It has been described to them in detail with alternate names included. In every instance a "no record" response is generated by the government.

Things did not end there, however. A FOIA request was made concerning the scientist involved, Dr. Hans Friedrich Gold. Again, "no record" responses were generated by the government's spy agencies. Below is an example, written on June 13, 2000 by the National Archives at College Park, MD., which says in part:

*   *   *   *   *   *

"This is in reply to your May 21, 2000 Freedom of Information Act inquiry regarding documentation on the Austrian scientist Dr. Hans Friedrich Gold.

Please note that our World War 11 records are declassified and in the public domain. It is not necessary to file for access under the Freedom of Information Act.

We have examined name indexes to pertinent records in our custody but were unable to locate any information of Dr. Gold. Many records of the Allied Control Commission, Austria, are not indexed by name. We are not staffed to undertake the substantial research that would be necessary to examine un-indexed material for information of one individual. Our staff would be pleased to assist you or your representative at our College Park, Maryland facility.

Sincerely,

Amy Schmidt
Archivist, Modern Military Records
Textural Archives Services Division

*   *   *   *   *   *   *

First, a request under the provisions of the FOIA is always necessary. This binds them to comply with the law imposed upon them by the Congress.

Second, the National Archive's World War ll holdings are not all declassified, for example, the German scientist Otto Maurer's file is full of references to material removed from public view because it is still secret. Without a request made under FOIA, the National Archives is under no obligation to make the requestor even aware that portions of the file have been withheld.

Third, files do exist under the name of Dr. Hans Friedrich Gold in the possession of the National Archives. The United States National Archives, have just simply lied. They are just simply liars. They just simply violate the law of the land and get away with it probably hundreds of times per day.

Fourth, the National Archives are under Federal Mandate to comply with all the provisions of the FOIA. Their staffing or their staffing problems are their own concern. Their only obligation as far as FOIA is concerned is to fully comply.

Fifth, the National Archives is not being asked to do "substantial research", they are being asked to pull a file, as any librarian could and should do.

Sixth, nowhere in the FOIA does it specify that requestors must put in an appearance at College Park, Maryland in order to receive a proper response. The location of either the requestor or the requester is irrelevant.

An example is made here to point out the fact that nothing comes easily out of the Federal Government. Everything is kept secret. It is simply their policy. They have no idea why this information is being requested and could not care less. Their policy is secrecy, pure and simple. This applies to everything. The National Archives is simply a de facto reclassification project.

But before turning to Dr. Gold, mention should be made of another government document, which greatly added to our knowledge in this matter. In 1999 a German researcher, Friedrich Georg, found what might be described as a mini-Rosetta Stone concerning secret German research and what the Americans knew about it. This document, "An Evaluation Of German Capabilities In 1945" was written in late 1944 and makes predictions of what to expect, militarily, from Germany in the new year. The relevant entry is shown here under "Gases Appli-

APPENDIX NO 1.

<u>COPY OF LETTER DIRECTED BY DR. GOLD TO HEADQUARTERS,</u>

<u>UNITED STATES FORCES, AUSTRIA, AS OF 23RD AUGUST, 1945.</u>

Graduate Engineer,
Hans Friedrich Gold,
Wien II Prater 150.   Vienna, 23 August, 1945.

Supreme Headquarters, U.S. Forces,
Attention: Technical Intelligence.

Re: Technical references connected with application.

  Unfortunately I do not speak your language well enough to use it
freely and therefore ask to excuse that I address you in German.
Following is a short survey about some matters of possible interest at
which I have worked. These are:

   1. Engine-stop-missile.
   2. Rockets and rocket fuels.
   3. Radioactive Research.

In connection with the two last items, it is suggested that in the
near future the problme of stratospheric aviation from England and
America will be taken up and the request is expressed to make use of
my service on ground of my specific knowledge.

  In regard to the Engine-stop-missile, I would like to mention
that during my activity at Aviation Research Institute in Braunschweig,
I succeeded in finding a substance which mixed with air in a special
proportion stops an engine immediately after a reaction of LESS THAN
ONE SECOND. The engine suffers damage, which in the best of cases
can be repaired only in a repair shop. The carrying out of large
scale tests which were already in preparation at Spandau did not
materialize owing to the evacuation of Spandau by the Army authorities.
The contemplated steps were primarily intended for tank defense.

  It should be stressed here, that this effective substance is not
one that would dirty the sensitive parts of the engine. With this
kind of stoppage substance the period leading to success is far too
long. At the Research Institute I was principally and quite independently engaged in research pertaining to rocket propulsion and I believe
gained interesting and valuable experience during my activities there.

RESTRICTED
-18-

Dr. Hans Friedrich Gold's post-war letter to U.S. Forces in Austria describing his scientific progress.

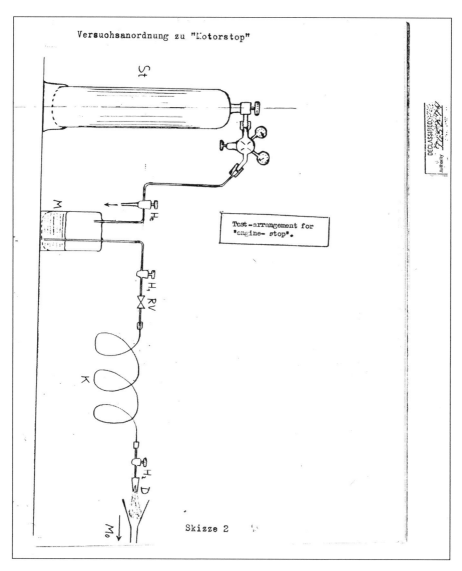

Diagram of the apparatus used by Dr. Gold to produce motor-stopping gas.

cable to Aircraft". As we can read, there were two gases under consideration for attacking Allied aircraft, one which caused pre-ignition of engines and another which caused motor oil the thin out to the point that engine protection disappeared and the engine seized.

From this document we learned that Vesco was not making this all up and that further work in this area was warranted.

The National Archives has always resisted providing any sort of index or catalogue of their holdings. Recently, they have provided a kind of computer index of their holding which they call by an acronym, NAIL. Unfortunately, NAIL will not even list items already produced by the U.S. National Archives under FOIA duress so one has to wonder what the real purpose of such a stealth index is.

Since the year 2000 and under pressure of the FOIA, the National Archives has provided a list, an index, of some titles of the Combined Intelligence Objectives Sub-Committee reports. Contained in that list was File Number XXXll-1109, "Interrogation Of Dr. Hans Friedrich Gold"[2]. With this new information an Appeal was filed with the National Archives concerning the previous "no record" Gold request. The National Archives handled this Appeal by ignoring it. Finally, a new request was made and the file was sent. Again, this violates the law.

Dr. Gold did work at the Luftfahrtforschungsanstalt, Hermann Goering, at Volkenrode. He was a chemist and chemical engineer who spent most of his time working on hypergolic fuels. These are fuels developed in pairs, such as "C-Stoff" and "T-Stoff". When both fuels are combined within the combustion chamber, combustion occurs automatically.

Somehow, in July of 1944 Dr. Gold's mind seemed to do a flip-flop because it came to him that it would also be possible to stop and engine using chemical means. Dr. Gold worked on the chemistry to do this as well as developing a test apparatus to measure the efficiency of this idea.

Dr. Gold used methylnitrate in one of his hypergolic rocket fuel mixtures in order to get oxygen into the combustion chamber. It occurred to him that this same chemical might be used to make an engine stop. A mixture of methylnitrate and methanol in a mixture of 75% to 25% respectively was used. With this mixture constitution only 2%, by weight, of the air drawn in by the target engine, a strong knocking occurred. With a 5% concentration, a metallic "hard hitting" and "heavy rattling" occurred. At 8%, within a fraction of a second a "strong bang" occurred, the engine stopped, and suffered a torsion of its crankshaft of about 30 degrees. In other words, it broke the engine apart.

Pictured is Dr. Gold's diagram of the testing device by which he came to these figures. The nitrogen from Bomb "St" presses, according to size, with 29 atmospheres upon the methylnitrate-methenol mixture (75/25) in the small bomb "M", so that the liquid rushes through nozzle "D" with open taps "H1" and "H2", across the check valve "RV" and the copper capillaries "K". A "Bosch" nozzle was used, with a spray angle of about 35 degrees. For the testing engine "M", a rather sturdy 500 cm "FN" motorcycle engine was used, its suction pipe "A" being provided with a funnel. The engine that was generally used for fuel tests was mounted on a test stand and connected with an oscillograph. "H" is a tap for reducing pressure.

Tests were to be carried out in a suburb of Berlin, Spandau, with the projected first use to be against tanks. Full scale testing was never done, according to Dr. Gold, because of the evacuation of that facility in the face of the Soviet advance. It is unclear if other testing or application of this weaponry was ever carried out.

Interestingly enough, there is a footnote to the Dr. Hans Friedrich Gold story. It is an Appendix, Appendix No. 2, to the CIOS report referenced above. This constitutes a statement by Dr. Gold on his personal views on future research. These views might seem fantastic coming from anybody other than such a well respected scientist. It is probably best to postpone Dr. Gold's discussion until a better foundation for his ideas have been built, but we will return to Dr. Gold later in the discussion.

SOURCES

1. Vesco, Renato, 1976, Intercept UFO, pages 137-138, Pinnacle Books, New York.

2. Combined Intelligence Objectives Sub-Committee report number XXXll-109, 1946, "Interrogation Of Dr. Hans Friedrich Gold, obtained from the National Archives, College Park, MD.

25 | Means To Stop Engines
Magnetic Wave—Motorstoppmittel

There have always been rumors of a secret German weapon which could cause ignition based engines, those with spark plugs, to stop running. These rumors started before World War Two and persisted well into the 1990s.

During the late 1980s or early 1990s, someone called me on the telephone that claimed to be an employee of a large defense firm. He told me that he was part of a group investigating the possibility that the Germans had built a beam weapon, but not directional as a laser beam, but an omni-directional weapon in which waves radiate out from a central point in all directions as does a pebble make waves when it is thrown into a pond. When in the range of this weapon, all ignition-based engines would stop running. He gave me some reports of this device from wartime Germany. I had never heard of such a thing before this time and, in consideration of the circumstances of the telephone call, took the whole thing with a grain of salt. But it did perk my interest and from this moment on, I was on the lookout for such descriptions.

Such descriptions of German devices that stopped engines did appear. Descriptions of this device seemed to abound with the genre of German writers who believed in and wrote of a wartime German technical history which had simply been kept secret after the war. Among the devices they described was something called "Motorstoppmittel", which translated literally is: "means to stop (a) motor".

What they seemed to be describing was different from the method described by Renato Vesco in his book about the history of flying saucers. Vesco described a device which he called "Feuerball", "fireball". This flying device used special chemicals in its fuel resulting in an over-ionized atmosphere near the target aircraft. This over-ionization caused the aircraft's engine to ground itself directly through the atmosphere, short-circuiting out the engine, thus causing it to fail. The difference is that nothing was ever mentioned about fuel or chemicals in reference to Motorstoppmittel.

One of the first accounts of a test involving this device comes from Germany's Axis ally, Italy, in 1936. It involves no less than the electric genius Dr. Guglielmo Marconi, Italian leader Benito Mussolini and Mussolini's wife.

It seems that in June of 1936 Mrs. Mussolini informed her husband of her intention to travel on the Rome-Ostia highway in the afternoon. Mussolini told his wife she would experience a something special if she made the trip between 3:00 and 3:30 P.M. As a matter of fact he said that she would be struck with wonder at seeing something. Mrs. Mussolini was at the prescribed place and time along with dozens of other cars both in front of her and behind her. What happened which was of such wonder was that their cars stopped running. Her Chauffeur as well as other stranded motorists attempted to restart their vehicles but to no avail. At exactly 3:35 P.M. all the cars mysteriously restarted and proceeded normally.

That evening Mussolini gave his wife the story behind her trouble. Marconi had invented something that halted engines. Pope Pius Xl got wind of the experiment and called it the work of the devil. Marconi died just over a year later, July 20, 1937.[1]

Of course, numerous Freedom Of Information Act requests were made of U.S. government agencies for information concerning Motorstoppmittel. It was described in as much detail as possible, as a German secret weapon capable of stopping ignition based engines. From every source a "No Record" response was generated.

When Freidrich Georg discovered the mini-Rosetta Stone, as described in the previous section, all this denial changed. Now we knew what the Germans called Motorstoppmittel was called "Magnetic Wave" by the US government. Besides the original document, An Evaluation Of German Capabilities In 1945, which described Motorstoppmittel, many other documents became available.

F.O.I.A. REPORTS ON MAGNETIC WAVE

The American intelligence reports are based on many sources. There are reports from German sources, there are reports from captured German scientists, from prisoners of war, and from the American military, all speaking of the same thing. They all describe an alleged German weapon able to make motor vehicles, including airplanes, stop running. Some of these reports are reproduced here.

The Americans and British went to some trouble to get to the bottom of all this. The American military even sent aircraft into areas suspected of being defended by this weapon in order to evaluate it. This is a report dated January 24, 1945, which involves two P-38 aircraft sent to fly over a suspect area near Frankfurt. Nigel Pennick tells us why this area was chosen for the American test[2]:

> "In connection with this high-enery research, various mysterious 'transmitters' were erected at several 'key points' in the Reich. In 1938 the Brocken, a celebrated peak in the Harz Mountains, was the site of feverish construction work. Holy mountain of the goddess Freyja, the Brocken is best known for the curious optical phenomenon known as the 'Brocken Spectre', which occurs when the shadow of a person on the summit is cast by the rays of the sun onto a cloud below. Under some conditions, this 'spectre' has a saintly halo around its head.
>
> This 'transmitter' was a strange contraption, a tower surrounded by an array of posts with pear-shapted knobs on top. At the same time a similar system was erected on the peak of the Feldberg near Frankfurt. When it began operation, there were soon reports of strange phenomena in the vicinity of the Brocken tower. Cars traveling along the mountain roads would suddenly have engine failure. A Luftwaffe sentry would soon spot the stranded car, and tell the puzzled motorist that it was no use trying to get the car started at present. After a while, the sentry would tell the driver that the engine would work again now, and the care would then start up and drive away."

ENGINE INTERFERENCE BY ELECTRO-MAGNETIC DISTURBANCES

AN EXAMINATION CONDUCTED BY U.S.S.T.A.F. TECHNICAL INTELLIGENCE SECTION

PREPARED BY:

DIRECTOR OF INTELLIGENCE
U.S.S.T.A.F.

Summary reports by American Intelligence on the German magnetic wave weapon.

SECRET

HEADQUARTERS
UNITED STATES STRATEGIC AIR FORCES IN EUROPE (REAR)
Office of the Director of Intelligence

AAF Sta 390
AFO 633 U.S.Army
24 January 1945

SUBJECT: Preliminary Report on Suspected Magnetic Ray.

TO : Brigadier General George C. McDonald, U.S. Strategic Air Forces in
Europe (Rear) APO 633 U. S. Army.

1. This is a preliminary report on investigation of the F-38 aircraft which
flew sortie No. 3832 over Frankfurt and the interrogation of the Pilot, Lt. Hitt.
Over this area the Pilot encountered a freakish condition which indicates that the
enemy may be using some new device (suspected as being a magnetic ray) as a
defence measure against our aircraft.

2. The Pilot made three passes over the target area which was the northern
part of Frankfurt for the purpose of taking aerial photographs. He took a number
of frames on his first two passes, at approximately 22,000 ft. and 20,000 feet,
but on his third pass at 17,500 ft. he ran into trouble with his aircraft. At this
time he was flying in a straight slightly climbing condition, no flak of any kind
was encountered and no evasive action was taken during the whole time over the
target area.

3. In beginning his third pass his instruments began acting up and his left
engine became very rough. He tried for approximately a minute and a quarter to
correct the engine condition, that is, changing mixture control to auto-rich and
back and changing RPM and manifold pressure. During this time the fuel pressure
gauge and RPM were fluctuating very excessively. Tuffs of black smoke were observed from the turbo. After trying to correct the condition he observed flames
coming from the turbo and fearing a fire he immediately feathered the engine.

4. The other gauges and instruments which were effected included the fuel
level gauges, gyro compass and the artificial horizon. The hands on the fuel
level gauges started spinning in the same direction. The gyro compass was also
spinning through 360° revolutions. The Pilot caged the compass at three differen
times and after uncaging each time the compass continued to spin through 360°
revolutions. The artificial horizon was floating in a peculiar attitude so that
it could not be used.

5. The Pilot stated that his right engine also ran rough but the coolant
temperature of both engines remained normal during the time that the trouble was
encountered.

6. Lt. Hitt had a Wing Mate who was covering the target in the Southern
part of Frankfurt. At no time was his Wing Mate closer than one mile of the
area in which Lt. Hitt encountered the trouble and apparently his Wing Mate did
not encounter the same peculiar troubles (his Wing Mate landed at Hanston for
refuelling and has not been interrogated to date).

7. After Lt. Hitt encountered this trouble he could not use his instrum-

- 1 -

APPENDIX C   SECRET

So the Americans chose this area near Frankfurt to see if they could determine the source and nature to the interference with their aircraft. At 17,000 feet in altitude and just North of Frankfurt, near the second tower mentioned above on the Feldberg, the pilot mentioned in the report, Lt. Hitt, encountered trouble. One of his engines began to "run rough". His fuel pressure indicator, rpm gauge, gyro gauge, artificial horizon gauge, all started to malfunction. The hands on his fuel level gauge started spinning in the same direction. The gyro compass started spinning through 360 degree revolutions. In the meantime, the pilot's other engine began to run rough.

While Lt. Hitt was experiencing such difficulty, the other P-38 pilot was flying over a Southern portion of Frankfurt. He encountered no trouble but was always at least a mile away from Lt. Hitt. Lt. Hitt' began heading for his base. After eight to ten minutes of trouble, Lt. Hitt's aircraft began running normally. Even his instruments returned to normal.

Upon landing an investigation was conducted and a mechanical and electrical inspection of Lt. Hitt's P-38 ensued. The title of the final report reflects the verdict of the inquiry: "Preliminary Report on Suspected Magnetic Ray". This report was given "Secret" status and was produced by Headquarters, United States Strategic Air Forces Europe (Rear), Office of the Director of Intelligence, dated January 24, 1945.

Even prior to this, a report had been generated by the Director of Intelligence, U.S.S.t.A.F., dated 12/6/44 and titled: "Engine Interference By Electro-Magnetic Disturbances". This was sub-titled on the second page: Project 1217, "Investigation Into German Possible Use Of Rays To Neutralize Allied Aircraft Motors".

Another interesting document is worth mentioning. It is marked secret, and from the American British Laboratory of Radio Research, dated January 30, 1945. In it calculations by J.M. Hollywood are discussed. Perhaps his ideas will give us a clue as to the real nature of Motorstoppmittel. It says in part:

> "Calculations by J. M. Hollywood of ABL-15 indicated that the most economical means of disturbing an aircraft's ignition system would probably employ electro-magnetic radio frequency transmissions recurrent at a rate near the frequency of the engine's ignition cycle."[3]

The report goes on to conclude that there is no real evidence for the German deployment of such an ignition suppression device but admits that intelligence information suggests that such a device exists and works on a short range basis. It goes on to say that an apparatus necessary to generate the required electromagnetic energy using ground-based coils would be enormous in size and therefore impractical.

Obviously, the actual German device was a little more intelligent, adaptable, flexible and target specific than a simple, huge, ground-based, gigantic coil pumping out a single, steady pulse as envisioned by Hollywood.

REPORTS FROM THE GERMAN SIDE

Thanks to the research in the German language publication "Waffen-Revue", January 1983, we are able to glimpse some of the real German work in this field. They published three documents. The first was from a commercial firm, ELEMAG. The second, a message sent by a sitting member or the Reichs Research Council, Dr. Werner Osenburg to Dr. Brandt of the SS. The third was from Dr. A. Meissner, also with a private research company. Each document is followed with my rough English translation.

English Translation of ELEMAG Document

*   *   *   *   *   *

```
ELEMAG ELECTROMAGNETIC DEVICE
CONSTRUCTION COMPANY HILDESHEIM
JANUARY 28, 1944
DISRUPTION OF THE FUNCTION OF DEVICES
AS A MEANS OF WARFARE
   It is to be striven for to put out or bring about or
disconnect that material of warfare used by the enemy via
the ability to disrupt the function of electronic appara-
tus.

UNDER THESE WEAPONS OF WAR ARE:
   Aircraft and motorized vehicles with an internal
combustion engine with spark plug ignition as used
in a propulsion method, whole intelligence services or
```

communications such as artillery adjustments.

To the attainment of this goal a long distance influence of the function of electronic devices will be put forward of the following basis.

The construction of electric devices consists of two fundamental elements together, voltage regulation and insulation. Disruption of electronic apparatus and devices is primarily attributed to suspension in voltage regulation or spanning of insulation.

A spanning of insulation, for example, a breakthrough of the blockage of the voltage path or circuit carried to the formation of eddy currents or short circuits and caused as a consequence of the latter interruption of voltage regulation, be it as a result of a melt-through of a fuse and lead or through the disfunction of the consumer of the electric energy itself.

Through a spanning of the insulation there is the possibility to cause the electric device to malfunction.

This brings up the problem of building of all electronic devices in fulfillment of finding insulation to make long distance influence ineffectual.

In the search for this suitable material it was found that the atmosphere contained the necessary provisions in sufficient measure.

Insulation atmosphere was found to be such a material, in its natural condition in general with no other special consideration. It produced insulation principle of electrics and without it any electronic device of known construction would be impossible. The present position of applied science offers the possibility of an influence of insulation atmosphere in the sense of accomplishing the solution of this problem.

It is known that ultra short electronic oscillations or waves of determined frequency, developed under specific proprietary work, and developed to force the atmosphere to ionize can cause an opposite electrical reaction to be released. That is, in other words, to cause the insulation atmosphere to alter in voltage regulation.

Trouble with the economic utilization of this knowledge was observed before the war, and, to be sure, concerns itself with the problem of the wireless communication of electric energy.

ELEMAG

Elektro-mechanische Apparatebaugesellschaft m. b. H.

HILDESHEIM · Goschestr. 14   Fernruf Nr. 3846   Bankkonten: Städt. Sparkasse, Hildesheim   Postscheckkonto : Hannover 670 92
Bankhaus Pagel, Hildesheim

Ihr Zeichen: Ihre Nachricht vom: Unsere Zeichen: Or/Wie.   Tag: 28.10.1944

Betrifft:

Störung der Funktion elektrischer Geräte als Mittel
der Kriegsführung.

Es wird angestrebt, auf der Feindseite eine Ausschaltung derjenigen
Kampfmittel herbeizuführen, deren Einsatzfähigkeit auf der Funktion
elektrischer Geräte beruht.

Unter diese Kampfmittel fallen:
Luft- und Landfahrzeuge mit einem Verbrennungsmotor mit Kerzenzündung
als Antriebsmittel, das gesamte Nachrichtenwesen, sowie einige artille-
ristische Einrichtungen.

Zur Erreichung dieses Zieles wird eine Fernbeeinflussung der Funktion
elektrischer Geräte auf folgende Basis vorgeschlagen.

Der Aufbau elektrischer Geräte setzt sich aus zwei Grundelementen
zusammen, aus Spannungsleitern und Isolatoren. Störungen an elektrischer
Geräten und Maschinen sind grundsätzlich auf Unterbrechungen in Spannungsleitern oder Überbrückungen von Isolatoren zurückzuführen.

Eine Überbrückung von Isolatoren z.B. durchbricht die Blockierung
der Spannungswege und führt zur Bildung von Kriechströmen oder Kurzschlüs-
sen, und verursacht als Auswirkung der letzteren Unterbrechungen in
Spannungsleitern, sei es infolge durchschmelzen von Sicherungen und Zu-
leitungen, oder durch Zerstörung der Verbraucher selbst.

Durch Überbrückung von Isolatoren ist also die Möglichkeit gegeben
jedes elektrische Gerät außer Betrieb zu setzen.

Es erwächst nun die Aufgabe einen, beim Aufbau sämtlicher elektrischer Geräte in Erfüllung ausreichend wichtiger Funktionen Anwendung
findenden Isolierstoff durch Fernbeeinflussung unwirksam zu machen.

Auf der Suche nach einem hierfür geeignetem Stoff wurde gefunden,
daß die Atmosphäre die erforderlichen Voraussetzungen in ausreichendem
Maße erfüllt.

Der Isolierstoff Atmosphäre findet zwar als Solcher infolge der Na-
türlichkeit dieses Zustandes im Allgemeinen keine besondere Beachtung,
er bildet aber letztenendes die isolatorische Grundlage der gesamten
Elektrotechnik, und es steht fest, daß eine Aufhebung der isolierenden
Wirkung der Atmosphäre den Betrieb irgend eines elektrischen Gerätes,
bekannter Konstruktion und Ausführung unmöglich macht.

Der gegenwärtige Stand der Technik bietet die Möglichkeit eine
Beeinflussung des Isolierstoffes Atmosphäre im Sinne der zu lösenden Auf
gabe durchzuführen.

Es ist bekannt, daß ultrakurze- elektrische Schwingungen bestimmter
Frequenzen unter Anderem auch die Eigenschaft entwickeln die von Ihnen
durchdrungenen Atmosphäre zu ionisieren, und damit eine umgekehrte elektrische Reaktion auslösen; das heißt mit anderen Worten, den Isolierstoff Atmosphäre in einen Spannungsleiter zu verwandeln.

Bemühungen zur wirtschaftlichen Nutzbarmachung dieser Erkenntnis
ließen sich vor dem Kriege beobachten, und zwar handelte es sich hierbei

Dokument 1, Seite 1

Three reports concerning stopping engines at a distance which were written during the war. English translations are in the main text.

ELEMAG

Elektro-mechanische Apparatebaugesellschaft m. b. H.

HILDESHEIM · Bahnhofstr. 14 Fernruf Nr. 5996 Bankkonten: Stödt. Sparkasse, Hildesheim Postscheckkonto: Hannover 67082 Bankhaus Pagel, Hildesheim

Blatt 2

hierbei um das Problem der drahtlosen Übertragung elektrischer Energien.
Wenn vorwiegend aus patentrechtlichen Gründen auch keine ausführlichen
Veröffentlichungen hierüber erfolgt sind, so kann die physikalische
Grundlage dieses Problemes heute doch im wesentlichen als gelöst ange-
sehen werden.

Bei einer Auswertung dieser Erkenntnis zur Realisierung des vorgeschla-
genen Kampfmittels kann zu einem großen Teil auf diese Unterlagen zurück-
gegriffen werden. Es istdaher zweckmäßig zunächst Ermittlungen darüber
anzustellen, welche Frequenzbereiche hinsichtlich ihrer yonisierenden
Wirkung bereits näher untersucht, und welche Ergebnisse dabei erzielt
worden sind.

   Im Einzelnen sind für jeden infragekommenden Frequenzbereich möglichst
unter Zugrundelegung verschiedener Sendeenergien folgende Feststellungen
zu treffen:

1. Welcher Leitwert wurde ermittelt. a) Bei Wellenbündelung
                                       b) " Rundstrahlung

2. Welche wirksame Reichweite wurde erzielt.
                                       a) Bei Wellenbündelung
                                       b) " Rundstrahlung

3. Welche Raumstreuung wurde bei Wellenbündelung beobachtet,(auszu-
    drücken durch Angabe der Bündelquerschnitte in den Entfernungen
    X_a bis X_z von Richtstrahler.)

4. Welche Leitwertänderungen wurden bei zunehmender Streuung in den
    Abständen X_a bis X_z festgestellt.

5. Einfluß der Leitwertänderungen auf den Kontakteffekt pro Kontakt-
    flächeneinheit.

   Nach Klärung dieser 5 Punkte, sei es durch Ermittlung bereits vorlie-
gender Ergebnisse oder durch Eigenversuche, kann ein zusammenfassender
Überblick über den Umfang der Wirkung und Anwendbarkeit dieses Kampfmittels gegeben werden.

   Da eine Klärung dieser Punkte unter den gegenwärtigen Verhältnissen
mit privaten Mitteln nicht durchführbar ist, im Interesse der Landes-
verteidigung jedoch von großer Wichtigkeit sein kann, wird nachgesucht,
die erforderlichen Mitteln durch das Reich zur Verfügung zu stellen.

Dokument 1, Seite 2

PROFESSOR Dr.-Ing. WERNER OSENBERG
LEITER
DES
PLANUNGSAMTES DES REICHSFORSCHUNGSRATES

(20) NORTHEIM/HANN, DEN 7. Februar 1945
POSTSCHLIESSFACH 148

FERNRUF: KATLENBURG   242/288
NORTHEIM   782
FERNSCHREIBER: 022 84

IHRE ZEICHEN:

IHRE NACHRICHT VOM

MEINE ZEICHEN 03/5 Dr.O/Eg.

Durch Boten!

An den
Persönlichen Referenten
des Reichsführers SS
SS-Standartenführer Dr. B r a n d t
Feldquartier des Reichsführers SS

Geheim!

Betreff: Störung der Funktion elektrischer Geräte als Mittel
der Kriegsführung (Vorschlag der Elektromechanischen
Apparatebaugesellschaft m. b. H. Hildesheim,
Goschenstraße 16)

Vorgang: Mein Vortrag beim Reichsführer SS am 8.1.45

Standartenführer!

Die Prüfung des mir von Reichsführer SS gelegentlich meines Vor-
trags am 8.1.45 übergebenen Vorschlages der Elemag Hildesheim für
die Störung der Funktion elektrischer Geräte durch Jonisierung
der Luft mit Hilfe von ultrakurzen elektrischen Wellen hat zu dem
Ergebnis geführt, daß dieser nach dem augenblicklichen Stand der
Technik nicht zu verwirklichen ist. Die Ausführungen der Elemag
selbst lassen jedes tiefere Verständnis für die behandelten tech-
nischen und physikalischen Vorgänge vermissen, so daß es nicht
empfohlen werden kann, diese Stelle mit der Durchführung entspre-
chender Forschungsarbeiten zu beauftragen.

Tatsächlich wird an der drahtlosen elektrischen Energieübertra-
gung und deren Anwendung für militärische Zwecke seit Jahrzehnten
eifrigst gearbeitet, bisher jedoch ohne greifbaren Erfolg.

Da ähnliche Anregungen immer wieder vorgebracht werden, habe ich
einige namhafte Wissenschaftler um eine grundsätzliche Stellungnahme zu den angeschnittenen Fragen gebeten. Leider haben sich
infolge der schwierigen Post- und Verkehrsverhältnisse die ange-
forderten Berichte verzögert, so daß ich Ihnen als Vorbescheid zunächst eine Beurteilung des Vorschlages der Elemag durch Herrn
Prof. Dr. Meißner (Anlage 1), der auf dem Gebiet der elektromagnetischen Wellen über besondere Erfahrungen verfügt, sowie eine
Stellungnahme des Leiters meiner Erprobungsabteilung, Dr. Badstein,
(Anlage 2) vorlege.

Nach Eingang der noch ausstehenden Gutachten werde ich Ihnen einen
umfassenden Überblick über den augenblicklichen Stand der Entwicklung auf diesem Gebiet geben.

Mit verbindlichsten Empfehlungen und

Heil Hitler!

W. [signature]

10. FEB. 1945
2 Anlagen

Dokument 9

Prof.Dr.A.Meißner
AEG FORSCHUNGS-INSTITUT
Fernsprecher: 49 71 91

Ergänzung zum Gutachten vom 27.1.1945 zum Erfindungsvorschlag der
"Elemag", Elektro-mechanische Apparatebaugesellschaft m.b.n.,
Hildesheim, Goschenstr.16

Die hier gemachten Vorschläge sind insbesondere im ersten Teil nicht
für den Fachmann bestimmt, sondern nur für den Laien. Es ist übrigens
nicht zum erstenmal, daß in dieser Art eine Erfindung gemacht wurde,
durch Fernübertragung elektrische Apparate unwirksam zu machen. Die
Grundlage sollte auch damals sein, daß "die Atmosphäre in außerordent-
lichem Maße die erforderlichen Voraussetzungen besitzt, daß sie durch
Fernbeeinflussung als Isolierstoff ausgeschaltet werden kann." Im
vorigen Krieg (1916) mußten auf höheren Befehl trotz heftigen Ein-
spruchs der Fachkreise mehrere Stellen an der Aufgabe arbeiten, durch
Röntgen- oder irgendwelche anderen Strahlen ("Todesstrahlen") die
Zündung in Flugzeugen unwirksam zu machen.

Outweighed by patent-right concerns, no ample publications concerning this resulted, so the physical reasons of this problem, even today, in reality can be considered lost. With an evaluation of this knowledge, a realistic proposition of a means of warfare can be reconstructed form this data. Hence, appropriate first research concerning this has not put forth as to which frequency range results in ionizing action. This needs to be more precisely investigated.

In particular for every possible frequency range makes possible various broadcast energies so that the following statements are to be met with:
1. Which values would be ascertained.
   A. By wave packets.
   B. By sweeping radiation.
2. What effective range would be realized.
   A. By wave packets.
   B. By sweeping radiation.
3. What spaces distributions would be observed with wave packets (expressed through statements of packet cross-section in the distance Xa to Xz.
4. What change of values would be established with increasing distribution in the distance from Xa to Xz.
5. What would be the influence of the change of values in the effect of constant per unit area.

Only after clarification of these five points, be it through inquiry into previously submitted results or through individual research, can an inclusive summary concerning the parameters of the workings and applicability of this means of warfare be given.

There is a clarification of these points under the present situation with private means is not feasible. In the interests of the nation's defense, notwithstanding potential greater importance, it will be researched in order to set for the necessary means of enactment throughout the Reich.

* * * * * *

English Translation of the Osenberg Document

Professor Dr. (Engineering) Werner Osenberg

Planning Department of the Reich's Research Council

By Messenger
To the personal Advise of the SS Reichsfuehrers

SS Standartenfuehrer Dr. Brandt
Field Headquarters of the SS Reichsfuehers

Regarding: Disruption of the function of electronic devices as a means of warfare. Proposal of the Electro-Mechanical Device Conductor Company Ltd., Hidesheim, Goschenstrasse 16

Procedure: My report to Reichsfuehrer SS on January 8, 1945

Standartenfuehrer:

The investigation of the proposal of the Elemag Heildesheim Company, that of the disruption of the function of electronic devices through ionization of the atmosphere through the use of ultra-short electromagnetic wave lengths has been brought to a conclusion. I reported to the Reichsfuehrer of the SS concerning this on January 8, 1945. The results are that this can not be realized in technical terms, instantly. The realization of the Elemag itself leaves many deep areas of understanding, concerning procedures of applied technology and physics, missing, so that it can not be comprehended how these positions correspond with the accomplishment of research work.

Actually, it will take decades to turn the wireless energy transmission to military goals even with zealous work. At this point, it is without tangible success.

There, similar stimulation has frequently been brought forth. I have a notable scientist whom I requested to fundamental opinion in dissection of this question. Unfortunately, as a result of the difficulties of mail and circumstances of communications, the preliminary, an evaluation of the proposal of the Elemag company can be arranged by Professor Dr. Meissner (appendix 1) who works in the area of electromagnetic waves on an especially practical level as well as an option of the leader of my testing division, Dr. Badstein (appendix 2).

After the input of these outstanding assessors, I will give you a comprehensive overview of the current position of development in this area.

Courteous regards and Heil Hitler,
Dr Werner Osenberg

*   *   *   *   *   *   *

English Translation of the Meissner Document

Professor Dr. A. Meissner
General Electric Company, Research Institute

Commentary of assessment of January 27, 1945 to the
research proposal of "Elemag" Elektro-mechaniche
Apparetebaugesellschaft m.b.n.(Electro-mechanical Device
Construction Co. Ltd.) Hildescheim, Goschenstrasse 16

   The proposal made, especially in the first part is not
for the technical person decidedly important. On the
contrary, it is meant for the lay person. It is not,
moreover, the first time this sort of discovery has been
made, through long distance transmission of electromagnetic energy a device being made dysfunctional. The
underlying principle was also formerly that the atmosphere, in a strong measure, possessed the necessary
prerequisite that in can be influenced remotely through
the insulation medium. In the previous war, 1916, an order
came from high up, in spite of severe protests, and technical circles worked on various positions concerning this
question, which was through Roentgen or some other ray
("death rays") to make the ignition in aircraft unworkable.

*   *   *   *   *   *   *

   It should be noted that we are going to run into Dr. Meissner again
in his position with the Kaiser Wilhelm Institute in which he worked
on a project in conjunction with the I.G. Farben company,
Ludwigshafen on laser weaponry.

POSSIBLE RELATED PATENT
   The first words of a report by the American British Laboratory of
Radio Research Laboratory, January 30, 1945, stamped "Secret" read:

   "Calculations by J.M. Hollywood of ABL-15 indicated

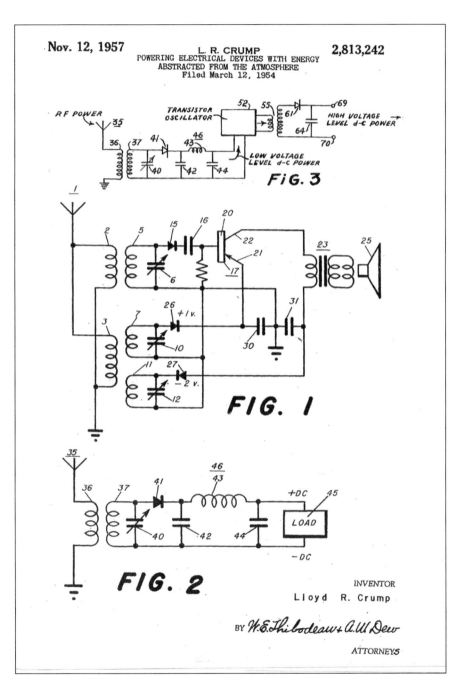

Nov. 12, 1957

L. R. CRUMP

2,813,242

POWERING ELECTRICAL DEVICES WITH ENERGY
ABSTRACTED FROM THE ATMOSPHERE
Filed March 12, 1954

FIG. 3

FIG. 1

FIG. 2

INVENTOR

Lloyd R. Crump

BY *W. E. Thibodeau + A. W. Dew*

ATTORNEYS

Dr. Gordon Freeman took one look at this patent and concluded that a similar principle may have been responsible for the workings of the magnetic wave weapon. In the patent, radio waves are received and turned into a small electric current which might charge up a battery, for instance. In the magnetic wave weapon, radio waves, generated by all ignition-based engines, would be received, amplified, and re-broadcast to be absorbed by all the metal parts of that same target engine. Absorption by the engine would cause a short circuit in the same wave frequency and wave length and ignition timing as the original signal coming from the engine. This would result in misfiring of the engine.

that the most economical means of disturbing an
aircraft's ignition system would probably employ electromagnetic radio frequency transmissions recurrent at a
rate near the frequency of the engine's ignition cycle."

Something in its name caused this writer to order a copy of a 1954
patent granted L. R. Crump titled: "Powering Electrical Devices With
Energy Abstracted Form The Atmosphere"[4]. Diagrams from that
patent are shown here. The patent does not quite live up to its promise. Instead of extracting energy from the atmosphere in a free-energy
manner, it captures energy from local radio stations, in the form of
their radio programming and turns this energy, not into sound as does
a radio receiver and speaker system, but into pulses of energy which
are gathered and smoothed into a small but useable energy flow.
Small electric devices can be powered using this device or small
batteries can be recharged using it.

I sent a copy of this patent to Dr. Gordon Freeman as I had told him
of the patent's name and its implied promise. Dr. Freeman wrote back
to me saying that the patent had value after all. In fact, he said that
this patent might have a bearing on the famous Motorstoppmittel
device. What he meant might be best illustrated using an automobile
engine.

In an automobile's engine it is common practice to keep each
ignition wire separate and separated from every other ignition wire
in that engine using air as insulating space as well as plastic spacers.
The reason for this is that sometimes, especially at high rpms, the
firing of one wire, when touching another wire, will induce a current
in that second wire which will cause its spark plug to fire out
of sequence. This is called misfiring. Misfiring can cause many
problems in an engine, including causing it to halt.

Now, suppose a special device were built with an antenna, which
could receive the electromagnetic waves generated by an engine
instead of a radio transmitter. This is not so hard since ignition
engines produce radio frequency signals all through their ignition
cycle. Special and specific shielding has to be incorporated into most
engines in order for us to hear our car radios as we drive. As soon as
our special device received the incoming ignition signals, they were
exactly duplicated and amplified. Then they are re-broadcast by
a powerful antenna right back to the original source. The source, the

COPY/   S E C R E T

HEADQUARTERS
EUROPEAN THEATER OF OPERATIONS
P/W and X Detachment
Military Intelligence Service
APO 887   US Army

SUBJECT: ETOIB/Ext No. 101   25 Jan 45

TO: Col H. G. Bunker
         Director of Technical Services
         Hq. USSTAF (REAR) APO 633 U.S.Army.

****

The following information was given by German P/W (W/T Specialist) on German Experiments with Remote Control of Automobile and Airplane Motors.

(This material was written originally by P/W in German and has since been translated into English.)

In the year 1934 successful experiments were made in Germany on the paralyzing of combustion in Automobile Engine viz. the stopping of the motors. Subject heard also last year from a Laboratory Engineer of the Weapons Office, that vehicles and motors could be stopped at a distance of 150 meters (about 166 yards).

An Engineer belonging to a Research Institute of the R.M.V. who attended these experiments, said that the same thing could be done with airplanes.

In 1938, two German Aircraft Plants were entrusted with the order to study motors for aircraft without electrical ignition.

Between Augsburg and Munich, experiments were made in driving an electric motor by wireless.

During the last experiments a small ventilator motor (in Augsburg) was set in motion by a dispatcher controlled in Munich. The power used by the dispatching station in Munich was reported to be very strong.

CERTIFIED A TRUE COPY

/s/ Taylor Drysdale.
/t/ TAYLOR DRYSDALE.
    Captain. A.C.

                    S E C R E T
                      -1-

SECRET

Extract of Information - Source: Letter #1172/EM, 11 Mar. 1944 to
Col. H.A. Kenyon from Col. A.J.P. Le Bel.

Source - SECRET

* * *

Notable Incidents.

a.) On November 19, on the outskirts of Lens at 5:30 P.M.
a British Plane was downed with no apparent struggle. The plane was
flying normally when all of a sudden, it pitched to the ground and
was crushed.

b.) English pilots, interned in Switzerland, have declared that
as they flew over the Eastern part of France their apparatus had
been deranged - also - reports have pointed to the fact that centers
for the transmission of these rays have been installed at Ardenes.

These two facts lead us to surmise that the Germans have
experimented with their secret weapon and that these rays or waves
are capable of hampering Electric parts of plane motors and to disturb
the apparatus on board.

Report Received from G-2, 12 April 1944 and Filed in Ski Site File.

A Secret report describing the downing of a British aircraft by magnetic wave.

engine, picks up our transmission thorough its metal parts and wires. Through these engine parts and wiring electrical energy is induced just as it is with the misfiring ignition wires in our earlier example. The result is the same, a misfiring engine. At best, this engine runs rough. Other small and sensitive electromagnetic devices such as the aircraft's gauges and gyros also malfunction. At worst, the aircraft's misfiring is so bad that the engine stalls or fires in complete opposition to its proper firing order so that it actually breaks apart.

Something similar to this simple description is the probable paradigm for the famous and super-secret Motorstoppmittel.

SOURCES

1. Haarmann, D.H., 1985, pages 26-27, lll Geheime Wunderwaffen Ueber den Krieg hinaus!, Hugn Gesellschaft fuer Politisch – Philosophische Studien E.V.

2. Pennick, Nigel, 1981, page 169, Hitler's Secret Sciences, Neville Spearman Limited.

3. American British Laaboratory of Radio Research Laboratory, Januray 30, 1945, Unexplained Interference with Allied Aircraft Engines over Enemy Territory", Great Malvern, Wores

4. United States Patent, Patent Number 2,813,242, 11/12/57, Granted to Lloyd R. Crump, titled: "Powering Electrical Devices With Energy Abstracted From The Atmosphere".

26 | "Death Rays"
X-Ray—Gamma Ray Weapon

Sometimes the magnetic wave/Motorstoppmittel is called a "death ray" but it was passive in nature and meant to kill engines, not people. The first type of real death ray we will encounter is of the x-ray or gamma ray type. We know this was worked upon during the Third Reich because we have the actual scientific study detailing the feasibility of such a weapon.

Perhaps most amazing is that the information contained in this chapter comes from the German government itself. This information comes in the form of a report from the Forschungezentrum at Karlsruhe. They graciously provided a copy of a report, upon a simple written request, which is titled: "Ueber die Moeglichkeit biologischer Wirkungen kurswelliger Roentgen-bsw. Gammastrahlen von Roentgenroehren besonderer Bauart auf groessere Entfernungen". This translates into English as something like: "Concerning the possibility of biologic effects of short wave x-rays, respectively, gamma rays from x-ray tubes of special construction at great distance".

This report dates from the Second World War, 1944, is of poor quality, and illegible in many sections. Sometimes reports copied on and off microfilm have the same fuzzy quality of this text, although the real reason for its fuzziness is unknown. Accompanying the document came a letter from the research center explaining that original material itself was of poor quality and was not possible to improve upon the copy as generated. Portions of that document are reproduced here.

This report could properly be called a design study

Prof.Dr.E.schiebold.

Leipzig S 36, den 19. Juli 1944.
Dankwartstr. 1.
Tel. 39 12 43.

G-284
Copy 1

An die
Forschungsführung
des Reichsministers der Luftfahrt
und Oberbefehlshaber der Luftwaffe
Herrn Prof.Dr. Georgii
B e r l i n S 68.
Jerusalemer Str. 65.

Betr. Forschungsstelle Groß Ostheim.

Sehr geehrter Herr Professor,

Anbei gestatte ich mir, Ihnen Abschrift eines Exposés zu überreichen,
welches ich am 12.d.M. Herrn Prof.Dr. Kulenkampff-Jena zur Begutach-
tung zugesandt habe.

Das Exposé stellt eine Ausarbeitung dar, welche ich auf Grund meiner
Unterlagen vorgenommen habe, über die ich in der Kuratoriumssitzung
selbst nur ganz summarisch berichten konnte.

Heil Hitler!

E. Schiebold

1 Exposé.

Cover page of a German design study concerning the utilization of an x-ray anti-aircraft weapon with translation following.

Prof. Dr. E. Schiebold

Leipzig, S 36, 7/19/44
Dankwartstr. 1
Tel. 39 12 43.

On the conducting of research of the
Reich Ministry of Aeronautics and
Commander in Chief of The Air Force
Herrn Professor Doctor Georgii
Berlin SW 68
Jerusalemer Str. 65.

In Reference to the Research Installation Gross Ostheim

Very Honored Herr Professor,

Enclosed permit me to present to you the transcript of an expose
which I have sent to Professor Dr. Kulenkampff at Jena for an
expert opinion.

This expose describes the carrying out of a plan which for reason
of support I have undertaken and about which I in the board of
trustees position am only able to report summarily.

                                    Heil Hitler,

Über die Möglichkeit biologischer Wirkungen kurzwelliger Röntgen-
bzw. Gammastrahlen von Röntgenröhren besonderer Bauart auf größere
Entfernungen.
Unterlagen zum Vortrag auf der Sitzung des Kuratoriums der Forschungs
stelle der Luftwaffe Großostheim am 6. Mai 1944.

I. Einleitung.

Die nachstehenden Ausführungen beziehen sich auf die Möglichkeit der
biologischen Strahlenwirkung in größeren Entfernungen als einander
von mir ins Auge gefaßten Anwendungsgebiete der Röntgen- und Elek-
tronenstrahlen als Mittel der Feindbekämpfung. Ich bin mir dabei be-
wußt, daß diese Darstellung meiner Gedankengänge in der vorliegende.
Form nur rein überschlägig ist, wobei ich mir eine tiefergehende
und ausführlichere Begründung vorbehalte. Mangels einer exakten Theorie habe ich mich vorläufig mit Abschätzungen begnügt, um Anhalts-
punkte zu gewinnen, welche Energiemengen primärseitig für eine aus-
reichende Wirkung am Beobachtungsort benötigt werden, wobei ich kei-
nen Anspruch darauf erhebe, daß die Zahlen auf eine oder zwei Zehner-
potenzen genau richtig sind.

Die quantenmechanische Theorie des Durchgangs sehr energiereicher
Elektronen und Gammastrahlenquanten durch Materie ist bekanntlich
von Bethe, Heitler, Sauter, v. Weizsäcker sowie von Sommerfeld u. sei-
nen Schülern entwickelt worden und kann hier als bekannt voraus-ge-
setzt werden. Die experimentelle Prüfung der Theorie ist bis-
bisher nur soweit erfolgt, wie man mit den härtesten künstlichen
Röntgenstrahlen, ferner bei radioaktiven Strahlen und den bei
künstliche Kernumwandlungen entstehenden Gammastrahlen prüfen
kann. Außerdem können Beobachtungen der Höhenstrahlung heran-ge-
zogen werden, welche das Verhalten energiereicher Teilchen be-
treffen. Im allgemeinen sei aber bemerkt, daß die In-
tensität der radioaktiven Strahlungen und der Un-einheit-
heit der Höhenstrahlung quantitative Aussagen über die Theorie
kaum zu erwarten sind und im ersten Fall eine Über-einstim-
mung zwischen Beobachtung und Rechnung befriedigend ist.
Genauere experimentelle Daten werden sich ...
nügend energiereiche Elektronen erhalten ...
Hochspannungsbeschleunigung oder ... in ...
elektromagnetischen Hilfsfeld (Wambacher ...
den und ihr Verhalten, insbesondere die ...

Concerning the Possibility of Biologic Effects of Short Wave X-Rays, respectively, Gammarays from X-Ray Tubes of Special Construction at Great Range.

1. Introduction

This exposition concerns the possibility of the biologic beam effects at great range as one means I have seized upon as a sphere of application of the x-ray and a beam of electrons as a means of fighting the enemy. I know that this description of my train of thought in the present form is quite rough whereby I reserve a deeper going basis and completeness of detail.

For want of an exact theory I have used a preliminary evaluation in order to obtain which energy admixtures primarily sided for a far reaching effectiveness of an observation spot will be necessary---claims arising that a number of one or two--are exactly correct.

(text not legible)

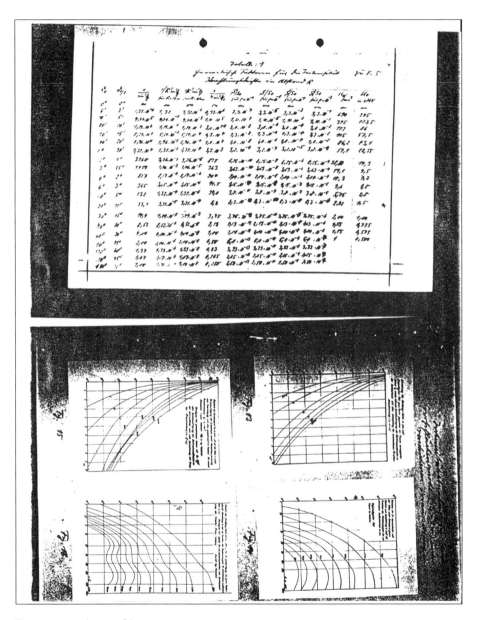

These are two sample pages of the report.

in America. It was written by a Professor Dr. E. Schiebold to the research effort of the Reich Ministers of the Air Transport and the Supreme Commander of the Air Force, Professor Dr. Georgii on July, 19, 1944.

A stamp on the face of the document, "Caution Restricted Data", which dates from the post-war occupational period, advises the reader that this document involves restricted data as defined by the Atomic Energy Agency as of 1946 and that disclosure of its contents to an unauthorized person is prohibited. Another stamp on the cover dated 1/1/50 or 4/1/50 declassifies the document.

Inspire of the fact that much of the text of the report is illegible, the summary can be read. From what can be learned Dr. Schiebold used mathematical models to evaluate three types of x-ray weapons. If physical models were constructed in order to obtain mathematical values is unknown to this writer. The weapons were designed for anti-aircraft purposes. Much of the report is technical.

These ray guns were to be mounted on an adjustable stand and aimed at enemy aircraft. The objective was not to shoot down the aircraft but to harm the pilot of the aircraft. An effective dose necessary to cause biologic harm was calculated. This dose varied in time depending upon the intensity of the x-ray beam itself. At weaker values the time on target had to be longer to be effective. Intensity of the beam depended upon the energy input, beam thickness and the scattering effect as the beam goes through the atmosphere as well as the distance from the target. Higher values of effectiveness, that is biologic harm, could be achieved with higher voltages and greater beam thicknesses. Beam thickness seems to be dependent upon the size of the anode in the gun's design. In practice one can see that various atmospheric conditions and high-speed aircraft only complicate the picture.

Three different ray-gun designs were evaluated. They were ascribed mathematical values for targets at various altitudes and time on target and given in two scenarios, under most favorable and least favorable circumstances. The first type was unacceptable for anti-aircraft purposes. The second type was only marginal under some of the most favorable circumstances. The third type was more acceptable. It featured a large surface anode. A dose of 7 rads per second at a distance of 5 kilometers with a time on target of 30 seconds, which was achievable with this weapon, was considered adequate to inflict irreversible biologic harm to the crew of the aircraft. This is a range of about three miles or a little over 15,000 feet. Of course, shorter time on target periods were possible for nearer targets.

One finding of the report involves the scattering effect. It was found that the metal skin of the aircraft scattered the radiation from this weapon and produced stronger biologic harm to the inhabitants of that aircraft than a dose straight from the beam weapon itself. In other words, the skin of the aircraft acted like a microwave oven, more efficiently cooking the crew.

Also according to the report the most sensitive parts of the human body, thus those most easily harmed, were the gonads which do not repair themselves once damaged in this manner. This means that even should the crew escape with their lives once hit with this weapon, they face the possibility of sterility, cancer or other long-term damage. Employment of this weapon certainly would have had negative effects on the morale of the enemy once these facts were understood.

The weapon was never fielded. The reason was probably the issue of "time on target". It does not seem likely that a weapon could be trained upon an enemy aircraft for the required time duration in a combat situation. One still wonders why it was not considered for ground combat applications. It might have had value defending fixed targets such as mountain passes or bridges.

Nevertheless, the work of Dr. Scheibold constitutes legitimate research into the concept of a death ray. Somehow, Dr. Schiebold found a way to weaponize x-rays and gamma rays. Somehow, they were focussed on a distant target. The possibility of using X-rays has been recently raised again in regards to the proposed "Star Wars" defense shield. This is another matter involving destruction of hardware, not people, but the German success in focussing X-rays should be kept in mind.

SOURCES

1. Schiebold, E. Professor Dr., 1944, Ueber die Moeglichkeit biologischer Wirkungen kurzwelliger Roentgen-bsw. Gammastrahlen von Roentgenroehren besonderer Bauart auf groessere Entfernungen. Forschungszenturm karlsruhe Technik und Umwelt, Karlsruhe, Germany

27 | "Death Rays"
Laser Weapon

It is almost inconceivable that almost sixty years ago anyone could have developed something with which we are struggling to develop at this very moment. Yet, there are many rumors and some evidence that the Germans were actively working on a laser weapon in the mid-1940s. We will dispense with some of the more vague, sensational evidence and focus on references to which, firstly, a name and a reputation are attached and, secondly, to evidence brought forth by the United States government.

Two bits of information come to us from sources which should have been informed. These are from German U-boat captains. U-boat captains were highly trained, highly selected individuals for whom the German military as well as the culture itself had the utmost respect. They would have received a great deal more information concerning the weaponry than the average citizen or fighting man.

Herbert Werner discusses death rays in his book *Iron Coffins*. This book was the principal source for the film "Das Boot". Captain Werner needed no sensationalism, his truth was sensational enough. He makes the comments in response to comments by a downed American pilot and explains Zhis thinking:

> "I was thinking about our much-discussed new weapons, including death rays and atom bombs, which were now in the development stage".[1]

"Death rays" are called "much-discussed" and

WAR DEPARTMENT
MILITARY INTELLIGENCE SERVICE
WASHINGTON

16 November 1944.

SUBJECT: Evaluation of Reports on Rays or Charges to Neutralize
Aircraft Motors.

TO: Major F. J. Smith, Post Office Box 2610, Washington, D. C.

1. The Military Intelligence Service is in receipt of various
reports dealing with rays for stopping or neutralizing aircraft motors
such as:

a.   An ultra-violet ray for stalling airplane motors is
being worked upon hard, but as yet without practical success.

b.   Experiments were being made on another electrical
apparatus whereby vehicles coming within its field could be stopped.

c.   The famous "Death Ray" is spoken of again and it is said
that several airplanes have been made to fall in the neighborhood of
this installation.

d.   The use of radio ray emits wave that slows down the
motors of Allied planes flying over region.

e.   In February it was reported that the Germans were
working on some mechanism to stop aircraft motors.

f.   A source who states that he has done much work for the
P.T.T. at Tempelhof in Berlin and for the Reichspostforschungsanstalt
claims that 80% of their laboratory work is on aviation. A high official
and an engineer there have informed him that they have completed a new
A/A weapon which will be turned out in mass production in two or three
months.

g.   Experiments with "Death Rays" were conducted by AEG -
Siemenstadt Berlin at Tempelhof in 1939. Guinea pigs were killed at
a distance of 200 meters.

h.   An individual employed "on electrical matters", not named,
or otherwise described, told the prisoner that the Germans had for
years been experimenting with these death rays.

A short summary-report dealing with German "death rays". Note item "g" which clearly deals with the killing of test animals. This is in contrast to the other entries which deal with stopping of ignition engines. Two pages.

C O P Y

SECRET

     i.   It is believed that it is a sort of magnetic beam, capable of stopping the motors of planes at a great distance.

     j.   Experiments of which he knew, (1) destroying the functions of aircraft motors with induced magnetic fields, (2) exploding aircraft in the air by direct ultra-violet ray.

     k.   This weapon which emits waves or rays based on piezo-electricity is a development of the death ray. It is known that tests were made in 1938 and that a distance of eight hundred meters an automobile motor was successfully stopped.

     l.   The Germans will use within next three weeks new generator which is capable of stopping motors.

     2.   An hypothesis has been received stating that by use of rays or charges the atmosphere surrounding the airplane engine could be ionized, causing the ignition system to spark at joints and also where the insulation has been cracked or broken, thereby causing a short circuit of the spark plug.

     3.   Any evaluation or opinion you may be able to render on the existence or practicability of any rays or charges, to include probable type of emission, range, size of installation required, would be highly appreciated.

     For the Chief, Military Intelligence Service:

                  MERILLAT MOSES,
                  Lt. Colonel, F.A.,
             Chief, Scientific Branch, MIS.

EIDM   1st Ind.

War Department, P. O. Box 2610, Washington, D. C., 30 November 1944.

To: Chief, Military Intelligence Service, Washington, D. C.
     (Attention: Lt. Col. Merillat Moses, Chief, Scientific Branch, MIS)

     Attached herewith is memorandum requested in basic communication.

                  F. J. SMITH,
                  Major, C.E.

Inclosure:
  Memo., 29/Nov/44.

C O P Y

SECRET

mentioned as concrete reality in the same breath as the German atomic bomb project.

Heinz Schaeffer, Captain of U-977, surrendered his U-boat at Mar del Plata Argentina nearly four months after the war in Europe ended. In making this trip from the North Atlantic to the South Atlantic, he did so almost entirely underwater using the newly installed Schnorkel device. In that era, this was the longest underwater voyage ever made.

In his book, Captain Schaeffer describes a chance meeting and conversation on a train in the twilight days of Nazi Germany:

> "Next to me sat an S.S. officer who, in spite of my flatly contradicting him, simply would not stop talking about decisive new secret weapons. I was fed up with secret weapons by now for I knew perfectly well from my own experience that if all the blueprints were there so were the air-raids on our factories. "Well, of course, you aren't really in a position to judge," he said, but he was, naturally, because he was working at some S.S. H.Q. or other and was out watching the tests every day. If I would only come and look him up I would see something that would make me sit up.

> When I got to Berlin I really did look him up, and after I had waited at the H.Q. entrance for some time my new acquaintance appeared and started showing me round. Everybody there was certain we were going to win, with a conviction I'd never seen the like of even after the fall of France. Among the fantastic contrivances of which I was shown photographs was one called a death ray which my friend wanted me to come back and see in action the next day.

> But I wasn't wasting any more time. I wanted to see my mother, for it was obvious the Russians were advancing on Berlin and that the last battle was going to be fought there."[2]

Captain Schaeffer saw photographs but missed the actual demonstration. From his account, we know that the project in question was run by the SS and that it was perhaps based in Berlin.

Mention of a death ray of the type under discussion also appears in an unlikely source. Michael Bar-Zohar, writing in the "Nazi Hunter" genre, raises death rays:

> "There was also a vague report on the mysterious

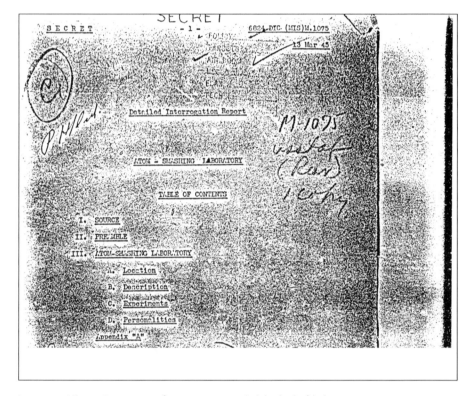

M-1075

Detailed Interrogation Report

ATOM - SMASHING LABORATORY

TABLE OF CONTENTS

Laser weapon! This is a Secret prisoner of war interrogation in which the details of the laser weapon experiment were explained including a diagram of the laser testing facility. This was taken from microfilm.

DETAILED INTERROGATION REPORT

I. SOURCE

Name	:	SCHNETTLER, Karl
Rank	:	Unteroffizier
Unit	:	PANZER 33
Captured	:	1 Dec 44, DIFFERTEN -
Interrogation	:	6824 DIC (MIS), 2 Mar 45

II. PREAMBLE

An 18 year old technician from LUDWIGSHAFEN. At first, he confirmed his previous story, as given in Report 2/32 (see NOTE, below). He was then questioned as to his technical knowledge of electronics, and it was found that he could not answer even elementary questions on the subject. He then stated that his original story was false.

PW now states that he was never, for any length of time, associated with a German University, or TECHNISCHE HOCHSCHULE, and that he cannot give information concerning the University of HEIDELBERG.

Although it is believed that PW is telling the truth, it is felt that his information should not be given a high reliability rating.

The information contained in this Report has been obtained at this Hq with the assistance of the Technical Liaison Division Office of the Chief Signals Officer, ETO.

Reliablity : C-5

    (NOTE: This Report should be read in conjunction with Mobile Field Interrogation Unit No 2 PW Intelligence Bulletin No 2/32, dated 30 Jan 45. See para 12, entitled "Atom-Smashing Experiments").

III. ATOM-SMASHING LABORATORY

A. Location

    Ref Map: GERMANY 1: 25,000 GSGS 4414
              Sheet 6416, FRANKENTHAL, Revised Oct 44

    Photo Ref: ACIU Interpretation Report K 3228, 2 Oct 44

5021 0050   PW stated that the experiments described in Report 2/32 (see NOTE, above) were carried out in an underground structure, located at MR, in the I.G.FARBEN Plant at LUDWIGSHAFEN.

In Sep 44, PW heard that the Experimental Station was to be moved to an unspecified location in either HEIDELBERG, or FREIBURG/Breisgau.

B. Description (See Appendix "A")

The laboratory consisted of a concrete underground shelter, approx 50 meters long, 25 meters wide, and 8 to 10 meters high. Concrete walls were between 75 cms and 1 meter thick. The shelter was entered at ground level, but was not visible from their.

The floor, and a strip 4 or 5 meters wide, along the inside walls approx 2 meters above floor level, were covered with a 3 to 5-cm thick plastic layer known as IGELIT.

One end of the laboratory contained a recess housing 5 or 6 Electronic Tubes, referred to as FANGPOLE and SPRUEHPOLE. These rested on special trolleys, and could be moved foward into the focusing area. The sides and rear of the tubes were shielded by a semi-circular quartz plate.

At the other end of the Laboratory was the Observation and Control Station, shielded in front and at the sides by a semi-cicular, transparent quartz plate. This station contained electrical controls.

Opposite this station was a target stand, consisting of a 1.25 to 1.5-meter high column, surrounded by a 5-cm thick, approx 1.25-meter long and 1.25-meter wide quartz plate. A vacuum system (details unspecified) was incorporated in the target stand. All parts of the stand had been sprayed with the plastic IGELIT.

C. Experiments

PW could add little to the information in Report 2/32.

Experiment with Rats

In the experiment of Apr 44 (See Report 2/32), PW stated that, when the rats were bombarded by the rays, a phosphorescent glow was observed over their bodies, lasting about a fifth of a second. PW believed that the rats had been reduced to a gaseous Sodium (?), which had been drawn into the vacuum system of the test stand.

D. Personalities

The following men took part in the laboratory experiments:

    1. KAISER WILHELM Institute

        KALB, Diplom Ingenieur
        MEISSNER, Diplom Ingenieur
        FALKE, Diplom Ingenieur
        H.ERINGER, Studienrat

    2. I.G.FARBEN/Ludwigshafen

        WENDT, Diplom Ingenieur
        RAITHEL, Diplom Ingenieur
        EDLEFSEN, Ingenieur

                  WHG (Ed: ARP)

        FOR THOMAS C. VAN CLEVE, LT COL
        Commanding 6824 DIC (MIS)

        IVO V GIANNINI
        Major, INF,
        Army Section

13 Mar 45

DISTRIBUTION

JIC., .FHQ........................4
SHAEF...........................8
ETOUC...........................8
6 Army Group.....................6
12 ArmyGroup.....................8
21 ArmyGroup.....................1
7 Army.........................8
MU 500..........................2
MI 14 (j)........................3
MI 19...........................3
MIRS...........................2
G-2 (CI), .FHQ..................2
1st French Army.................1
CIS Washington D.C..............2
PW &X Det, U.S..................1
U.S.Group C.C...................3
HQ FID.........................3
O.S.S.........................3
P.J.D.........................3
Sigs Off Washington D.C.........6
T.A.Div Sigs Off Com Z..........8
File..........................7

APPENDIX "A"

<u>ATOM - SMASHING LABORATORY</u>

I.C.FARBEN/Ludwigshafen

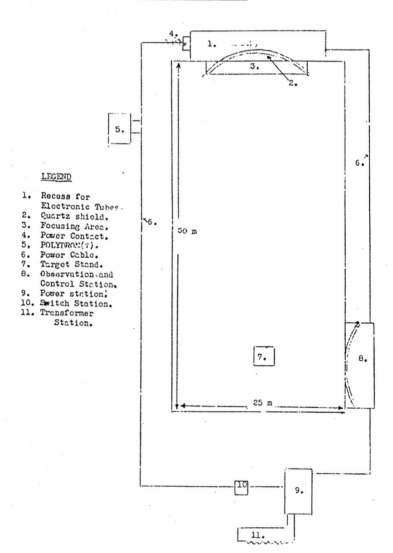

LEGEND

1. Recess for
   Electronic Tubes.
2. Quartz shield.
3. Focusing Area.
4. Power Contact.
5. POLYTRON(?).
6. Power Cable.
7. Target Stand.
8. Observation and
   Control Station.
9. Power station.
10. Switch Station.
11. Transformer
    Station.

50 m

25 m

Zimmermann—the man believed to have invented the
"death ray" and even to have used it effectively against
the Russian in the Carpathians on 30 August 1944."[3]

Bar-Zohar's focus is on the moral ambiguity of German scientists
working in the United States. He asks: "How could they reconcile
themselves to their ambiguous moral position?". The point for us is
that Bar-Zohar is certainly not interested in aggrandizing the technical
achievements of these scientists.

Now that we have picked up the scent of a possible German death
ray, we might fairly ask what our government found out when they
sent teams of technical investigators into Germany to acquire such
exotic technology, even before the final surrender. What they found is
obviously still a secret but there are hints. These "hints" are probably
nothing more than the failure of government censors to do their job
effectively. They simply cannot catch everything, every reference,
every off-handed mention of something which appear in the voluminous government record concerning wartime Germany.

German researcher Friedrich Georg made a huge discovery in
uncovering microfilm evidence of the laser testing facility at I.G.
Farben facility in Ludwigshafen. The reference is reproduced here[4].
The report uses an 18-year-old prisoner of war as an informant for the
text of the report. As was the usual practice in using informants, the
report tears down his credibility but then ends up using him as a
source. The reason for this is that the Allies had no idea if this was the
truth or not and wanted to cover their butts either way.

It is also interesting to note that the Allies were given a list of
scientists who participated in the laser experimentation at I.G. Farben,
Ludwigshafen: engineers Meissner, Ike, and their advisor, Eringer.
None of their testimony appears in this report.

Besides the detail of the layout, it is most impressive to note that
when the test targets of the weapon, rats, were hit with the ray,
their bodies glowed for a fraction of a second before they
completely disintegrated.

Also please note that on page three of the government document
shown and under the heading Kaiser Wilhelm Institute, we find the
name "Meissner, Deplom Ingenieur". This is the same Meissner we
encountered in the Magnetic Wave discussion.

SOURCES

1. Werner, Herbert A., Captain, 1978, page 228, *Iron Coffins*, Bantam Books, Inc., N.Y., NY.

2. Schaeffer, Heinz, Captain, 1952, page 104, *U-boat 977*, Ballantine Books, Inc., N.Y., NY.

3. Bar-Zohar, Michael, 1967, page 152, *The Hunt For German Scientists*, Avon Books, N.Y., NY.

4. Detailed Interrogation Report, 3/13/45, "Atom-Smashing Laboratory" report 6824-DTC (MIS)M.1075, taken from U.S. government microfilm

28 | Distillation of Crude Oil Using Sound Waves

We have all heard that the Germans made oil from coal using the Fischer-Topische method as well as a method of hydrogenation. Something which is totally unknown is that they may have invented a revolutionary technology to refine the oil, separating it into gasoline, oil, wax, diesel oil, etc., using sound waves of a special kind.

The informant used by the British to get this information was a prisoner of war named Josef Ernst. The British say of Ernst:

> "In the course of interrogation it became clear, that Ernst was not at all reliable, and through there may in some cases be a factual basis for some of his claims, they are as a whole inaccurate and of doubtful value".[1]

In spite of their badmouthing of Ernst, the British used him as a primary source on no less than seven different aspects of captured German technology. Like the Americans, the British found it necessary to cover their butts.

There is an error in the report, however. It has to do with the name of the inventor for the distillation process, which is given in the British report as "Kelly". Even from the brief description given, it is evident that the correct name of this inventor is "Keely", as in John Worrall Keely.

Keely was born in Philadelphia in 1837. Therefore, he did most of his work in the latter part of the nineteenth century. Keely put forth a theory of the reso-

(g) Production of petrol from oil

Ernst claimed to have invented a process for the separation of petrol from oil by the use of vibrations of audible frequency. This method was developed from the Kelly process in use in the U.S.A. The crude oil is passed through glass tubes suspended above a plate of "Pertinax", which is caused to vibrate at frequencies on the Pythagoras tone-scale. The frequency is altered according to the product required. Cold air is passed over the glass tubes in the reverse direction to the liquid flow, the air being cooled to nearly liquid air temperatures by means of an Auto-Union cold air plant. By this means the crude oil was separated into petrol, paraffin, and wax fractions, which are collected in a tank, and remain in separate liquid layers. This process was operated at the wells near Hamburg owned by the S.S. and many tons of petrol were produced. These factories were probably destroyed, but the apparatus is possibly in the south of Germany. Ernst stated that the method "destroys" the mutual solubility of petrol and paraffin, but it seems possible that this may be a process depending on the continuous fractional freezing of the crude oil, the function of the vibration being to prevent supercooling and possibly to keep the tubes from becoming choked. A process for the freezing out of wax fractions from crude oil is in fact well known.

Refining Oil Using Sound Waves. This is from British Intelligence Objectives Sub-Committee report number 142. This is yet another SS lost technology.

nance of light and sound. His inventions, which he kept secret, synthesized vibrations into a machine capable of practical value. Some of his machines used rows of vibratory bars, all resonating at a frequency specific to the target material of the machine. Frequencies for hydrogen and oxygen where the targets of a water-based machine, for instance, which caused the cavitation of water using this resonance.

The short text of the British Intelligence Objectives Sub-Committee report is reproduced here. It is clear from the text that it is Keely's theory, which is being used to distill oil.

From the text we are given to understand that SS alchemists are keeping this process to themselves, for themselves, on oil reserves that they themselves exclusively hold. The real question is what became of this technology? Certainly, if it is true, it would be of enormous benefit to the modern world. Is this one of those secret technologies held and kept by the post-war SS to be used as barter with the victorious Allied Powers? Or is this technology already in the hands of one or more of the Allies but being kept secret? Or was this technology given to an employee or consultant of a petroleum giant as a favor for work done during the war? Whatever happened, whatever this report is, fact, fiction or fable, no adequate explanation for it has been offered by the British or anyone else.

Dr. Ronald Richter will say a few words in this respect in an upcoming section.

SOURCES

1. British Intelligence Objectives Sub-Committee report number 142,
   "Information Obtained From Targets Of Opportunity In The Sonthofen Area,
   no date given, pages 8 and 9, 32 Bryanston Square, London

29 | Synthetic Production of Gasoline

Most everybody has heard that the Germans produced large volumes of gasoline and other petroleum products by chemically cracking coal during the war. Besides gasoline, diesel fuel, lubricating oils and greases were manufactured using this process. Huge underground refineries were rumored to be under construction as the war ended which would have allowed the Germans to fuel their war machine indefinitely. Following the war, this process of coal to gasoline conversion never seemed to materialize in spite of cyclic gasoline shortages which, naturally, threw doubt on the technical and economic feasibility of turning America's vast coal reserves into something other than polluting smoke-stack industry.

From time to time, this subject would re-emerge such as an article in The Dallas Morning News, dated Tuesday, September 4, 1990. This article was titled: "Scientists Seek To Study Nazi Paper" and contained all the oft reported statements such as a post-war US plant in Louisiana, Mo. which used this German technology to produce gasoline at 1.6 cents per gallon. Mentioned in the story was a storehouse of German technical documents at Texas A&M University and a Professor Arnold Krammer.

The promise of a treasure of captured German documents was enough for me to attempt contact. Contact was established with Professor Krammer, Professor of Modern German History, as well as Dr. David Chappman, Curator of the Cushing Library, which housed the material. Both gentlemen were very gracious with their time. Professor Krammer sent me a

TABLE 1

Germany's Largest Synthetic Fuel-producing Installations

Name	Location	Products of Interest to Technical Oil Mission
Reichs-Marineamt (Admiralty)	Kiel	Diesel fuel
Betriebstoff Laboratorium	Wilhelmshaven	Fuel standards
Rhenanin-Ossag (Mineralowerke A.G.)	Hamburg	Petroleum products
Deutsche Vacuum Oel A.G.	Hamburg	Petroleum products
I. G. Farbenindustrie A.G.	Leuna	Synthetic fuel and by-products
I. G. Farbenindustrie A.B.	Ludwigshafen-Oppau	Synthetic fuel and by-products
Braunkohle Benzin A.G.:		
Brabag I	Bohlen-Rotha	Synthetic liquid fuels
Brabag II	Magdeburg	Synthetic liquid fuels
Brabag IV	Troglitz-Zeitz	Synthetic liquid fuels
Gelsenberg Benzin A.G.	Gelsenkirchen	Hydrogenation
Hydrierwerke Scholven A.G.	Scholven-Buer	Hydrogenation
Union Rheinische Braunkohlen Kraftstoff A.G.	Wesseling	Hydrogenation
Ruhrol A.G. (Matthias Stinnes)	Bottrop-Welheim	Hydrogenation
Wintershall A.G.	Lützkendorf Mucheln	Gasification
Ruhrchemie und Ruhrbenzin A.G.	Sterkrade-Holden	Gas synthesis or Fischer-Tropsch process
Friedrich Krupp	Wanne Eickel	Synthetic liquid fuels
Klochner Werke A.G., Gewerkschaft "Victor"	Castro-Rauxel	Gas synthesis
Hoesch Benzin A.G.	Dortmund	Gas synthesis
Gewerkschaft Stein:		
Kohlenbergwerk	Homberg	Gas synthesis
Rheinpreussen	Homberg	Gas synthesis
Chemische Werke, Essener Stein-Kohle A.G.	Kamen-Dortmund	Gas synthesis
Braunkohle-Benzin A.G.:		
Brabag III	Ruhland-Schwarzheide	Synthetic liquid fuels
Schaffgotsche Benzin A.G.	Odertal (Deschowitz-Beuthen)	Synthetic liquid fuels
Kaiser Wilhelm Institute für Kohlenforschung	Mulheim-Ruhr	Research on gas-synthesis process
Studien und Verwertungs G.m.b.H.	Mulheim-Ruhr	Synthetic liquid fuels

Source.—W. C. Schroeder, "Investigation by the U.S. Government Technical Oil Mission" (paper presented to the Twenty-fifth Annual Meeting of the American Petroleum Institute, Chicago, November 14, 1945), pp. 3–4.

Bureau of Mines
1951 Design for Coal Hydrogenation Plants

	Single Plant (Wyoming)	Single Plant (Kentucky)	Multi-Plant (8) Industry
Coal (tons/calendar day)	14,800	14,720	117,920
Products (bbl/cd)			
Gasoline	18,600	16,300	142,000
Liquefied Petroleum gas	7,100	8,290	63,800
Totals	25,700	24,590	205,800
Chemicals			
Benzene (gals/yr)	11,750,000	12,400,000	97,900,000
Toluene (gals/yr)	39,350,000	41,450,000	327,400,000
Phenol (lbs/yr)	43,800,000	84,300,000	593,400,000
Cresol (lbs/yr)	56,750,000	177,300,000	237,000,000
Ammonia (tons/yr)	131,000	129,000	—
Sulfur (tons/yr)	17,000	80,000	—
Construction materials			
Steel (tons)	217,130	210,865	1,699,450
Investment capital (millions of $)	411	400	3,222
Cost/gallon of product with 5.7 to 6.2 per cent return on equity capital (cents)	10.9	10.75	10.8
Cost/gallon of gasoline equivalent	9.12	7.96	8.19

Source: U.S. Department of Interior, Bureau of Mines. "Cost Estimate for Coal Hydrogenation," DOI, NPC, 1951, "Synthetic Fuels File," October 25, 1951.

Top: A partial list of German installations producing synthetic petroleum products from coal.

Bottom: A U.S. Bureau of Mines chart showing the actual cost of gasoline produce in their test facilities using the German hydrogenation method in 1950's money.

letter and some publications explaining the German coal to oil conversion processes and events in the USA after the war.

Before the war there had been processes by which coal was cracked and converted to oil (and so gasoline and so forth). The Germans came up with two new methods for doing so which were an advance on previous methods.

The first method was developed by Friedrich Bergius and for which he won the Nobel Prize. It is sometimes called the "Bergius process" or the "hydrogenation process". It involves forcing a mixture of powdered coal, recycled oil, and a catalyst into a high-pressure vessel filled with hydrogen. This resulted in the liquefaction of the coal. The liquified coal was then separated into gasoline, middle oil and heavy oil. The final products were diesel fuel and gasoline. Four to five tons of coal was necessary to make a ton of gasoline[1].

The second method is often called the "Fischer-Tropsch process", after its inventors, Franz Fischer and Hans Tropsch. In this process, powdered coal was broken up by super heated steam to produce a mixture of hydrogen and carbon monoxide gases. This gas mixture was then purified to remove all sulfur compounds. It was then passed over a metal catalyst to produce low-octane gasoline and high-grade diesel oil as well as wax, the latter being further processed into lubricating oils. This process could be done at lower pressure and temperature than the Bergius process. And like the Bergius or hydrogenation process, it yielded one ton of petroleum product for about four or five tons of coal[2].

In fact, the Germans had 14 separate projects involving synthetic petroleum products made from coal with about 112 separate facilities of various sizes[3]. The plan was to relocate these facilities underground in bombproof shelters. At the cessation of hostilities, 2,708,000 square feet of underground facilities were planned for synthetic petroleum production. Only 689,000 square feet had been completed, however, leaving 2,019,000 under construction[3]. By German standards, underground synthetic petroleum production was not a large project. The SS planned a total of 11,298,000 square feet of underground facilities just for their own private use[4].

Unlike some other German secrets, it seems that the Allies, particularly the British and Americans, got all the information on synthetic petroleum product that they desired. As much as 175 tons of German documents regarding synthetic petroleum production fell into the hands of the Allies[5]. This information was translated, evaluated, and if appropriate, given to the major oil companies without cost[6]. Imagine, two whole new breakthrough energy technologies were simply handed to some of the most wealthy companies which have ever existed without the cost of research and development or even the cost for the patents.

The question arises, what did we do with this technology after the war? The answer is that in 1949 the Bureau of Mines built a demonstration coal conversion plant in Louisiana, Missouri. This facility used the Bergius or hydrogenation process as developed by I.G. Farben in Germany. For three years this plant remained in operation. They first tested various types of coal from all over the United States. After satisfying themselves about the method, they seemed to have focussed on improving the procedure itself. Defrayed by the sale of byproducts, the cost to produce a gallon of gasoline was 10.6 cents per gallon. This meant, at the time, a cost at the pump of about 15. or 16. cents per gallon. Unfortunately, this figure was about 25% higher than the cost of natural petroleum gasoline at the time.

This is the basic problem. At any given time it is cheaper to import crude oil or imported refined gasoline than it is to produce synthetic gasoline at home from coal. Given the flux in the crude oil price, nobody, no oil company, no government, wants to invest the money which large-scale conversion from coal to gasoline requires. The Louisiana, Missouri plant was shut down in 1953 by the Eisenhower Administration as a result of opposition to it from the oil industry itself[7].

The subject comes up, and probably will continue to come up, with each cyclic spike in gasoline prices. Perhaps, once the public realizes that this spike is cyclic and not an aberration, pressure will be placed on industry and the appropriate elected officials and a source of energy at a relatively stable price will finally be made available.

SOURCES

1. Krammer, Prof. Arnold, 1981, "Technology Transfer as War Booty: The U.S. Technical Oil Mission To Europe, 1945", page 69, Reprinted for private circulation from Technology And Culture, Vol.22, No.1, The Society for the History of Technology, The University of Chicago

2. ibid

3. Krammer, Prof. Arnold, 1982, "German Underground Industrial Facilities During World War ll", page 481, ASEE Annual Conference Proceedings.

4. ibid

5. Krammer, Prof. Arnold, 1981, page 97

6. Krammer, Prof. Arnold, 1981, page 110

7. Krammer, Prof. Arnold, 1982, page 467

30 | Super Lubricants

You have probably seen the advertisements on late-night television for automobile super lubricants. These additives are touted as doing amazing things. Claims are made for increased gas milage with the addition of a small bottle of their product. Claims are made for reduced engine or transmission wear. Claims are made that an auto's engine will run after the motor oil has been drained out of it with the use of a super lubricant.

We already know the Germans invented synthetic oil during World War Two. They synthesized a standard-size oil molecule out of oil or even coal using one of two processes developed at that time. Naturally occurring crude oil is "cracked" into lighter oils, some of which can be used as motor oil. Even these oils, however, are really a mixture of longer and shorter chains of oil molecules. The viscosity index used to grade oils is, in part, just and average which reflects the average molecular chain length of a mixture of molecules. The German synthetic oil molecules were almost carbon copies of each other and this uniformity led to lubrication benefits for the user. Mobil Oil Company, for instance, used captured German technology to create a synthetic oil, Mobil-One, in the mid-1970s.

This is not the technology under discussion, however. What is under discussion is more than re-working existing oil molecules or even creating oils out of ester base products. What we are talking about is a treatment involving new chemicals.

Of course, these are products surrounded in proprietary secrecy. None of the companies making this class of lubricants advertises or even lists what their products contain. But a clue came from a competitor, Slick 50, which markets the best selling Teflon additive for automobile application. Their advertising compared their product to "chlorinated hydrocarbons", to which Slick 50 fared favorably in terms of bearing corrosion. So we learn that the product in question was some sort of chlorinated hydrocarbon.

These words rang a bell. The reference in question was titled "Secrets By The Thousands" by C. Lester Walker. It concerned astounding yet little-known developments made by the Germans during the war. Interestingly enough, it had appeared in Harper's Magazine. The date of the article is most significant. It is dated from October of 1946.

1946 was a time of good feelings. The war was over and we had won. The Russians were still technically our allies. The Cold War had not, as yet, materialized. There was a thaw in censorship and in the press. For a brief time, only months, not years, things about captured German technology were reported openly, almost proudly, as if to underscore our victory over people who could produce such wonders. The Harper's report was one of these. It described many things. One of these was a night vision device that allowed the viewer to see in darkness as if it was daytime. It ran on a small motor:

> "The diminutive generator—five inches across—stepped up current from an ordinary flashlight battery to 15,000 volts. It had a walnut-sized motor, which spun a rotor at 10,000 rpm—so fast that originally it had destroyed all lubricants with the great amount of ozone it produced. The Germans had developed a new grease: chlorinated paraffin oil. The generator then ran 3,000 hours!"[1]

Chlorinated paraffin oil certainly qualifies as a chlorinated hydrocarbon. There may be others.

Calls were made to each of the four or five companies making these products to ask, point blank, if this technology was of a German origin. All denied any connection to wartime Germany. One company spokesman whispered to me, as if telling a secret, that the technology came from NASA, the space agency. Somehow, their stories did not ring true.

A search of the technical literature of wartime Germany was done to see if my suspicions, and the Harper's article, could be verified.

Without too much difficulty a reference appeared. This was from the Combined Intelligence Objectives Subcommittee[2]. It comprised a report titled: "The Preparation Of Tetrahydrofuran Polymers As A Synthetic Lubricant For Metals".

This report was based upon an interview of Dr. Delfts of I.G. Farben, the largest chemical company in the world at the time. Dr. Delfts reported that tetrayhdrofuran polymers produced desirable properties as a lubricant including a high flash point (temperature at which it will burn), high viscosity index (resists thinning at high temperature), and extremely low pour point (lowest temperature at which it will flow). Polymers were produced from tetrahydrofuran using a catalyst. The best catalysts, it was found, were ferric chloride and thionyl chloride. These are the chlorinated hydrocarbons in question.

The report went on to describe high temperature applications of this product in conjunction with glycol and its esters as crankcase additives for automobile engines. These were surely the chlorinated hydrocarbons described in the Harper's article and in the competitor's advertising.

The CIOS report did not mention bearing wear nor did it endorse or dissuade the use of these additives for automobiles. The producers of these products all denied that they caused bearing corrosion. A maker of manual transmission fluid did mention chlorinated hydrocarbons at a website and seemed to indicate that they were not suitable for a closed system. It indicated that they were better in a vented system, one open to the air. I am not a chemist and cannot recommend or condemn these products. I can only report on their history.

As history, it is certainly safe to say that Dr. Delfts never envisioned his work on super lubricants as providing such wonder late-night infomercial entertainment.

SOURCES

1. "Secrets By The Thousands", October, 1946, page 331, by C. Lester Walker

2. Combined Intelligence Objectives Sub-Committee report, item no. 30, File no. XXX-70, November 15, 1945, "The Preparation Of Tetrahydrofuran Polymers As A Synthetic Lubricant For Metals".

31 | What is Happening in Antarctica?

Recently, an anonymous letter was written to Scientific American describing something very odd. The report came out of Australia's Casey Station in Antarctica. Two women were attempting to ski across Antarctica when they were interrupted. A U.S. Navy Special Forces team, working out American Samoa, abducted the women, against their wishes, and under protest from the crew at the Australian Casey Station. The two adventurers were then held in seclusion for reasons never given[1].

What is going on here? Ufologists are always describing UFOs as originating in Antarctica. Certainly, the theme is familiar to everyone through science fiction movies. Some think Atlantis may be buried deep under the ice. Many nations currently have research bases in Antarctica. The German base at Neuschwabenland was active, at least on some level, during the Second World War and may have served as a last refuge for Nazi die-hards after the conflict.

Not only do these theories exist but there are all sorts of combinations of the theories mentioned above. Did the Germans locate their base in Antarctica because the Ahnenerbe, the SS racial-archeological organization, found evidence of a lost civilization? Or did the Germans or any of the other nationalities involved in Antarctica make contact with an extraterrestrial presence located on that continent, a theory recently revamped by Dr. Michael E. Salla[2].

Geologically speaking, Antarctica is almost split in half by a huge rift valley, which runs from the South Pole toward Africa, then up East Africa to the Dead

Sea. This entire rift valley is overflowing with geothermal activity. It was on this very rift valley that the Germans located their Antarctic base. Hot water ponds, named the Schumacher Ponds by the Germans, are teaming with algae, and found on surface rock deep within Antarctica. These ponds never freeze over. Interestingly enough, each pond is populated by a different species of algae, giving each pond a different color. It is not far-fetched to believe that a sustainable base could be located over one of these geothermal vents, especially deep within a large crevice or cave. Also located in a glacial environment, the Icelanders rely of geothermal energy to produce electricity for their daily needs. Why could not have inhabitants of Antarctica?

But recently much more strangeness has been uncovered in Antarctica than some old rumors, geothermal vents or two abducted women.

One strange thing is Lake Vostok. Lake Vostok is one of those poorly kept secrets that no government really wants to deny but, at the same time, doesn't really want to talk about. For example the Jet Propulsion Laboratory (JPL) announced on 1/24/01 that it has terminated all further study of Lake Vostok in Antarctica and deferred study, according to their spokeswoman Debra Shinteller, to the National Security Agency (NSA). The NSA is spook-central, hardly the type of organization one would think equipped to do a scientific study of a lake. But Lake Vostok is no ordinary lake.

Lake Vostok is located 300 miles from the South Pole in Antarctica near the Russian research station, Vostok. Evidently, for some time an international team has been carrying on research at this lake and it is exactly this research that JPL headed. The reason for this mystery becomes apparent as details of the lake emerge. Lake Vostok is not located on the surface rock as are the Schumacher Ponds. Lake Vostok is a very large subterranean lake situated over three-quarters of a mile beneath the Continental Ice Sheet. The lake is up to 2000 feet deep. Thermographic images from space yield a water temperature of 50 degrees Fahrenheit as an average with hot spots going up to 65 degrees. Such high temperatures could only be the result of geothermal activity.

What seems even more astounding is the fact that this lake was completely hidden from view. This is because there is a roof of ice over the lake, forming a dome, which is up to one-half a mile in height. This opaque dome admits enough sunlight during the summer months to allow for a strange, twilight world of continuous morning light. Lake Vostok is a lost world. It is a lost subterranean world so strange it is almost beyond the realm of science fiction writers. Of course JPL is interested in this lake for its unique strangeness. This environment, it seems, may duplicate or at least approximate a frozen moon of Jupiter, covered by a frozen sea and bottom-heated by geothermal energy. Isolated for millions of years, Lake Vostok could also provide some answers concerning the evolution of life on earth. Yet, these reasons alone cannot possibly account for the extreme secrecy evidenced by is take-over by the National Security Agency.

The reason for the NSA's involvement has nothing to do with biology and everything to do with physics. It seems that the lake has been scanned by low-level flights, which for some reason were looking for gravitational and magnetic anomalies. Admiral Byrd did the same thing in his short-lived 1946 Antarctic "invasion". The recent effort was probably related to something Byrd first uncovered. What they found was a huge magnetic anomaly covering the entire Southeast portion of the shore of the lake[3]. This anomaly's strength registered 1,000 nanoteslas of variance with the surrounding vicinity. One scientist jumped on this publicly and began to debunk its significance[4] but the fact remains that the best and most probably answer as to the origin of this vast magnetic disturbance is the presence of a massive amount of metal. Metal as in a buried city.

This brings us right back to the mystery-school of Antarctica. Is this metal the remains of Atlantis? Is it the underground city said by some to have been built by the Germans, Neu-Berlin? Is this an extraterrestrial base? With the NSA involved, the only thing for certain is that we won't be told the answer to this mystery anytime soon nor will we be allowed to visit the lake without U.S. Delta Orcs swooping down on us as they did with the two women skiers.

But besides Lake Vostok, there is a second strangeness going on in Antarctica. Unlike the Lake Vostok mystery, even you at home can monitor this strangeness.

Countries maintaining Antarctic bases usually do geological research. Among the instruments employed are seismographs. Besides seismographs in Antarctica itself, neighboring countries also monitor seismic events in the frozen continent.

Recently, researcher Rainer Daehnhardt, who knows a great deal about Antarctica, sent me a printout of a German language website[5]. Strange and interesting things are explored here, among them the work of two researchers, Kawi Schneider and Christian Saal. What they uncovered and presented are actual Antarctic seismographs that are quite out of the ordinary. These charts show a 24 hour cycle, broken down hour by hour on the vertical axis and minute by minute on the horizontal, so that for any given hour a line running from left to right yields the intensity and duration of earth movement. In fact, this web-site offers links to current seismological monitoring in real time so that the viewer can actually see what typical day in Antarctica looks like in terms of earth movement. What we are talking about, however, is anything but typical.

I would like to first call your attention to these seismological graphs and then repeat what Christian Saal has to say about them.

The first graph is a typical day in Antarctica.

The second, dated 3/19/03, shows massive, intense long-wave movement which is quite unnatural.

The third, dated 3/24/03, shows a strong earthquake for comparison.

The fourth, dated 3/20/03, shows the long-wave activity and a sudden, powerful jolt at 17 hours, 20 minutes.

The fifth, dated 3/21/03, shows a somewhat less powerful jolt at 20 hours, 20 minutes.

The Americans at the Amundsen South Pole station took these readings. This station actually consists of three stations, according to the author, which are located surrounding the old German area called Neuschwabenland.

Christian Saal's interpretation is as follows. The first graph is a typical day, a baseline with which to compare abnormal graphs. Graph two shows tremendous long-wave energy, which is unnatural. Saal explains this in a surprising way. He says this energy is being produced at the German facility of Neuschwabenland, apparently by Germans still inhabiting the facility. Christian Saal goes on to suggest that this energy is defensive in nature, an energy umbrella that has been activated by the Germans there in response to an attack.

Graph three shows that graph two is unique, since this is what a naturally occurring earthquake looks like.

Graph four again shows the long-wave energy but also shows a sharp anomaly at 17.20 hours. Saal interprets this to be an American

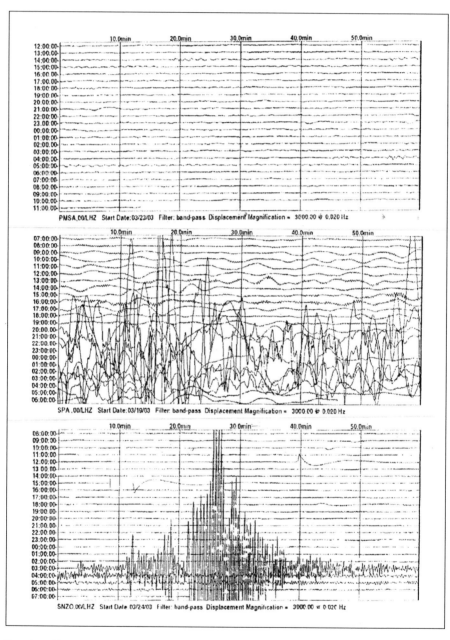

Seismological Antarctica.

Top: Typical, quiet day in Antarctica.

Middle: South Pole gone wild! On 3/19/03 there was massive long wave movement. Is this a Tesla-type standing wave (scalar wave) weapon?

Bottom: This is a strong earthquake, 03/24/03. Notice the difference between this graph and the one above.

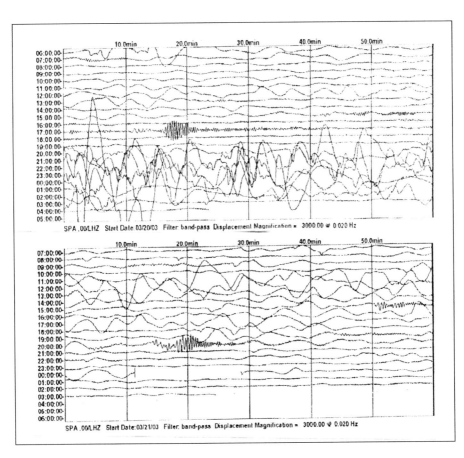

SPA .00/LHZ Start Date:03/20/03 Filter: band-pass Displacement Magnification = 3000.00 @ 0.020 Hz

SPA .00/LHZ Start Date:03/21/03 Filter: band-pass Displacement Magnification = 3000.00 @ 0.020 Hz

Seismological Antarctica.
Top: Dated 3/20/03, this is a graph of a sudden, powerful jolt at 17 hours, 20 minutes.

Bottom: Finally, on 3/21/03, there was a somewhat less powerful jolt at 20 hours and 20 minutes. Was this the U.S. test of an atomic bunker buster bomb and a somewhat less powerful conventional bunker buster on the next day?

attack on Neuschwabenland using the new boring atomic weapon announced at the time of the Iraq invasion. Look at the date on this graph, 3/20/03, the very day the United States began its massive bombardment of Baghdad, the start of the second Iraq war. Saal goes further in suggesting that the Iraq bombing served as a cover, it diverted the world's attention, so that nuclear weapons could be again used in Antarctica.

Evidently, Neuschwabenland's defenses held because as seen in the fourth graph, another, similar but smaller jolt was experienced in this area. Christian Saal again goes back to the words of the Americans who designed "leaks" talking about a MOAB bomb at this time. The MOAB, called popularly "Mother Of All Bombs" is a conventional explosive, an advanced form of the fuel-air bomb designed by Dr. Zippermeyr.

I really don't know if Christian Saal's interpretation is correct or not. What is most important to me is that there is real data here that shows something unusual and unexplained by "the authorities". This hard seismological data, an acknowledged mystery lake in the center of Antarctica, and the interjection of the National Security Agency all point to something as yet unexplained happening on our southern-most continent.

SOURCES

1. "The Secret Of Lake Vostok, William P. Eigles, Atlantis Rising (magazine), number 29, page 60

2. Salla, Michael E., Ph.D., 2003, Foundations for Globally managing Extraterrestrial Affairs-The Legacy of the Nazi Germany-Extraterrestrial Connection, Research Study #6, www.exopolitics.org

3. "The Secret Of Lake Vostok, William P. Eigles, page 60

4. ibid

5. www.unglaublichkeiten.info

32 | Large German Mystery Rockets
"The Hammer of Thor"

By the term "Large German Mystery Rockets" what is meant here are rockets larger than the V-1 or V-2 with which we are all familiar.

To the best of my knowledge, the first people to raise the possibility that the German ever built anything larger than the V-2 were Colonel Howard A. Buechner and Kapitan Wilhelm Bernhart in 1988[1].

Colonel Buechner was a U.S. Army medical doctor and later Professor of Medicine at Tulane University and Emeritus Professor of Medicine at Louisiana State University. During the war, he was among the first Americans to enter Dachau concentration camp.

Kapitan Wilhelm Bernhart is an alias. The reason for the use of an alias is obvious as we assess his resume. Bernhart was a German officer who served aboard the famous U-530. U-530 surrendered, not in May of 1945 when the war in Europe ended, but on July 10, 1945 at Mar del Plata, Argentina. The nature of this U-boat and its mission have been the subject of much speculation and controversy. Kapitan Bernhardt is now a U.S. citizen and has been engaged in commercial shipping for 32 years.

The nature of the V-2 controversy starts with its time frame. Dr. Werhner von Braun and his rocket team finished work on the V-2 in August of 1943. After that, the V-2 was taken to the vicinity of Nordhausen in Thuringia. There, in a vast underground factory, it was mass-produced. The question for us is what in the world occupied Dr. von Braun's time between August of 1943 and May of 1945 when he surrendered to the United States military?

Pictures of the A4-b "Bastard" under testing as the war closed. This winged V-2 glided down to its target, increasing its range. The "Bastard" was a half way measure between the A-9 and the A-4. There is an Enlargement of the A4-b on the following page. On the page following the A-4b enlargement is a diagram of the A-9/A-10. Note how the A-9 is embedded inside the cowling of the A-10. Also, note the lengths of the two rockets and compare these with the prisoner of war testimony.

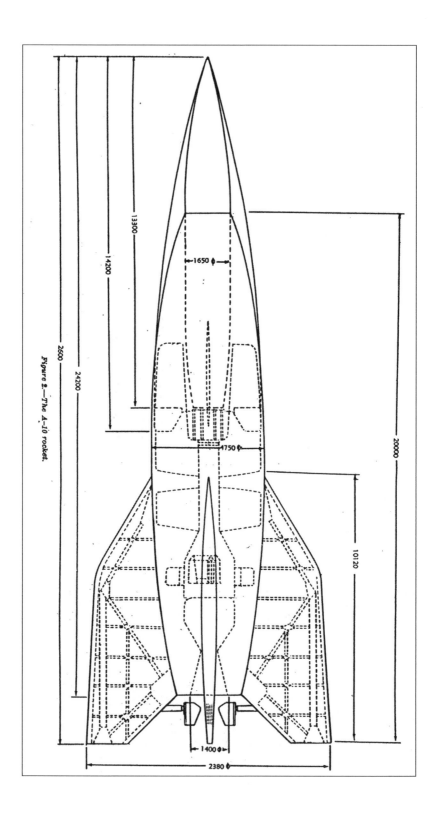

Figure 2.—The A-10 rocket.

We are all familiar with Dr. Werhner von Braun. He was one of our space heros. He, more than anyone else on the planet, was responsible for the trip we earthlings took to the moon in 1969. We remember him as an intelligent, articulate, and energetic scientist and as advocate for the space program. Returning to the wartime situation in late 1943, we again ask ourselves if a man such as this would have simply kicked back and rested on his laurels after developing the V-2 or would he have gone on to other projects? Officially, we are told that he did just this; he sat on his butt for twenty months, doing nothing. And even if Dr. von Braun wanted to kickback and do nothing, do you think the Nazi government would allow him to do so? This is not likely.

What is more likely, much more likely, is that he and his team went on to the next rocket slated for development, the A-9/A-10. Most of us are familiar with that rocket also even though we are told it existed only on paper. It was a huge, two stage rocket. The second stage, the A-9, resembled a modified V-2, which already existed but the larger, lower stage and to be designed and built.

In 1989 the two aforementioned writers, Buechner and Bernhart, described rumors of this project:

> "Finally, there was the A-10, the most advanced missile in the series. It was a massive, supersonic rocket with a high stratospheric trajectory, which was designed for Trans – Atlantic bombardment. It had an estimated range of 2800 miles. It was actually a two-stage rocket consisting of a booster and payload similar in principle to the space shuttles of today. Officially the A-10 was never brought to production. However, there are persistent rumors that the A-10 or an even larger intercontinental ballistic missile was produced, although a total of only four were completed. It was called the "Hammer of Thor" and nicknamed The "America Rocket" since it was intended to be fired at major cities in the U.S., such as Washington, Boston, New York and Philadelphia. Four rockets are said to have been launched from the research base at Peenemuende just before the rocket center was captured by Russian soldiers. Three missiles were test fired into the Atlantic Ocean and one was sent into orbit or into outer space for unknown reasons."[2]

In one sense we do know what became of the "Hammer of Thor". Hollywood picked up on the provocative description and used it as the basis of an X-File episode. The plot had nothing to do with a mystery missile, wallowed in sentiment, and was otherwise totally forgettable.

But there is evidence that actual rockets, of the type described by Buechner and Bernhardt, were actually built by the Germans and flown. This voluminous evidence has been produced by three German researchers and published in German language[34]. The evidence that they present is based upon eyewitness testimony of several individuals, but it does not end there. These researchers have some actual photographic evidence and professional photo-interpretation that supports this hypothesis. The evidence has convinced me of the validity of their hypothesis: that the A-9/A-10 rocket was actually built and flown. It is sincerely hoped that anyone deeply interested in this topic who can read German language will go to the books referenced and experience this discovery "first-hand" as the author's tell it. I will not even try to translate and regurgitate their data, second-hand. What I will do is to describe some proof for the existence of this rocket that comes from English language sources.

For this evidence we will go to the U.S. government itself, in the form of a document titled: "Headquarters, United States Strategic Air Forces In Europe Office Of The Director Of Intelligence An Evaluation Of German Capabilities In 1945", or as it has been already called, the "Rosetta Stone". The reality of each and every weapon's system described in this document is proven by a sentence in the first paragraph of this report that reads:

"No consideration is given to those for which there is lacking evidence of possible use for some time to come".

In other words, these are weapons in which we can expect the enemy to employ; now, yet there may be others in the distant future. After describing the V-2, section 2.b. describes "larger rockets":

"Larger rockets (68 feet in length as against 45 feet) are known to exist, and may appear in small quantities during the year. They would have a considerably larger warhead".

The 45-foot rocket they are describing was the V-2. A 68-foot rocket is officially unknown, but here it is not only acknowledged to have existed but a warning is being posted to the Allied military to watch out for this weapon. It should be mentioned again that this report does not contain speculation. This report is a distillation of intelligence from many sources concerning concrete threats to the Allied war effort. But the question remains, what could this weapon be?

Here are the facts that we are told. It is a rocket. It is 68 feet long. It was produced in small quantities. It has a considerably larger warhead, larger payload, than the V-2. What fits this description?

The one thing that fits this description best is the first stage of the A-9/A-10. The first stage of this project was never built according to official history. The second stage, the A-9, looked like a somewhat modified V-2 (A-4) rocket with longer, swept-back wings. The diagram of the A-9/A-10 shows us that the A-10 was a short, stocky rocket whose upper half encased the A-9.

According to reliable sources, the A-9/A-10, together, stood 30 meters, about 90 feet, in height[5]. The A-9, the second stage, is 45 feet long. If the first stage, the A-10, is 68 feet long, the total length of the rocket would be 113 feet. But the second stage A-9 is set inside the cowling of the A-10 with approximately only half of its surface showing (see diagram). Half of 45 is 22.5 feet. If we add the correct figures together, 68 feet for the A-10 and 22.5 feet for the portion of the A-9, which can be seen, we get the figure of 90.5 feet. This is a good approximation of the height of the combined A-9/A-10. In reality, the 68-foot rocket described in the government report can not be a description of anything other than the A-10.

One more point. The government intelligence report says that these rockets "are known to exist". This obviously means that they were built, not on paper, but in metal. The government intelligence report also says that they "may appear in small quantities during the year". The government is not talking about capturing these rockets at this point in time. The words "may appear" really means "may fly". For a description of the lift-off of the A-9/A-10 please see the sources[3] and[4] listed below.

But if the A-10 was actually built, would not there be some sort of confirmation on the ground from the German rocket scientists them-selves? Of course there should be testimony concerning this but it seems that all the testimony was in the negative. The German rocket scientists denied making rockets beyond the V-2. Now, we know that these German scientists were under extreme pressure, pressure generated by the cold war, to do and say exactly what their new employers and benefactors, the government of the United States of America, said they should say. Most of these same scientists, for instance, denied that German flying discs were built during the war. This claim has now turned out to be completely false. Time and research work have put a chink in this cold war propaganda armor.

The question for us here is if there is a chink regarding the A-10? Is there any German source that affirms its existence? Recently, such a source has been found. Not only was such a German source found, it was heavily relied upon by the intelligence agencies of the United States of America. As with many sources within government itself, this one was found by accident, while researching something else.

The topic in question then was the "V-3". A "V" weapon was purely a political designation. "V" stood for Vergeltung which means "vengeance", perhaps better expressed in the vernacular, "payback". It seems there were several weapons on their way to being designated as the V-3. A F.O.I.A. request was made concerning the V-3 since the name appeared in a government index.

The government's source was declassified in 1993 and was a German prisoner of war who fell into the hands of the U.S. Seventh Army[5]. A date stamp indicates this was on or about December 14, 1944. The prisoner was a disgruntled German who had tried to immigrate to Australia before the war but was drafted before this could take place. He was made a paratrooper and later served as a field chemist. He was caught listening to a BBC broadcast and as punishment he was sent to Peenemuende in March of 1943 and placed under the auspices of the Luftwaffe. He was given work described as "danger-ous" to complete his punishment. He was later assigned to Nancy, France, where he deserted and contacted U.S. forces.

The information this prisoner provided on Peenemuende was quite wide-ranging, including descriptions of the hardware being devel-oped there, personnel, maps, organizational information, and security information. The prisoner described the V-3 as follows:

> "d) V-3 This is a radio-controlled glider bomb launched by a HE 177 and is intended to be guided into enemy bomber formations. PW, who personally timed it, noted

that it remained in the air seven minutes. When PW left PEENEMUENDE in July 44 the bombs were not yet considered satisfactory, sometimes dropping into the sea before the seven minutes had elapsed. He believes that this weapon may now have a higher number in the V series."

This little description is important because it will tie in with information about this missile developed from another source, which will be discussed later. The big surprise coming from this F.O.I.A. request did not come from any disclosure concerning the V-3, however, but concerning something the prisoner described under another section, "V-2 Glider Bombs".

In this section the same prison describes two different types of V-2s. One is called the A-4 and is described as about 18 meters long and 2.5–3 meters in diameter. This is the 45-foot V-2 of which we are familiar. But there is a second rocket present. This one is called "Type A 1" It is described as being about 23 meters long and 4.5 meters in diameter. Only the smaller, 18 meter V-2 was in mass production according to the report. The prisoner states that V-2s have attained a height of 12-15 kilometers in altitude. At that altitude, 15 kilometers, its range is said to be 500 kilometer. This is long but otherwise not surprising. What is surprising is that the prisoner says that he heard that technicians intended to launch "them" to an altitude of 120 kilometers, "which would have permitted them to reach NEW YORK." The difference between 15 and 120 kilometers is considerable. Obviously, the difference is the difference between the two rockets under discussion with the higher altitude and range going to the larger rocket.

How big was this larger rocket? Please look at the diagram of the A-9/A-10. A 23-meter rocket is about 70 feet long. Likewise, the diameter, 4.3 meters, corresponds to "about" the dimensions of the A-10 and the source, the prisoner, does use the word "about" in describing these dimensions. The target discussed, New York City, indicates its range and this also corresponds to the A-10.

Now we come to the name given it by the prisoner. He lumps it together with the V-2, indicating that it was a second version of that weapon which was not yet in mass production. He calls it or it is called in this report "Type A 1". Note that there is no hyphen between

D. V-2 GLIDER BOMBS

The V-2 flying bombs are assembled in the EAST Works (see Appendix A) which has about 3,000 engineers and workers. Two types of V-2 have been built: Type A 1, which is about 23 m long and 4.5 m in diameter, and Type A 4, which is about 18 m long and 2.5-3 m in diameter. Only the latter is in mass production. The experimental launching of V-2 used to take place every Saturday afternoon from Mar 43 to Mar 44. At the latter time it was rumored that HITLER had visited the center and had demonstrated his anger at the slow progress of the experiments. From this time on the frequency of the bomb launchings was increased to every other day. When PW left the center in July 44 there were still some launchings which were not successful due to the fact that the bombs were not able to be radio-guided, although they were launched successfully.

All experiments conducted with V̄-2 were done without explosive charges, except once, in HITLER's presence. It is rumored that on that occasion the bomb was guided to HELA Island, near DANZIG. Invariably a small explosive charge with a fuze is placed in all bombs lest a bomb drop intact into some foreign country - Sweden, for example.

When a V-2 bomb is launched all the workers of all four factories listen to the noise of the bomb as it climbs to the stratosphere. When it becomes apparent that control is lost over the bomb, everybody makes a mad rush for a shelter, since sometimes the bomb returns and hits a factory.

PW once had an opportunity to observe the launching of one of these bombs from a distance of 200 m. The bomb stands on a concrete platform, inclined about five degrees in the direction of fire. It is

ignited from an underground concrete bunker which is about 30 m away. The detonation is similar to that of a large-caliber arty gun going off. The firing produces a white smoke cloud which reaches a height of 50 m. Up to a height of 1,000 m, 10 m-long red flames can be seen. From 1,000 to 3,000 m the sight picture is that of a blue flag waving under the projectile. Beyond 3,000 m it has a long vapor trail. V-2 bombs have attained heights of 12-15 km. PW heard that German technicians intended to launch them to an altitude of 120 km, which would have permitted them to reach NEW YORK. At a height of 15 km the bombs have a range of 500 km. When the bomb drops from the stratosphere to a lower level, it becomes red through friction.

This is from a U.S. Army document, declassified 7-13-93, titled: Ref No 579, MU 500, CSDIC (West), Seventh Army APO 758 US Army. A prisoner of war, a chemist, tells of work being done in Peenemuende around March, 1943 (over two years before the end of the war). Please note his reference to tow types of V-2s, the A-4 and the A-1. From the description given, we can see that this "A-1" reference is a corruption of the A-10 or a censored deletion of the word by the U.S. Army so it would not surface in a search of records

A and 1. Considering the description in its totality, it can be argued that this "Type A 1" is a mistake or a typographical error or a deliberate deception—an attempt at a cover-up. All this was done simply by omitting one zero. This rocket's true designation certainly should have been given as Type A-10.

This prisoner had no reason to lie. His other information was mostly very accurate. There was no attempt on the part of the U.S. intelligence to hedge his testimony (in case it proved false) as was their most common practice. The U.S. Seventh Army believed it was getting the best information this particular individual could supply. Shouldn't we also? The A-10 was a reality but produced in limited quantity.

SOURCES

1. Buechner, Howard A. Col. and Kapitan Wilhelm Bernhardt, 1989, pages 286-289, Hitler's Ashes, Thunderbird Press, Inc., Metairie, Louisiana

2. Buechner, Howard A. Col. and Kapitan Wilhelm Bernhardt, 1989, pages 162-163

3. Mayer, Edgar and Thomas Mehner, 2002, *Die Atombombe und das Dritte Reich Das Geheimnis des Drieiecks Arnstadt-Wechmar-Ohrdruf*, Jochen Kopp Verlag, Rottenburg

4. Georg, Friedrich, 2003, *Hitlers Siegeswaffen Band 2 Star Wars 1947 Band2, Teil B,* Amun-Verlag, Schleusingen

5. MU 500, CSDIC (WEST), SEVENTH ARMY APO 758 US ARMY, reference No. 579, PEEMUENDE EXPERIMENTAL CENTER (KARLSHAGEN), December 14, 1944, Declassified Authority NNO750122, 7/13/93

Note: There are two new books in German language describing in even more detail the reality of the A-10:

A.   Georg, Friedrich, 2004, Hitlers Siegeswaffen Band 2: Star Wars 1947 Teilband B: Von der Amerikarakete zur Orbitalstation-Deustshlands Streben nach interkontinentalwaffen und das erste Weltraumprogramm, Amun-Verlag, Schleusingen

B.   Georg, Friedrich and Thomas Mehner, 2004, Atomziel New York Geheime Grossraketen-und Raumfahrtprojekte des Dritten Reiches, Jochen Kopp Verlag, Rottenburg

33 | Yet Another "V-3" Rocket

As mentioned earlier, when one speaks of the "V-3" one never knows what the specific response will be. There have been so many weapons called by so many people the V-3. Examples of these are the Hochdruckpumpe, the high pressure cannon, the Me-262 jet fighter/bomber, one of many German flying discs, a further development of the Henschel HS-293 for purposes other than floating targets and various missiles and rockets under development by the Germans at the time. It is one of these latter rockets that is the subject of this report.

While the report described above did mention the V-3, a much better report came bundled up with various other reports under the heading of "Werwolf"[1]. (There is just no figuring out the government's filing system.)

The informant in this case was a prisoner of war, a Czech of German ancestry named Joseph Koch. Koch was an engineer who was assigned in May of 1944 to the Flottmannwerke in Breslau. He worked there for three weeks before it was learned that he was a Czech, which, somehow, made him ineligible for continued employment at Flottmannwerke so he was returned to the Army. During his three-week stint at Flottmannwerke he had access, on about ten occasions, to the director's office. On the wall of that office was a diagram of a new rocket, which he overheard officials speak of as the "V-3". But before describing Flottmannwerke or the V-3 more fully, the reader should be made aware of the unique circumstances of the plant's site itself, Breslau.

SECRET

Name: KOCH, Joseph
Rank: Pvt.
Unit: 385 Pz
Capt: 26 Nov 44.
Interrogated: 6824 DIC MIS, 12, 13 Dec 44.

JAN 27 1945

FILE

Preamble

P/W is a 28 year old Czech who served in the German army from
26 Jul 42 until his surrender to Allied forces 26 Nov 44. Before his
induction he was employed by the HUTEMBERG GESELLSCHAFT in TRINEC, Czechoslovakia, as an engineer making and checking plans for the manufacture
of Martin furnaces. In May 44, while still in military service, he was
assigned to FLOTTMANNWERKE, BRESLAU, but, according to him, he was returned to the army when the factory discovered after three weeks that he
was a Czech. He seems sincere and anxious to help, but has a tendency
to exaggerate which makes it advisable to consider his information with
reserve. Since the subject, at least, is of such prime importance, we are
sending at once to our User Agencies this report containing all PW seems
to know about V-3 (?)

        Reliability: C-5. Source fair - truth of information cannot be
                judged.

New Secret Weapon (V-3?) See sketch-May 44 - FLOTTMANNWERKE, BRESLAU

During the time of his employment May 44 at FLOTTMANNWERKE P/W
says that on about ten occasions he had the opportunity of seeing hastily
a sketch on the wall of the director's room which, he claims, was the
plan of a new secret weapon. On several occasions he overheard some officials speak of it as V-3. It is principally intended to be a large rocket
which functions on practically the same principle as a rifle grenade. P/W
described it as 33,100 mm in length, 3200 mm in diameter and consisting
of eight sections containing nitroglycerine and compressed air. (see
sketch). On contact with the target these charges explode the rocket which
is supposed to cause sufficient concussion to destroy anything in its path.

Propulsion of Proposed Secret Weapon

P/W had no knowledge of the proposed method for starting the
rocket in flight and could not reveal any information regarding the force
whereby it would be sustained in flight. From hearsay, however, he was
made to believe that the new weapon was to be partially inserted into
the end of an immense gun barrel, estimated to be 25 m in length, from
which the rocket was to be shot somewhat in the manner of a rifle grenade.

PRODUCTION at FLOTTMANNWERKE

Until May 44 this firm assembled 5 or 6 V-1 and 3 or 4 V-2 weapons. Shortages of materials lessened the production of both during
the month of May 44. Evidently acquisition of light metals for producing the interior parts of the V-bombs has delayed the output. Steel
strips, however, with an overall length of 15 m had continued to arrive
as well as prefabricated hulls for the V-weapons. P/W claims that twice
weekly five flat-car loads of steel and hulls continued to arrive at the
plant. There was no specific time or day for the arrival of these cars.

In addition to interior parts for V-weapons, the firm also manufactures tank treads for Panzers, half tracks and heavy Tigers. The
average output as of May 44 was 36 treads per week.

SECRET

This is the cover page of a secret intelligence report. It is the testimony of a young German-Czech engineer who stumbled upon at least one of Dr. Hans Kammler's pet projects. Pehaps Kammler was building a second long range rocket or series of rockets in his eastern sphere of influence centered upon the Kammler Group Headquarters near Pilsen/Prague. Was this an SS empire within an empire?

Breslau was a city in the German state of Silesia. Silesia was the eastern-most state or Provence within the German Reich. Breslau was a large city in the west-central part of Silesia that contained, for instance, a large governmental presence and a university. Breslau and this entire Silesian region were also somewhat of a center in the German testing and development of secret weaponry. As the Soviets pushed westward at the end of the war, Breslau became isolated. The Reich propaganda of the times called it as "Fortress Breslau". In fact, it held against the Soviets surprisingly well. Hitler Youth learned new defense tactics during the siege and formed a major component in the defense of Breslau. Hitler Youth were so successful that some of their leaders were flown to Berlin to organize the defense of that city. In fact, Breslau held out against the Soviets longer than Berlin held out. But today neither Silesia nor Breslau no longer exists.

After the war all of Silesia was ceded to Poland and became part of that country. The Germans living in Breslau as well as the remainder of Silesia were all relocated west into the Soviet zone of East Germany. The German population of Silesia and Breslau were entirely replaced, almost overnight by Poles. This movement of peoples brought with it a cultural disconnect. Current residents of western Poland had no connection with the pre-war population whatsoever. Silesia and Breslau, like the American Confederacy after the Civil War, were "gone with the wind".

The point of this history review is that all happenings in Silesia during the war cannot be verified or traced in any meaningful manner. The German industrial plants are gone. The university is gone. The streets and the names of the cities themselves have been changed. All we have of what happened there during the war came out of there on the backs and in the minds of the German refugees who were displaced. This report is, then, one of those scraps of evidence we have concerning this important region.

The Flottmannwerke consisted of thirteen buildings and a work force of 2000 individuals working three shifts per day. A railroad ran directly into the plant from which raw materials were unloaded and, presumable, from which finished weaponry was shipped to its point of insertion. A special police force enforced security and secrecy at the plant.

The Flottmannwerke made tank treads for German tanks and tracked vehicles but its highest priority work concerned making

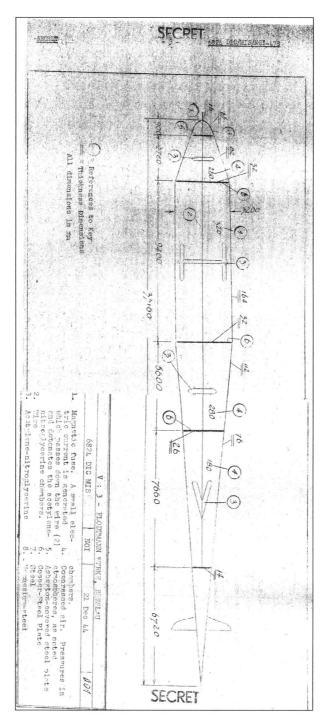

6824 DIC/MIS/NOI-478

= References to Key.
= Thickness Dimensions
All dimensions in mm

V : 3 - FLOTTMANN WERKE, BRESLAU

6824 DIC MIS	NOI	21 Dec 44	1008

1. Magnetic fuse. A small electric current is generated which passes down the wire (2) and detonates the acetylene-nitroglycerine chambers.
2. Wire
3. Acetylene-nitroglycerine

4. chambers.
5. Compressed air. Pressures in atmospheres, as noted
6. Asbestos-covered steel plate
7. Copper-steel Plate
8. Steel
8. Magnesium-steel

This is the Flottmann V-3, drawn from memory by the German-Czech engineer, Joseph Koch.

interior parts for V-weapons. Prefabricated hulls for these weapons were delivered by rail along with steel strips measuring 15 meters in length. Shortages were experienced, according to Koch, concerning light metals necessary for finishing the weapons. Five or six V-1s had been assembled by May, 1944 as well as 3 or 4 V-2s.

Koch saw the diagram of the new V-3 weapon well enough to make a drawing of it and memorize some of its details. He said it is intended to be a large rocket that functions on practically the same principle as a rifle grenade. From this description we might say today that this was a ballistic weapon. The rocket itself was 33.1 meters long and 3.2 meters in diameter. These figures put the rocket in the neighborhood of 100 feet long and over 10 feet in diameter. Koch reports it had eight sections containing nitroglycerine and compressed air. This is somewhat confusing since we do not know if he is talking about rocket stages or construction modules. The statement about nitroglycerine and compressed air is further confused by Koch's admission that he had no knowledge of the proposed method for starting the rocket in flight and "could not reveal any information regarding the force whereby it would be sustained in flight. In other words, he did not know its method of propulsion. Koch relayed what he termed "hearsay" on the subject that the new weapon was to be partially inserted into the end of an immense gun barrel, estimated to be 25 meters in length, from which the rocket was to be shot somewhat in the manner of a rifle grenade.

From Koch's description we certainly can see that a large rocket was under consideration. He indicates this was a ballistic device, not a device under continuous power. He admits his lack of understanding concerning its exact propulsion method.

Recently, evidence has surfaced from German sources concerning a large, previously unknown rocket2 which matches this description in many details and yields answers to gaps in Koch's description. This is called the V-101 or "European rocket" as opposed to the A-9/A-10, called the "America rocket".

The V-101 was the result of a design by Dr. Buedewald and Dr. Teichmann at the Skoda works in conjunction with the SS think-tank, the Kammler Group. This was a three-stage, solid fuel rocket with thrust of 100 tons and a range of 1800 kilometers. The rocket was designed to reach an altitude of 200 kilometers. Its payload was most likely larger than that of the V-2[3].

Because it was a solid fuel rocket it was considered superior for storage in rocket silos where complicated liquid fueling was awkward. Dr. Kammler did plan to use this rocket in a large underground launching facility whose exact location remains unknown to this day. Likewise, until Koch's diagram surfaced, no plans of the V-101 had seen the light of public scrutiny. Both the expectation cited by the German language source and Koch's description show that this rocket was far larger than the V-2 and exceeded it in performance.

On the other hand, German researchers who have seen this report are not of the opinion that this rocket was the V-101. They report that there was a V-3 under development at Nordhausen under the direction of the Peenemuende team[4]. This rocket was 26.14 meters long and had a weight of 102 tons.

The V-101, the same researchers report, was strictly a Kammler project run out of Skoda. It was a three-stage, solid fuel rocket, 30.26 meters long, 2.82 meters wide, and 146 tons in weight. It had three wings or vanes (Fluegel). Besides Kammler, Dr. Walter Reidel, Dr. Kurt Diebner and Albert Speer were said to be involved in its development[5]. It may have been this rocket which was the delivery device for the bomb mentioned in the "La Fussee Pilotte 'T'", mentioned in a previous chapter. In fact, it may have been this rocket whose test stand was photographed from the air by the Americans at Rudisleben along with a whole complex devoted to rocketry according to these same researchers.

Rudisleben is in or very near the Jonas Valley. Couple this with their connection of this work to the places mentioned: Skoda, the site of the Flottmannwerke in Breslau documented here and to the Owl Mountains[6] which was the site of the huge "Der Riese" underground complex and a new picture emerges of secret work within Nazi Germany.

It seems that Dr. Hans Kammler and his SS ran its or his own little country or sphere of influence within the Reich. He had his own atomic scientist, Diebner, his own rocket people, his own research and development scientists, his own production facilities, his own intelligence and security, and, of course, he ran all the underground facilities within Germany. His empire within an empire seems to run to the east of Germany's centerline, possibly from the Baltic facility of Stettin to Breslau, through Silesia (what is now Western Poland), into Moravia and Bohemia in what is now the Czech Republic and perhaps even into Austria. The very presence of this rocket under discussion here may point to the nature of the relationship between Kammler's world and the "outside" world of the remainder of Nazi Germany. This inner world may contain secrets that are far stranger than we can imagine, both in the technical sense and in the political sense.

Returning to the rocket, this rocket, whether it is the "V-3" or the "V-101" is the spiritual predecessor for the American Minuteman rocket series, a solid fuel intercontinental ballistic rocket housed in underground silos, throughout the Cold War. It this is true, and it is, then its spiritual godfather of the Minuteman and of those under-ground bases must be none other than Dr. Hans Kammler.

But, on the other hand, a German researcher just told me he thought the giant rocket was actually a giant torpedo, so the search for the truth of the Flottmann rocket is still the subject of some discussion.

SOURCES

1. C.S.D.I.C. (U.K.) S.I.R. 1632 20 Apr. 45, 5/5/45, *Consolidated report on information obtained from various PW, interrogation of whom did not warrant the issue of separate reports,* number: 015001 declassification number NND 750122, date illegible

2. Georg, Friedrich, 2003, *Hitlers Siegeswaffen Band 2: Star Wars 1947-Die Geheimgeschichte der Raketen und Flugkoerper des Dritten Reiches Teilband A: Von der V-1 zur A-9 – Unkonventionelle Kurz-und Mittelstreckenraketen,* page 186-187, Amun-Verlag, Schleusingen

3. ibid

4. Georg, Friedrich and Thomas Mehner, 2004, page 259, Atomziel New York Geheime Grossraketen-und Raumfahrtprojekte des Dritten Reiches, Jochen Kopp Verlag, Rottenburg

5. ibid, pages 259-260

6. ibid, page 261

34 | "Y" Communication Facilities

There have always been rumors that the Germans developed special ELF wave communications devices by which a U-boat drug a one-mile antenna so that world-wide communications were possible. A further rumor goes that this same system was used, not only for communication, but for recharging the U-boat's batteries via some long distance Tesla-type of technology. In this rumor the mile-long antenna receives electrical energy propagated directly through the earth by a mysterious generator somewhere in Germany. I have even heard it said by a knowledgeable person that Dr. W.O. Schumann was involved in this work. I cannot confirm nor deny these rumors, but I can relate the existence of another rumored secret communication system.

There are hints that the Germans developed a super-secret, high-tech, long distance communication system. This system was said to be new and totally independent of other German communication systems[1]. Thomas Mehner and Edgar Mayer as well as other researchers have investigated a whole series of huge underground installations in and around the Jonas Valley in Thuringia. One of these facilities, code-named "Burg" is generally thought to have, as at least one of its ultimate aims, the function of a huge communications switch-board connecting the Reich together. Keeping this in mind, Mr. Mehner obtained an American intelligence document describing such a communications network (PW Intelligence Bulletin No. 2/32, January 30, 1945, USAF Archives, Alabama, microfilm roll A 5370, Nr. 519.6501-2).

29. Fg-Werk: Telephone Devices
    (Fernsprechgeraet)   unknown   SPANDAU

30. Y-Werk: amplifying Devices
    (Verstaerkergeraet)   Dir Dr RABANNUS   Bldg 10

31. EL-Werk: Electrochemical plant
    (Elektrochemie)   Dir Dr ILLIG

C. Research Laboratory

32. Research Laboratory   Prof Dr HERTZ*
33.   (Forschungslabor)   Prof TREULEINBURG**

                                                              corner of
                                                              Rohrdamm &
            * a nephew of Heinrich HERTZ   Motardstr.,
           ** accoustic specialist   in cellar
                                                              of new bldg.

34. The main research work is at present concerned with the destruction of atoms (Zyklotron). Experiments are conducted in accordance with
principles formulated by U.S. scientists. Prof Dr HERTZ witnessed some of
these experiments in the States in 1939.

35. According to P/W SIEMENSSTADT was about 50% destroyed as of Oct 44,
practically every building suffering considerable damage, but all available
space is still being used for production. (Source for III MU 500 AZ)

IV. SIGNALS

    A. REIHER

36. This is the code name of a new 10 channel decimeter set developed
by SIEMENS & HALSKE and intended for use in RUSSIA, but as far as P/W knows
it has not yet been put into production.

37. Specifications as follows:

        Code Name   REIHER
        Purpose   Directional Link
        Capacity   Multi-Channel (10)
        Frequency   600-660 MC's
        Wave Length   45-50 cm.
        Range   5 relays, each having range of 60-100 km.
        Antenna   similar to DMG 36, but with fewer dipoles.
        Transmitter   2 LD 2's. normal triodes - push pull.
                         Magnetrons not used as they did not give the de-
                         sired stability.

                         SECRET

A page of the Secret report: Coil Research Laboratory Siemens Halske Berlin which we first saw in a previous chapter.
Here, please notice item number 30, Y-Werk: amplifying Devices and item IV. Signals, which describes the Reiher device.
Was this part of the Y-communications system?

This document is based on the interrogation of a German prisoner of war. In summary, he said that there were six facilities in Germany fitted with the "Y" communication system. They were built between 1943 and 1944. These were for communications purposes of a special kind and supported the Luftwaffe.

Using this document and a living informant, Mr. Mehner and Mr. Mayer add that the firm Siemens was the contractor involved in building this top-secret, stand-alone network. Such a network was closely associated with the work going on at the facility named "Burg".

The reason this is being mentioned is that another American document has come to light using the FOIA and search-words involving "Y" and "communications"[2]. This document also uses the information gathered from a prisoner of war. In this case the PW was a graduate engineer of the Technische Hochschule, Dresden where he majored in electrical engineering. In 1938 the subject came to work for Siemens & Halske where he did coil research. From September of 1942 to July of 1943 he worked with a Dr. Heinrich in an ultra-short wave laboratory. They developed a 10-channel decimeter set with the codename of "Reiher". Actually, the entire facility was employed in all aspects of the construction of this system from the ultra-short wave technology itself to the relays, amplifiers, transformers, condensers, transmitters and antennae. One of the production plants was specifically designated "Y Werk". The Reiher system itself was intended for use in Russia, which gives an idea of its intended range. Technical specifications of the system are given in the report.

Of huge interest is the fact that this system was separate from existing systems, secret, long-range, and destined for high-value, secret underground installations such as "Burg". We will return to Burg later, with other rumors.

SOURCES

1. Mayer, Edgar and Thomas Mehner, 2002, pages 71-73, Die Atombombe und das Dritte Reich Das Geheimnis des Driecks Arnstadt-Wechmar-Ohrdruf, Jochen Kopp Verlag, Rottenburg

2. JICA Med. Alhq. No R-1198/45, 6824 DIC/MIS/NOT-533, March 14, 1945, "Coil Research Laboratory Siemens Halske Berlin Oct.44."

35 | Experiments in Time

There are a lot of old rumors of work in time experimentation. During the early 1990s one or several individuals went around the country giving lectures at UFO conferences and writing books hyping the "Montauk Project". As time went by, the individuals involved continued to enlarge these rumors at every conference and with every book in a seeming game of one upmanship with each other. As this story evolved it was said to dovetail into the Philadelphia experiment. These were great stories but the problem was always a lack of proof.

There was a German connection to these time experiments, according to these stories. Some of the technology and even some of the funding are rumored to have come from Nazi Germany. German U-boats were said to surface off the New Jersey coast, secretly off-loading mysterious cargos. In our quest for suppressed German science, this is intriguing because most of what has actually proven to be true first originated as a story or rumor. This has happened over and over again as with German flying discs, Magnetic Wave, and beam weapons.

A great example is the story told to me by researcher Friedrich Georg. This came to him by an individual he knows and trusts and in-fact is related to him by marriage. As a young person, this man was a soldier in the German Wehrmacht like thousands of others at the time. And like so many others, at the close of the war, in April, 1945, this person found himself in American-run prison detention camp. There, he met a fellow prisoner, a SS soldier, with a strange tale to tell.

According to the SS man, Hitler had a hidden facility in the mountains of the Harz region. There, deep under a mountain Hitler had constructed a time machine. Unfortunately, this machine was no longer accessible from the surface.

Now, sixty years later, we do know that Hitler had a series of huge underground facilities in the Harz region at the Jonas Valley. Some of the exact functions of some of these facilities are still under debate today. The reason for this, in part, is that these tunnels were sealed with explosives before the American 3rd Amry under Patton could secrue them. Later they fell into the Soviet Zone but nobody ever bothered to investigate what went on down there.

As with most rumors stemming from the 3rd Reich, there was usually a kernel of truth to it. There have always been real scientists as well as tinkerers who experiment in time, then as now, so the very fact that some physics laboratory experiments were done in those days by the Germans should be of surprise to nobody. Now, however, some new developments bring these rumors all back into focus.

The first is the work of Igor Witkowski. Witkowski is a Polish researcher who is deeply into finding the truth behind German flying discs. Mr. Witkowski has made a remarkable discovery. He has found a truly unique site or laboratory or test site in Poland, then Lower Silesia, which was a part of Germany during and before the war. It is located at the Wenceslas Mine part of the larger German facility called "Der Riese", The Giant.

Witkowski was visited and interviewed by aerospace writer Nick Cook and the amazing story is featured in Nick Cook's book, The Hunt For Zero Point One Man's Journey to Discover The Biggest Secret Since The Invention Of The Atom Bomb. (This text appears in English, so those interested in more detail may consult the source.) Witkowski had the opportunity to view secret Soviet NKVD files which put him on to the story. The German code name given in the NKVD report was "Laternentrager" and "Chronos". Laternentrager is lantern-carrier in English. The word Chronos is almost self-explanatory.

Witkowski's research shows that this was a top-secret SS experiment originating from a facility in Leubus, northwest of Breslau (now Wroclaw), but moved to Fuerstenstein (Ksiaz) 34 km to the south in late 1944 because of the Soviet advance. Finally, it was moved south again to Ludwigsdorf (Ludwwikowice) in the Owl Mountains very near Der Riese[1]. Two physical structures are associated with this project. One structure is now gone and one still in existence.

Gone but known to Witkowski through his peek into Soviet intelligence files is "Die Glocke", the Bell. The Bell was just that: a hard, metallic bell-shaped object. Within the bell there were situated two cylinders that were rapidly spun in opposite directions. Each cylinder was filled with a mercury-like substance, code named "Xerum 525"[2]. Other substances included in Xerum 525 were thorium and beryllium peroxides. The substance had a violet color. Here we have a liquid compound of mercury, violet in color, housed at a German nuclear research facility. Does this ring a "bell" with anybody? Mercury has no fluid compounds according to conventional wisdom. So if this liquid is as Witkowski says that it is, then the conclusion is inescapable. It is red mercury.

Still present is a structure that stands above ground and associated with these experiments. This is a circle of Stonehenge-like columns, joined the in the same manner as Stonehenge, at the top. The structure is about ten meters tall and about 30 meters in diameter. Strangely, high-strength steel hooks are set into the tops of the columns[3].

Witkowski's research shows that the Bell was always operated underground. This leaves us to wonder at the purpose of the Stonehenge-like structure with the hooks at its top.

Speculation about the purpose of this experimentation is divided. Some think the Bell was a field propulsion engine destined for some exotic aircraft. Some think the whole apparatus, Bell and stone circle, concerned itself with experiments in time. An alternative is that it was both.

This is because Nick Cook links Russian experiments with spinning superconductors to the spinning, liquid, mercury-like compound contained in the Bell[5]. Could red mercury be a superconductor? Could this be its real secret? A superconductor would allow the generation of monstrous magnetic fields and perhaps other types of energy. Cook calls this other type of energy a "torsion field" and says it bends the four dimensions as well as bending time[6].

What makes this account credible? We have physical evidence that something was going on. We have the mysterious Stonehenge-like structure. We have Igor Witkowski whose peek into the NKVD secret files led him to this unexplained place.

This is where I stood in the Winter of 2002 when a chance conversation occurred with a friend of mine. His name is Greg Rowe and I have corresponded with him for several years as the result of a chance contact. Greg is a trained engineer as was his father. Once Greg told me that his father had worked for NASA at the Huntsville, Alabama facility. Knowing that some German Paperclip scientists worked there, I asked Greg if any of these worked with his father.

Greg replied with a list of German scientists with whom his father had worked and a few words about each one of them. One of these, Otto Cerny, seemed particularly interesting from Greg's description so I pressed him for more information. What follows is a compilation of several e-mails on the subject of Otto Cerny.

Cerny was Greg's father's boss. Greg knew the whole family and went to school with Cerny's son whom Greg called by name. Greg also referred to Cerny's wife by her first name and gave other small details of their family life. When he was somewhere between 12 and 14 years old, Greg and his family were invited to dinner at the Cerny's house. This would have been between the years 1960-62. Greg sat and listened as the older men talked.

Otto Cerny was an engineer and physicist. He had worked at Peenemuende on a variety of projects. That was why he was in the United States, to work on rockets, and why he was a Paperclip scientist to begin with. But it is his work prior to coming to Peenemuende, which was the subject of discussion that night. Cerny said that he had worked near Breslau in the early years of the war. It was there that he met his wife who worked in Breslau at a hospital where she was employed doing physical rehabilitation work.

Cerny continued describing this work that night in Alabama, dismissing it at first as "weird experiments on the nature of time". Greg's father must have picked up on this comment because the two men quickly became involved, according to Greg, in a deep discussion concerning the nature of time. Greg told me that it seemed to him now, that, at all times Cerny was a little vague in his statements, choosing his words and being careful of what he said, almost as if he were under some sort of hidden duress.

Greg listened to the two men attentively but did not enter into the conversation himself. At that time and place in polite adult company, as Greg explains, a child did not speak unless spoken to. In considering what follows and what was relayed to me, it should be remembered that Greg had not yet read Nick Cook's book or ever heard of the work of Igor Witkowski.

Greg remembers that Cerny drew a circle of stones, which Greg said was "like a Greek Temple", with a ring around the top". Then Greg added a feature not mentioned by Cook or Witkowski, "and some sort of ring inside of that". This second ring was like a hoop of metal from which something hung—like an oscilloscope or a TV screen. Greg went on to mention the atomic symbol as a means of description. The atomic symbol has a nucleus around which orbit electrons. The electrons have two orbits, one within the other and are moving independently from each other. From this description it follows that this structure contained two movable and independently adjustable fixtures from which something hung, perhaps as with a gyroscope.

Cerny said that it was possible to "go back and witness things". With this statement a Greg's father asked why it was not possible to go forward if it were possible to go backward. Evidently there was some discussion between the two men on this point. Cerny responded that it simply did not work that way.

Greg reports that, after a pause, Cerny cut more pastry and poured another cup of coffee, then changed the subject to a jet engine, which had been built at Peenemuende, for an unmanned rocket other than the V-1.

Naturally, I was dumbfounded by the turn of events. This was mid-January, 2002. Greg had not read my book on German saucers or Cook's book containing discussion of Igor Witkowski. As a matter of fact, Greg had never heard of Igor Witkowski. I told him of these references and sent him a copy of my book. I quickly re-read Cook's passages on the subject. Then something else occurred to me. I quickly found my partial list of Paperclip scientists and looked for Otto Cerny's name. Sure enough, it was there. I wasted no time in ordering the file from the National Archives under the F.O.I.A. I had no idea of what to expect. Greg had provided so much detail into their personal lives that I was a little apprehensive that my friend might have been wrong about some of this. Would the F.O.I.A. file confirm what Greg overheard? Fortunately, Paperclip files are packed with what we would call today "personal information".

Ninety days pass and the file arrives[4]. In it are the names and birth dates of Otto Cerny and all his family. The name Greg gave for Mrs. Cerny was correct. The name Greg gave for his son was correct and his year of birth puts him in Greg's grade in school. They had lived in Huntsville where Otto was employed by NASA. There was no doubt that this was the person Greg had described and his description matched very well.

The file included a time-line and a statement of Cerny's work at Peenemuende. Many "deletion" pages were inserted into the file telling the reader that portions of the file were being withheld for security reasons. But the censor was somewhat uneven. It seemed that sensitive information was pulled out at various times by various censors. Some of these censors only read English, it seemed, because the English translation of Cerny's work history consisted of nine pages while the original had consisted of twenty-five pages in German language. Fortunately, twenty-four pages in the original German edition remained. It included a description of a previously unknown weapon.

The weapon in question was a special edition of the Henschel HS-292. The regular HS-292 was a air-to-ship guided missile which was fired from a carrier aircraft, such as a two-engine He-111 bomber, and steered towards the target ship though the a thin wire linkage and an operator using a joy stick. The new weapon was a high-altitude air-to-air weapon that was again launched from an aircraft and guided via wire and joystick but its target was not a ship beneath it but an enemy bomber formation above it.

Was this the weapon Greg had commented upon?

Unfortunately, no mention is made of experiments in time in the Paperclip file. This could hardly be expected, however. The file had been gone over many times and items pulled for security reasons. But the time-line was very complete and in it Cerny accounts for his every move since college. I went directly to the war years.

From May, 1939 to September, 1939 (September, 1939 was the date Germany invaded Poland, beginning the Second World War), Cerny attended a flight school at Braunschweig, the Deutsche Versuch-sanstalt fuer Luftfahrt (German Flight Research Institution). This is a heavyweight school. Cerny received an A2 Degree (Acrobatics).

From September, 1939 to April, 1940, Cerny worked at three Air Force test bases including one at Rechlin. Rechlin is next door to Peenemuende and was a test site for exotic aircraft. This would put him in the proper region at the proper time. His next assignment, May, 1940 to April, 1945 was at Peenemuende, immediately to the west.

NND 843012
BX 25
RG-330

Tab 26
1/1c

ACCESS RESTRICTED

The item identified below has been withdrawn from this file:

File Designation _Cerny, OTTO Franz_

MSG TT 9334

Date _18 Feb, 1957_

From _—_

To _—_

In the review of this file this item was removed because access to it is
restricted. Restrictions on records in the National Archives are stated
in general and specific record group restriction statements which are
available for examination. The item identified above has been withdrawn
because it contains:

WITHDRAWAL NOTICE

[X] Security-Classified Information

[ ] Otherwise Restricted Information

OSD
Authority

5 Sept 84
Date

, LDS

GENERAL SERVICES ADMINISTRATION

GSA FORM **7117** (2-72)

GPO : 1973 O - 503-659

This is a government deletion slip. About 20 or so of these were inserted into the Cerny file and appropriate material
withdrawn. Additionally, one page of his twenty-five page employment time-line in German is missing. The English
translation omits this altogether and is only nine pages long. This is impressive redaction for a mere mechanical engineer
with a master's degree.

A-1769

the form of reports presenting most recent theories and concepts in solution
of existing problems.

5. Contacts agencies and contractors involved in the research of propulsion
systems of missiles to exchange information, obtain additional views, coordi-
nating efforts, work, etc. Keeps abreast of latest developments in specialized
field, by reviewing reports, pertinent literature, scientific publications,
etc. Attends conferences and meetings concerning projects and programs to
utilize the latest and best knowledge for application to the work of the organizational segment.

    Performs other duties as assigned.

NOTE: I N T E R D I S C I P L I N A R Y position with duties and qualifications
requirements characteristic to a comparable degree of positions allocable to the
following additional series and classes; Power Plant Engineering, GS-834-0;
Physics (General) GS-1310-0; Mechanical Engineering, GS-830-0, and Chemical
Engineering Series, GS-893-0.

Top: The "Greek temple" (from Nick Cook) described to me by Greg Rowe, recounting the conversation between his father
and Otto Cerny. Greg witnessed and overheard this conversation as a child. Suspended from the top was some sort of
concave mirror in which "images from the past" were seen during operation of the mechanism.

Bottom: The end of Cerny's Paperclip resume in which he lists "Power Plant Engineering" as interdisciplinary duties and
qualifications. Is this what Cerny did for Projekt Chronos?

Taken as a whole, Greg's account of what Cerny said and what Cerny's Paperclip file show are remarkably consistent. I have to believe that the rendition concerning Cerny's work on an unknown jet engine for use in an advanced missile is factual and possibly be the new type of HS-292 or even the recently described V-4, the replacement for the V-1[7].

I also must believe that Cerny was telling the truth when he said that prior to coming to Peenemuende he worked on a German program involving time experimentation. What he disclosed fits into the evidence provided by Mr. Witkowski and provides some new data. The details of this program remain yet to be discovered as does its place in the German war effort.

Based upon my new respect for the possibility of German time experimentation, I contacted Thomas Mehner, the researcher and publisher famous for his work at the Jonas Valley site in Germany. I asked Mr. Mehner about references to German time experimentation one finds here and there and if he knew of any such evidence coming from the Jonas Valley. Mr. Mehner replied via e-mail on 7/9/03 that there was no hard evidence for German time experimentation, but there were hints. He said that recent opinion among researchers there (so there must be ongoing discussion of the possibility) is that time machine experiments would originate at least 200 meters below the surface. There has been no attempt to describe the technology involved at Jonastal and no attempt yet to dig it up. This area is still, today, a German military base.

The most exciting statement made by Mr. Mehner was that recently, researchers there are of the opinion that the Germans experimented with what he described as "interdimensional trips". If this is ever proven, it would be just as explosive as successful time experimentation itself.

There is another story that comes to mind that now rests squarely in the realm of science fiction. It appeared in a 1997 edition of the magazine "Wissenschaft ohne Grenzen" which was responsible for placing the concept of the lost underground facilities at Jonastal in the public eye.

This tale involves the disappearance of up to 3,000 people. These people included SS personnel and scientists. Just prior to capture by Patton's 3rd Army, these people including their women and children, all of "pure Aryan origins", disappeared DOWN into an underground facility in the Jonas Valley called "Burg". After the people were inside the entrance was then sealed with explosives[8]. It should be noted that this is not referred to as a mass suicide. We are left with the impression that these people wished to escape the 3rd Reich. So many other wild rumors of the past have been based upon fact. Could this escape have been into another time or another dimension? Could it really be true?

SOURCES

1. Cook, Nick, 2001, *The Hunt For Zero Point One Man's Journey To Discover The Biggest Secret Since The Invention Of The Atom Bomb*, page 188, Century, London

2. ibid, page 192

3. ibid, page 197

4. Project Paperclip "Foreign Scientist Case Files, 1945-1958 (Record Group 330, Box 44, file of Otto F. Cerny

5. Cook, Nick, 2001, page 194

6. ibid, page 228

7. Georg, Friedrich, 2003, *Hitlers Siegeswaffen Band 2: Star Wars 1947 Teil A: Von der V-1 bis zur A-9: unkonventionelle Kurz – und Mittelstreckenwaffen*, pages 132, 204-207, Amun-Verlag, Schleusingen

8. Georg, Friedrich, 2000, *Hitlers Siegeswaffen Band 1: Luftwaffe und Marine Geheime Nuklearwaffen Des Dritten Reiches Und Ihre Traegersysteme*, page 126, Amun-Verlag, Schleusingen

36 | Dr. Ronald Richter

If we remember Dr. Richter today at all, it is not for his stunning achievements in physics, but for a press fiasco involving the Argentine leader Juan Peron in the 1950s. At this time, Richter was employed by Peron to do nuclear research and evidently had some promising results. Peron jumped ahead of the research and prematurely announced that Argentina had bypassed fission power and had succeeded in producing fusion power.

Around the world "experts" were enlisted to condemn Richter's work. It seems the US government was on particularly high alert and wanted this development contained. Peron could not deliver fusion on the spot and Richter suddenly fell out of favor. As a matter of fact, Dr. Richter was jailed by Peron, thus effectively ending the affair and discrediting Richter. After Peron was ousted and Richter released, the incoming political party considered Richter a Peron favorite and as such he could never regain the funds, laboratory or momentum to further his work. Richter ended up in the mid to late 1950s looking for a job. Eventually, he fell off the world scene.

The late Dr. Eugene F. Mallove has written of the affair:

> "Magnetic confinement fusion had a very strange beginning. Argentine dictator Juan Peron announced on March 24, 1951, that his country had mastered controlled fusion, bypassing completely the development of fission power that was then

in vogue in various nations. Peron, a Germaophile,
had set up an island laboratory for a certain obscure
German scientist, Ronald Richter, who supposedly had
brought the secret fusion work to fruition, or so head-
lines in the United States had allowed. The press was
much less circumspect in those days about amazing
scientific claims"[1].

Now, it may seem like everything which is to follow refutes the
above paragraph, so it is necessary to point out that it was Dr. Eugene
Mallove who originally directed me in Richter's direction when I
inquired of him about alleged German scientists working for Peron
concerning nuclear power. What has changed my mind about his
matter is that the United States government, through various agencies,
compiled an intelligence file on Dr. Richter, which was shocking. This
file was obtained using the Freedom of Information Act. In fact, it was
a Paperclip file, even though Richter never came to the USA to work
as a scientist. Equally shocking was the tone of the Paperclip file itself.

Normally, a Paperclip file contains biographical and educational
information about the particular scientist. It usually contains
a description of his specialty as well as where he worked and who
he worked for in Germany. There is a discussion of his alleged
political leanings, which are always considered satisfactory. Then
there is a background check, again politically motivated. Then,
there are immigration details and perhaps which companies or
government agencies which are interested in employing this individual. It is then up to the researcher to follow up these leads for additional information.

Sometimes, there is a description of actual work in Germany and
actual hardware that was created, but this is rare. Also rare is any
discussion about applications of his specialty in the United States or
any proposed future research in the United States. Dr. Richter's file
is the big exception to all of this.

But even before I had obtained Dr. Richter's Paperclip file from the
US National Archives and Record Administration via the Freedom Of
Information Act, Dr. Mallove's original letter naming him struck me
like my head was a bell. This is because Dr. Ronald Richter was not an
"obscure German scientist" to me. His name was a name I had run into
repeatedly in investigating German scientific research. In fact, the

Austrian physicist, Dr. Friedrich Lachtner, in a letter, published in my last book, names Dr. Richter.

From the Paperclip file, it is evident that the US government and its scientists given the job of investigating Dr. Richter were torn between two opposing poles. There were those who considered Dr. Richter a fraud. There were those who openly admitted that they did not have the expertise to fully evaluated Dr. Richter and clearly wanted to take themselves out of the game of doing so. And there were those who recognized, even in 1957, that Dr. Richter "was working in 1970", an understatement which can only now be fully appreciated.

We should start our investigation of Dr. Richter with his own chronological biography. There are two or three accounts of his personal and professional history in his Paperclip file. Perhaps the best is the Air Intelligence Information Report. Dr. Richter and so states provided the information in this report.

Richter was born February 21, 1909 in Eger, Bohemia. Bohemia was then Austria but was included in Czechoslovakia as it was formed. Dr. Richter entered the German University at Prague in 1928 to study physics, chemistry and geophysics. He graduated on March 2, 1935 with a Doctor of Natural Sciences degree.

Richter's parents were involved in directing a coalmine. It was in this same industry where Dr. Richter was to make his entrance into the world of science and industry. In 1935 Dr. Richter ran a private research laboratory near Falkenau A.D. Eger, "sponsored by industrial circles". In this first venture the foundation was laid for all that followed in Richter's work. In the words of the Air Intelligence Report:

> "Research on the activation of catalysts, catalyst –
> controlled high-pressure coal hydrogenation and coal
> cracking processes, development of an image-converter-
> like activity-contract-microscope, based on scanning of
> hydrogen or deuterium absorbing border surfaces by
> protons, deuterons, or electrons: for the first time, it
> became possible to see and to photograph activity
> contrasts which cannot be made visible by light nor by
> electron microscopes. Activation of catalysts take place
> under continuously activity-controlled conditions.

Research work and design studies on electric arc
furnaces systems, development of new types of arc
plasma analyzing instruments and methods. In 1936,
discovery of a plasma shock wave generating process,
conception of a completely new type of industrial arc
reactor system, based rather on plasma shock wave
reactivity than on heat transfer. Development of a
basis of operation for testing plasma shock wave
conditions by means of plasma-collision-induced
nuclear reactions."

Plasma happens when a gas is heated to the point where its
electrical structure is somewhat altered. Normally, each element will
have a specific electrical charge, either positive or negative. When
a gas is heated to the point that plasma is created, that gas is altered
in such a way that the numbers of positively and negatively charged
particles are the same. Richter did this using shock wave technology.

In the years 1937 to 1938, Richter was in charge of a research
laboratory connected to the Berlin-Suhler-Waffen und Fahrzeugwerke
at the Gustloff-Werke in Suhl, Thuringia. Suhl and the Gustloff-Werke
are in the Jonas Valley which was to become a center of several
Nordhausen-sized underground facilities, all doing secret work
on weapons and science. In another part of Richter's statement
he lists the physical addresses in which he lived. At this time an
address of Muehltorstr. 11, Suhl is listed as Richter's home address.
German researcher and publisher Thomas Mehner actually went
to this address when he received a copy of the Paperclip file.
Mr. Mehner reports that the house is now gone but the street still
exists. Suhl is Mr. Mehner's home area.

In Suhl, Richter worked on a hydrogen storage system as well as
continuing his shock wave research. During this period he complains
about the lack of measuring equipment that could withstand such
high temperature stress.

With the outbreak of World War Two in 1939, Dr. Richter joined the
research staff of the Junkers Aircraft and Motor Works at Dessau,
Germany. The Dessau facility for Junkers could be compared to the
Skunk Works for Lochkeed. Dessau was the facility for cutting edge
research. Dr. Richter worked on vibrational problems associated with
supersonic aircraft at Dessau. He found that the instruments needed

to do this could be used to benefit his shock wave research, which he obviously had not put aside.

During this time Richter was invited by Dr. Busemann and Prof. Dirksen to join them at the Aircraft Research Facility, Hermann Goering near Braunschweig. Unfortunately, Richter was a Czech citizen and the Gestapo took a dim view of his presence at Braunschweig. They took away Richter's passport and essentially put him under day-to-day scrutiny. This situation simply was not working out well.

By 1942-1943 Richter found himself at the Berlin-Lichterfelde-Ost facility of Baron Manfred von Ardenne. Von Ardenne ran one of the major German nuclear research groups. This group, strangely enough, was the German Post Office. The German Post Office was responsible for communications and was loaded with technical expertise. At this time Dr. Richter met Prof. Abraham Essau, then in charge of all nuclear energy research in Germany. Later in 1943 Richter joined the research staff at the German Research Facility for Air Transport at Berlin-Adershof. This happened after a falling out occurred between Richter and Baron von Ardenne. At Berlin-Adershof, Richter developed turbulence detectors for use in wind tunnels and again furthering his own shock wave research goals.

In 1944 and 1945 Dr. Richter was sponsored by the Speer Ministry for Armament and Munitions as well as by the Reichs Research Council who directed all important war-related research within the Reich. He worked on light-weight battery research at the AEG (General Electricity Company) in Berlin as well as becoming the scientific and technical advisor to Ruhrchemie Aktiengesellschaft at Muehlheim. In addition to his duties in these positions, Richter found time to further his own work in arc plasma experiments using the large test installations available at the AAEG transformer factories at Berlin-Oberschoeneweide.

After the war Richter visited France, England and Holland looking for work. In London, Richter met and became somewhat acquainted with Prof. Kurt Tank, the famous Focke-Wulf aircraft designer, who showed particular interest in the development of nuclear powered propulsion for aircraft. In 1947 Tank went to Argentina.

Dr. Richter went to work for the French Petroleum Institute in Paris but this was not a permanent position. In May 1948, Professor Tank contacted Dr. Richter. He was asked to join with Professor Tank on work in Argentina. The Argentine government also extended an invitation. Richter was being asked to do work involving nuclear reactor development.

By August 1948, Dr. Richter was talking with Juan Peron about the development of nuclear power in Argentina. Argentina had no supply of uranium nor was Dr. Richter interested in developing a fission reactor for Peron. As stated in the Air Intelligence Information Report:

> "…I was not interested in the development of nuclear
> fission reactor systems but anxious to develop a control-
> lable thermonuclear reactor system; there was a certain
> probability that the chain-reacting schemes, developed in
> the fall of 1942, ignited by a shock-wave-controlled arc
> plasma might turn out to become a controllable reactor
> system."

"Thermonuclear" means fusion. "Chain-reacting scheme developed in the fall of 1942" mean just that. Dr. Richter had managed to initiate a chain reaction using fusion in 1942. What is the mystery here? Dr. Richter had succeeded in producing fusion power in 1942. What he needed to do was fine-tune the procedure to achieve better control of it.

Dr. Richter states that in October of 1948, he signed a five-year contract with the Argentine authorities and became head of a thermo-nuclear reactor project. June, 1949 saw start of construction of a laboratory and reactor on Huemul Island. Huemul Island was situated in a mountain lake and virtually isolated from the outside world. The location of this facility was within an area habituated or perhaps even controlled by Germans of the Nazi era. It has even been called "Colonia Dignidad" by some, referring to the fact that perhaps here and no other place on the planet could a former German soldier walk about in uniform without condemnation.

Dr. Richter claimed success in his work on Heumul Island. Again, from the Air Intelligence Information Report:

> "On 16 February 1951 an exponential reactor system was
> ready for test. In the first test, the injection of lithium-6-
> enriched lithium into a shock-wave-controlled proton
> hydrogen plasma, for a short interval, produced series of
> primary and secondary reactions, the helium-3 helium 3
> reaction giving proof for the existence of self-reproducing

reaction chains. In a second test, by jetting lithium-6-
enriched lithium into avalanche of neutron-reproducing
reaction chains were monitored. In both tests, the self-
reproducing-reaction chains were analyzed by means of
excitation-energy discriminating ultraviolet sensitive
proportional counter tubes. At that time, a large-scale
reactor system was under construction in which a self-
sustaining chain reaction should have been realized;
however, this reactor system has never been completed,
probably for reasons for sabotage."

This statement is very important. Dr. Richter is saying that he
succeeded in sustaining a controlled fusion reaction using his shock
wave technology as the containment system.

"Against my strict advice, President Peron announced these results
with a great display of propaganda", says Richter. We must remember
that although Argentina declared war on Nazi Germany in the final
days of the war, being pressured to do so by the United States,
Argentina had basically backed the wrong side in World War Two.
Peron had marched alongside Hitler in Paris. So, in the 1950s,
Argentina and Peron were in a state of somewhat disrepute. Peron
saw this development as an instantaneous step to recognition and
possibly greatness for himself and Argentina. No great power, not
the United States, not the Soviet Union nor Great Britain or France
had a fusion reactor. This was a big propaganda coupe for Peron.

Richter returned to reactor tests. On October, 26, 1951 a third test
was performed. Richter injected boron into an avalanche of neutron-
reproducing reaction chains, which had resulted from the injection of
lithium into the shock wave, controlled, neutron producing deuterium
plasma. The result was that the boron kept the reaction going. The Air
Intelligence Information Report goes on:

"Later on, the plasma-collision-induced isomerization of
indium – and rhodium nuckei has been proven by
monitoring the radioactive emission of gamma quan-
tums; signal discrimination had to be provided against
the shock-wave-induced bremsstrahlung background."

In December, 1951 Richter, according to the report, advised Peron
to accelerate development of a commercial reactor by joining with a
highly industrialized county "like the United States". Richter was

attempting to move away from a political and propaganda usage of his work. Peron was interested in doing just this, and, according to the report, authorized preliminary industrial negotiations.

By March, 1952 the political winds had changed. Richter claims his work was being physically sabotaged on Huemul Island. On September 2, 1952, a commission arrived on the island to investigate progress there. Richter believed its real purpose was to paralyze work there for political reasons having to do with Argentine internal politics. By November, 1952, Richter found himself expelled from his own project and work on it stopped. He was not able to contact Juan Peron.

Dr. Richter now lived day to day in a sort of limbo. He was unable to find work with a private firm for some reason. Richter believed they feared government reprisal. He was forced to sell possessions to put food on the table for his family. Richter was under constant surveillance. In spite of these difficulties, Richter continued with non-nuclear aspects of his research:

> "I immediately changed over to intensive design work on shock-wave-controlled industrial chemical arc reactor systems and arc melting furnace systems, which has no bearings on nuclear research at all and, so I hoped, might get me a new position.
>
> At the same time I was developing an improved shock-wave-control ram jet system (a thermonuclear exponen-tial reactor system has so much in common with and looks like a test installation for rocket and jet engines, and all new types of plasma-analyzing and plasma-controlling instruments and processes turn our to be useful in this development)."

In September of 1954 governmental deputies in internal hearings concerning Dr. Richter's alleged negative test results denounced Richter. Dr. Richter responded with a series of telegrams to the President of the Chamber and to President Peron protesting what he saw as unjust accusations made against him. Evidently the President of the Chamber was angered by Richter's telegrams because he was jailed for five days in the congress building without hearings or any sort of trial.

Richter's position did not change with a change in government. The new Lonardi government wanted nothing to do with Richter whom they regarded as a Peron supporter. Richter's state of limbo continued until the date of the Air Intelligence Report, February 18, 1956.

It is quite evident from the tone of Richter's correspondence with the Americans, as evidenced by the full disclosure that he makes, that he was interested in employment in the United States.

Another point, which surfaces again and again in Richter's biography, is his inability to "get along" with co-workers or administrators.

Three other observations should be made about Richter's work, even before we fully review it. First, Dr. Richter was a well know physicist within Nazi Germany and had worked on a wider variety of secret scientific wartime projects within the Reich than most other scientists. Second, Dr. Richter did not follow the standard game plan of physicists of his day. There is no talk of Einstein, except references to a Unified Field Theory, which certainly is not Einstein's domain alone). There is no work in sub-atomic physics, particle accelerators, cyclotrons, neutron generators, etc. Dr. Richter followed completely different path. Third, this path involves shock-wave technology. Everything that Dr. Richter did from day one in 1935 at Falkenau a.d. Eger derived from shock-wave applications. This includes containment of his fusion reaction, which is not the containment via a magnetic field which is and was the vogue in "hot fusion" up until the present.

In this introduction to Dr. Richter, the reader was introduced to Dr. Richter and his work through his biography. One reason for doing this was so that his work will not come as such a "shock" to you, pardon the pun. Dr. Richter advanced science and technology in five areas:

1. The ultra-sound fusion furnace.

2. His ramjet ideas.

3. A sustainable fusion reaction.

4. Direct thermonuclear to electric conversion of energy through plasma induction.

5. Zero Point Energy

Again, quite frankly, the author is more than a little concerned that the reader will simply think these claims and this report is nothing more than a bazaar a fabrication. For this reason, I have decided to use Richter's actual words from his Paperclip file, the file belonging to the United States government, itself. Those interested in verification can obtain a copy of the Paperclip file from the National Archives using the designation given in Sources, below. The topics listed above involve a separate sub-file and statement by Dr. Richter in the overall Paperclip file. Two of these preliminary reports are missing, naturally the latter two, numbers 4 and 5. The reports are out of sequence in internal numbering and so it can safely be surmised that reports do exist which were not included in the National Archive's F.O.I.A. response. These are described, somewhat, in another part of the Paperclip file, however, and that portion will be reproduced also. These preliminary reports will be re-typed here for clarity. Nobody can possibly explain these ideas better than the inventor. A sample page of the original text will be shown. It should be understood that his is a word for word account as if it were enclosed by quotation marks.

★   ★   ★   ★   ★   ★

Air Intelligence Information Report IR-79-56

"IMPROVED RAM JET ENGINE"

SUMMARY
Report contains the preliminary report of Dr. Ronald Richter on his work to develop a ram jet engine of radical design by substitution shock waves for the valves of an intermittent ram jet system.

APPROVED:
George R. Herrman
Colonel USAF
Air Attache

1. The following prepared statement was obtained from Dr. Ronald Richter (IR-76-56) and represents his preliminary report on his work to develop a new type of ram jet engine.

IMPROVED RAM JET SYSTEM
  The development of an aircraft with a thrust greater

than its weight will be the next major step in the evolution of high-speed flight. It is the author's conviction that this goal can be achieved by developing a new type of jet propulsion system, based on the continuously controlled conversion of rocket and ram jet operations within the same propulsion system.

INTRODUCTION

A turbo jet system has many drawbacks. The turbine wheel is in the path of the hot expanding gases. The velocity of the jet increases as the square root of the temperature within the combustion chambers. Besides the constant blast of very hot gases from the combustion chambers with no relief, the high-speed rotation of the turbine subjects the blades to very considerable centrifugal forces, which will pull them out of shape as soon as the metal weakens from the heat attack. The turbine is also subjected to stresses from the aerodynamic effects of the hot gasses which can cause severe vibration and buffeting, and may eventually result in the turbines fluttering to limits at their full rated speed, so that overspeed or overtemperatures, even for a short duration, may be very detrimental. Accordingly, temperature and speed must be controlled with narrow limits and with a high degree of accuracy and stability of the full range of possible operating conditions such as change in altitude, air temperature, air speed, a.s.o., to avoid excess speed or temperature for even a short period. Since the allowable creep stresses are a function of temperature while the actual stresses are a function of speed, both speed and temperature must operate the power controls. At last, the turbo jet system is limited by the ultimate speed of the mechanical revolutions. Therefore, the main problem of the development of turbo jet systems has been and still is to find suitable materials of construction for the turbine to withstand the very high temperatures and stresses.

The ram jet system is based on the straightforward propulsion by thermal energy alone and its propulsive power is not subject to any limitations from moving parts. Whilst in the case of the intermittent ram jet system the air inlet is still controlled by some valves, a steady flow ram jet system has not even a valve as

a moving part, but is a simple tunnel in which fuel is
burned continuously.

Unfortunately, the thermo-propulsive duct cannot operate at a speed under 200 m.p.h. But at this speed, the
ram jet system becomes self-operative, and the faster the
forward speed of the aircraft, the greater the compression of air entering the duct and the greater is thrust
and efficiency. Since speed automatically breeds more
speed, the propulsive power of a ram jet system rises
quite extraordinarily with speed, thus leading to power
capacities which probably never can be obtained by single
turbo jet units. Moreover, the maximum speed to be
attained from the thermo-propulsive duct will be limited
only by the resistance of the airframe structure to the
heat generated by skin friction. Due to the lack of
moving parts in the high temperature zone of a ram jet
system, ceramics and cerments can be used as materials
of construction which would otherwise fail to withstand
the combine thermal and mechanical attacks taking place
in the moving parts of the turbo jet system.

Besides all the promising aspects of a ram jet system, –
no moving parts within the high temperature zone, no
centrifugal stresses, no limitation by the ultimate speed
of mechanical revolutions, no defects caused by disintegrating moving parts, no losses in turbine and compressor,
the theoretically unlimited increase of propulsive power
with increasing speed, less control problems, highest
climbing speeds, altitude limitation probably in the
region of about 100,000 ft, and more (in the case of
nuclear powered propulsion), reduced construction costs
and easier construction, a.s.o., – there exists a limiting factor which does not allow to take full advantage
of such a propulsion system yet; the necessity for some
initial means of acceleration, such as rockets or turbo
jet systems, until sufficient speed is obtained for the ram
jet system to take over its natural thermo-propulsion. For
the same reason, it becomes necessary to prevent too low
a velocity of the ram jet system with a consequent loss of
flight. Owing to the critical velocity by which a ram jet
system becomes self-operative, take-off and landing operations are complex.

The reheat device supplies the principle of the ram jet

system to the turbo jet system, giving short bursts of extra speed in an emergency as well as at take-off.

A rocket is just another branch of jet propulsion and becomes a ram jet system when the mass (and the oxygen, in case of chemical combustion processes) to be discharged is taken from the outside atmosphere instead of being stored in the aircraft fuselage itself.

A jet propulsion system has to be developed which is operating as a rocket system at take-off and becomes self-operative as an intermittent and steady flow ram jet system gradually with increasing speed of flight. The continuously controlled conversion of one propulsion phase into the other can be achieved by the control of the combustion process itself.

For many years, the author was experimenting with a new shock wave generating process, the shock waves being generated by an electro-magnetically controlled extremely hot arc plasma zone. By the same process technique, shock waves can also be generated in combustion chambers and in gaseous zones heated by the impact of nuclear energy.

The analysis of the injection of gaseous jets into a superposition of powerful shock waves revealed interesting data in regard to the penetrability of shock-wave-controlled zones. In the course of these investigations, it became obvious, for instance, that the valves of an intermittent ram jet system can be substituted by shock waves, thus providing for the continuously controlled conversion of an intermittent into a steady flow ram jet system.

In the explosion phase, an intermittent ram jet system is operating as a rocket system. The explosion closes the entrance valve and the hot expanding gases escape at high speed through the exhaust. In the same way, a shock-wave-controlled intermittent ram jet system, in the very instant of the shock-wave-generation explosion, behaves like a rocket system. On that basis, it should become possible to start an intermittent shock-wave-controlled ram jet system without the help of acceleration-assisting means by a series of shock-wave-generating explosions.

The operation of a shock-wave-controlled ram jet system can be considerably improved by dividing the combustion reactor system into two partial reactor units;

the one reactor unit near the exhaust will be operating
as a rocket system as long as the other, shock-wave-
controlled reactor, unit will substitute a more or less
impenetrable valve. As soon as the shock-wave-controlled
ram jet system becomes self-operative as a steady flow ram
jet system, both partial reactor units are operating
without shock waves.

In the case of chemical combustion processes, the rocket
phase of shock-wave-controlled ram jet systems will probably cause an extravagant fuel consumption. In general,
the fuel consumption of a rocket system is up to six times
the rate of a ram jet system and from ten to twenty times
as much as the turbo jet consumption. But in the case of
defensive jet fighters, for instance, which need to be
airborne with a minimum of delay, economy is a second
consideration to performance; the use of rockets to assist
take-off and to reduce runways seemed to be the simplest
and most economic solution. In the first line, the advantages of a shock-wave-controlled ram jet system lies in
the fact that all the different systems of propulsion are
combined in one, making also possible the continuously
controlled conversion of one propulsion system into the
other, in flight. Like in the case of the reheat device,
by the conversion of the ram jet phase into the rocket
phase in flight, short bursts of extra speed can also be
produced, thus providing, for instance, for the highest
possible climbing rate, s.s.o.

The continuous covertibility of ram jet and rocket
operations in flight will also improve the safe operation
of high-speed aircraft and will especially supply the ram
jet system with all the flexibility necessary to make it
the most powerful and efficient aircraft in atmospheric
flight. Even vertical take-off and landing operations
could be attainable with shock-wave-controlled ram jet
systems.

The problem of fuel consumption, especially in the
rocket phase, becomes obsolete in case of the substitution of the chemical combustion system by a nuclear reactor system. Although the heat from nuclear reactor systems
can be transferred normally only by means of heat
exchange processes and not by direct 'combustion', means
can be developed, by which the suitable control charac-

271

teristics of highly enriched fission reactor systems and
of shock-wave-ignited lithium and boron consuming fusion
reactor systems and their enormous power capacity can be
suitably be used in the operating of shock-wave-
controlled convertible ram jet systems.

The economy of shock-wave-controlled ram jet systems
will undoubtedly increase with the power capacity of the
system; in other words, the author is not in the position
yet to estimate accurately whether jet fighter development
will be influenced by this new ram jet system at once. But
it seems to be reasonable to assume, that the development
of larger-hypersonic aircraft (bomber, transport, passen-
ger planes, a.s.o.) will be based on the improved ram jet
systems, outlined in this preliminary report.

COMMENTS OF PREPARING OFFICER:
2. Dr. Richter is very desirous of obtaining a position
   with an aircraft engine manufacturing company in the
   United States. He would like to continue working on
   ram jet engine development. This office, if desired
   can obtain additional information.

VERGIL N. NESTOR
Lt. Colonel USAF
Assistant Air Attache

* * * * * * *

AUTHOR'S COMMENTS OF THE RICHTER RAM JET

Not only could the ram jet designs of Dr. Richter be used in a
standard fighter jet, they could also be used in a vertically rising
aircraft, even one powered by nuclear fission or even nuclear fusion.
This brings UFOs to mind.

* * * * * *

Air Intelligence Information Report IR-80-56

"THERMONUCLEAR EXPONENTIAL EXPERIMENTS"

1. Report contains a summary of his work by
   Dr. Ronald Richter in developing a completely new
   type of arc melting furnace based on a shock wave
   reactivity rather than a heat transfer process through

utilization of a chemical arc reactor system. To prove
his theory, he developed a reactor simulator utilizing
thermonuclear exponential experiments based on
shock-wave-ignited self-reproducing chains consuming
lithium and boron isotopes.

2. Approving Officer is not technically qualified to
comment
on the subject presented. However, Dr. Richter is,
in the opinion of qualified German scientists resident
in Argentina, a complete fraud who has "parlayed"
a limited scientific background and a glib tongue
to obtain much publicity: i.e., the explosion of
the so-called "Argentine Atomic Bomb" in 1952.
In the opinion of these qualified German scientists,
the disgrace and obscurity that Dr. Richter now
enjoys is better than he deserves.

APPROVED:
George R. Herrman
Colonel USAF
Air Attache

1. The following statement was prepared by
   Dr. Ronald Richter (IR-76-56) and given
   to Preparing Officer.

The advantage of a high-speed reaction is that for a
given capital investment more product can be run through
a chemical or metallurgical plant or a smaller plant can
be built to yield a given amount of reaction product.

In general, the reaction rate of a chemical reactor
system depends on temperature, pressure, and catalyst.
An electric arc between electrodes of carbon is the most
intense source of heat used commonly in industrial practice. Such an arc plasma reactor can be operated in any
atmosphere at any desired pressure and any kind of material can be introduced into the arc plasma zone and thus
vaporized and heated up to plasma temperatures. The operation of a plasma reactor system can be considerably
improved by jetting a mixture of reactants through the
high energetic arc plasma zone at very high velocities.

Although arc furnaces are used to the greatest extent
in the melting of metals and the production of ferroal-

loys, they figure prominently in the chemical operations
requiring high temperatures, such as calcium carbide,
elemental phosphorus, a.s.o. Arc furnaces up to 30,000 kw
are in service.

In 1936, I was experimenting with reflector-controlled
arc reactor systems. When studying self-stabilization of
arc plasma zones by instantaneous strong overloading, I
quite incidentally observed the occurrence of explosion-
like plasma fluctuations, generating powerful shock waves.
The analysis of the shock wave promoting factors revealed
how to improve the shock wave generating process by means
of andyzer-controlled feedback operations.

In the course of these investigations, it has been
found, that about 50% of the arc plasma energy can be
converted into powerful plasma shock waves, thus creating
a completely new type of chemically and metallurgically
reactive zone of operation. Such a reflector-controlled
superposition of powerful plasma shock waves produces
tremendous intensities of sound and ultra-sound, generated by the gaseous plasma zone itself, thus providing
for the highest possible rate of energy transfer at all.
All the before-known ultra-sound generating methods were
characterized by a very poor coupling of the ultrasound
energy to be fed into the reacting zone. For all these
reasons, a shockwave-controlled reactor plasma is representing the strongest source of ultra-sound. The operation of such a powerful ultra-sound generating arc reactor
plasma is quite a simple affair, but precautions have
to be taken for preventing structural damage by ultra-
sound and the shock-wave-induced corrosion. Data-teleme-
tering operations and remote reactor control have to be
applied, to avoid a considerable health hazard for the
reactor-operating crew.

The combined reaction of non-Maxwellian heat transfer,
intense shock wave and ultra-sound reactivity leads to the
most radical mechanical disintegration of all the materials to be fed into the reacting zone. In consequence of
this, basic physical and chemical conditions can be
achieved with never before could be obtained by other
reactor systems. Owing to the incomparable high reaction
rates that only can be obtained by shock-wave-controlled
arc plasma systems, in many industrial chemical and

metallurgical processes processing time ad production
costs can be considerably reduced.
   There exists a wide field of industrial
applications, as:

> The production of extremely purified and degassified
> metals and alloys, cheap tonnage processing
> of zirconium, titanium, beryllium, uranium,
> thorium and other metals.

> Improved steel alloys with reduced production costs,
> wide range of variation of the mechanical and
> thermal properties of steel alloys (in general,
> of any kind of alloy) by applying different shock
> wave: heat ratios,

> The production of completely new types of ultra-
> sound-induced alloys and cements, improved cerments
> and ceramics for rocket and jet engines, improved
> ceramics and cerments with desirable nuclear
> properties of nuclear power reactors,

> Ultra-sound-cracking of petroleum, ultra-sound
> induced disintegration of macromolecules,

> De-gasification of liquids and fused
> materials, a.so.o.,

> Considerable increase of the reaction rate
> of chemical processes induced by the high
> temperatures and pressure peaks, resulting form
> the plasma shock fonts, a.s.o.

> A reactor simulator has been developed by which
> industrial application problems can be studied
> without building up the large-scale reactor system
> itself, thus reducing initial costs of industrial
> projects considerably. No further research work
> is necessary to construct large-scale shock-wave
> furnaces and reactors.

In brief:

   Thermonuclear exponential experiments, based on shock-
wave-ignited self-reproducing reaction chains, consuming
lithium and boron isotopes
   When developing a shock-wave-controlled arc reactor

system, one fundamental problem was the thermodynamic analysis of the plasma shock waves.

After a considerable amount of experimenting on the photoelectric analysis of highly luminous shock fronts, it seemed to be promising to improve the thermodynamic analysis of shockwave-controlled arc plasma zones by employing plasma-collision-induced nuclear reactions. Owing to the high temperatures and pressure obtained in a gas behind of strong shock waves, it became very probable that in the case of deuterium gas, some high energetic deutrons might undergo deuteron-deuteron reactions, the reaction yield being a suitable basis for testing non-equilibrium thermodynamics. Since the reaction rate of a thermonuclear reaction depends exponentially on temperature, and since the temperature increases rather rapidly toward the center of the arc plasma zone, especially in the case of shockwave-induced plasma pulsations, it was to be hoped that a detectable reaction rate might be achieved. But it was unlikely that the detection of statistically fluctuating plasma-collision-induced thermal nuclear reaction chains might become a reality.

In order to improve the deductibility of plasma-shockwave-induced nuclear reactions in the fall of 1942, – by using nuclear mass data just having been published by J. Mattauch and S. Fluege, (Kernphysikalische Tabellen, Springer Verlag, Berlin, 1942) – I developed nuclear reaction schemes, based on the chain-reacting consumption of the lithium and boron isotopes.

The neutron-induced conversion of lithium-6 into tritium and helium, the neutron-multiplying tritium-tritium reaction, and other neutron-multiplying and lithium-7 into lithium-6 converting secondary reactions were taken into consideration as being useful components of controllable self-reproducing reaction chains. By providing for a sufficient number of initial neutrons and sufficiently high reaction rate of the neutron-multiplying processes, it was to be expected that the ignition of bursts of reaction chains might become feasible by jetting lithium or lithium-6-enriched lithium into a shock wave controlled neutron-producing deuterium high-pressure plasma. Since the reaction rate of such a reaction scheme depends equally on temperature and on multiplication factor, a shock-wave-induced neutron-reproducing reaction chain must be far more sensitive to temperature than a plasma-collision-induced thermal nuclear reaction chain ever can be.

The source of neutrons for the neutron-reproducing thermonuclear exponential experiments was a shock-wave-controlled, 300 kw, deuterium high pressure plasma. In such a deuterium plasma, due to the persistent isotropic plasma-collision-induced bombardment, not only the basic deuteron-deuteron reactions, but also plasma-collision-induced secondary reactions, like the deuterium-tritium and the tritium-tritium reaction will occur. By these reactions a spectrum of fast neutrons is produced. A contribution to the number of plasma-produced neutrons and thus a substantial increase in reactivity can be obtained by surrounding the plasma zone with a neutron-multiplying beryllium reflector. For helium-5 being a strong neutron absorber in the low energy range the balance between neutron-producing and neutron-absorbing processes will finally be controlled by the scattering-induced moderation of the neutron energies and by the plasma-collision-induced reaction rate of the helium-3-producing and helium-3-consuming secondary reactions. Tritium enrichment follows from the two-dimensional bombardment of a deuterium target with deuterons. In the case of the plasma-collision-induced three-dimensional deutron-deutron bombardment, tritium will not only be produced but will also be consumed by secondary reactions. This criterion is useful when it comes to prove the existence of plasma-collision-induced secondary nuclear reactions.

By the injection of lithium into a neutron producing deuterium plasma, an avalanche of tritium-producing and neutron-multiplying primary and secondary processes will develop. The lithium-5 converting reactions, having a relatively high cross section in the low as well as in the high-energy range, with a remarkable capture resonance near 258 kev, starts the avalanche of reaction chains by producing tritium. The shockwave induced reaction rate of the neutron-multiplying processes (tritium-tritium, tritium-lithium-7, tritium-lithium-6) determines the intensity of the bursts of reaction chains. The

tritium-producing process can to a certain extent be
controlled by inserting neutron absorption rods into the
neutron-reflecting structure, thus controlling back-scattering into the plasma region. For lithium-7 being
a poor neutron absorber, there is no parallel to the
resonance absorption in uranium-238. The gradual enrichment of helium-4 will increase non-reactive scattering
but indications exist, that the enrichment of helium-6
might turn out to be even useful in regard to the safe
operation of such a reactor system. The lack of reactor-
contaminating radioactive reaction products adds to the
outstanding features of neutron-reproducing thermonuclear
reactor systems.

As one can see, the shock-wave-controlled arc plasma
system became involved in thermonuclear exponential
experiments by accident rather than design but turned out
to become a useful tool in research on controlled thermonuclear reactor systems. For the first time, an arc plasma
has been transformed into a zone of intense shock waves,
accompanied by an extraordinarily high degree of plasma
turbulence; a practically invisible reactor plasma
(as a consequence of the non-Maxwellian characteristics
of plasma shock waves, most of the photons emitted belong
to the ultra-violet and bremsstrahlung region of the
electromagnetic spectrum), emitting an almost unbearable
intensity of sound and ultra-sound, the whole reactor
structure oscillating under the impact of the feed-back-
controlled plasma shock waves, – that's the basis of
operation for the ignition of self-reproducing plasma
reaction chains, and this shock-wave-induced ignition
process will undoubtedly substitute nuclear-fission-
induced ignition, and make possible the gradual transformation of a thermonuclear exponential reactor system into
a self-sustaining chain-reacting system.

On February 15, 1951, an exponential reactor system was
ready for test. In the first test, a series of primary and
secondary nuclear reactions was produced for a short
interval by jetting lithium-6-enriched lithium into
a shockwave-controlled proton hydrogen plasma. Some of
the reactions (the helium-3, helium-3 reaction) were
multiplying the primary protons by ejecting two high
energetic protons.

In a second test, a rapidly developing avalanche of neutron-reproducing reaction chains was produced by jetting lithium-6-enriched lithium into a shock-wave-controlled deuterium high-pressure plasma.

In both tests, the self-reproducing reaction chains were analyzed by means of excitation-energy-discriminating ultraviolet-sensitive proportional counter tubes, a tele-analyzing method, having been developed and applied for the first time in 1938, when analyzing powerful plasma shock fronts.

By these exponential experiments, it has been demonstrated (1) that the shock-wave-induced ignition of self-reproducing thermonuclear reaction chains is possible, and (2) that the ignition of such reaction chains can be accomplished under controllable conditions.

On October 26, 1951, in a third decisive exponential experiment, it has been proven that the avalanche of neutron-reproducing reaction chains, resulting from the injection of lithium into a shock-wave-controlled neutron-producing deuterium high-pressure plasma, can be kept going on by injecting boron. Boron-11 like lithium-7 is an excellent neutron-multiplier when being bombarded with tritium particles. The fast-neutron-induced conversion of boron-10 into tritium and helium and the slow-neutron-induced conversion of boron-10 into the neutron-multiplying lithium-7 and helium are providing for tritium production and neutron multiplication. It might be of interest to note that the mechanism of the hydrogen bomb is based on the same reaction schemes. As has already been mentioned, a lithium and boron injected deutrerium plasma is a chain-reacting source of fast neutrons. When injecting natural uranium into such a plasma zone, fast-neutron-fission of uranium-238 occurs, the so-called 'thermo-fission'.

A serious disadvantage from the point of view of reactor control seems to be arising from the fact that in all the plasma-induced neutron-reproducing reaction chains only prompt neutrons are emitted. It is evident that the absence of delayed neutron emission would demand an exceedingly fine and extremely fast operating adjustment of the reactor controls. Fortunately, ignition, control and heat exchange of thermonuclear reactor systems can

considerably be improved by providing for a reflector-
controlled pulsating reactor plasma. In the case of a
nuclear fusion reactor system, not a critical size of
reactive material by a critical compression of the reactive plasma will be responsible for reaching a sufficiently
high reaction rate of the neutron-multiplying processes,
thus developing a controllable self-repeating cycle of
plasma pulsation. In other words, during the compression
period, the central temperature of the compressed reactor
plasma should become comparable with the temperature
needed for a sufficiently high reaction rate of the
neutron-reproducing reaction chains, to make the reactor
system a self-sustaining one. The absence of delayed
neutrons will only alter rise time and delay time of the
compression-induced impulse of reaction chains. The self-
stabilizing features of pulsating reactor operation will
suitably control supercritical bursts of self-reproducing
reaction chains. By compressing the reactive plasma zone
briefly to supercriticality, the gaseous zone quickly
heats up and then cools itself by expansion, thus eliminating the formidable heat transfer obstacles.

Much work has been done in regard to the control of
chain-reacting plasma zones by magnetically and electrodynamically induced plasma deformation, magnetically-
controlled plasma pulsation, electronic simulation of
pulsating reactor plasma conditions, a.s.o.

Monte Grande
February, 1, 1956

COMMENTS OF PREPARING OFFICER:
 2. Material contained above is beyond the technical
    ability of the Preparing Officer to evaluate.

Vergil N. Nestor
Lt. Colonel USAF
Assistant Air Attache

                  *   *   *   *   *   *   *

Air Intelligence Information Report IR-145-56

"THERMONUCLEAR PROPULSION SYSTEM"

Report describes the work and theory of Dr. Ronald Richter
in development of aircraft thermonuclear propulsion
system.

APPROVED:
George R. Herrman
Colonel UFAF
Air Attache

1. The following is extracted from a paper written by
   Dr. Ronald Richter (IR-76-56):

In nuclear fission powered propulsion systems, thermal
energy cannot be generated by 'direct combustion' but has
to be applied to the propulsion system by means of indirect heat transfer. For this reason, the efficiency of
such a propulsion system – jet or rocket system – depends
mainly on the technology on the heat-transfer-promoting
materials of construction.

The gradual contamination of the hermetically sealed-
off reactor system with highly radioactive nuclear fission
products and the protection of the flight personal against
neutron, gamma, and radioactive hazard, demands for voluminous any heavy shielding structures. Leakage or fully
destruction of the reactor system by flight accident
causes severe contamination of the atmosphere by radioactive fission products.

In nuclear fission powered propulsion systems – homoge-
neous or heterogeneous systems – only highly enriched
and very costly reactor fuels can be used. Based on the
results of shock-wave-ignition controlled thermonuclear
exponential experiments, the conception for a thermonuclear propulsion system has been developed.

The shock-wave-controlled arc plasma system of project
1 became involved in thermonuclear exponential experiments
by accident rather than design. A fundamental problem
connected with the development of shock-wave-controlled
reactor systems was the thermodynamic analysis of the
plasma shock waves produced. After a considerable amount
of experimenting of the photoelectric analysis of highly
luminous shock fronts, it seemed to be promising, to
improve the thermodynamic analysis of shock-wave-

controlled arc plasma zones by employing plasma-collision-
induced nuclear reactions.

Owing to the high temperatures and pressures obtained
in a gas behind strong shockwaves, it was very probable
that in the case of a deuterium high pressure plasma,
some high energetic deuterons might undergo deuteron-
deuteron reactions, and even secondary tritium-deuteron
and tritium-tritium reactions, the reaction yield being
a suitable basis for testing non-equilibrium thermodynamics. Since the reaction rate of a thermonuclear reaction
depends exponentially on temperature, and since the
temperature increases rather rapidly toward the center of
the arc plasma zone, especially in the case of shock-wave-
induced plasma pulsations, it was to be hoped, that a
detectable reaction rate might be achieved. The detection
of statistically fluctuating plasma-reaction rate might be
achieved. The detection of statistically fluctuating
plasma-collision-induced thermal nuclear reaction chains
was unlikely then (in 1936).

In order to improve the deductibility of plasma-shockwave-induced nuclear reactions, I developed nuclear reaction schemes, (in 1942), based on the chain-reacting
consumption of the lithium and boron isotopes.

The neutron-induced conversion of lithium-6 into
tritium and helium, the neutron-multiplying tritium-
tritium reaction, and other neutron-multiplying and
lithium-7 into lithium-6 converting secondary reactions
were taken into consideration as being useful components
of a controllable self-reproducing reaction chain.
By providing for a sufficient number of initial neutrons
and a sufficiently high reaction rate of the neutron-
reproducing processes, it was to be expected that the
ignition of bursts of reaction chains might become feasible by jetting lithium or lithium-6-enriched lithium
into a shock-wave-controlled neutron-producing deuterium
high pressure plasma. The reaction rate of such a reaction scheme depends equally on temperature and reproduction factor, a shock-wave-induced neutron-reproducing
chain of reactions must be far more temperature-sensitive
than a plasma-collision-induced thermal nuclear reaction
can ever be. The experimental analysis of the non-
Maxwellian thermodynamic conditions in a shock-wave-

controlled arc plasma zone by shock-wave-ignited self-reproducing nuclear reaction chains is practically a thermonuclear exponential experiment.

By injecting lithium into a neutron-producing deuterium plasma, an avalanche of tritium-producing and neutron-multiplying primary and secondary reactions develops. The lithium-6 converting reaction, having a relatively high cross section in the low as well as in the high-energy range, with a remarkable capture resonance near 258 kev, starts the avalanche of reaction chains by producing tritium. The shock-wave-induced reaction rate of the neutron-reproducing processes (tritium-tritium, tritium-lithium-7, tritium-lithium-6) will determine the intensity of the bursts of reaction chains. The tritium-producing process can to a certain extent by controlled by inserting neutron absorption rods into the neutron-reflecting structure, thus controlling back-scattering into the plasma region. For lithium-7 being a poor neutron-absorber, there is no parallel to the resonance absorption in uranium-238. The gradual enrichment of helium-4 will increase non-reactive scattering but indications exist, that helium-4 enrichment might turn out to be even useful in regard to the safe operation of such a reactor system, when it becomes self-sustaining. The lack of reactor-contaminating radioactive reaction products adds to the outstanding features of neutron-reproducing thermonuclear reactor systems.

The avalanche of neutron-reproducing reaction chains, resulting from the injection of lithium into a shock-wave-controlled neutron-producing deuterium high-pressure plasma, can be maintained by injection boron. Boron-11 like lithium-7 is an excellent neutron-multiplier, when bombarded with tritium. The fast neutron-induced conversion of boron-10 into tritium and helium and the slow-neutron-induced conversion of boron-10 into the neutron-multiplying lithium-7 and helium are providing for tritium production and neutron multiplication.

A serious disadvantage from the point of view of reactor control seems to be arising from the fact that in all the plasma induced neutron-reproducing reaction chains, only prompt neutrons are emitted. It is evident that the absence of delayed neutron emission would demand for an exceedingly fine and extremely fast operating adjustment of the reactor controls. Fortunately, ignition, control, and heat exchange of thermonuclear reactor systems can be considerably improved by providing for a reflector-controlled pulsating reactor plasma. In the case of a nuclear fusion reactor reactant plasma will be responsible for reaching a sufficiently high reaction rate of the neutron-reproducing processes, thus developing a controllable self-repeating cycle of plasma pulsation. The absence of delayed neutrons will only alter rise time and decay time of the compression-induced impulse of reaction chains. The self-stabilizing features of pulsating reactor operation will suitably control supercritical burst of self-reproducing reaction chains. By compressing the reactant plasma zone briefly to supercriticality, the gaseous zone quickly heats up and then cools itself by expansion, thus eliminating the formidable heat transfer obstacles.

(Much work has been done in regard to the control of chain-reacting plasma zones by magnetically and electrodynamically induced plasma deformation, magnetically-controlled plasma pulsation, the direct conversion of nuclear energy into electricity in plasma reactor systems due to the high ionization rate of the plasma zone and its interaction with a static magnetic field.)

Development of a pulsating plasma reactor system, the compression period providing for a sufficiently high reaction rate and reproduction factor, the expanding period providing for thrust and heat dissipation. Such a pulsating thermonuclear propulsion system, based on the chain-reacting consumption of the lithium and boron isotopes, depends in the first line of the realization of a shock-wave-controlled ignition process. It is to be expected that in the very near future the United States or Russia will demonstrate, by exploding a thermonuclear device, that such an explosion can be ignited by shockwaves, i.e. without the use of an initial nuclear fission device.

Since there are no highly radioactive reaction products, the tail-pipe can be directly connected to the reactor vessel, thus avoiding indirect heat transfer. The critical diameter of such a 'direct combustion' system depends on reaction rate and reproduction factor of the compression period of the plasma pulsation, which in turn depends on the isotope ratio of the reactant materials injected.

Accurate neutron dosage by accurate injection dosage of the reactant materials reduces shielding volume and weight considerably.

Practically no reactor contamination. No atmospheric contamination.

Vertical start and landing operations.

Near target, the propulsion reactor system of a guided missile can be converted automatically into a thermonuclear bomb reactor system by providing for the necessary overloading of the reactor system.

PROGRAM OF DEVELOPMENT

Installation and operation of a shock-wave-controlled arc plasma reactor system
(like project 1),

Shock-wave-ignition controlled thermonuclear exponential experiments, based on the injection of lithium and boron into the shock-wave-controlled deuterium plasma, analysis of injection characteristics,

Performance of a self-sustaining neutron-reproducing reactor system when directly connected to the tail-pike, they representing a thermonuclear propulsion system, combine injection and thrust analysis, analysis of control characteristics,

Development of a safe ignition process,

Minimum diameter of the reactor vessel vs. isotope ration, a.s.o.

INSTALLATIONS AND EQUIPMENT

Reactor system, analyzing and controlling equipment practically the same as in project 1.

Tele-operating nuclear reaction analyzer of special design,

Non-equilibrium thermodynamics-analyzer of specialdesign,

Reactor controls of special design,

285

Plasma turbulence analyzer of special design,

Digital computer components,
pressure-analyzing equipment,

Photoelectric cell of special design,

Sealers, counting rate meters, pulse
height analyzers,

Neutron, gamma, and radioactivity detecting
and analyzing equipment,

Shock-wave-ignition reactor bombs,

Thrust analyzing equipment as in project 2, a.s.o.

As you can see, all the three projects have shock-wave-operations in common. In all the projects, an explosion-proof structure for the reactor system and an explosion-protected control station are needed. Most of the analyzing and controlling equipment (also that of special design) is practically the same in ll the projects. The task is to build up an automatically self-recording test installation, providing for a maximum of automatically plotted characteristics curves of the reactor system in question, thus requiring just a minimum of scientifically trained personnel. In all the three projects, operational progress can be achieved faster by setting up electronic analog systems.

2. The project number 1 referred to in the above was
   reported in IR-80-56. Installation and equipment
   for this project is as follows:

   A tele-controlled reactor system, (shock-wave-induced noise hazard),

   Reactor vessel and electrodes immersed in an
   explosion-proof structure of reinforced concrete.

   Dimensions and shape of the reactor structure
   depend on the power input and industrial
   application of the reactor system (melting
   furnace, chemical reactor system, a.s.o.),

   Although principal demonstrations of the process
   in question can be carried out with a rector system
   consuming around 100 kw, it is recommended to start

the shock-wave-reactor program with a power input
of about 1,000-5,000 kw, for higher power input
means higher output of reaction products, alloys,
ceramics, cermets, a.s.o., i.e. to arrive
at large-scale operations (and large-scale
business faster,

Power transformer, rectifier installations, power
controls, stabilizing equipment, rectifier controls,
electrode controls,

Shock-wave-analyzers of special design,

Shock-wave-controls of special design,

Blowers, cooling water installations,

A travelling crane for handling the reactor system,

Explosion-protected control station, containing all
the controls, analyzers, automatic power switches,

Injection systems, electromagnetically
controlled valves,

Relays and automatic switches, switchboard
instruments,

Electronic instruments of special design.

Recording multichannel galvanometers and
cathode ray detectors,

Ultra-sound spectrum analyzers, ultra-sound
intensity meters,

Polar-coordination recorders for ultra-sound
field recording,

Pulse height analyzers, pulse counting rate meters
(recording),

X-Y recording instruments and plottingboards,
digital computer components,

D.C.-D.C. cathode ray oscilloscopes, with cameras,

Microwave spectrum analyzers (Plasma
oscillation spectrum),

Height-speed framing camera, Kerr cell cameras,

Television equipment, monitoring the reactor core,

Multichannel magnetic data recorder,

Reaction product analyzers (when the reactor system is used as a chemical reactor system-recording infrared and mass spectrometer analysis,

Carbon electrodes,

Reactor simulation for design work on industrial reactor system,

3. The project number 2 referred to in the above was reported in IR-79-56. Installation and equipment for this project is:

A complete ram jet system with a flight simulator (compressor unit for the performance of subcritical, critical, and supercirtical flow conditions), immersed in an explosion-proof test-pit,

Injection systems of special design, electromagnetically controlled valves,

Fuel and oxygen tanks,

Explosion-protected control station,

Thrust-analyzing equipment (recording),

Shock-wave-analyzers of special design,

Shock-wave-controls of special design,

Most of the analyzing and controlling equipment of project 1, especially multichannel recording instruments, pulse height analyzers, pulse spectrum and ultra-sound analyzers, pulse counting rate meters, a photoelectric reaction analyzer of non-equilibrium thermodynamics,

Temperature and pressure recording instruments,

Flow recording instruments.

COMMENTS of Preparing Officer:

4. The material contained in this report is beyond the technical ability of the Preparing Officer to evaluate. Conversation with dr. Cooper and Dr. Multhopp, scientists of The Glen L. Martin Company of the United States who have interviewed Dr. Richter,

```
        revealed that there may be something of value in
        the work and theory of Dr. Richter.
Vergil N. Nestor
Lt. Colonel USAF
Assistant Air Attache

COMMENTS of Approving Officer:

 5. Material contained in this report was submitted to
    the Air Attache by Dr. Ronald Richter, whose scientific
    reputation in Argentina is not good. (See IR-80-56).

G. R. H.
```

                    *   *   *   *   *   *   *

These are the three main reports submitted by Dr. Richter to the
American authorities, obviously hoping for employment. The reports
have been reproduced as accurately as possible, including minor
spelling errors. The positive and negative comments of the American
personnel preparing these reports indicate either a split opinion of
Dr. Richter's value or an attempt to cover all contingencies. In other
words, if Dr. Richter and his work were to turn out to be of great
value, then these individuals would be in line for credit for his
"discovery". On the other hand, if naught came from all of this
or something negative developed, the same command could say
"I told you so".

All three examples of Dr. Richter's work involve shock waves.
Ultra-sound was harnessed and set into a feedback loop to accomplish
his ends. Two projects that he has written on above involve fusion.
The ignition procedure and the containment field are provided for by
means of his a shock wave technology. If this were all Dr. Richter had
done, he would have been guaranteed inclusion in this book for that
work alone, but Dr. Richter's mind had already moved beyond the
production of a sustained fusion reaction and the technological
implication, thereof. A clue to this broader thinking is given in his
specialties:

        "...development and testing of highly-turbulent,
        magnetic-field-controlled fission and fusion plasma
        systems, Experimental approach to solar flare conditions
        and to the explosion-tendency of the solar plasma,

ultraviolet excess analysis, excitation of space structure
by pulsation-controlled plasma implosion, testing the
limitations of quantum mechanics and quantum dynamics, Experimental approach to the unified field theory
and to the velocity of propagation of gravity, a.s.o."

Dr. Richter was thinking on a much grander scale. It is clear that
Dr. Richter's method was experimentation, not merely conducting
"research" by scribbling mathematical babble on a chalkboard and
then insisting on a Spinosian set of definitions of exactly what the
physical universe actually is.

Dr. Richter's laboratory work led to two striking spin-offs of the
shock-wave research. He was working on furthering both this
concepts as well as refining the work already described in 1956,
contemporaneously with the creation of the Paperclip file by the US
intelligence services.

The first is the direct conversion of nuclear energy into electric
energy. Again, this was an offshoot of the research already described
above. It involves venting the moving plasma through a magnetic
field, which causes a plasma induction of electric energy.

Dr. Richter indicates that the concept and testing occurred in 1951
with the original experimentation being derived from his work in
Germany in 1944. Dr. Richter did "Preliminary work" in 1953 and he
cites an unpublished letter to the editor of "Nucleonics" on September
22, 1956 as documentation. Dr. Richter mentions that the charge
carried by some of the substances he worked with might prove to be
better than others.

Dr. Richter also mentions direct conversion of nuclear energy into
radio frequency energy in fission and fusion plasma systems. He
claims the year of the concept was 1949 and the report, again, in 1956.
We have all heard of this phenomena; it is the pulse of electromagnetic
energy that occurs during detonation of a nuclear or thermonuclear
bomb. This pulse knocks out sensitive electronic equipment and radio
communications devices.

But there was another discovery made by Dr. Richter that dwarfs
everything except, perhaps, controlled fusion. This discovery is of
another and entirely different sort of energy whose discovery also
resulted from Dr. Richter's work on shock waves. Dr. Richter even
coined a phrase for it, (although he is never given credit for doing so),

and it is a term which we hear frequently now. It is called "Zero Point Energy".

Dr. Richter writes:

> "experimental approach to zero point energy (and probably to a new source of energy at all), deriving from the analysis of exponential fusion experiments in 1951,"

So, Dr. Richter was working on fusion experiments when he hit upon something else. In another statement we learn that the experiments that led to the discovery of zero point energy were the experiments of directly converting plasma energy into electrical energy (as he wrote it minor errors included):

> "...still in 1944, I have been using the coupling between plasma jets and a magnetic field as a means for analyzing non-Maxwellian plasma conditions; experimental research of a plasma-controlled, energy-converting system (converting nuclear energy directly into electrical energy by the induction effect) has been carried out on a preliminary non-nuclear basis in 1951 and 1952, (deriving from the analysis of plasma induction spectra), in 1954, a push-pull plasma reactor system has been analyzed theoretically, based on two interconnected reactor vessels which become plasma-critical alternately, only one vessel becomes critical at a time; when it goes plasma-critical, a plasma jet is firing through a magnetic field, producing electrical energy by the induction effect, in the fall of 1951, when analyzing the induction spectrum of an extremely turbulent, shock-wave-superimposed plasma of ordinary proton hydrogen, a specific class if signals revealed the existence of sort of 'decaying structures', not resulting from eventual electron capture by protons, forming decaying neutrons, another class of signals, characterized by extremely large amplitudes and very small pulse width was even indicating the existence of a certain exchange mechanism of energy, the source of the energy being still a mystery; sort of extremely irregular fluctuations spectrum was developing at the very moment of optimal plasma compression, during the past four years of exile, much theoretical work has been done

to clarify this matter; it has been found, at least, that an explanation can be given for the large-amplitude 'exchange signals' when we assume, that highly compressed electron gas becomes a detector for energy exchange with what we call zero point energy, zero point energy derives from the exclusion principle, the exclusion principle derives from empirical data, in a shock-wave-superimposed, turbulence-feed-back controlled plasma zone exists a high probability for cell-like super-pressure conditions, gas represents an enormously high energy capacity of exchange processes, about 10 to the 10th kwh per unit volume, on the basis of exchange coupling, it seems to be possible to 'extract' a compression-proportional amount of zero point energy by means of a magnetic-field-controlled exchange fluctuation between the compressed electron gas and sort of cell structure in space (dimensions about 10 to the minus 13th cm) (author's note: Dr. Richter abbreviated this figure as scientific notation), representing the source of what we call zero point energy, it seems even possible that the large-amplitude fluctuation signals derive from a mechanism of energy-conversion unknown to us yet which becomes detectable only in highly compressed electron gas, (it would be of interest to repeat these experiments not with a proton hydrogen plasma-proton spin and electron spin identical – but with a helium-4 plasma, the spin discrepancy supporting energy extraction, it would also be worth-while to search for exchange signals in high-power pulsating fission plasma systems), in case, all these interpretations are fully correct, plasma implosion analysis might turn out to become an approach to a completely new source of energy, probably superior to nuclear energy, the present status of this matter can best be compared with the situation when nuclear fission was discovered, but when the development of a chain-reacting fission reactor system was still depending on the realization of controllable neutron reproduction, (the compression-induced 'decay signals' can be explained as resulting from wave-mechanical coupling of groups from these theoretical studies derives, that such a shock-wave-controlled pulsation-controlled fission (or fusion) plasma system must be an enormously powerful source of shock-wave-induced ultra-sound, (converting nuclear energy directly into ultra-sound energy),

theoretically, a chain-reacting controllable plasma reactor system (fission or fusion type) will be the only one which can produce nuclear power in the range of millions of kilowatts, when based on the controlled pulsation of supercritical chain-reacting zones; therefore, the optimal output of nuclear-power-induced ultra-sound will be determined and limited by the reactor structure demoloshing effects of the ultra-sound itself,

still in 1944, I have been using the coupling between plasma jets and a magnetic field as a means for analyzing non-Maxwellian plasma conditions; experimental research on a plasma-controlled, energy-converting system (converting nuclear energy directly into electrical energy by the induction effect) has been carried out on a preliminary non-nuclear basis in 1951 and 1952, (deriving from the analysis of plasma induction spectra),

in 1954, a push-pull plasma reactor system has been analyzed theoretically, based on two interconnected reactor vessels which become plasma-critical alternately,

only one vessel becomes critical at a time; when it goed plasma-critical, a plasma jet is firing through a magnetic field, producing electrical energy by the induction effect,

in the fall of 1951, when analyzing the induction spectrum of an extremely turbulent, shock-wave-superimposed plasma of ordinary proton hydrogen, a specific class if signals revealed the existence of sort of 'decaying structures', not resulting from eventual electron capture by protons, forming decaying neutrons,

another class of signals, characterized by extremely large amplitudes and very small pulse width was even indicating the existence of a certain exchange mechanism of energy, the source of the energy being still a mistery; sort of extremely irregular fluctuation spectrum was developing at the very moment of optimal plasma compression,

during the past four years of exile, much theoretical work has been done to clarify this matter; it has been found, at least, that an explanation can be given for the large-amplitude 'exchange signals', when we assume, that highly compressed electron gas becomes a detector for energy exchange with what we call zero point energy,

zero point energy derives from the exclusion principle,
the exclusion principle derives from empirical data,
in a shock-wave-superimposed, turbulence-feed-back-controlled plasma zone exists a high probability for cell-like super-pressure conditions,
zero point energy in balance with the mass energy of the electron gas represents an enormously high energy capacity for exchange processes,

This is a copy of the actual text written by Dr. Richter. Did he coin the words "Zero Point Energy" sometime between 1956 and 1958? This text was declassified for the author on April 26, 1999.

Separate Sheet No. <u>1</u>.

3. Professional Field or Occupation: Include specialized fields of work
or interest.

experimental and applied physics,

analysis of stress and vibration under extreme thermodynamic and mechanical conditions (hypersonic flight conditions,
radiation corrosion, a.s.o.),
development of new materials of construction for rocket
and jet motors, nuclear propulsion systems, a.s.o., to be produced
in shock-wave- and ultra-sound-controlled arc melting furnaces,
high-pressure plasma physics and plasma implosion analysis,
shock-wave physics and chemistry, interested in rocket and jet plasma analysis, solar plasma physics,
analysis of nuclear reactions in chain-reacting fission
and fusion plasma zones,
development and testing of plasma-type, pulsation-controlled fission and fusion reactor systems,
development and testing of propulsion reactor systems,

experimental approaches to new concepts,

development and testing of highly-turbulent, magnetic-field-
controlled fission and fusion plasma systems,
experimental approach to solar flare conditions and to the
explosion-tendency of the solar plasma, ultraviolet excess analysis,
excitation of space structure by pulsation-controlled plasma implosion, testing the limitations of quantum mechanics and quantum dynamics,
experimental approach to the unified field theory and to the
velocity of propagation of gravity, a.s.o.

This is another page of Dr. Richter's declassified text highlighting some of his accomplishments.

about 10^{10} kwh per unit volume,

on the basis of exchange coupling, it seems to be possible to 'extract' a compression-proportional amount of zero point energy by means of a magnetic-field-controlled exchange fluctuation between the compressed electron gas and sort of cell structure in space (dimensions about 10^{-13} cm), representing the source of what we call zero point energy,

it seems even possible that the large-amplitude fluctuation signals derive from a mechanism of energy-conversion unknwon to us yet which becomes detectable only in highly compressed electron gas,

(it would be of interest to repeat these experiments not with a proton hydrogen plasma - proton spin and electron spin identical - but with a helium-4 plasma, the spin discrepancy supporting energy extraction,

it would also be worth-while to search for exchange signals in high-power pulsating fission plasma systems),

in case, all these interpretations are fully correct, plasma implosion analysis might turn out to become an approach to a completely new source of energy, probably superior to nuclear energy,

the present status of this matter can best be compared with the situation, when nuclear fission was discovered, but when the development of a chain-reacting fission reactor system was still depending on the realization of controllable neutron reproduction,

(the compression-induced 'decay signals' can be explained as resulting from wave-mechanical coupling of groups of electrons, the repulsive forces between the electrons becoming neutralized gradually by wave-mechanical coupling with increasing compression),

first, there was the discovery of the shock-wave-generating process in 1936, the discovery of a feed-back loop between shock-wave-induced plasma turbulence and plasma-turbulence-induced promotion of shock-wave-generating plasma explosions,

the concept of testing shock-wave conditions by means of plasma-collision-induced nuclear reactions,

the development of nuclear reaction schemes, based on the chain-reacting consumption of the lithium and boron isotopes in 1942,

the concept of a controllable fusion reactor system, ignited by a shock-wave-controlled deuterium high-pressure plasma,

then came the first series of exponential fusion experiments in February, 1951, and the second series of exponential fusion experiments in October, 1951, giving proof for the existence of self-reproducing reaction chains,

from these experiments derived the discovery of field-interaction-accelerated particles, initiating a completely new concept of reactor systems, and the discovery of two specific classes of flash signals, the 'decaying type', deriving from wave-mechanical coupling of electron groups, and the 'large-amplitude-type', deriving from a possible exchange process with a new source of energy, probably the zero point energy,

from the development of super-plasma conditions derives fluctuating plasma implosion as a concept for fusion reactor systems, and as a probable approach to a new source of energy (in any case, as a method for exploring space structure physics),

from the development of a shock-wave-controlled arc melting furnace probably derive series of new materials of construction for rocket and jet engines, and for nuclear propulsion systems, under hypersonic flight conditions,

from the analysis of the penetrability of shock-wave-controlled plasma zones derives the concept for an improved ram jet propulsion system, which will allow to take full advantage of the feed-back loop existing between thrust and air-intake,

from the theoretical analysis of a pulsating fission plasma system derives the conception of a nuclear-energy into ultra-sound converting reactor system, the conception of a nuclear-energy into electrical energy converting reactor system, and the conception of a nuclear-energy into radiofrequency energy converting reactor system,

during the past four years of exile, much theoretical work has been done in space-time physics, and in unified field theory (having been interested in possible experimental approaches).

More of Dr. Richter's text. Standing ultrasound waves were the basis for all of his work of electrons, the repulsive forces between eh electrons becoming neutralized gradually be wave-mechanical couplings with increasing compression,"

This has been a glimpse into the mind of Dr. Ronald Richter. It has also been a glimpse into a probable post-war world if the Nazi government had survived and Dr. Richter has gone on with his work, in Germany, without breaks in funding.

The media, especially the American media, wanted to brand Dr. Richter as a charlatan. The American intelligence services which put together the Paperclip report on Dr. Richter, spent a great deal of time and effort researching Dr. Richter while, at the same time, repeating negative things said about him in an effort to cover their butts no matter what became of him and his work. This tactic should not surprise us. We have seen them do this time and time again.

The question arises as to what we are to think of Dr. Richter today. Opinion was split in the mid-1950s. As an example of this, there is a technical evaluation of Dr. Richter included in the Paperclip file. It is a report from The Foreign Service of the United States of America, Office of the Air Attache, United States Embassy (Argentina). It is dated 7/3/56 and so is concurrent with the file and reports cited A whole group of scientists were sent by the US government to Argentina to evaluate Richter. Interestingly enough, a medical doctor also accompanied the team. Cold war political implications are noted. The report was done for and directly submitted to the Director of Intelligence, USAF, and it must be concluded that this is a high-level intelligence report. It is re-written here word for word:

*   *   *   *   *   *   *

CONFIDENTIAL

The Foreign Service of the United States Of America
Office of the Air Attache
United States Embassy
Buenos Aires, Argentina
175-R&D 3 July 1956
(Ucl)

SUBJECT: Dr. Ronald Richter (See IR-76-56, 79-56, 80-56 and 145-56)

TO: Director of Intelligence

Headquarteres, USAF

ATTN: Air Attache Branch

Washington 25, D.C.

1. A recent visit by a group of U.S. atomic energy
   scientists to Argentina, headed by Dr. John Hall,
   resulted in a conversation among Dr. Richter,
   Dr. Hall and two other scientists in the group.
   The undersigned officer attended a meeting with
   Dr. Hall subsequent to this conference and the
   following items of interest relative to Dr. Richter
   are being forwarded for information and whatever
   action is required:

   a. Dr. Richter is considered by Dr. Hall to be
      "a mad genius". Along the same lines Dr. Hall
      stated that Dr. Richter is thinking in the year
      1970. Dr. Hall was quite impressed with the
      knowledge, theories and work of Dr. Richter.
      He will attempt to send to Argentina an atomic
      scientist thoroughly familiar with Dr. Richter's
      field of work to further interrogate Dr. Richter
      and thus properly evaluate his capabilities. One
      of the visiting group who attended this conference
      was a medical doctor and has diagnosed Dr. Richter
      as being close to the verge of a complete breakdown

   b. Dr. Richter has visited the undersigned officer
      several times during the past four months. He has
      become increasingly concerned about his future
      inasmuch as he cannot secure employment in
      Argentina and has completely exhausted all his
      personal funds. Dr. Richter has repeatedly
      indicated his desire to work for the U.S. or
      for any country that is opposed to the Communists.
      It isknown to this officer that Dr. Richter has been
      approached four times in the past six months by
      "pink" Germans residing in Buenos Aires and has
      been urged to visit the Russian attache who would
      completely solve all of his problems. His condition
      at present is such that the undersigned feels that
      unless he has some definite encouragement for
      obtaining employment in the U.S. or with

a Western Bloc country, he will accept employment
with the Communist Bloc.
175-R&D, USAIRA, Buenos Aires, Argentina,
Subj Dr. Ronald Richter

2. It is urged that this office be advised if there
is any interest on the part of private concerns
or governmental agencies in securing Dr. Richter's
services. Dr. John Hall of the Atomic Energy
Commission may be contacted on this subject.

Vergil N. Nestor
Lt. Col USAF
Air Attache

* * * * * * *

A second memo of the exact same date, July 3, 1956
contains a significant paragraphs:

3. Dr. Richter's work in Argentina should be reviewed by
a competent specialist. The recommendation of Dr. Hall
to interrogate Dr. Richter is concurred in.
Specifically, this headquarters desires the following
information:

    a. Technical data, diagrams and plans concerning his
    experiments in Argentina and Germany in 1943
    (reference IR-76-56) with discussion of his
    problems and results.

    b. Resume of his research activity, problems and
    results while at Berlin-Suhler-Waffen-und-
    Fahrzeugwereke during 1937/38 (reference IR-76-56).

4. The headquarter's interest in foreign activities
in the nuclear field covered by Dr. Richter in
Argentina requires the utilization of technically
qualified persons. Should there be no interest
in other government agencies or private industry
of Dr. Richter's services, this headquarters would
attempt to retain Dr. Richter, either in the U.S.
if he can be permitted to enter, or in Argentina.
Dr. Richter's evaluation of unclassified literature
of various foreign nations in this field would

Home
Back to the home page.
Discussion Forum
Science discussion,
science waffle and science
brouhaha from assorted
boffins.
Hot Topics
- **Global Warming**
- **Health**
- **Nature & The
  Environment**
- **Particle Physics &
  Nanotech**
- **Space**
News Archive
- **2005 Archive**
- **2004 Archive**
- **2003 Archive**
- **2002 Archive**
- **2001 Archive**
- **2000 Archive**
- **1999 Archive**
- **1998 Archive**
Forum Archive
Stuff that people wish they
hadn't said, but that is now
immortalized until the next
server crash.
Search
Go
Science Books
Books for every interest
including space exploration,
evolution, the philosophy of
science, nature and
physics.
Science Shopping
Lego
For budding boffins
Space Stuff
Flight suits, toys, models,
astronaut gear
Science Toys
Great fun and educational

3 March 2004

Nuclear Fusion From Bubbles Blasted With Sound

Physical Review E has announced the publication of an article by a team of researchers from Rensselaer Polytechnic Institute (RPI), Purdue University, Oak Ridge National Laboratory (ORNL) and the Russian Academy of Science (RAS) stating that they have replicated and extended previous experimental results that indicated the occurrence of nuclear fusion using a novel approach for plasma confinement.

The approach - called bubble fusion - and the experimental results are being published in an article which is scheduled for publication in the *Physical Review* journal this month.

The research team used a standing ultrasonic wave to help form and then implode the cavitation bubbles of deuterated acetone vapor. The oscillating sound waves caused the bubbles to expand and then violently collapse, creating strong compression shock waves around and inside the bubbles. Moving at about the speed of sound, the internal shock waves impacted at the center of the bubbles causing very high compression and accompanying temperatures of about 100 million Kelvin.

These new data were taken with an upgraded instrumentation system that allowed data acquisition over a much longer time than was possible in the team's previous bubble fusion experiments. According to the new data, the observed neutron emission was several orders of magnitude greater than background and had extremely high statistical accuracy. Tritium, which also is produced during the fusion reactions, was measured and the amount produced was

Three pages describing "new" fusion research using standing ultrasound waves.

Dinosaurs
Dinosaur everything!

found to be consistent with the observed neutron production rate.

Earlier test data indicated that nuclear fusion had occurred, but these data were questioned because they were taken with less precise instrumentation.

"These extensive new experiments have replicated and extended our earlier results and hopefully answer all of the previous questions surrounding our discovery," said Richard T. Lahey Jr. at Rensselaer and the director of the analytical part of the joint research project.

Other fusion techniques, such as those that use strong magnetic fields or lasers to contain the plasma, cannot easily achieve the necessary compression, Lahey said. In the approach to be published in Physical Review E, spherical compression of the plasma was achieved due to the inertia of the liquid surrounding the imploding bubbles.

Professor Lahey also explained that, unlike fission reactors, fusion does not produce a significant amount of radioactive waste products or decay heat. Tritium gas, a radioactive by-product of deuterium-deuterium bubble fusion, is actually a part of the fuel, which can be consumed in deuterium-tritium fusion reactions.

Researchers Rusi Taleyarkhan, Colin West, and Jae-Seon Cho conducted the bubble fusion experiments at ORNL. At Rensselaer and in Russia, Professors Lahey and Robert I. Nigmatulin performed the theoretical analysis of the bubble dynamics and predicted the shock-induced pressures, temperatures, and densities in the imploding vapor bubbles. Robert Block, professor emeritus of nuclear engineering at Rensselaer, helped to design, set up, and calibrate a state-of-the-art neutron and gamma ray detection system for the new experiments.

In the first experiments, with the less sophisticated equipment, the team was only able to collect data during a small portion of the five-millisecond intervals between neutron pulses. The new equipment enabled the researchers to see what was happening over the entire course of the experiment.

The data clearly show surges in neutrons emitted in precise timing with the light flashes, meaning the neutron emissions are produced by the collapsing bubbles responsible for the flashes of light, Taleyarkhan said.

"We see neutrons being emitted each time the bubble is imploding with sufficient violence," Taleyarkhan said.

Fusion of deuterium atoms emits neutrons that fall within a specific energy range of 2.5 mega-electron volts or below, which was the level of energy seen in neutrons produced in the experiment. The production of tritium also can only be attributed to fusion, and it was never observed in any of the control experiments in which normal acetone was used, he said.

Whereas data from the previous experiment had roughly a one in 100 chance of being attributed to some phenomena other than nuclear fusion, the new, more precise results represent more like a one in a trillion chance of being wrong, Taleyarkhan said.

"There is only one way to produce tritium - through nuclear processes," he said.

The results also agree with mathematical theory and modeling.

Future work will focus on studying ways to scale up the device, which is needed before it could be used in practical applications, and creating portable devices that operate without the need for the expensive equipment now used to bombard the canister with pulses of neutrons.

| HOME |
| SCIENCE DISCUSSION FORUM |
| SCIENCE DISCUSSION FORUM ARCHIVE |
| SCIENCE BOOKS | CONTACT US |

HOT TOPICS
| GLOBAL WARMING | HEALTH | NATURE AND THE ENVIRONMENT |
| PARTICLE PHYSICS AND NANOTECH | SPACE |

NEWS ARTICLE ARCHIVE
| 2005 | 2004 | 2003 | 2002 | 2001 | 2000 | 1999 | 1998 |

Press Release

FOR RELEASE: IMMEDIATE
March 2, 2004

CONTACT: Theresa Bourg
(518) 276-2840
bourgt@rpi.edu

Researchers Report Bubble Fusion Results Replicated

Physical Review E **publishes paper on fusion experiment conducted with upgraded measurement system**

TROY, N.Y. — *Physical Review E* has announced the publication of an article by a team of researche Rensselaer Polytechnic Institute (RPI), Purdue University, Oak Ridge National Laboratory (ORNL), a Russian Academy of Science (RAS) stating that they have replicated and extended previous experin results that indicated the occurrence of nuclear fusion using a novel approach for plasma confineme

This approach, called bubble fusion, and the new experimental results are being published in an extensively peer-reviewed article titled "Additional Evidence of Nuclear Emissions During Acoustic Cavitation," which is scheduled to be posted on *Physical Review E*'s Web site and published in its jo this month.

The research team used a standing ultrasonic wave to help form and then implode the cavitation bu of deuterated acetone vapor. The oscillating sound waves caused the bubbles to expand and then v collapse, creating strong compression shock waves around and inside the bubbles. Moving at about speed of sound, the internal shock waves impacted at the center of the bubbles causing very high compression and accompanying temperatures of about 100 million Kelvin.

These new data were taken with an upgraded instrumentation system that allowed data acquisition much longer time than was possible in the team's previous bubble fusion experiments. According to new data, the observed neutron emission was several orders of magnitude greater than backgroun had extremely high statistical accuracy. Tritium, which also is produced during the fusion reactions, measured and the amount produced was found to be consistent with the observed neutron producti rate.

Earlier test data, which were reported in *Science* (Vol. 295, March 2002), indicated that nuclear fus occurred, but these data were questioned because they were taken with less precise instrumentatic

"These extensive new experiments have replicated and extended our earlier results and hopefully a all of the previous questions surrounding our discovery," said Richard T. Lahey Jr., the Edward E. H Professor of Engineering at Rensselaer and the director of the analytical part of the joint research p

Other fusion techniques, such as those that use strong magnetic fields or lasers to contain the plasi cannot easily achieve the necessary compression, Lahey said. In the approach to be published in *Pl Review E*, spherical compression of the plasma was achieved due to the inertia of the liquid surrour the imploding bubbles.

Professor Lahey also explained that, unlike fission reactors, fusion does not produce a significant ar

Another internet article describing replication of the sonofusion experiments.

of radioactive waste products or decay heat. Tritium gas, a radioactive by-product of deuterium-de(
bubble fusion, is actually a part of the fuel, which can be consumed in deuterium-tritium fusion rea(

Researchers Rusi Taleyarkhan, Colin West, and Jae-Seon Cho conducted the bubble fusion experim(
ORNL. At Rensselaer and in Russia, Professors Lahey and Robert I. Nigmatulin performed the theor(
analysis of the bubble dynamics and predicted the shock-induced pressures, temperatures, and der
in the imploding vapor bubbles. Robert Block, professor emeritus of nuclear engineering at Rensseli
helped to design, set up, and calibrate a state-of-the-art neutron and gamma ray detection system
new experiments.

Special hydrodynamic shock codes have been developed in both Russia and at Rensselaer to suppo(
interpret the ORNL experiments. These computer codes indicated that the peak gas temperatures a
densities in the ORNL experiments were sufficiently high to create fusion reactions. Indeed, the the
shock code predictions of deuterium-deuterium (D-D) fusion were consistent with the ORNL data.

The research team leaders are all well known authorities in the fields of multiphase flow and heat t(
technology and nuclear engineering. Taleyarkhan, a fellow of the American Nuclear Society (ANS) a
program's director, held the position of Distinguished Scientist at ORNL, and is currently the Ardent
Bement Jr. Professor of Nuclear Engineering at Purdue University. Lahey is a fellow of both the ANS
the American Society of Mechanical Engineers (ASME), and is a member of the National Academy o
Engineering (NAE). Nigmatulin is a visiting scholar at Rensselaer, a member of the Russian Duma, {
president of the Bashkortonstan branch of the Russian Academy of Sciences (RAS). Block is a fellov
ANS and is the longtime director of the Gaerttner Linear Accelerator (LINAC) Laboratory at Rensseli
The bubble fusion research program was supported by a grant from the Defense Advanced Researc
Projects Agency (DARPA).

About Rensselaer

Rensselaer Polytechnic Institute, founded in 1824, is the nation's oldest technological university. Th
school offers degrees in engineering, the sciences, information technology, architecture, manageme
and the humanities and social sciences. Institute programs serve undergraduates, graduate studen(
working professionals around the world. Rensselaer faculty are known for pre-eminence in research
conducted in a wide range of research centers that are characterized by strong industry partnershi(
Institute is especially well known for its success in the transfer of technology from the laboratory to
marketplace so that new discoveries and inventions benefit human life, protect the environment, ar
strengthen economic development.

```
be quite valuable considering his reported first
hand experience.
```

$$\star \quad \star \quad \star \quad \star \quad \star \quad \star \quad \star$$

Two points emerge form this. The U.S. government wanted to know more about his early fusion research, the chain-reaction consumption via jetting lithium and boron isotopes into the shockwave ignited fusion reaction and he research done at the (spelled correctly) Berlin-Suhler-Waffen und Fahrzeugewerk, Gustloff-Werke, Suhl, Thuringia, Germany. In other words, the research work he did for the Gustloff Aircraft Works in Suhl, in the Jonas Valley, Nazi Germany's Area 51.

On November 21, 1956, the USAF declined sponsoring Dr. Richter but left the door open to other U.S. governmental or private agencies if they wished to do so. In the meantime, it was their recommendation that Dr. Richter be kept under lock and key, either in the USA or in Argentina.

As said earlier, the statement saying that Dr. Richter was "thinking in the year 1970" turns out to be one of the greatest understatements of the scientific 20th Century. Even today, after billions and billions of dollars and the careers of two generations of atomic scientists have been poured into sub-atomic particle research, we still do not, today, have controlled atomic fusion.

Anyone having doubts the validity of Dr. Richter's work should review the articles below concerning the state of nuclear fusion research from almost a half-century later.

Somehow, for some reason, Dr. Richter and his work were simply allowed to fade away into history.

SOURCES

The National Archives and Records Administration, 8601 Adelphi Rd., College Park, MD. 20740-6001, Foreign Scientist Case Files 1945-1958, Paperclip File of Dr. Ronald Richter, Box 54 of record Group 330.

37 | Dr. Friedrich Gold, Again

Once the reader has had time to re-read and digest the magnitude of Dr. Richter's discoveries, one small item should be injected into consideration concerning the future implications of his work. This small item comes from Dr. Friedrich Gold, which we encountered in the discussion of gaseous means to stop engines from running.

In addition to his research on gas, Dr. Gold had given considerable thought to the limitations of rocketry, nuclear propulsion, the conversion of nuclear energy into other forms of energy as well as travel through deep space. This is such a short document that it is better posted in its entirety.

The reason for the consideration of these ideas at this point is that they can only be considered in light of Dr. Richter's innovations. In particular are the similar ideas concerning nuclear propulsion, utilization of Dr. Richter's method direct conversion of atomic plasma energy to electrical energy and the utilization of "energy within 'space'" as Dr. Gold seems to call zero point energy.

While we are comparing Dr. Richter's "zero point energy" to Dr. Gold's "energy within 'space'", we might throw in Hans Coler's energy source for his machine, "Raumenergie" or "space energy". Coler's work was reviewed by both Dr. Frolich and Dr. Schumann at an early date. This means that thought about this new form of energy would have had years to foment within Nazi Germany.

In fact, these scientist's ideas dovetail so perfectly that one has to wonder as to whether there was actual

APPENDIX NO. 2.

DR. GOLD'S PERSONAL VIEWS ON FUTURE RESEARCH .

His primary interests lie in the subject of rockets and nuclear physics,
both fields being closely interconnected. He claims that, even though
he undertook some private research and gained some practical experiences on the latter, his knowledge was still somewhat insufficient.
He was therefore contemplating to continue specialized studies in
physics so as to be able to work on further developments of rockets
which will utilize atomic energy. Besides that, he is planning to
undertake some research on the still very little known subject of
"UNIVERSAL-SPACE-AVIATION ". Gold has some definite ideas pertaining
to the propulsion and control of aircraft flying through space by
means of "REPELLING MAGNETIC FIELDS OF IDENTICAL POLARITY", of which
one is fitted into the aircraft, the other , so to say, being derived
from energy within "space", thus driving the aircraft .

He professes to be quite aware of the fact that this might sound rather
fantastic - but at present it is common knowledge that the performance
of a rocket depends on the speed of the rocket itself and the speed
of particles expelled by it.

The greater the difference between these 2 figures, the worse is the
performance. With the direct use of the recoil of atomic processes
(The speed of the particles thrown out is about 30.000 Km/sec,) the
efficiency will be only a fraction of a promille. This ratio of
necessary energy and actual performance , however , is not good enough
even for nuclear processes. It will,therefore, be necessary in due
course to find a suitable transformation of the released atomic energy
for the propulsion of"universe- crafts."This is why the above idea
has been conceived. He does not know whether this suggestion can be
carried out or not. In the affirmative case, however, he is convinced
that the efforts will be worth while.

Another internet article describing replication of the sonofusion experiments.

personal communication between them. Further, one has to wonder at the general level of communication and mutual understanding of all those scientists involved in cutting-edge, high technology during the Third Reich. Also, one has to ask about the very underpinnings of how this communication and understanding could take place.

SOURCES

Combined Intelligence Objectives Sub-Committee report, Item No. 1,4,&5, file No. 32-109, page 22, Interrogation Of Dr. Hans Friedrich Gold, Jan. 17, 1946, G-2 Division, SHAEF (Reer) APO 413

38 | Why?

Let's finish the question raised in the previous chapter.

What was the reason for so many scientific and technical breakthroughs in Germany at this time? Was it simply the result of the educational system of the time? Was it the pressure of the losing war effort? Was it a culture of high expectation?

I think it was all these things and yet something else. What I mean by this statement is that the Germans anticipated making breakthroughs as a matter of course because they believed in paradigms unique to Nazi Germany. In other words, one of the answers to my question could be Nazi culture itself. Of course the words "Nazi culture" does not mean something monolithic inspite of propaganda efforts to say exactly that. It involved many paradigms.

But one of these paradigms comes specifically to mind in our discussion of German science and technology. It has to do with new energy. Contemporaries might have relegated this paradigm to the world of the occult even as they reviewed the technical achievements of the 3rd Reich immediately after the war—and so discarded. Or, it might never have been recognized as a part of Nazi thought at all, and so overlooked. Today, using a wider viewing perspective, it may be worth reconsideration.

Dr. Richter was responsible for several lines of new research. Most of us who have read his FOIA file would conclude that his work on atomic fusion was the most important. But that might not be the case in the long run. Dr. Richter coins the term "zero point energy" in 1957. Now, almost 50 years later, this is a concept is receiving a great deal of attention from researchers today who are interested in new ways of energy production.

But, it is quite obvious from his commentary that Dr. Richter first had to reconstitute his laboratory and confirm his results from earlier work. Dr. Richter, for instance, began his shock wave fusion research in Germany in 1942. His work was decades old before coming to the attention of the American CIA. Is it not reasonable to assume that the basic work done to formulate his ideas on zero point energy were from those times also? And is it not reasonable to conclude from the comments of Dr. Gold and his "energy within 'space'", that knowledge of Dr. Richter's work was desciminated though inner circles of the Reich?

"Zero point energy" is today a buzzword of a kind of fringe, cutting-edge, physics. At first glance, it seems almost impossible for this word-phrase to have been coined by an old Nazi-era German scientist. But zero point energy would not have been quite such a strange concept in Germany during the Nazi period as it seems to some now.

The Germans were working on alternative means to produce energy. Karl Schappeller, discussed in my first book, was a great example. His work was continued to the Nazi period through the Reichsarbeitsgemeinschaft. Viktor Schauberger received state funding and facilities from the Nazi government. Hans Coler continued his work during those years and his continuing research was eventually was funded by the German Navy while at least one of his devices was being produced by a division of Siemens. He called the source of energy "Raumenergie" which is "space energy" in English. In the discovery of zero point energy, Dr. Richter may have been looking for experimental confirmation of theoretical ideas already held for some time within some circles. Dr. Gold went so far as to try to explain ideas of energy within space to the Americans but they were obviously not ready to listen.

The point we should keep in mind is that all of these devices and ideas involved the vortex. A vortex device produces a torsion field according to Nick Cook, Aviation editor of Jane's Defense Weekly. Drawing from Igor Witkowski, the Bell was a machine that spun cylinders of a violet, liquid, mercury-compound-based substance. Known mercury compounds are all solids. We are left to conclude that the material used in the Bell was red mercury, which also can be violet in color.

Cook compares properties of the Bell with experiments done on spinning superconductors[1]. We already know that red mercury could be used as a semiconductor. Inserting impurities into other substances such as silicon makes semiconductors.

But was a pure form of red mercury a superconductor? Or perhaps stated better: Are certain types of red mercury superconductors? Mercury is a great conductor of electricity and used for that purpose in a variety of electric switches, including household thermostats. If red mercury is even close to being a superconductor then a vortex of red mercury given a shot of electric current would have induced a huge electric/magnetic field in the surrounding area or field.

Cook mentions that a torsion field bends 4 dimensions and so bends time. It also radiates energy, including electromagnetic energy throughout the spectrum[2]. With a vortex, it is simple. If energy goes in, then energy must come out. Think of the energy implications for tornados and hurricanes, for instance. The energy coming out doesn't necessarily take the same form of what went in. A conversion takes place. Cook mentions that efforts at tuning the bell were taking place[3]. "Tuning" means converting the output energy into a form you want.

Cook points out that a torsion field is capable of directing zero point energy. Zero point energy is aether, or ether energy by another name. A machine that can also generate an electromagnetic field is especially valuable in directing this energy[4].

Cook describes the torsion field as being something like a mixer found in a kitchen. In this analogy, the mixer puts the batter or whatever is being mixed into motion, which is the same as that of the torsion field. But instead of batter, energy itself is being put into this new pattern of motion. The result is a huge increase in the field energy being moved and so a huge increase in the energy available to be put to use.

Returning to tuning a tuned output means that a field of electromagnetic energy or perhaps even zero point energy is possible. This would certainly power any machine including one that flies. Such a powerful torsion field could also bend space and alter time. It would also function as an energy device since it would activate more energy than was inputted, just as did the simpler Schauberger vortex machines that used only air and water.

Now we can return to the question posed at the beginning of this chapter: Why did this and other breakthroughs come during the period of the Third Reich? Do you think this is all an accident? Do you think this came about, step by step, as a series of random, non-directed, unrelated discoveries that somehow got pieced together into a coherent whole? Do you think there was no overall game plan involved?

"The Germans ignored Einstein and developed an approach to gravity based on quantum theory, Wikowski said. Don't forget that Einsteinian physics, relativity physics, with its big-picture view of the universe, represented Jewish science to the Nazis. Germany was where quantum mechanics was born. The Germans were looking at gravity from a different perspective to anyone else. Maybe it gave them answers to things the pro-relativity scientists hadn't even thought of."[5]

"Some of it, however – notably the non-conventional science pursued by the SS – came from a different culture altogether."[6]

"When the Americans tripped over this mutant strain of non-linear physics and took it back home with them, they were astute enough to realize that their homegrown scientific talent couldn't handle it. That it was beyond their cultural terms of reference. That's why they recruited so many Germans. The Nazis developed a unique approach to science and engineering quite separate from the rest of the world, because of their ideology, unrestrained as it was, supported a wholly different way of doing things. Von Braun's V-2s are a case in point, but so was their understanding of physics. The trouble was, when the Americans took it all home with them they found out, too late, that it came infected with a virus. You take the science on, you take on aspects of the ideology, as well."[7]

This is a huge point. German science was influenced by German culture – a German culture of those Nazi times. To understand how all these futuristic ideas came into being, an understanding of that esoteric culture must be considered. Fortunately, the concepts under consideration, the vortex, the torsion field, zero point energy and the singularity illustrate an important aspect in their belief system.

The SS took inspiration from older mysterious groups. So did the parent organization, the Nazis themselves. The swastika, for instance, is now almost universally interpreted as a sun sign. No doubt this is true. But the swastika, as Hitler chose the symbol, was black and tipped on its side. The impression is of a spinning, hooked cross. This is the best static representation one can make of a vortex in motion. Yet, it was a black vortex. Why?

The swastika as we know it is not the only swastika to surface in Nazi Germany. The SS used round swastikas. The SS, Heinrich Himmler's rather strange creation, also drew swastikas with many more arms than the four we are accustomed to seeing.

In fact, at the SS headquarters Himmler built, Wewelsberg Castle, there is a huge stylized swastika mosaic that forms a floor of a central rotunda. This swastika has twelve arms and they are bent twice. This is the Black Sun swastika.

The Black Sun was a kind of all-seeing eye in the minds of the SS. It was allegedly located at the center of the galaxy around which our sun and all other stars made one rotation every 26,000 years. The Black Sun was a huge vortex. It could not be seen by the naked eye as our solar sun is seen. Instead, they believed, it emitted invisible radiation that extended throughout the galaxy all the way to earth. Only the initiated knew of the Black Sun.

For these initiated, the very words upon which the abbreviation "SS" is based was not the commonly held "Schutz Staffel" or body-guard in English, but "Schwarze Sonne" or Black Sun in English. So, the SS was really the Schwarze Sonne in the minds of initiates while for the masses it was Schutz Staffel. Each group gave the symbol a totally different meaning.

Today we know the Black Sun is no idle myth. Today we know that at the heart of each galaxy there lies what we call today a black hole. Today we know that this black hole and the galaxy surrounding it are part of an integrated system. We know today that there is a precise mathematical relationship between the speed of the outermost stars orbiting the black hole and the strength of that black hole itself. We know the black hole sucks in matter via a huge vortex and yieldsa tremendous amount of energy, including electro-magnetic radiation right across the spectrum. It also produces a tremendous magnetic field.

But the speed of the outer stars has nothing to do with the "attrac-tion" of gravity produced by the black hole. That black hole is much too far away. Nor does it have anything to do with the huge magnetic field generated by the black hole. Yet, the mathematical relationship is so strong that there does exist a cause and effect relationship between

A New Theory That Unifies The Forces of Nature

By
Prof. A. Zielinski*

The earth is expanding. All celestial bodies have magnetic fields that are circular or polar dependent on spin. The magnetic north- and south poles are produced by the earthís spin. The magnetic poles are moving but are on the same spot at the same hour. Every galaxy has more or less a "black hole" that is not a hole at all. The universe is not expanding, there was never a "BIG BANG". Electric power can be generated from eather.

Abstract

A new exciting discovery of the existence and behavior of aether leads to a new concept of the essence of aether, that is able to explain why the famous Michelson-Morley aether experiment of 1887 failed, explain and unify the forces of nature, explain why quantum theory works and even explain where the universe comes from, and last but not least, shows the gateway to the new source of energy of the future.

THE MICHELSON-MORLEY AETHER EXPERIMENT

Introduction

In 1887, Albert Michelson and Edward Williams Morley [1,2], assuming that aether was uniform and at rest in space, wanted to measure the absolute motion of the earth in space. In order to do so, a special sensitive interferometer was pointed in various compass directions. The interferometer readings, however, indicated that the earth had no relative motion to the aether in any horizontal direction. The interpretation of the result of the experiment was that it would mean that the earth had no relative motion in space, which was obviously not the case. Michelson and Morley could not explain this mystery and, therefore, thought that their experiment had failed. Even today, many scientists believe that the Michelson-Morley aether experiment is probably the most important experiment that did not work, in the entire history of science. One of the explanations given by numerous physicists, including Albert Einstein, is that there is no such thing as aether at all. Unill today, many mysterious forces and phenomena are still puzzling the minds of astronomers and physicists because of the unsolved mystery of the aether, that kept concealed the nature of mass, inertia, gravity, the powers of attraction and repulsion, magnetism, light, heat, electricity, superconductivity, twin stars, the source of energy of stars, volcanic and tectonic activities, black holes, and the expansion of the universe.

The mistake in the experiment

The assumption of Michelson and Morley that aether was uniform and at rest in space, was a fundamental error [1,2]. Had Michelson and Morley pointed their interferometer in a vertical plane, they would have concluded that the earth is moving in a perpendicular direction to the surface of the earth into space. A worldwide verification of their experiment would have indicated that the earth is moving everywhere simultaneously in a vertical direction into

This is an internet article in which Professor A. Zielinski proposes a unifying aether explanation of energy, matter and gravity. This is a densification and transmutation explanation of aether in which matter is a aether/gravity shield. If we add re-radiation, as in a black hole, and the theory is complete. Scientists within the 3rd Reich must have known or must have been moving toward this realization.

http://www.viewzone.com/unified.field.html

space, which is, of course, not possible. The only conclusion therefore is: aether is constantly moving towards the earth in straight perpendicular lines, just like reversed rays of energy (**Fig. 1**). I have termed this phenomenon the "Charan effect." The Charan effect is the cause of many sub-effects, as we shall discover further on. Consequent experiments and observations were so coherent that the existence of aether could not be ignored any longer, and the need of a concept or theory that would describe the essence, qualities and behavior of aether, was required for me to continue my own research in the field of quantum electrodynamics, which is my field of activity.

A concept of the nature of aether, based on the Charan effect.

The true nature of aether cannot be conceived by the human intellect since it cannot be perceived by human senses. However, conclusions may be drawn based on the actions of aether or on phenomena caused by aether actions that probably may be true or closer to the truth than present assumptions. In this view, I have developed the following theory with which almost all the phenomena mentioned earlier can be explained in a logical, coherent, and conclusive manner: Aether is a pure form of subtle, active energy, in which all the forces of nature are vested. Aether is the subtle energy tissue out of which matter has been made and is still being made and sustained. Subatomic interaction of aether and matter causes the phenomena of inertia, mass, gravity, cohesion and all the forces in nature. On its way to the center of cosmic systems such as galaxies, the solar system, and atoms, the density of aether increases, causing higher speeds of the solar planets and of the subatomic particles interacting with it. The Charan effect is fundamental for the movement, control, and equilibrium of the cosmos.

The consequences of the Charan effect

The Charan effect, as simple and innocent as it may look, may have a bearing on science and stir up many aspects of it, even in industry, economy, and society. Many ideas, theories, concepts, formulae, definitions and units in physics, even of such great men as Isaac Newton and Albert Einstein, may have to be reviewed, redefined, adjusted, or corrected. The following examples may clarify what the logical consequences could be if the Charan effect were applied just in physics and astronomy:

Inertia would mean subatomic interaction with aether.

Mass would mean concentration of aether, due to the Charan effect, which is mainly in the center of a subatomic particle or the center of a celestial body, because of the higher density (concentration) of aether there. Consequently, mass may be just a flow of aether, a flow of energy, or an absorption of aether, a phenomenon, an effect, a force. It also means that mass is not a function of velocity, as postulated by Albert Einstein, but a function of aether concentration (aether density), which subsequently causes the velocity of a particle or a celestial body.

Mass is also an indication of the amount of aether that is being absorbed by the subatomic particle or the celestial body. The closer to the sun, the higher the speeds of the solar planets, because of the higher density of aether, caused by the Charan effect.

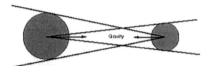

Fig. 3

Gravity would mean obstruction of the flow of aether, a kind of "aether shadow" that bodies or particles cast upon each other; less energy on one side as a result of the Charan effect (**Fig. 3**).

Binding energy or cohesion of matter would mean gravity on a molecular level, which means aether energy.

Fig. 2

Bending of light, caused by the Charan effect, may be the cause for all sorts of distortions if objects move between the eye of an observer and a source of light - twin stars? pulsars? (**Fig. 2**).

Magnetism would be caused by the movement of matter in space (in aether) or of electrons in matter (in aether).

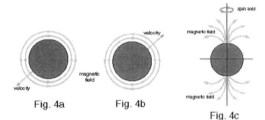

Fig. 4a   Fig. 4b   Fig. 4c

The magnetic poles of spinning celestial bodies or of spinning subatomic particles are vested in aether (**Fig. 4a, 4b**, and **4c**).

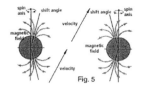

Fig. 5

Shift angles between magnetic axes and spin axes of celestial bodies are caused
by the relative motion of the body to the aether motion (**Fig. 5**). Since aether is
not at rest in space, nor uniform, measuring the shift angle and its position
would not reveal the absolute movement of the body in space. There is no such
thing as a fixed point in space; everything is moving, magnificently controlled
by one law, vested in aether.

The solar energy and the temperature of celestial bodies may be caused by the
concentration of aether due to the Charan effect; the bigger the star, the higher
the aether density and the higher the temperature.

Fig. 6

Volcanic and tectonic actions may be caused by the concentration of aether inside
or at the center of the earth (**Fig 6**). The earth may be growing, its mass may be
increasing and its temperature may be rising.

Black holes may not be black holes at all, but gigantic concentration of masses
in the center of galaxies, absorbing aether at such enormous speed, causing a
Doppler shift of the light frequency far beyond the sensitivity of our eyes and
therefore creating the impression of a black hole.

The big bang, presumably causing the expansion of the universe, may be just an
impression caused by the movement of aether towards the center of our galaxy.
Most probably, there has never been such a thing as a big bang. The Doppler red
shift of light is not only the foundation of the big bang theory, it is also the
fundamental basis of measurements in astronomy. Now, if the movement of aether in
space may cause a Doppler red shift, then a review of all the data in astronomy
is due.

Electric power can be generated from aether

Great scientists such as **Nikola Tesla** [right], Paul Dirac
and Werner Heisenberg have predicted the introduction of a
new source of energy, which they called·

"electromagnetic quantum energy," "zero-point energy" and
also "vacuum-field energy," which are different names for
aether energy. Recently, I successfully concluded
fundamental research in the field of aether energy
conversion, which has resulted in a new technology for

producing engines, generators and batteries, in an economical and technically feasible manner. The very high energy density of aether allows such a flexibility of the aether absorption/conversion units, that they can be integrated on a silicon chip, for powering the chip of a wrist watch or a computer, but can also meet the requirements of a 4,000 megawatt power plant. This means that soon a new source of energy will be powering automobiles, trains, ships, aircraft, tractors, electric power plants, homes, industries, portable computers, telephones, etc. The aether technology in which I am involved, is environmentally clean and unlimited. Its application is neither restricted nor limited by materials or resources.

Once again in history, the cards are being shuffled anew and distributed in industry, like in the days of Thomas Alva Edison, and hopefully without too much turbulence at the international stock exchanges. Let us hope that the first application of aether energy will not be for military purposes, or for one nation to take advantage of other nations, as has so often been the case in history with epochal discoveries and inventions, but for the improvement of the conditions of humanity.

References:

[1] A.A. Michelson, Am. J. Sci. 3rd ser., 22, 252-253 (1881), and Univ. of Chicago Press, 1902.

[2] A.A. Michelson & E.W. Morley, Am. J. Sci. 3rd ser., 34, 277 (1887).

Prof. Zielinski conducts research i.a. in the field of quantum electrodynamics. He is an active member of the Russian Academy of Science and is ambassador of the International Scientists Club with its headquarters at St. Petersburg, Russia. Prof. Zielinski can be contacted via the Internet at the Email address: scorpionsyndrome@hotmail.com

ViewZone || Comments? || Read Comments

Supermassive Black Holes in Galactic Nuclei

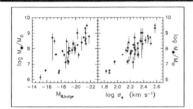

Black holes with masses of a million to a few billion times the mass of the Sun are believed to be the engines that power nuclear activity in galaxies. Active nuclei range from faint, compact radio sources like that in M31 to quasars like 3C 273 that are brighter than the whole galaxy in which they live. Some nuclei fire jets of energetic particles millions of light years into space. Almost all astronomers believe that this enormous outpouring of energy comes from the death throes of stars and gas that are falling into the central black hole. This is a very successful explanation of the observations, but until recently, it was seriously incomplete: we had no direct evidence that supermassive black holes exist.

For the past twenty years, astronomers have looked for supermassive black holes by measuring rotation and random velocities of stars and gas near galactic centers. If the velocities are large enough, as in the Sombrero Galaxy, then they imply more mass than we see in stars. The most probable explanation is a black hole. About 37 have been found as of 2001 March. Their masses are in the range expected for nuclear engines, and their numbers are consistent with predictions based on the energy output of quasars

2003 June census of supermassive black hole mass measurements (postscript) from my review paper at the Carnegie Symposium on "Coevolution of Black Holes and Galaxies"

2003 June census of supermassive black hole mass measurements (PDF)

The plot at the top of the page shows two of the main demographic results found so far:

(Left) Black hole mass correlates with the luminosity of the elliptical-galaxy-like "bulge" part of the host galaxy. The bulge luminosity is given by the absolute magnitude in the blue "B" band. Distances are based on a Hubble constant of Ho = 80 km/s/Mpc. Blue points are based on the motions of stars, green points are based on the motions of hot gas, and red points are based on the motions of cold gas in which water molecules emit maser radiation. The correlation says that more luminous galaxies -- that is, more massive galaxies -- contain more massive black holes. Probably, the reason is that bigger galaxies have more fuel to feed black holes.

(Right) Black hole mass versus the average line-of-sight random velocity ("velocity dispersion") of the stars in the host galaxy. These are not the stars near the center that are used to find the black holes; rather, they are the stars in the main body of the galaxy. How fast one of these stars moves is not affected appreciably by the black hole, it is determined by the other stars. If the black hole were taken away, these stars would not know the difference. Despite this, there is a tight correlation between their velocities and the black hole mass. The correlation says that more massive black holes live in galaxies whose stars move faster. How fast the stars move is determined by how much the galaxy collapsed inside its dark matter halo before stars formed. We conclude that there is a very close connection between galaxy formation and black hole fueling. Probably the major events that made the bulge and the major periods of black hole growth were the same events. Galaxy formation directly results in the black hole feeding that makes quasars shine.

To get gif or color postscript versions of the above figure, click on it. To get a more detailed discussion of supermassive black holes, click on one of the following review papers.

Review article for the general public (from Stardate magazine)

Review article for generalist scientists (from Encyclopedia of Astronomy and Astrophysics)

Perspective: Astronomy article for generalist scientists (from Science) (postscript)

Review article for professional astronomers: Kormendy and Richstone (1995) "Inward Bound: The Search for Supermassive Black Holes in Galaxy Nuclei" Annual Review of Astronomy and Astrophysics, 33, 581 [0.33 Mb postscript file]

- Table 1
- Figure 1 | Figure 2 | Figure 3 | Figure 5
- Figure 7 (top) | Figure 7 (bottom)
- Figure 8 | Figure 9 | Figure 10 | Figure 14 | Figure 15

Review article for professional astronomers: March 2001 update including Hubble Space Telescope results(astro-ph/0105230)

John Kormendy's Home Page

University of Texas Astronomy Home Page

HST Nuker Team Home Page

The larger the galaxy, the stronger the black hole; the stronger the black hole, the faster the stars in that galaxy rotate. But, the star speed is not accountable through the effects of "gravity". Does a black hole re-radiate the energy it captures, thereby generating energy with glues the galaxy together? Is this energy glue aether and is not aether what we call "gravity" when aether is being absorbed (or shielded) locally, by matter?

Date: 2002-06-04

Black Hole Dynamo May Be Cosmos' Ultimate Electricity Generator

ALBUQUERQUE, N.M., June 3, 2002 – Researchers at the U.S. Department of Energy's Los Alamos National Laboratory believe that magnetic field lines extending a few million light years from galaxies into space may be the result of incredibly efficient energy-producing dynamos within black holes that are somewhat analogous to an electric motor. Los Alamos researchers Philipp Kronberg, Quentin Dufton, Stirling Colgate and Hui Li today discussed this finding at the American Astronomical Society meeting in Albuquerque, N.M.

This is an internet article with compares the energy output of a black hole to an electric motor.

Black Hole Mystery Mimicked By Supercomputer

Advanced supercomputers have simulated extremely powerful energy jets squirted out by black holes, the most exotic and powerful objects in the Universe.

"This research helps us unlock the mysteries of rotating black holes and confirms that their rotation actually produces power output," said Dr. David Meier, an astrophysicist at NASA's Jet Propulsion Laboratory, Pasadena, Calif. Meier is co-author of a paper that will appear in the journal Science. The leader of the research team is Dr. Shinji Koide of Toyama University, Toyama, Japan.

A black hole is an object so dense and powerful that nothing, not even light, can escape. A black hole gobbles up stars and other material that approaches it, including other black holes. These odd objects form in one of two ways - when a dying star collapses, or when many stars and black holes collapse together in the center of a galaxy, like our Milky Way.

Both types of black holes can rotate very rapidly, dragging along the space around them. When more material falls in, it swirls and struggles wildly before being swallowed. Astronomers have witnessed this violence, including the ejection of jets, with radio and X-ray observations, but they are not able to see a black hole itself.

"We can't travel to a black hole, and we can't make one in the lab, so we used supercomputers," Meier said. This simulation process is similar to weather-prediction techniques, which create animation of how clouds are expected to move, based on current satellite views and knowledge about Earth's atmosphere and gravity effects. In much the same way, the scientists combined data about plasma swirling into a black hole with knowledge about how gravity and magnetic fields would affect it.

"We have modeled a rotating black hole with magnetized plasma falling into it," said Koide. "We simulated the way that the magnetic field harnesses energy from the rotation of the black hole."

"In this case, jets of pure electromagnetic energy are ejected by the magnetic field along the north and south poles above the black hole," Meier added. "The jets contain energy equivalent to the power of the Sun, multiplied ten billion times and then increased another one billion times."

This jet phenomenon had been predicted by Professor Roger Blandford of the California Institute of Technology, Pasadena, Calif., and his colleague, Roman Znajek, in the 1970s, but the new computer simulation confirms that prediction. The latest research was conducted in late 2001 using supercomputers at Japan's National Institute for Fusion Science.

Scientists have theorized the existence of black holes since the 1700s and identified jet-producing objects in the centers of galaxies since the early 1900s. In the 1960s, scientists explored the possibility that these jet-emitting objects were supermassive black holes between one million and several billion times heavier than our Sun. In the 1990s, it was discovered that such jets also are ejected by much smaller black holes in double star systems. A black hole ten times as massive as the Sun can form when the center of a dying star, 20 to 30 times the mass of the Sun, collapses on itself. This creates a tiny object, only a few miles across, with an intense gravitational pull. The other supermassive type of black hole is formed when many stars and black holes collapse together in the center of a galaxy.

In addition to Koide and Meier, the team includes colleagues Dr. Kazunari Shibata, Kyoto University, Kyoto, and Dr. Takahiro Kudoh, National Astronomical Observatory, Mitaka. Images of the research are available at http://www.jpl.nasa.gov/images/blackholes .

The research was partially funded by an Astrophysics Theory Grant from NASA. The California Institute of Technology in Pasadena manages JPL for NASA.

Editor's Note: The original news release can be found here.

This story has been adapted from a news release issued by NASA/Jet Propulsion Laboratory.

This is a NASA/JPL internet article. It describes the energy output of a black hole. It says in part: "This research helps us unlock the mysteries of rotating black holes and confirms that their rotation actually produces power output." In other words, a spinning black hole is a vortex and it is the vortex which makes power output possible.

the two. The black hole's sphere of influence extends to its outermost stars, which demonstrates that the whole thing, the black hole, stars and vortex galaxy are part of one huge system—one huge field.

We all know that a black hole sucks in matter and energy. Now we know that this input is matched by a huge output of energy. Along with the energy output from this black hole is it not reasonable to assume that these Nazi theoreticians might also speculate that it was the source for the mysterious, all pervasive, zero point energy? Would they have not considered this huge, powerful black hole, the Black Sun, to be a source of this power just as an electric motor generates an electric field?

Somehow, the SS had this knowledge. Somehow this concept found its way into their lore. Should the Nazis have won the war, one triangular section of Wewelsberg Castle was to form the tip of a huge architectural spear. Forming the remainder of this spear was to be something like a whole city. This city was to be a university. This university would have been dedicated to the teaching of concepts that are totally unknown, forgotten, or little appreciated today. It would have been a center for Nazi thought, culture, alternative leaning and new science.

Given their belief in the Black Sun and zero point or aether energy, is it not reasonable to assume that they would seek experimental confirmation of the basic vortex concept? Is it not reasonable to assume that, once confirmed, scientific validation and actual technical exploitation of this new source of power would be a high priority for an energy-staved country at war? In other words, is it not reasonable to assume that the Germans were pre-disposed to making the break-through that they did and, conversely, isn't it reasonable to assume that the Western Allies, for instance, were not even close to this mind-set? Further, isn't it reasonable to assume that even when confronted by the hardware and ideas of this vanquished group of scientists, these ideas would be minimized or rejected out-of-hand by outsiders simply because it had gone far beyond their own circle of thinking?

"As above, so below" is an old occult saying. In fact, the Schauber-ger devices, the Schappeller device and well as the Bell function as miniature versions of our galaxy following this line of thought. The Germans brought the knowledge of the larger concept, literally their world-view, and applied it to their specific technology.

This brings us full circle back to the SS fountainhead in

Skoda/Pilsen, the Kammler Group, and to its scientific overseer and spiritual father, Dr. Hans Kammler.

SOURCES

1. Cook, Nick, 2001, page 194, The Hunt for Zero Point One Man's Journey to the Biggest Secret Since the Invention of the Atom Bomb, Random House Group, Ltd., London

2. ibid, pages 229, 232

3. ibid, page 233

4. ibid, page 232

5. ibid, page 194

6. ibid, page 251

7. ibid, page 270

39 | Kammler Again

As mentioned in our first discussion of Kammler, all the science, technology and weaponry we have seen so far as well as much, much more awaiting to be re-discovered, were all part of the Kammler hoard hidden somewhere near Pilsen and the Skoda Works.

Kammler was careful in amassing this technological treasure. He certainly had enemies or at least those within government who were jealous of his rapid rise and the power he had taken. It is almost certain that Nazi bigwigs were kept "out of the loop" regarding this technological magic. Kammler would be, then, in a position to unveil his wonder weaponry and save the Reich, forever securing his position within the Nazi Party. The fact that this would never be realized is more chance and circumstance which was out of Kammler's control, although there are hints that he recognized political uncertainties and was involved in that arena also[1]. This part of Kammler's history, as well as his many "deaths" and possible post-war survival and hidden ascendence, should properly await telling by the researchers responsible for this startling information, hopefully, in English[2].

The immediate problem we will deal with now is attempting to make the advanced science and technology, which has been discussed in these pages, concrete, in the eyes of the reader. This is especially difficult since this same information has purposely been suppressed by all those interests who have had access to it. Only small dribbles of this vast sea of knowledge have oozed their way to the surface in the last sixty

Fernspruch - Fernschreiben - Funkspruch - Blinkspruch

Nachr.-Stelle	Nr.	an	Befördert Tag	Zeit	durch	Rolle
Funkstelle SS-Oberabschnitt Süd	140		23.4.	1658		

Durch die Nachr.-Stelle auszufüllen

Vermerke: Geheim

Geheim

Geheim 17/45

Angenommen oder aufgenommen

von	Tag	Zeit	durch

Abgang	
Tag:	
Zeit:	
Dringlichkeits-Vermerk	KR-Blitz

An SS-Sturmbannführer Grosch
Bauinspektion der Waffen-SS und Polizei
Böhmen-Mähren,
Prag
Muspillistr. 19
zur Weiterleitung an SS-Ostuf. Schürmann
Berlin

Absende-Stelle

Fernsprech-Anschluß:

DH-43

O.U., den 23.4.1945

Geräte V 1 bei Berlin sofort sprengen.
SS-Ostuf. Schürmann sofort zum Meldekopf München-Oberföhring,
Muspillistr. 19 in Marsch setzen.

(Dr.Ing.Kammler)
SS-Obergruppenführer und General
der Waffen-SS

Erledigt:

Kammler's last (official) sign of life – nuclear V-1 2 planned use against Russia

Quittung	Fernspruch / Fernschreiben / Funkspruch / Blinkspruch	Nr.	Von	An	Tag	Zeit	Annehmender Offz. (Uffz.) Name	Dienstgrad

WH-2145a
Verlag W. F. Mayr, (13b) Miesbach

This document is really the last trace of Dr. Hans Kammler. It is dated April 23, 1945. It orders SS Sturmbanfueher Grosch in Prague to order another SS officer, Schuermann, in Berlin, to immediately blow up something called a "V-1 device" there and to then report to a command in Munich. Why Kammler would waste time with a single V-1 buzz-bomb in Berlin at this time seems more than a little strange. Perhaps this was not a standard V-1 or this device was not a Vergeltungs weapon at all and so the "V" stood for something else entirely. This order is marked with a hand-written "Geheim" (Secret) and is signed by Kammler, personally, not simply issued by his office in his name. This is a strange way to exit the world stage.

years, and all that has surfaced has done so with a false and/or clouded developmental history.

Perhaps the reader will remember the discussion in my first book, Hitler's Flying Saucers, of a strange letter from Prague dated March, 1944[3]. This cryptic letter began with the words which, in English are: "Still Alive" and go on to describe recent events in Prague. It was of interest in the previous book because this letter recounted developments in one of the German flying discs at Prague.

Klaus-Peter Rothkugel has pointed out something else about this letter and it is something very important to the larger story of lost German technology. It is the first mention of the name "Achenbach". Achenbach's name is affixed by the word "Diplom.". This might either mean he was a diplomat or it might mean he had received a degree in engineering although in the latter case it is usually written with the word for engineer, "Ing.", added. Achenbach's name is written in same paragraph as describes the progress made with the flying disc and in the company of other names about which questions of their current presence and status are asked. In the case of Aschenback, it is asked "Where is Diplom. Achenbach? To Canaris –". Admiral Wilhelm Canaris was in command of the Abwehr, the German military intelligence. So connecting the dots here, Ashenbach was among a knowledgeable inner circle who knew of secret weaponry under development and had connections to the highest levels of German military intelligence.

Now, let's quickly review page 133, third and fourth paragraphs, of Hitler's Flying Saucers. These two paragraphs are based on a 1998 book in Czech by Dr. Milos Jesensky and Robert Lesniakiewicz[4]. These two paragraphs are reproduced here:

> "On October 13, 1945, over five months after the hostilities in Europe had ended, the French embassy in Prag notified the Czechoslovakian Foreign Ministry that an SS officer in a French detention camp had given them information that a cache of secret documents existed near Prag. This cache took the form of a tunnel in which 32 boxes of secret documents were hidden and were wired with explosives before being sealed at its opening. The French offered their services and the information given to them by the SS officer in question, Guenther Achenbach.

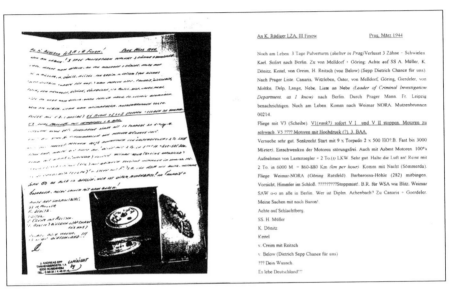

An K. Rüdiger LZA, III Finow   Prag, März 1944

Noch am Leben 3 Tage Pulverturm (*shelter in Prag*)/Verlusst 3 Zähne - Schwielen Karl. Sofort nach Berlin. Zu von Melldorf + Göring: Achte auf SS A. Müller, K. Dönitz, Keitel, von Greim, H. Reitsch (von Below) (Sepp Dietrich Chance für uns). Nach Prager Liste. Canaris, Witzleben, Oster, von Melldorf, Göring, Gierdeler, von Moltke, Delp, Lange, Nebe. Liste an Nebe (*Leader of Criminal Investigation Department, as I know*) nach Berlin. Durch Prager Mann. Fr. Leipzig benachrichtigen. Noch am Leben. Komm nach Weimar NORA. Mutzenbrunnen 00214.

Fliege mit V3 (Scheibe). V1(*rank?*) sofort V I und V II stoppen. Motoren zu schwach. V5 ???? Motoren mit Hochdruck (?). 3. BAA.

Versuche sehr gut. Senkrecht Start mit 9 x Torpedo 2 x 500 HO?.B. Fast bis 3000 M(*eter*). Einschwenken der Motoren störungsfrei. Auch mit Asbent Motoren. 100°s Aufnehmen von Lastensegler = 2 To.(*t*) LKW Sehr gut. Halte die Luft an! Reise mit 2 To. in 6000 M = 860-880 Km (*km per hour*). Komm mit Nacht (Sömmerda). Fliege Weimar-NORA (Göring Ratsfeld). Barbarossa-Höhle (282) mitbingen. Vorsicht, Himmler im Schloß. ????????Stoppmist!. B.R. für WSA wie Blitz. Weimar SAW o-o an alle in Berlin. Wer ist Diplm. Achenbach?. Zu Canaris + Goerdeler. Meine Sachen mit nach Baron!.

Achte auf Schlachtberg.

SS. H. Müller
K. Dönitz
Keitel
v. Creim mit Reitsch
v. Below (Dietrich Sepp Chance für uns)
??? Dein Wunsch.
Es lebe Deutschland!!!

The "Still Alive" letter from Prague, March, 1944. This letter was in the possession of Josef Andreas Epp until his death in 1997. It describes the developmental progress on a German flying disc in Prague as well as poor conditions in Prague to a person named K. Ruediger. Of interest now is the mention of a Diplm. Achenbach. The writer asks where he is now, to Canaris and Goedeler? Canaris ran the Naval Intelligence Agency, the Abwehr. He was later hung for treason. Today, there are rumors and a novel linking Canaris to a contingency plan in the event that Germany lost the war as well as secret, high technology. Achenbach was involved in the post-war leaking of a secret cache of information on microfilm to French authorities. Evidently, the French did not act but the Americans did once they got wind of the tip. This action provoked an international incident between the East and West. Thanks to Gerhard Peluk (Kadmon) who set this letter into legible text which appears a the right.

(f) Microfilmed documents

An agency had been set up in Berlin for the microfilming of important technical and political papers
under the control of Oberst Sauer who had his office at
88 Potsdamerstrasse. He came under the control of Speer's
ministry, but also copied all the important papers of
the S.S. Hauptamt. After the first heavy attacks on Berlin in 1943 it was decided to conceal three or more sets
of the film copies at various dispersal points, probably
in southern Germany. Gen.Ing. Herrmann and Oberst Diesing of the R.L.M. were thought to be responsible for the
evacuation order. Manfred von Brauchitsch was charged
with the transport of the films. Obersts Kneemeier and
Diesing of the R.L.M., Oberst Geist who worked with Sauer
and the head of the Beschaffungs and Rüstungsliefer-
ungsamt of the army should know the location of one or
more of the hiding places. This information has been
passed to Air Intelligence and they are dealing with the
matter.

This is a British Intelligence Objectives Sub-Committee report, number 142, which describes a cache of secret documents on microfilm.

But even after months of waiting, the French from the Czechoslovakian Foreign Ministry received no response.

Somehow the Americans got wind of this information. Incredibly, the Americans on February 13, 1946, mounted an armed incursion into Czechoslovakiam, which was in the Soviet sphere of occupation, retrieved this hoard of information and escaped back into occupied Germany. Naturally the Czechoslovakians were furious and demanded and got an apology from the Americans. They also demanded the return of the German documents stolen from their sovereign territory. The Americans did return documents but probably not those sensitive documents for which the expedition was mounted."

Achenbach was the source of a piece of intelligence describing a hoard of documents near Prague, which, as it turned out, interested the Americans enough to mount in incursion, that is, mount an invasion, breaking international law at a very sensitive moment in time. The only reasonable explanation for this series of events is that this hoard of documents represented the microfilmed records of the Kammler Group and the entire cache of secret German weapons, science and technology.

Now, new evidence has surfaced that the Americans did have prior knowledge of this cache of documents. This evidence takes the form of an intelligence report produced by the United States Strategic Air Force In Europe, Office Of The Assistant Chief of Staff A-2, Exploitation Division APO 033 dated July 29, 1945[5]. This report deals with any possible information or weaponry produced at Skoda by the Germans, which could have been sent to the Japanese. In late July, 1945, the atomic bomb had not yet been dropped on Hiroshima, so hostilities were still on-going in the Pacific. The report has been edited using a favorite method of the government. They have made much of the report illegible. Because it was taken off microfilm the government feels it has plausible deny-ability in rendering it illegible. Fortunately, the first few and last page can be made out and with some processing, read. The very last paragraph jumps out. The last page is reproduced here and the last paragraph reads:

"4. Investigation should be undertaken of report that

microfilms of 2 1/2 million Skoda drawings had been
hidden in three caves immediately East of SRBSKO (L-
5863) in the event that Ordnance personnel are not
satisfied with completeness of previous investigations."

What is meant by "not satisfied" is what was described in the first
two pages of the report. The basic problem is that at least two
American intelligence units were sent to Skoda but got little coopera-
tion from the Czechs in charge of the facility. These Czechs quickly
realized how their bread was buttered. They and their country would
remain in the Soviet sphere so it was with the Soviets that their future
lay, not the Western Allies. Giving sensitive information to the
Americans would not be viewed upon favorably by the Soviets.

Once the war with Japan was over, the Americans returned to the
topic of the Kammler Group and its files. They realized that the
Czechs had given them less than the truth. They also had intelligence
of a large cache of sensitive documents, intelligence that was
confirmed by the French. Apparently, the Soviets had not been given
this information for whatever reasons. The Americans did act, seizing
the microfilmed documents, some of which were later returned.

As to the question if the Americans, British, French or Russians ever
found all of the German secret high-technology they sought, well, the
answer is that it certainly has to be doubted[6].

Another source, Kurt Kreutzfeld, a German prisoner of war interviewed and cited in the British Intelligence Sub-Committee report
number 142, page 4, shows us how widespread microfilming of this
type was:

"An agency had been set up in Berlin for the microfilming
of important technical and political papers under the
control of Oberst Sauer who had his office at 88
Potsdamerstrasse. He came under the control of Speer's
ministry, but also copied all the important papers of the
S.S. Hauptamt. After the first heavy attacks of Berlin in
1943 it was decided to conceal three or more sets of the
film copies at various dispersal points, probably in
southern Germany. Gen. Ing. Herrmann and Oberst
Diesing of the R.L.M. were thought to be responsible for
the evacuation order. Manfred von Brauchitsch was
charged with the transport of the films. Obersts

330

Kneemeier and Diesing of the R.L.M., Oberst Geist who worked with Sauer and the head of the Beschaffungs and Ruestungslieferungamt of the army should know the location of one or more of the hiding places. This information has been passed to Air Intelligence and they are dealing with the matter."

Indeed, one witness claims that still, today, the 2.5 tons of archival material remain under the control of former SS members and are still intact[7].

Sources

1. Mayer, Edgar and Thomas Mehner, 2002, page 19, *Die Atombombe und das Dritte Reich Das Geheimnis des Dreiecks Arnstadt-Wechmar-Ohrdruf*, Jochen Kopp Verlag, Rottenburg

2. ibid

3. Stevens, Henry, 2003, page 50, 135, *Hitler's Flying Saucers A Guide To German Flying Discs Of The Second World War*, Adventures Unlimited Publishing, Kempton, Illinois

4. Jesensky, Milos Ph.D., and Robert Lesniakiewicz, 1998, page 98-102, *"Wunderland" Memozemske Technologie Treiti Rise*, Aos Publishing

5. United States Strategic Air Forces In Europe Office Of The Assistant Chief Of Staff A-2 Exploitation Division APO 033, Maxwell AFB, microfilm roll A5730, 1955, Maxwell AFB

6. Mayer, Edgar and Thomas Mehner, 2002, page 23

7. Georg, Friedrich and Thomas Mehner, 2004, page 257, Atomziel New York Geheime Grossraketen – und Raumfahrtprojekte des Dritten Reiches, Jochen Kopp Verlag, Rottenburg

40 | Conclusion

Does our government keep files of German technology suppressed to this day? I certainly think so. In fact, I think there is a whole history of World War Two German scientific and technical development that has been kept from us.

As has been mentioned, rarely are the implications of any technology discussed in government files. There seems to be some unwritten system by which only a general description of the technology is given in a government report. From there government people must go to a more secret and detailed report or contact the individuals responsible for compiling that report. Should their security clearance suffice, a briefing might follow. The final stage might involve a trip to the government facility involved with further development of this technology.

People high up in government often retire to work for private industry. It is suspected that sometimes a reward is given to these individuals if they have distinguished themselves and endeared themselves in some way while in government service. What better way to reward someone than to throw a technological pearl their way, or rather, in the way of the private industrial firm in which they are now employed and in which the individual in question has stock options. In this way German technology was slowly and secretly spread throughout American industry to the benefit of certain insiders. We have already touched upon one example involving exactly this scenario, but let me go over this excellent example again, making this second point.

German tank crews on the Eastern Front found that low temperature winter conditions turned their crankcase oil into asphalt. The tanks wouldn't start. German soldiers actually had to build fires under their tanks to heat the oil in order for their tanks to start in the morning. Starting each day by building a fire under your tank isn't exactly safe. German chemists needed to get busy.

Oil gets thicker as it cools. This is one measure of oil, its flow rate, which is called viscosity. This is familiar to as by numbers: 30 weight oil, 10w-30 oil, as so forth. The lower the number, the thinner the oil. Longer oil molecules flow more slowly than shorter ones. Actually, each "weight" of oil is an average containing both long and short molecular strands. The average strand length for 10w oil is shorter than for 20w oil but each grade represents an average, each contains both long and short oil molecules.

What the German chemists did was to re-synthesize new oil molecules from existing mineral oil. The new re-synthesized molecules were more uniform in length as compared with normal mineral oil. They found that the new synthetic oil flowed much better at low temperatures because of this internal consistency. This meant that the tanks were able to start in cold weather. As a byproduct of this new process it was found that the new molecules were much tougher than conventional oil and could lubricate at much higher temperatures. After the war this technology disappeared for thirty years.

Then, in 1975, Mobil Oil Company announced a new product, "Mobil One". This was based upon the German process for re-synthesized mineral oil. It was a huge financial success. Somehow, and for some reason, Mobil Oil got the secrets to the German synthetic oil process after a lapse of thirty years and made a ton of money. This revelation spawned a whole new lubrication industry, that of synthetic motor oil.

Another factor is timing. With new times come new priorities. After May, 1945, the priority was using German technology to defeat the Japanese, as we did with the atomic bomb. Later, the priority was deterrence of the Communist Block. Energy has become a priority. It is interesting that the British only made the discovery of Hans Coler public after the first energy crisis of the early 1970s. Evidently they were afraid of the accusation of suppression of this technology and wanted to come clean before the next energy crisis.

I think we can expect large American companies to "invent" some of these technologies in the near future as the need arises. I also think that any further economic deterioration in the lands of the former Soviet Union also might produce some of this technology on the open or black market as was the case with red mercury. There is also the possibility that the former Allied Powers did not corner all of this German technology. To this day the Germans keep secrets, even from other NATO and EU countries. The underground high-tech facilities at Jonastal are proof that there remains an untold story or two.

Besides the technology itself, I think whole suppressed or hidden histories of how this technology came to pass will slowly surface as it become feasible to do so in the political climate. The final history of World War Two has not yet been written.

Thanks

I have many people who have helped me with this book to thank. Some have contributed material. Some have contributed information, opinions, ideas or even done translation work. These include: Joseph Altairac, Dr. David Chapman, Remy Chavilier, Rainer Daehnhardt, Dr. Gordon Freeman, the late Heiner Gehring, Friedrich Georg, Professor Arnold Krammer, "Leo", Lea McDonald, Thomas Mehner, Gerhard Petak, Jeff Rense, Klaus-Peter Rothkugel, Greg Rowe and Milos Vnenk. Special thanks to Lisa Stevens for proofreading/editing this book.

LOST CITIES

LOST CITIES OF ATLANTIS, ANCIENT EUROPE & THE MEDITERRANEAN
by David Hatcher Childress

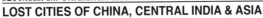

Atlantis! The legendary lost continent comes under the close scrutiny of maverick archaeologist David Hatcher Childress in this sixth book in the internationally popular *Lost Cities* series. Childress takes the reader in search of sunken cities in the Mediterranean; across the Atlas Mountains in search of Atlantean ruins; to remote islands in search of megalithic ruins; to meet living legends and secret societies. From Ireland to Turkey, Morocco to Eastern Europe, and around the remote islands of the Mediterranean and Atlantic, Childress takes the reader on an astonishing quest for mankind's past. Ancient technology, cataclysms, megalithic construction, lost civilizations and devastating wars of the past are all explored in this book. Childress challenges the skeptics and proves that great civilizations not only existed in the past, but the modern world and its problems are reflections of the ancient world of Atlantis.
524 PAGES. 6x9 PAPERBACK. ILLUSTRATED. BIBLIOGRAPHY & INDEX. $16.95. CODE: MED

LOST CITIES OF CHINA, CENTRAL INDIA & ASIA
by David Hatcher Childress

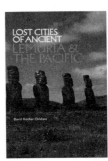

Like a real life "Indiana Jones," maverick archaeologist David Childress takes the reader on an incredible adventure across some of the world's oldest and most remote countries in search of lost cities and ancient mysteries. Discover ancient cities in the Gobi Desert; hear fantastic tales of lost continents, vanished civilizations and secret societies bent on ruling the world; visit forgotten monasteries in forbidding snow-capped mountains with strange tunnels to mysterious subterranean cities! A unique combination of far-out exploration and practical travel advice, it will astound and delight the experienced traveler or the armchair voyager.
429 PAGES. 6x9 PAPERBACK. ILLUSTRATED. FOOTNOTES & BIBLIOGRAPHY. $14.95. CODE: CHI

LOST CITIES OF ANCIENT LEMURIA & THE PACIFIC
by David Hatcher Childress

Was there once a continent in the Pacific? Called Lemuria or Pacifica by geologists, Mu or Pan by the mystics, there is now ample mythological, geological and archaeological evidence to "prove" that an advanced and ancient civilization once lived in the central Pacific. Maverick archaeologist and explorer David Hatcher Childress combs the Indian Ocean, Australia and the Pacific in search of the surprising truth about mankind's past. Contains photos of the underwater city on Pohnpei; explanations on how the statues were levitated around Easter Island in a clockwise vortex movement; tales of disappearing islands; Egyptians in Australia; and more.
379 PAGES. 6x9 PAPERBACK. ILLUSTRATED. FOOTNOTES & BIBLIOGRAPHY. $14.95. CODE: LEM

LOST CITIES OF NORTH & CENTRAL AMERICA
by David Hatcher Childress

Down the back roads from coast to coast, maverick archaeologist and adventurer David Hatcher Childress goes deep into unknown America. With this incredible book, you will search for lost Mayan cities and books of gold, discover an ancient canal system in Arizona, climb gigantic pyramids in the Midwest, explore megalithic monuments in New England, and join the astonishing quest for lost cities throughout North America. From the war-torn jungles of Guatemala, Nicaragua and Honduras to the deserts, mountains and fields of Mexico, Canada, and the U.S.A., Childress takes the reader in search of sunken ruins, Viking forts, strange tunnel systems, living dinosaurs, early Chinese explorers, and fantastic lost treasure. Packed with both early and current maps, photos and illustrations.
590 PAGES. 6x9 PAPERBACK. ILLUSTRATED. FOOTNOTES. BIBLIOGRAPHY. INDEX. $16.95. CODE: NCA

LOST CITIES & ANCIENT MYSTERIES OF SOUTH AMERICA
by David Hatcher Childress

Rogue adventurer and maverick archaeologist David Hatcher Childress takes the reader on unforgettable journeys deep into deadly jungles, high up on windswept mountains and across scorching deserts in search of lost civilizations and ancient mysteries. Travel with David and explore stone cities high in mountain forests and hear fantastic tales of Inca treasure, living dinosaurs, and a mysterious tunnel system. Whether he is hopping freight trains, searching for secret cities, or just dealing with the daily problems of food, money, and romance, the author keeps the reader spellbound. Includes both early and current maps, photos, and illustrations, and plenty of advice for the explorer planning his or her own journey of discovery.
381 PAGES. 6x9 PAPERBACK. ILLUSTRATED. FOOTNOTES. BIBLIOGRAPHY. INDEX. $16.95. CODE: SAM

LOST CITIES & ANCIENT MYSTERIES OF AFRICA & ARABIA
by David Hatcher Childress

Across ancient deserts, dusty plains and steaming jungles, maverick archaeologist David Childress continues his world-wide quest for lost cities and ancient mysteries. Join him as he discovers forbidden cities in the Empty Quarter of Arabia; "Atlantean" ruins in Egypt and the Kalahari desert; a mysterious, ancient empire in the Sahara; and more. This is the tale of an extraordinary life on the road: across war-torn countries, Childress searches for King Solomon's Mines, living dinosaurs, the Ark of the Covenant and the solutions to some of the fantastic mysteries of the past.
423 PAGES. 6x9 PAPERBACK. ILLUSTRATED. FOOTNOTES & BIBLIOGRAPHY. $14.95. CODE: AFA

24 hour credit card orders—call: 815-253-6390 fax: 815-253-6300
email: auphq@frontiernet.net   www.adventuresunlimitedpress.com   www.wexclub.com

TECHNOLOGY OF THE GODS
The Incredible Sciences of the Ancients
by David Hatcher Childress

Popular *Lost Cities* author David Hatcher Childress takes us into the amazing world of ancient technology, from computers in antiquity to the "flying machines of the gods." Childress looks at the technology that was allegedly used in Atlantis and the theory that the Great Pyramid of Egypt was originally a gigantic power station. He examines tales of ancient flight and the technology that it involved; how the ancients used electricity; megalithic building techniques; the use of crystal lenses and the fire from the gods; evidence of various high tech weapons in the past, including atomic weapons; ancient metallurgy and heavy machinery; the role of modern inventors such as Nikola Tesla in bringing ancient technology back into modern use; impossible artifacts; and more.

356 PAGES. 6x9 PAPERBACK. ILLUSTRATED. BIBLIOGRAPHY. $16.95. CODE: TGOD

VIMANA AIRCRAFT OF ANCIENT INDIA & ATLANTIS
by David Hatcher Childress, introduction by Ivan T. Sanderson

Did the ancients have the technology of flight? In this incredible volume on ancient India, authentic Indian texts such as the *Ramayana* and the *Mahabharata* are used to prove that ancient aircraft were in use more than four thousand years ago. Included in this book is the entire Fourth Century BC manuscript *Vimaanika Shastra* by the ancient author Maharishi Bharadwaaja, translated into English by the Mysore Sanskrit professor G.R. Josyer. Also included are chapters on Atlantean technology, the incredible Rama Empire of India and the devastating wars that destroyed it. Also an entire chapter on mercury vortex propulsion and mercury gyros, the power source described in the ancient Indian texts. Not to be missed by those interested in ancient civilizations or the UFO enigma.

334 PAGES. 6x9 PAPERBACK. RARE PHOTOGRAPHS, MAPS AND DRAWINGS. $15.95. CODE: VAA

LOST CONTINENTS & THE HOLLOW EARTH
I Remember Lemuria and the Shaver Mystery
by David Hatcher Childress & Richard Shaver

Lost Continents & the Hollow Earth is Childress' thorough examination of the early hollow earth stories of Richard Shaver and the fascination that fringe fantasy subjects such as lost continents and the hollow earth have had for the American public. Shaver's rare 1948 book *I Remember Lemuria* is reprinted in its entirety, and the book is packed with illustrations from Ray Palmer's *Amazing Stories* magazine of the 1940s. Palmer and Shaver told of tunnels running through the earth—tunnels inhabited by the Deros and Teros, humanoids from an ancient spacefaring race that had inhabited the earth, eventually going underground, hundreds of thousands of years ago. Childress discusses the famous hollow earth books and delves deep into whatever reality may be behind the stories of tunnels in the earth. Operation High Jump to Antarctica in 1947 and Admiral Byrd's bizarre statements, tunnel systems in South America and Tibet, the underground world of Agartha, the belief of UFOs coming from the South Pole, more.

344 PAGES. 6x9 PAPERBACK. ILLUSTRATED. $16.95. CODE: LCHE

A HITCHHIKER'S GUIDE TO ARMAGEDDON
by David Hatcher Childress

With wit and humor, popular Lost Cities author David Hatcher Childress takes us around the world and back in his trippy finalé to the Lost Cities series. He's off on an adventure in search of the apocalypse and end times. Childress hits the road from the fortress of Megiddo, the legendary citadel in northern Israel where Armageddon is prophesied to start. Hitchhiking around the world, Childress takes us from one adventure to another, to ancient cities in the deserts and the legends of worlds before our own. Childress muses on the rise and fall of civilizations, and the forces that have shaped mankind over the millennia, including wars, invasions and cataclysms. He discusses the ancient Armageddons of the past, and chronicles recent Middle East developments and their ominous undertones. In the meantime, he becomes a cargo cult god on a remote island off New Guinea, gets dragged into the Kennedy Assassination by one of the "conspirators," investigates a strange power operating out of the Altai Mountains of Mongolia, and discovers how the Knights Templar and their off-shoots have driven the world toward an epic battle centered around Jerusalem and the Middle East.

320 PAGES. 6x9 PAPERBACK. ILLUSTRATED. INDEX. $16.95. CODE: HGA

IN QUEST OF LOST WORLDS
Journey to Mysterious Algeria, Ethiopia & the Yucatan
by Count Byron Khun de Prorok

Finally, a reprint of Count Byron de Prorok's classic archeology/adventure book first published in 1936 by E.P. Dutton & Co. in New York. In this exciting and well illustrated book, de Prorok takes us into the deep Sahara of forbidden Algeria, to unknown Ethiopia, and to the many prehistoric ruins of the Yucatan. Includes: Tin Hinan, Legendary Queen of the Tuaregs; The mysterious A'Haggar Range of southern Algeria; Jupiter, Ammon and Tripolitania; The "Talking Dune"; The Land of the Garamantes; Mexico and the Poison Trail; Seeking Atlantis—Chichen Itza; Shadowed by the "Little People"—the Lacandon Pygmie Maya; Ancient Pyramids of the Usamasinta and Piedras Negras in Guatemala; In Search of King Solomon's Mines & the Land of Ophir; Ancient Emerald Mines of Ethiopia. Also included in this book are 24 pages of special illustrations of the famous—and strange—wall paintings of the Ahaggar from the rare book *The Search for the Tassili Frescoes* by Henri Lhote (1959). A visual treat of a remote area of the world that is even today forbidden to outsiders!

324 PAGES. 6x9 PAPERBACK. ILLUSTRATED. $16.95. CODE: IQLW

THE LAND OF OSIRIS
An Introduction to Khemitology
by Stephen S. Mehler

Was there an advanced prehistoric civilization in ancient Egypt? Were they the people who built the great pyramids and carved the Great Sphinx? Did the pyramids serve as energy devices and not as tombs for kings? Mehler has uncovered an indigenous oral tradition that still exists in Egypt, and has been fortunate to have studied with a living master of this tradition, Abd'El Hakim Awyan. Mehler has also been given permission to present these teachings to the Western world, teachings that unfold a whole new understanding of ancient Egypt and have only been presented heretofore in fragments by other researchers. Chapters include: Egyptology and Its Paradigms; Khemitology—New Paradigms; Asgat Nefer—The Harmony of Water; Khemit and the Myth of Atlantis; The Extraterrestrial Question; more.

272 PAGES. 6x9 PAPERBACK. ILLUSTRATED. COLOR SECTION. BIBLIOGRAPHY. $18.95. CODE: LOOS

ANTI-GRAVITY

THE FREE-ENERGY DEVICE HANDBOOK
A Compilation of Patents and Reports
by David Hatcher Childress

A large-format compilation of various patents, papers, descriptions and diagrams concerning free-energy devices and systems. *The Free-Energy Device Handbook* is a visual tool for experimenters and researchers into magnetic motors and other "over-unity" devices. With chapters on the Adams Motor, the Hans Coler Generator, cold fusion, superconductors, "N" machines, space-energy generators, Nikola Tesla, T. Townsend Brown, and the latest in free-energy devices. Packed with photos, technical diagrams, patents and fascinating information, this book belongs on every science shelf. With energy and profit being a major political reason for fighting various wars, free-energy devices, if ever allowed to be mass distributed to consumers, could change the world! Get your copy now before the Department of Energy bans this book!
292 PAGES. 8x10 PAPERBACK. ILLUSTRATED. BIBLIOGRAPHY. $16.95. CODE: FEH

THE ANTI-GRAVITY HANDBOOK
edited by David Hatcher Childress, with Nikola Tesla, T.B. Paulicki, Bruce Cathie, Albert Einstein and others

The new expanded compilation of material on Anti-Gravity, Free Energy, Flying Saucer Propulsion, UFOs, Suppressed Technology, NASA Cover-ups and more. Highly illustrated with patents, technical illustrations and photos. This revised and expanded edition has more material, including photos of Area 51, Nevada, the government's secret testing facility. This classic on weird science is back in a 90s format!
• How to build a flying saucer.
• Arthur C. Clarke on Anti-Gravity.
• Crystals and their role in levitation.
• Secret government research and development.
• Nikola Tesla on how anti-gravity airships could
  draw power from the atmosphere.
• Bruce Cathie's Anti-Gravity Equation.
• NASA, the Moon and Anti-Gravity.
253 PAGES. 7x10 PAPERBACK. BIBLIOGRAPHY/INDEX/APPENDIX. HIGHLY ILLUSTRATED. $16.95. CODE: AGH

ANTI–GRAVITY & THE WORLD GRID
Is the earth surrounded by an intricate electromagnetic grid network offering free energy? This compilation of material on ley lines and world power points contains chapters on the geography, mathematics, and light harmonics of the earth grid. Learn the purpose of ley lines and ancient megalithic structures located on the grid. Discover how the grid made the Philadelphia Experiment possible. Explore the Coral Castle and many other mysteries, including acoustic levitation, Tesla Shields and scalar wave weaponry. Browse through the section on anti-gravity patents, and research resources.
274 PAGES. 7x10 PAPERBACK. ILLUSTRATED. $14.95. CODE: AGW

ETHER TECHNOLOGY
A Rational Approach to Gravity Control
by Rho Sigma

This classic book on anti-gravity and free energy is back in print and back in stock. Written by a well-known American scientist under the pseudonym of "Rho Sigma," this book delves into international efforts at gravity control and discoid craft propulsion. Before the Quantum Field, there was "Ether." This small, but informative book has chapters on John Searle and "Searle discs;" T. Townsend Brown and his work on anti-gravity and ether-vortex turbines. Includes a forward by former NASA astronaut Edgar Mitchell.
108 PAGES. 6x9 PAPERBACK. ILLUSTRATED. $12.95. CODE: ETT

ANTI–GRAVITY & THE UNIFIED FIELD
edited by David Hatcher Childress

Is Einstein's Unified Field Theory the answer to all of our energy problems? Explored in this compilation of material is how gravity, electricity and magnetism manifest from a unified field around us. Why artificial gravity is possible; secrets of UFO propulsion; free energy; Nikola Tesla and anti-gravity airships of the 20s and 30s; flying saucers as superconducting whirls of plasma; anti-mass generators; vortex propulsion; suppressed technology; government cover-ups; gravitational pulse drive; spacecraft & more.
240 PAGES. 7x10 PAPERBACK. ILLUSTRATED. $14.95. CODE: AGU

TAPPING THE ZERO POINT ENERGY
Free Energy & Anti-Gravity in Today's Physics
by Moray B. King

King explains how free energy and anti-gravity are possible. The theories of the zero point energy maintain there are tremendous fluctuations of electrical field energy imbedded within the fabric of space. This book tells how, in the 1930s, inventor T. Henry Moray could produce a fifty kilowatt "free energy" machine; how an electrified plasma vortex creates anti-gravity; how the Pons/Fleischmann "cold fusion" experiment could produce tremendous heat without fusion; and how certain experiments might produce a gravitational anomaly.
190 PAGES. 5x8 PAPERBACK. ILLUSTRATED. $12.95. CODE: TAP

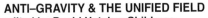

24 hour credit card orders—call: 815-253-6390 fax: 815-253-6300
email: auphq@frontiernet.net   www.adventuresunlimitedpress.com   www.wexclub.com

ANTI-GRAVITY

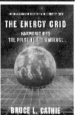

THE A.T. FACTOR
A Scientists Encounter with UFOs: Piece For A Jigsaw Part 3
by Leonard Cramp
British aerospace engineer Cramp began much of the scientific anti-gravity and UFO propulsion analysis back in 1955 with his landmark book *Space, Gravity & the Flying Saucer* (out-of-print and rare). His next books (available from Adventures Unlimited) *UFOs & Anti-Gravity: Piece for a Jig-Saw* and *The Cosmic Matrix: Piece for a Jig-Saw Part 2* began Cramp's in depth look into gravity control, free-energy, and the interlocking web of energy that pervades the universe. In this final book, Cramp brings to a close his detailed and controversial study of UFOs and Anti-Gravity.
324 PAGES. 6x9 PAPERBACK. ILLUSTRATED. BIBLIOGRAPHY. INDEX. $16.95. CODE: ATF

COSMIC MATRIX
Piece for a Jig-Saw, Part Two
by Leonard G. Cramp

Cosmic Matrix is the long-awaited sequel to his 1966 book *UFOs & Anti-Gravity: Piece for a Jig-Saw*. Cramp has had a long history of examining UFO phenomena and has concluded that UFOs use the highest possible aeronautic science to move in the way they do. Cramp examines anti-gravity effects and theorizes that this super-science used by the craft—described in detail in the book—can lift mankind into a new level of technology, transportation and understanding of the universe. The book takes a close look at gravity control, time travel, and the interlocking web of energy between all planets in our solar system with Leonard's unique technical diagrams. A fantastic voyage into the present and future!
364 PAGES. 6x9 PAPERBACK. ILLUSTRATED. BIBLIOGRAPHY. $16.00. CODE: CMX

UFOS AND ANTI-GRAVITY
Piece For A Jig-Saw
by Leonard G. Cramp
Leonard G. Cramp's 1966 classic book on flying saucer propulsion and suppressed technology is a highly technical look at the UFO phenomena by a trained scientist. Cramp first introduces the idea of 'anti-gravity' and introduces us to the various theories of gravitation. He then examines the technology necessary to build a flying saucer and examines in great detail the technical aspects of such a craft. Cramp's book is a wealth of material and diagrams on flying saucers, anti-gravity, suppressed technology, G-fields and UFOs. Chapters include Crossroads of Aerodynamics, Aerodynamic Saucers, Limitations of Rocketry, Gravitation and the Ether, Gravitational Spaceships, G-Field Lift Effects, The Bi-Field Theory, VTOL and Hovercraft, Analysis of UFO photos, more.
388 PAGES. 6x9 PAPERBACK. ILLUSTRATED. $16.95. CODE: UAG

THE ENERGY GRID
Harmonic 695, The Pulse of the Universe
by Captain Bruce Cathie.
This is the breakthrough book that explores the incredible potential of the Energy Grid and the Earth's Unified Field all around us. Cathie's first book, *Harmonic 33*, was published in 1968 when he was a commercial pilot in New Zealand. Since then, Captain Bruce Cathie has been the premier investigator into the amazing potential of the infinite energy that surrounds our planet every microsecond. Cathie investigates the Harmonics of Light and how the Energy Grid is created. In this amazing book are chapters on UFO Propulsion, Nikola Tesla, Unified Equations, the Mysterious Aerials, Pythagoras & the Grid, Nuclear Detonation and the Grid, Maps of the Ancients, an Australian Stonehenge examined, more.
255 PAGES. 6x9 TRADEPAPER. ILLUSTRATED. $15.95. CODE: TEG

THE BRIDGE TO INFINITY
Harmonic 371244
by Captain Bruce Cathie
Cathie has popularized the concept that the earth is crisscrossed by an electromagnetic grid system that can be used for anti-gravity, free energy, levitation and more. The book reveals a new analysis of the harmonic nature of reality, acoustic levitation, pyramid power, harmonic receiver towers and UFO propulsion. It concludes that today's scientists have at their command a fantastic store of knowledge with which to advance the welfare of the human race.
204 PAGES. 6x9 TRADEPAPER. ILLUSTRATED. $14.95. CODE: BTF

THE HARMONIC CONQUEST OF SPACE
by Captain Bruce Cathie
Chapters include: Mathematics of the World Grid; the Harmonics of Hiroshima and Nagasaki; Harmonic Transmission and Receiving; the Link Between Human Brain Waves; the Cavity Resonance between the Earth; the Ionosphere and Gravity; Edgar Cayce—the Harmonics of the Subconscious; Stonehenge; the Harmonics of the Moon; the Pyramids of Mars; Nikola Tesla's Electric Car; the Robert Adams Pulsed Electric Motor Generator; Harmonic Clues to the Unified Field; and more. Also included are tables showing the harmonic relations between the earth's magnetic field, the speed of light, and anti-gravity/gravity acceleration at different points on the earth's surface. New chapters in this edition on the giant stone spheres of Costa Rica, Atomic Tests and Volcanic Activity, and a chapter on Ayers Rock analysed with Stone Mountain, Georgia.
248 PAGES. 6x9. PAPERBACK. ILLUSTRATED. BIBLIOGRAPHY. $16.95. CODE: HCS

MAN-MADE UFOS 1944—1994
Fifty Years of Suppression
by Renato Vesco & David Hatcher Childress
A comprehensive look at the early "flying saucer" technology of Nazi Germany and the genesis of man-made UFOs. This book takes us from the work of captured German scientists to escaped battalions of Germans, secret communities in South America and Antarctica to todays state-of-the-art "Dreamland" flying machines. Heavily illustrated, this astonishing book blows the lid off the "government UFO conspiracy" and explains with technical diagrams the technology involved. Examined in detail are secret underground airfields and factories; German secret weapons; "suction" aircraft; the origin of NASA; gyroscopic stabilizers and engines; the secret Marconi aircraft factory in South America; and more. Introduction by W.A. Harbinson, author of the Dell novels *GENESIS* and *REVELATION*.
318 PAGES. 6x9 PAPERBACK. ILLUSTRATED. INDEX & FOOTNOTES. $22.95. CODE: MMU

FREE ENERGY SYSTEMS

HARNESSING THE WHEELWORK OF NATURE
Tesla's Science of Energy
by Thomas Valone, Ph.D., P.E.
A compilation of essays, papers and technical briefings on the emerging Tesla Technology and Zero Point Energy engineering that will soon change the entire way we live. Chapters include: Tesla: Scientific Superman who Launched the Westinghouse Industrial Firm by John Shatlan; Nikola Tesla—Electricity's Hidden Genius, excerpt from The Search for Free Energy; Tesla's History at Niagara Falls; Non-Hertzian Waves: True Meaning of the Wireless Transmission of Power by Toby Grotz; On the Transmission of Electricity Without Wires by Nikola Tesla; Tesla's Magnifying Transmitter by Andrija Puharich; Tesla's Self-Sustaining Electrical Generator and the Ether by Oliver Nichelson; Self-Sustaining Non-Hertzian Longitudinal Waves by Dr. Robert Bass; Modification of Maxwell's Equations in Free Space; Scalar Electromagnetic Waves; Disclosures Concerning Tesla's Operation of an ELF Oscillator; A Study of Tesla's Advanced Concepts & Glossary of Tesla Technology Terms; Electric Weather Forces: Tesla's Vision by Charles Yost; The New Art of Projecting Concentrated Non-Dispersive Energy Through Natural Media; The Homopolar Generator: Tesla's Contribution by Thomas Valone; Tesla's Ionizer and Ozonator: Implications for Indoor Air Pollution by Thomas Valone; How Cosmic Forces Shape Our Destiny by Nikola Tesla; Tesla's Death Ray plus Selected Tesla Patents; more.
288 PAGES. 6x9 PAPERBACK. ILLUSTRATED. $16.95. CODE: HWWN

THE ENERGY MACHINE OF T. HENRY MORAY
by Moray B. King
In the 1920s T. Henry Moray invented a "free energy" device that reportedly output 50 kilowatts of electricity. It could not be explained by standard science at that time. The electricity exhibited a strange "cold current" characteristic where thin wires could appreciable power without heating. Moray suffered ruthless suppression, and in 1939 the device was destroyed. Frontier science lecturer and author Moray B. King explains the invention with today's science. Modern physics recognizes that the vacuum contains tremendous energy called the zero-point energy. A way to coherently activate it appears surprisingly simple: first create a glow plasma or corona, then abruptly pulse it. Other inventors have discovered this approach (sometimes unwittingly) to create novel energy devices, and they too were suppressed. The common pattern of their technologies clarified the fundamental operating principle. King hopes to inspire engineers and inventors so that a new energy source can become available to mankind.
192 PAGES. 6x8 PAPERBACK. ILLUSTRATED. REFERENCES. $14.95. CODE: EMHM

QUEST FOR ZERO-POINT ENERGY
Engineering Principles for "Free Energy"
by Moray B. King
King expands, with diagrams, on how free energy and anti-gravity are possible. The theories of zero point energy maintain there are tremendous fluctuations of electrical field energy embedded within the fabric of space. King explains the following topics: Tapping the Zero-Point Energy as an Energy Source; Fundamentals of a Zero-Point Energy Technology; Vacuum Energy Vortices; The Super Tube; Charge Clusters: The Basis of Zero-Point Energy Inventions; Vortex Filaments, Torsion Fields and the Zero-Point Energy; Transforming the Vacuum with a Zero-Point Energy Experiment; Dual Vortex Forms: The Key to a Large Zero-Point Energy Coherence. Packed with diagrams, patents and photos. With power shortages now a daily reality in many parts of the world, this book offers a fresh approach very rarely mentioned in the mainstream media.
224 PAGES. 6x9 PAPERBACK. ILLUSTRATED. $14.95. CODE: QZPE

THE TIME TRAVEL HANDBOOK
A Manual of Practical Teleportation & Time Travel
edited by David Hatcher Childress
In the tradition of The Anti-Gravity Handbook and The Free-Energy Device Handbook, science and UFO author David Hatcher Childress takes us into the weird world of time travel and teleportation. Not just a whacked-out look at science fiction, this book is an authoritative chronicling of real-life time travel experiments, teleportation devices and more. The Time Travel Handbook takes the reader beyond the government experiments and deep into the uncharted territory of early time travellers such as Nikola Tesla and Guglielmo Marconi and their alleged time travel experiments, as well as the Wilson Brothers of EMI and their connection to the Philadelphia Experiment—the U.S. Navy's forays into invisibility, time travel, and teleportation. Childress looks into the claims of time travelling individuals, and investigates the unusual claim that the pyramids on Mars were built in the future and sent back in time. A highly visual, large format book, with patents, photos and schematics. Be the first on your block to build your own time travel device!
316 PAGES. 7x10 PAPERBACK. ILLUSTRATED. $16.95. CODE: TTH

THE TESLA PAPERS
Nikola Tesla on Free Energy & Wireless Transmission of Power
by Nikola Tesla, edited by David Hatcher Childress
David Hatcher Childress takes us into the incredible world of Nikola Tesla and his amazing inventions. Tesla's rare article "The Problem of Increasing Human Energy with Special Reference to the Harnessing of the Sun's Energy" is included. This lengthy article was originally published in the June 1900 issue of The Century Illustrated Monthly Magazine and it was the outline for Tesla's master blueprint for the world. Tesla's fantastic vision of the future, including wireless power, anti-gravity, free energy and highly advanced solar power. Also included are some of the papers, patents and material collected on Tesla at the Colorado Springs Tesla Symposiums, including papers on: •The Secret History of Wireless Transmission •Tesla and the Magnifying Transmitter •Design and Construction of a Half-Wave Tesla Coil •Electrostatics: A Key to Free Energy •Progress in Zero-Point Energy Research •Electromagnetic Energy from Antennas to Atoms •Tesla's Particle Beam Technology •Fundamental Excitatory Modes of the Earth-Ionosphere Cavity
325 PAGES. 8x10 PAPERBACK. ILLUSTRATED. $16.95. CODE: TTP

THE FANTASTIC INVENTIONS OF NIKOLA TESLA
by Nikola Tesla with additional material by David Hatcher Childress
This book is a readable compendium of patents, diagrams, photos and explanations of the many incredible inventions of the originator of the modern era of electrification. In Tesla's own words are such topics as wireless transmission of power, death rays, and radio-controlled airships. In addition, rare material on German bases in Antarctica and South America, and a secret city built at a remote jungle site in South America by one of Tesla's students, Guglielmo Marconi. Marconi's secret group claims to have built flying saucers in the 1940s and to have gone to Mars in the early 1950s! Incredible photos of these Tesla craft are included. The Ancient Atlantean system of broadcasting energy through a grid system of obelisks and pyramids is discussed. •His plan to transmit free electricity into the atmosphere. •How electrical devices would work using only small antennas. •Why unlimited power could be utilized anywhere on earth. •How radio and radar technology can be used as death-ray weapons in Star Wars.
342 PAGES. 6x9 PAPERBACK. ILLUSTRATED. APPENDIX. $16.95. CODE: FINT

24 hour credit card orders—call: 815-253-6390 fax: 815-253-6300
email: auphq@frontiernet.net   www.adventuresunlimitedpress.com   www.wexclub.com

STRANGE SCIENCE

REICH OF THE BLACK SUN
Nazi Secret Weapons and the Cold War Allied Legend
by Joseph P. Farrell
Why were the Allies worried about an atom bomb attack by the Germans in 1944? Why did the Soviets threaten to use poison gas against the Germans? Why did Hitler in 1945 insist that holding Prague could win the war for the Third Reich? Why did US General George Patton's Third Army race for the Skoda works at Pilsen in Czechoslovakia instead of Berlin? Why did the US Army not test the uranium atom bomb it dropped on Hiroshima? Why did the Luftwaffe fly a non-stop round trip mission to within twenty miles of New York City in 1944? *Reich of the Black Sun* takes the reader on a scientific-historical journey in order to answer these questions. Arguing that Nazi Germany actually won the race for the atom bomb in late 1944, *Reich of the Black Sun* then goes on to explore the even more secretive research the Nazis were conducting into the occult, alternative physics and new energy sources. The book concludes with a fresh look at the "Nazi Legend" of the UFO mystery by examining the Roswell Majestic-12 documents and the Kecksburg crash in the light of parallels with some of the super-secret black projects being run by the SS. *Reich of the Black Sun* is must-reading for the researcher interested in alternative history, science, or UFOs!
352 PAGES. 6x9 PAPERBACK. ILLUSTRATED. BIBLIOGRAPHY. $16.95. CODE: ROBS

HITLER'S FLYING SAUCERS
A Guide to German Flying Discs of the Second World War
by Henry Stevens
Learn why the Schriever-Habermohl project was actually two projects and read the written statement of a German test pilot who actually flew one of these saucers; about the Leduc engine, the key to Dr. Miethe's saucer designs; how U.S. government officials kept the truth about foo fighters hidden for almost sixty years and how they were finally forced to "come clean" about the foo fighter's German origin. Learn of the Peenemuende saucer project and how it was slated to "go atomic." Read the testimony of a German eyewitness who saw "magnetic discs." Read the U.S. government's own reports on German field propulsion saucers. Read how the post-war German KM-2 field propulsion "rocket" worked. Learn details of the work of Karl Schappeller and Viktor Schauberger. Learn how their ideas figure in the quest to build field propulsion flying discs. Find out what happened to this technology after the war. Find out how the Canadians got saucer technology directly from the SS. Find out about the surviving "Third Power" of former Nazis. Learn of the U.S. government's methods of UFO deception and how they used the German "Sonderbueroll" as the model for Project Blue Book.
388 PAGES. 6x9 PAPERBACK. ILLUSTRATED. INDEX. $18.95. CODE: HFS

LEY LINE & EARTH ENERGIES
An Extraordinary Journey into the Earth's Natural Energy System
by David Cowan & Chris Arnold
The mysterious standing stones, burial grounds and stone circles that lace Europe, the British Isles and other areas have intrigued scientists, writers, artists and travellers through the centuries. They pose so many questions: Why do some places feel special? How do ley lines work? How did our ancestors use Earth energy to map their sacred sites and burial grounds? How do ghosts and poltergeists interact with Earth energy? How can Earth spirals and black spots affect our health? This exploration shows how natural forces affect our behavior, how they can be used to enhance our health and well being, and ultimately, how they bring us closer to penetrating one of the deepest mysteries being explored. A fascinating and visual book about subtle Earth energies and how they affect us and the world around them.
368 PAGES. 6x9 PAPERBACK. ILLUSTRATED. BIBLIOGRAPHY. INDEX. $18.95. CODE: LLEE

MIND CONTROL AND UFOS
Casebook on Alternative 3
by Jim Keith
Drawing on his diverse research and a wide variety of sources, Jim Keith delves into the bizarre story behind *Alternative 3*, including mind control programs, underground bases not only on the Earth but also on the Moon and Mars, the real origin of the UFO problem, the mysterious deaths of Marconi Electronics employees in Britain during the 1980s, top scientists around the world kidnapped to work at the secret government space bases, the Russian-American superpower arms race of the 50s, 60s and 70s as a massive hoax, and other startling arenas.
248 PAGES. 6x9 PAPERBACK. ILLUSTRATED. $14.95. CODE: MCUF

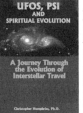

UFOS, PSI AND SPIRITUAL EVOLUTION
A Journey through the Evolution of Interstellar Travel
by Christopher Humphries, Ph.D.
The modern era of UFOs began in May, 1947, one year and eight months after Hiroshima. This is no coincidence, and suggests there are beings in the universe with the ability to jump hundreds of light years in an instant. That is teleportation, a power of the mind. UFOs sometimes float along close to the ground, in complete silence. That is levitation, another power of the mind. If it weren't for levitation and teleportation, star travel would not be possible at all, since physics rules out star travel by technology. So if we want to go to the stars, it is the mind and spirit we must study, not technology. The mind must be a dark matter object, since it is invisible and intangible and can freely pass through solid objects. A disembodied mind can see the de Broglie vibrations (the basis of quantum mechanics) radiated by both dark and ordinary matter during near-death or out-of-body experiences. Levitation requires warping the geodesics of space-time. The latest theory in physics is String Theory, which requires six extra spatial dimensions. The mind warps those higher geodesics to produce teleportation.
274 PAGES. 6x9 PAPERBACK. ILLUSTRATED. REFERENCES. $16.95. CODE: UPSE

SAUCERS OF THE ILLUMINATI
by Jim Keith, Foreword by Kenn Thomas
Seeking the truth behind stories of alien invasion, secret underground bases, and the secret plans of the New World Order, *Saucers of the Illuminati* offers ground breaking research, uncovering clues to the nature of UFOs and to forces even more sinister: the secret cabal behind planetary control! Includes mind control, saucer abductions, the MJ-12 documents, cattle mutilations, government anti-gravity testing, the Sirius Connection, science fiction author Philip K. Dick and his efforts to expose the Illuminati, plus more from veteran conspiracy and UFO author Keith. Conspiracy expert Keith's final book on UFOs and the highly secret group that manufactures them and uses them for their own purposes: the control and manipulation of the population of planet Earth.
148 PAGES. 6x9 PAPERBACK. ILLUSTRATED. $12.95. CODE: SOIL

24 hour credit card orders—call: 815-253-6390 fax: 815-253-6300
email: auphq@frontiernet.net   www.adventuresunlimitedpress.com   www.wexclub.com

ANCIENT SCIENCE

THE GIZA DEATH STAR
The Paleophysics of the Great Pyramid & the Military Complex at Giza
by Joseph P. Farrell
Physicist Joseph Farrell's amazing book on the secrets of Great Pyramid of Giza. *The Giza Death Star* starts where British engineer Christopher Dunn leaves off in his 1998 book, *The Giza Power Plant*. Was the Giza complex part of a military installation over 10,000 years ago? Chapters include: An Archaeology of Mass Destruction, Thoth and Theories; The Machine Hypothesis; Pythagoras, Plato, Planck, and the Pyramid; The Weapon Hypothesis; Encoded Harmonics of the Planck Units in the Great Pyramid; High Fregquency Direct Current "Impulse" Technology; The Grand Gallery and its Crystals: Gravito-acoustic Resonators; The Other Two Large Pyramids; the "Causeways," and the "Temples"; A Phase Conjugate Howitzer; Evidence of the Use of Weapons of Mass Destruction in Ancient Times; more.
290 PAGES. 6x9 PAPERBACK. ILLUSTRATED. $16.95. CODE: GDS

THE GIZA DEATH STAR DEPLOYED
The Physics & Engineering of the Great Pyramid
by Joseph P. Farrell
Physicist Joseph Farrell's amazing sequel to *The Giza Death Star* which takes us from the Great Pyramid to the asteroid belt and the so-called Pyramids of Mars. Farrell expands on his thesis that the Great Pyramid was a chemical maser, designed as a weapon and eventually deployed—with disastrous results to the solar system. Includes: Exploding Planets: The Movie, the Mirror, and the Model; Dating the Catastrophe and the Compound; A Brief History of the Exoteric and Esoteric Investigations of the Great Pyramid; No Machines, Please!; The Stargate Conspiracy; The Scalar Weapons; Message or Machine?; A Tesla Analysis of the Putative Physics and Engineering of the Giza Death Star; Cohering the Zero Point, Vacuum Energy, Flux: Synopsis of Scalar Physics and Paleophysics; Configuring the Scalar Pulse Wave; Inferred Applications in the Great Pyramid; Quantum Numerology, Feedback Loops and Tetrahedral Physics; and more.
290 PAGES. 6x9 PAPERBACK. ILLUSTRATED. BIBLIOGRAPHY. INDEX. $16.95. CODE: GDSD

PIRATES & THE LOST TEMPLAR FLEET
The Secret Naval War Between the Templars & the Vatican
by David Hatcher Childress
The lost Templar fleet was originally based at La Rochelle in southern France, but fled to the deep fiords of Scotland upon the dissolution of the Order by King Phillip. This banned fleet of ships was later commanded by the St. Clair family of Rosslyn Chapel (birthplace of Free Masonry). St. Clair and his Templars made a voyage to Canada in the year 1398 AD, nearly 100 years before Columbus! Chapters include: 10,000 Years of Seafaring; The Knights Templar & the Crusades; The Templars and the Assassins; The Lost Templar Fleet and the Jolly Roger; Maps of the Ancient Sea Kings; Pirates, Templars and the New World; Christopher Columbus—Secret Templar Pirate?; Later Day Pirates and the War with the Vatican; Pirate Utopias and the New Jerusalem; more.
320 PAGES. 6x9 PAPERBACK. ILLUSTRATED. BIBLIOGRAPHY. $16.95. CODE: PLTF

CLOAK OF THE ILLUMINATI
Secrets, Transformations, Crossing the Star Gate
by William Henry
Thousands of years ago the stargate technology of the gods was lost. Mayan Prophecy says it will return by 2012, along with our alignment with the center of our galaxy. In this book: Find examples of stargates and wormholes in the ancient world; Examine myths and scripture with hidden references to a stargate cloak worn by the Illuminati, including Mari, Nimrod, Elijah, and Jesus; See rare images of gods and goddesses wearing the Cloak of the illuminati; Learn about Saddam Hussein and the secret missing library of Jesus; Uncover the secret Roman-era eugenics experiments at the Temple of Hathor in Denderah, Egypt; Explore the duplicate of the Stargate Pillar of the Gods in the Illuminists' secret garden in Nashville, TN; Discover the secrets of manna, the food of the angels; Share the lost Peace Prayer posture of Osiris, Jesus and the Illuminati; more. Chapters include: Seven Stars Under Three Stars; The Long Walk; Squaring the Circle; The Mill of the Host; The Miracle Garment; The Fig; Nimrod: The Mighty Man; Nebuchadnezzar's Gate; The New Mighty Man; more.
238 PAGES. 6x9 PAPERBACK. ILLUSTRATED. BIBLIOGRAPHY. INDEX. $16.95. CODE: COIL

EXTRATERRESTRIAL ARCHAEOLOGY NEW EDITION!
by David Hatcher Childress
Using official NASA and Soviet photos, as well as other photos taken via telescope, this book seeks to prove that many of the planets (and moons) of our solar system are in some way inhabited by intelligent life. The book includes many blow-ups of NASA photos and detailed diagrams of structures—particularly on the Moon.
•NASA PHOTOS OF PYRAMIDS AND DOMED CITIES ON THE MOON. •PYRAMIDS AND GIANT STATUES ON MARS. •HOLLOW MOONS OF MARS AND OTHER PLANETS. •ROBOT MINING VEHICLES THAT MOVE ABOUT THE MOON PROCESSING VALUABLE METALS. •NASA & RUSSIAN PHOTOS OF SPACE-BASES ON MARS AND ITS MOONS. •A BRITISH SCIENTIST WHO DISCOVERED A TUNNEL ON THE MOON, AND OTHER "BOTTOMLESS CRATERS." •EARLY CLAIMS OF TRIPS TO THE MOON AND MARS. •STRUCTURAL ANOMALIES ON VENUS, SATURN, JUPITER, MERCURY,URANUS & NEPTUNE. •NASA, THE MOON AND ANTI-GRAVITY. PLUS MORE. HIGHLY ILLUSTRATED WITH PHOTOS, DIAGRAMS AND MAPS!
320 PAGES. 8x11 PAPERBACK. BIBLIOGRAPHY & APPENDIX. $19.95. CODE: ETA

THE ORION PROPHECY
Egyptian and Mayan Prophecies on the Cataclysm of 2012
by Patrick Geryl and Gino Ratinckx
In the year 2012 the Earth awaits a super catastrophe: its magnetic field will reverse in one go. Phenomenal earthquakes and tidal waves will completely destroy our civilization. Europe and North America will shift thousands of kilometers northwards into polar climes. Nearly everyone will perish in the apocalyptic happenings. These dire predictions stem from the Mayans and Egyptians—descendants of the legendary Atlantis. The Atlanteans had highly evolved astronomical knowledge and were able to exactly predict the previous world-wide flood in 9792 BC. They built tens of thousands of boats and escaped to South America and Egypt. In the year 2012 Venus, Orion and several others stars will take the same 'code-positions' as in 9792 BC! For thousands of years historical sources have told of a forgotten time capsule of ancient wisdom located in a labyrinth of secret chambers filled with artifacts and documents from the previous flood. We desperately need this information now—and this book gives one possible location.
324 PAGES. 6x9 PAPERBACK. ILLUSTRATED. BIBLIOGRAPHY. $16.95. CODE: ORP

MYSTIC TRAVELLER SERIES

THE MYSTERY OF EASTER ISLAND
by Katherine Routledge
The reprint of Katherine Routledge's classic archaeology book which was first published in London in 1919. The book details her journey by yacht from England to South America, around Patagonia to Chile and on to Easter Island. Routledge explored the amazing island and produced one of the first-ever accounts of the life, history and legends of this strange and remote place. Routledge discusses the statues, pyramid-platforms, Rongo Rongo script, the Bird Cult, the war between the Short Ears and the Long Ears, the secret caves, ancient roads on the island, and more. This rare book serves as a sourcebook on the early discoveries and theories on Easter Island.

432 PAGES. 6x9 PAPERBACK. ILLUSTRATED. $16.95. CODE: MEI

MYSTERY CITIES OF THE MAYA
Exploration and Adventure in Lubaantun & Belize
by Thomas Gann
First published in 1925, *Mystery Cities of the Maya* is a classic in Central American archaeology-adventure. Gann was close friends with Mike Mitchell-Hedges, the British adventurer who discovered the famous crystal skull with his adopted daughter Sammy and Lady Richmond Brown, their benefactress. Gann battles pirates along Belize's coast and goes upriver with Mitchell-Hedges to the site of Lubaantun where they excavate a strange lost city where the crystal skull was discovered. Lubaantun is a unique city in the Mayan world as it is built out of precisely carved blocks of stone without the usual plaster-cement facing. Lubaantun contained several large pyramids partially destroyed by earthquakes and a large amount of artifacts. Gann shared Mitchell-Hedges belief in Atlantis and lost civilizations (pre-Mayan) in Central America and the Caribbean. Lots of good photos, maps and diagrams.
252 PAGES. 6x9 PAPERBACK. ILLUSTRATED. $16.95. CODE: MCOM

IN SECRET TIBET
by Theodore Illion
Reprint of a rare 30s adventure travel book. Illion was a German wayfarer who not only spoke fluent Tibetan, but travelled in disguise as a native through forbidden Tibet when it was off-limits to all outsiders. His incredible adventures make this one of the most exciting travel books ever published. Includes illustrations of Tibetan monks levitating stones by acoustics.
210 PAGES. 5x9 PAPERBACK. ILLUSTRATED. $15.95. CODE: IST

DARKNESS OVER TIBET
by Theodore Illion
In this second reprint of Illion's rare books, the German traveller continues his journey through Tibet and is given directions to a strange underground city. As the original publisher's remarks said, "this is a rare account of an underground city in Tibet by the only Westerner ever to enter it and escape alive! "
210 PAGES. 5x9 PAPERBACK. ILLUSTRATED. $15.95. CODE: DOT

DANGER MY ALLY
The Amazing Life Story of the Discoverer of the Crystal Skull
by "Mike" Mitchell-Hedges
The incredible life story of "Mike" Mitchell-Hedges, the British adventurer who discovered the Crystal Skull in the lost Mayan city of Lubaantun in Belize. Mitchell-Hedges has lived an exciting life: gambling everything on a trip to the Americas as a young man, riding with Pancho Villa, questing for Atlantis, fighting bandits in the Caribbean and discovering the famous Crystal Skull.
374 PAGES. 6x9 PAPERBACK. ILLUSTRATED. BIBLIOGRAPHY & INDEX. $16.95. CODE: DMA

IN SECRET MONGOLIA
by Henning Haslund
First published by Kegan Paul of London in 1934, Haslund takes us into the barely known world of Mongolia of 1921, a land of god-kings, bandits, vast mountain wilderness and a Russian army running amok. Starting in Peking, Haslund journeys to Mongolia as part of the Krebs Expedition—a mission to establish a Danish butter farm in a remote corner of northern Mongolia. Along the way, he smuggles guns and nitroglycerin, is thrown into a prison by the new Communist regime, battles the Robber Princess and more. With Haslund we meet the "Mad Baron" Ungern-Sternberg and his renegade Russian army, the many characters of Urga's fledgling foreign community, and the last god-king of Mongolia, Seng Chen Gegen, the fifth reincarnation of the Tiger god and the "ruler of all Torguts." Aside from the esoteric and mystical material, there is plenty of just plain adventure: Haslund encounters a Mongolian werewolf; is ambushed along the trail; escapes from prison and fights terrifying blizzards; more.
374 PAGES. 6x9 PAPERBACK. ILLUSTRATED. BIBLIOGRAPHY & INDEX. $16.95. CODE: ISM

MEN & GODS IN MONGOLIA
by Henning Haslund
First published in 1935 by Kegan Paul of London, Haslund takes us to the lost city of Karakota in the Gobi desert. We meet the Bodgo Gegen, a god-king of Mongolia similar to the Dalai Lama of Tibet. We meet Dambin Jansang, the dreaded warlord of the "Black Gobi." There is even material in this incredible book on the Hi-mori, an "airhorse" that flies through the sky (similar to a Vimana) and carries with it the sacred stone of Chintamani. Aside from the esoteric and mystical material, there is plenty of just plain adventure: Haslund and companions journey across the Gobi desert by camel caravan; are kidnapped and held for ransom; witness initiation into Shamanic societies; meet reincarnated warlords; and experience the violent birth of "modern" Mongolia.
358 PAGES. 6x9 PAPERBACK. ILLUSTRATED. BIBLIOGRAPHY & INDEX. $16.95. CODE: MGM

One Adventure Place
P.O. Box 74
Kempton, Illinois 60946
United States of America
Tel.: 815-253-6390 • Fax: 815-253-6300
Email: auphq@frontiernet.net
http://www.adventuresunlimitedpress.com
or www.adventuresunlimited.nl

ORDERING INSTRUCTIONS

✓ Remit by USD$ Check, Money Order or Credit Card

✓ Visa, Master Card, Discover & AmEx Accepted

✓ Prices May Change Without Notice

✓ 10% Discount for 3 or more Items

SHIPPING CHARGES

United States

✓ Postal Book Rate $\left\{\begin{array}{l}\text{\$3.00 First Item}\\ \text{50¢ Each Additional Item}\end{array}\right.$

✓ Priority Mail $\left\{\begin{array}{l}\text{\$4.50 First Item}\\ \text{\$2.00 Each Additional Item}\end{array}\right.$

✓ UPS $\left\{\begin{array}{l}\text{\$5.00 First Item}\\ \text{\$1.50 Each Additional Item}\end{array}\right.$
NOTE: UPS Delivery Available to Mainland USA Only

Canada

✓ Postal Book Rate $\left\{\begin{array}{l}\text{\$6.00 First Item}\\ \text{\$2.00 Each Additional Item}\end{array}\right.$

✓ Postal Air Mail $\left\{\begin{array}{l}\text{\$8.00 First Item}\\ \text{\$2.50 Each Additional Item}\end{array}\right.$

✓ Personal Checks or Bank Drafts MUST BE

USD$ and Drawn on a US Bank
✓ Canadian Postal Money Orders OK

✓ Payment MUST BE USD$

All Other Countries

✓ Surface Delivery $\left\{\begin{array}{l}\text{\$10.00 First Item}\\ \text{\$4.00 Each Additional Item}\end{array}\right.$

✓ Postal Air Mail $\left\{\begin{array}{l}\text{\$14.00 First Item}\\ \text{\$5.00 Each Additional Item}\end{array}\right.$
✓ Payment MUST BE USD$

✓ Checks and Money Orders MUST BE USD$
   and Drawn on a US Bank or branch.

✓ Add $5.00 for Air Mail Subscription to
   Future *Adventures Unlimited* Catalogs

SPECIAL NOTES

✓ RETAILERS: Standard Discounts Available
✓ BACKORDERS: We Backorder all Out-of-
   Stock Items Unless Otherwise Requested

✓ PRO FORMA INVOICES: Available on Request

Please check: ☑

☐ This is my first order   ☐ I have ordered before

Name		
Address		
City		
State/Province		Postal Code
Country		
Phone day	Evening	
Fax		

Item Code	Item Description	Qty	Total

Please check: ☑

	Subtotal ▶	
	Less Discount-10% for 3 or more items ▶	
☐ Postal-Surface	Balance ▶	
☐ Postal-Air Mail (Priority in USA)	Illinois Residents 6.25% Sales Tax ▶	
	Previous Credit ▶	
☐ UPS	Shipping ▶	
(Mainland USA only)	Total (check/MO in USD$ only) ▶	

☐ Visa/MasterCard/Discover/Amex

Card Number

Expiration Date

10% Discount When You Order 3 or More Items!